MS. MARVEL'S AMERICA

Ms. Marvel's America

No Normal

EDITED BY
JESSICA BALDANZI AND HUSSEIN RASHID

UNIVERSITY PRESS OF MISSISSIPPI / JACKSON

The University Press of Mississippi is the scholarly publishing agency of the Mississippi Institutions of Higher Learning: Alcorn State University, Delta State University, Jackson State University, Mississippi State University, Mississippi University for Women, Mississippi Valley State University, University of Mississippi, and University of Southern Mississippi.

Designed by Peter D. Halverson

www.upress.state.ms.us

The University Press of Mississippi is a member of the Association of University Presses.

Copyright © 2020 by University Press of Mississippi
All rights reserved
Manufactured in the United States of America

First printing 2020

∞

Library of Congress Cataloging-in-Publication Data

Names: Baldanzi, Jessica, editor. | Rashid, Hussein, editor.
Title: Ms. Marvel's America : no normal / edited by Jessica Baldanzi and Hussein Rashid.
Description: Jackson : University Press of Mississippi, 2020. | Includes bibliographical references and index.
Identifiers: LCCN 2019034315 (print) | LCCN 2019034316 (ebook) | ISBN 9781496827029 (hardback) | ISBN 9781496827012 (trade paperback) | ISBN 9781496827036 (epub) | ISBN 9781496827043 (epub) | ISBN 9781496827050 (pdf) | ISBN 9781496827067 (pdf)
Subjects: LCSH: Khan, Kamala (Fictitious character) | Marvel, Ms. (Fictitious character) | Comic books, strips, etc.—History and criticism. | BISAC: LITERARY CRITICISM / Comics & Graphic Novels | LCGFT: Essays. | Literary criticism.
Classification: LCC PN6714 .M75 2020 (print) | LCC PN6714 (ebook) | DDC 741.5/9—dc23
LC record available at https://lccn.loc.gov/2019034315
LC ebook record available at https://lccn.loc.gov/2019034316
Library of Congress Cataloging-in-Publication Data

British Library Cataloging-in-Publication Data available

CONTENTS

Introduction   vii
    JESSICA BALDANZI AND HUSSEIN RASHID

PART ONE: Precursors

Mentoring Ms. Marvel
Marvel's Kamala Khan and the Reconstitution of Carol Danvers   3
    J. RICHARD STEVENS

Placing Ms. Marvel and Dust
Marvel Comics, the New York Metro Area, and the "Muslim Problem"   21
    MARTIN LUND

PART TWO: Nation and Religion, Identity and Community

Ms. Marvel Is an Immigrant   47
    HUSSEIN RASHID

"The Only Nerdy Pakistani-American-Slash-Inhuman in the Entire Universe"
Postracialism and Politics in the New Ms. Marvel   65
    SIKA A. DAGBOVIE-MULLINS AND ERIC BERLATSKY

"I Would Rather Be a Cyborg"
Both/And Technoculture and the New Ms. Marvel   89
    JESSICA BALDANZI

Hope and the *Sa'a* of Ms. Marvel   116
    A. DAVID LEWIS

PART THREE: Pedagogy and Resistance

The Transformational Resistance of Ms. Marvel in America   133
PETER E. CARLSON AND ANTERO GARCIA

Classroom Heroes
Ms. Marvel and Feminist, Antiracist Pedagogy   152
WINONA LANDIS

More than a Mask, Burkini, and Tights
Fighting Misrepresentations through Ms. Marvel's Costume   170
KRISTIN M. PETERSON

PART FOUR: Fangirls, Fanboys, and the Culture of Fandom

"Wow. Many Hero. Much Super. Such Girl"
Kamala Khan and Female Comics Fandom   191
AARON KASHTAN

Kamala Khan, Miles Morales, and Marvel NOW!
Challenging the Traditional White Male Fan   207
NICHOLAUS PUMPHREY

CODA: Conversations

Madina on the Light Rail (That Girl Is Me)   229
JOSÉ ALANIZ

Interview with G. Willow Wilson   230
SHABANA MIR

Acknowledgments   247

Contributors   249

Index   255

INTRODUCTION

JESSICA BALDANZI AND HUSSEIN RASHID

Kamala Khan, the new Ms. Marvel, appeared in 2014 at the forefront of a wave of character diversification in Marvel Comics. When longtime Ms. Marvel Carol Danvers became the latest Captain Marvel, editors Steve Wacker and Sana Amanat decided that the new Ms. Marvel should be a Muslim American. They also wanted her to be authentic, so they looked at their options for a female Muslim American writer with solid experience in comics. G. Willow Wilson was the only one who fit the description (Wilson, Interview). Wilson was excited to take the job, especially after talking with Amanat, a Pakistani American Muslim like Khan (Tolentino).

Khan joined the ranks of the revived Black Panther, as well as other high-profile superheroes with new alter egos, like Spider-Man, Captain America, Thor, Iron Man, and Hulk. However, Khan, a Muslim teen from Jersey City, stands out as the first to open up new fan bases—which many comics executives seemed unaware even existed—of young Muslim readers, as well as women and girls on a spectrum of faiths. As Wilson comments in her interview at the end of this collection, "This book should not have sold. It should have been dead on arrival by the old industry manual."[1] Yet *Ms. Marvel* has consistently topped digital comics sales lists, and the collections of these issues in paperback form have also placed high on *New York Times* bestseller lists. Khan is a critical success as well, and the series has won prestigious awards, including an Eisner and a Hugo award.

This new Ms. Marvel has several unique characteristics. A second-generation Pakistani immigrant, she was first conceived and written by two women, both of whom bring their own experiences as American Muslims to her character. She is also the first Muslim superhero to headline her own series. Ms. Marvel is an ideal topic for a scholarly volume, not only because of these firsts but also because of the myriad fronts on which she challenges traditional comics character tropes. Comics studies needs diverse methods to match the growing diversity within comics themselves.

Khan also appears at a time when anti-Muslim rhetoric in the United States is increasing, in ways that seem to be tied to the political trajectory of the country. Our contributors focus on scholarly analysis of the character, more than real-world political events, so a brief overview and record of political highlights and low points since Khan's debut is useful here. Both notable and hopeful are the ways Khan's fans have deployed her image to counter anti-Muslim rhetoric, as well as to develop her role as a positive Muslim icon in the United States and beyond. In one particularly high-profile example,[2] in January 2015, the American Freedom Defense Initiative, classified by the Southern Poverty Law Center as an anti-Muslim hate group, ran bus ads in San Francisco that implied connections between the Muslim faith and Nazism. When the bus company cited free-speech protections to claim that it was unable to remove the ads, a public art collective in the city took matters into its own hands. Rather than destroy the ads to counter the Islamophobic message, it pasted images of Ms. Marvel over the ads' grossly decontextualized photos of Hitler shaking hands with an anti-Zionist former Palestinian leader. Then the group pasted phrases like "Calling all bigotry busters" and "Free speech isn't a license to spread hate" over most of the text, turning the remaining words against their original meaning to create phrases like "STOP THE HATE . . . to Islamic countries."[3]

However, the bus ad campaign was only a brief respite from a recent, prominent wave of Islamophobia, much of which originated in the United States' highest political office. As a US presidential candidate, Donald Trump's rhetoric was xenophobic on a number of fronts, including his promise to build a wall between Mexico and the United States. A large part of his fear and loathing of so-called outsiders, however, was centered on Muslims: he talked repeatedly about restricting immigration of Muslims and even suggested a "database" of all Muslims in the United States, before walking the statement back in more official rhetoric (Carroll, Muaddi). Particularly appalling was candidate Trump's reaction to the 2016 Democratic National Convention, where the bereaved gold-star parents of a fallen US soldier spoke out against Trump's anti-Muslim statements and for the place of Muslims in American history. Trump mockingly played upon US stereotypes about Muslims by suggesting that religion had kept the mother silent while the father did the talking (Haberman). The couple themselves—Khizr and Ghazala Khan, from Pakistan like Kamala Khan's parents—clarified later that Ghazala's silence stemmed not from patriarchal control, but from grief. Fortunately, the news surrounding this saga was not entirely negative: fellow gold-star families of many faiths publicly came to the couple's defense (Bruton). At the same

Introduction ix

Figure 1.1 Fan art by Matt Stefani

time, this incident highlighted the ways in which Muslims are permitted to exist in this country: as terrorists, as victims, or as servants of the state. They are too often not allowed to have an identity outside of the lens of national security (see Abu-Lughod, Mamdani).

During that same period, as Trump's anti-Muslim campaign rhetoric began to escalate, fans of the new Ms. Marvel witnessed a cathartic, though controversial, unauthorized response. In an echo of the famous 1941 comic book cover of Captain America punching Hitler, one fan illustrated Kamala Khan, as Ms. Marvel, punching Donald Trump (Baker-Whitelaw; figure 1.1). Once Trump was inaugurated and attempted to enact the so-called "Muslim ban" as one of his first presidential endeavors, comics artist Phil Noto revised his variant cover image for *Civil War II* to show Khan ripping up a photo, not of her formerly beloved mentor and namesake Carol Danvers as in the original image (Cox), but of Donald Trump (Romano, Siefert).

Images like these have tremendous power to affect readers' perceptions of real-life women like Khan, and real-life Muslims in general. As Douglas Rushkoff argues in his foreword to the comics-and-religion essay collection *Graven Images*, "Picture, word, then connection.... This gives the author an amazing opportunity: to instill word and image into a reader's mind before the reader has a context for this information. This is the tremendous power behind comics' ability to generate cultural iconography—to create modern mythology" (qtd. in Lewis and Kraemer, x). Since, as A. David Lewis and Christine Hoff Kraemer further suggest in their introduction to the same collection, these "complex combinations ... frequently give images the final authority" (2), is the current circulation of Ms. Marvel images mostly positive or negative? Are the images of punching and ripping too violent, the bus ads too localized, or do all of these images, plus the comic itself, do enough positive work in the world to counter a dominant political narrative of Islamophobia? After all, as Robyn Wiegman has suggested, "the 'optics of race' reside less in the material existence of the 'ambiguous' racialized body than in the ways we learn to see that body" (*American Anatomies* xiv; qtd. in Berlant). These images may not have been created for the classroom, but there is little doubt that they are doing educational work in the world. As Khan gains this power, it becomes increasingly important not just to celebrate but also to examine her complexity, as well as the complexity of her friends and family. Kamala Khan may be fictional, yet like real Muslims, she lives a rich, multifaceted life, which bears no resemblance to any Islamophobic narrative.

This interdisciplinary anthology hopes to do justice to the breadth of Khan's symbolism, exploring her meaning and significance for a broad readership, both academic and nonspecialist. To that end, we have limited the scope of the analysis mainly to the first volume of the new Ms. Marvel—issues 1 through 19—although a few of the essays examine Khan's precursors or gesture beyond issue 19.[4] This focus allows our authors to delve deeply into the genesis of the series, before Khan's appearances extended into more volumes, and several multicharacter titles. Thus, we aim to provide a multifaceted yet solid groundwork for continuing discussion of how the character and the series have developed, as well as where they have yet to go.

Our approach emphasizes Ms. Marvel's superpower as a polymorph. Just as she can become what she needs to be as the situation demands, we work to see her in multiple forms at once: the multiple ways scholars from different disciplines read the same source material, and even the same secondary material. The humanities is about "both/and" much more than "either/or." Ms. Marvel is both a figure of independent Muslima empowerment, and a reaction to stereotypes of Muslims. For us, as humanities scholars, observation creates multiple states of being, rather than resolving and oversimplifying them.

Ms. Marvel has heroically broken through many boundaries in the world of comics and popular culture, and we hope that these essays serve similar purposes in academia. As Henry Jenkins argues in his introduction to *Critical Approaches to Comics,* media like comics are "best understood through an approach that is broadly comparative, looking across different platforms and modes of representation, rather than seeking exclusivity and specificity" (6). As coeditors and scholars equally committed to popular culture and public discourse, as well as trained in two different fields—literary/cultural and religious studies—our expertise is already broad. At root, however, Khan's story is a human story, and we are both humanities scholars, tasked with reading cultural texts to analyze and illuminate the myriad facets of the human condition. To do justice to Khan as a complex cultural figure, we have gathered scholars from numerous fields beyond our own specific expertise, including education and curriculum, visual rhetoric, media studies, and anthropology. The topics of these essays range from comics history to composition classrooms, fan culture to fashion, and future imaginings, such as what this series and this character mean for all of our stories in the face of a real possibility of apocalypse. The essays also address a range of intersectional categories, from Khan's religion, to her gender, age, location, family, and ethnicity, as well as her relations to other heroes in the Marvel Universe.

"Muslims in the U.S. and around the world grapple with a basic, burning question," writes Zareena Grewal in *Islam Is a Foreign Country,* "who defines Islam today?" (16). By entering the realm of fantasy, Ms. Marvel's storylines make real-world parallels more digestible and comprehensible. Yet as much positive work as Khan does, it remains important to note that one thing missing in these early issues is a truly broad diversity of Muslims. Readers learn through Kamran, Khan's brother Aamir, and her best friend, Nakia, among others, that there are different types of Muslims, yet these characters are not fully developed at this stage in the series. Even the head of Khan's mosque community, Sheikh Abdullah, who is key to Khan's desire to be a hero, is presented in fascinating yet mere thumbnail fashion. All these characters are also Sunni, which is an internally diverse community, but the Shi'ah branch of Islam is absent in this volume.

Fortunately, although it lies beyond the scope of this collection, the second volume offers more opportunity for broader inquiries, particularly into race and sexuality. Aamir becomes engaged to an African American Muslim woman, Tyesha. She is a "blerd," a black nerd, who bonds with Khan over Frank Herbert's *Dune*. Thus, volume 2 contains specific discussion of interracial relationships in Muslim communities and acknowledges the existence of racism within those same communities. In addition, Zoe, a popular girl in Khan's high school who initially serves as an antagonist to Khan in volume 1, is forced in volume 2 to come out as a lesbian. As this storyline develops, readers find out that Zoe has a crush on Nakia. The crush is unreciprocated, but Nakia still reaches out to Zoe as a friend. In yet another new arc, Khan travels to Pakistan and discovers that being a hero in Pakistan is different than being a hero in New Jersey. Clearly, there is more material to be mined in the move away from the first nineteen Khan-centric issues, and we look forward to these conversations continuing and deepening in future Ms. Marvel scholarship.

However, current and future discussions around Ms. Marvel will require context and history. To that end, the first two essays in this collection look back to Khan's two most prominent precursors: Carol Danvers, the first Ms. Marvel; and Dust, an Afghani Muslim member of the X-Men, who first appeared in 2002. J. Richard Stevens's essay on Danvers not only details her long history, but it also locates Khan as a generational youth ambassador who bridges feminist and postfeminist readerships. Stevens also raises important questions of gendered violence. In addition to the direct ways in which Carol Danvers is mistreated, this essay implicitly asks whether Danvers's story would have been different if women had been more involved in the inception and development of her early narrative.

In a second essay about Khan's precursors, "Placing Ms. Marvel and Dust," Martin Lund examines how crucial place and location are to Khan's identity, in particular in her role as a character who combats and transcends the Muslim female stereotypes that hampered Dust, her most prominent Muslim superhero precursor. Lund's analysis makes a seemingly obvious but important and—especially in the United States—too-often-forgotten point: not all Muslim women are the same. History and place make a difference in how people choose to present themselves, and their representations are shaped by their reactions to the world. Lund's essay makes a crucial contribution to a growing body of scholarship that analyzes Muslim women as fully realized human beings—a self-evident, yet unfortunately still necessary, corrective.

The second section, "Nation and Religion, Identity and Community," the largest section of the book, fleshes out Khan's significance and iconography, while also harboring rich and productive disagreements. Both of our essays are in this section, and both predominantly revel in Khan's triumphs over

Islamophobic stereotypes, whether through her identity as a South Asian immigrant, as detailed in Hussein's essay, or through her technocultural iconography, as in Jessica's piece. In contrast, Sika A. Dagbovie-Mullins and Eric Berlatsky, while acknowledging these positive gains, also detail what they see as an assimilationist and sometimes apolitical narrative in *Ms. Marvel* as a whole. A. David Lewis ends this section on a hopeful note, coalescing the "religion, identity, and community" themes, while agreeing that views of "nation" remain contentious and in flux.

The third section, "Pedagogy and Resistance," develops the idea of community first addressed in section 2 and asks how that community can be and already has been shaped by Khan's presence in real-world classrooms, comics conventions, and beyond. Peter E. Carlson and Antero Garcia map Khan's process of maturity and her journey to productive resistance as a way to reach students who might be struggling through a similar process themselves. Winona Landis addresses politics in the classroom from a different angle, citing students from her college composition and literature classes as they narrate their growth into a more complex understanding not only of Khan but also of themselves as political agents. Finally, Kristin M. Peterson employs theories of fashion and resistance to analyze the visual rhetoric of Khan's clothes and costume and to study the ways that Ms. Marvel's image has been disseminated into society, whether through cosplay or the San Francisco bus ads. All of these essays provide specific examples of the theoretical propositions offered in the first two sections, highlighting the ways that Khan has real impact in the real world.

Since fans have been so instrumental to Ms. Marvel's success, we close the academic portion of the book with two essays about fandom. In "Fangirls, Fanboys, and the Culture of Fandom," our fourth section, two scholars examine Khan's fans and Khan's own fandom from two different disciplines. English and media studies scholar Aaron Kashtan takes a closer look at the overlap between *Ms. Marvel*'s fans and Khan's character as a "fangirl," while religious studies professor Nicholaus Pumphrey surveys the recent history of "fanboys" and their resistance to change—especially in terms of gender and race. Both authors also note the potential for *Ms. Marvel* to disrupt the resistance of traditional male fans, whether from the top, within Marvel's corporate offices, or in fan-based stories that sprout from the grassroots. These two essays also force readers to think about their roles as both consumers and creators. If literary and cultural theorist Roland Barthes is right, and the author is dead, both readers and fans create their own expected and unexpected meanings around the text (Barthes). Both Kashtan and Pumphrey provide space for future fandom study of Ms. Marvel, the Marvel Universe, and the changing face of comics.

The book closes with a coda, which begins with a single-panel piece by scholar and artist José Alaniz and then launches into a wide-ranging interview with G. Willow Wilson by anthropology and education scholar Shabana Mir. Wilson and Mir's discussion touches on virtually every theme addressed by this collection's essays: race, ethnicity, gender, religion, and generational differences, as well as representation, modern statehood, and the way the series as a whole both maps and resists our national political landscape. This return to Ms. Marvel's political context brings the collection full circle, while the specific touchstones of youth and the future of community and plurality in America—present in both of the coda pieces—close the book on a positive note.

Our predominant hope for this book is that it inspires our readers and colleagues to continue to reach across the many border walls or "incursion zones" that we all encounter in the real world on a daily basis. As fans, as well as researchers, we also want to amplify what we see as most hopeful about this series and to help our nation and its citizens forge a better future, in particular for the youth whom Ms. Marvel's creators strive most to reach. We are, after all, a nation that aspires to pluralism, which means that we need to continue to welcome different people—whether immigrant or otherwise marginalized—as full citizens. Whether working in science, architecture, medicine, teaching, community organizing, or productive storytelling, people do not need costumes or special permission to put their talents and expertise into practice. Our worth should not be measured by economics or by recognition from those in power. Our worth is innate in who we are, as well as in how well we use our talents to create community.

In *No Normal*, the first collected trade, when Kamala Khan is about to engage in her first superheroic act, she remembers a verse from the Qur'an about the value of saving a life. She seems to act, generally, upon another verse of the Qur'an that she does not explicitly quote, which says to strive with each other in good works (2:148). As she puts the finishing touches on her costume, she simplifies the phrasing to "Good is not a thing you are, it's a thing you do." We hope that these essays continue, like Kamala Khan, to inspire this simple but powerful and necessary edict: Do good.

NOTES

1. "It was known throughout the industry that (1) solo titles headed by female characters do not sell; (2) new titles do not sell, ever; and (3) minority characters don't sell" (Mir, in this volume).

2. See also Peterson's essay in this volume.

3. Hearts covered up the middle of this sentence, "end all aid" ("Comic Heroine Ms. Marvel").

4. Issue 1 of the Kamala Khan Ms. Marvel is technically the first issue of volume 3. Volume 1 of Ms. Marvel began with the first appearance of Carol Danvers in the 1970s. For the purposes of this collection, however, we number issue 1 of Kamala Khan's Ms. Marvel as part of volume 1.

BIBLIOGRAPHY

Abu-Lughod, Lila. *Do Muslim Women Need Saving?* Cambridge: Harvard University Press, 2013.

Baker, Peter, and Eileen Sullivan. "Trump Shares Inflammatory Anti-Muslim Videos, and Britain's Leader Condemns Them." *The New York Times* (November 29, 2017): https://www.nytimes.com/2017/11/29/us/politics/trump-anti-muslim-videos-jayda-fransen.html.

Baker-Whitelaw, Gavia. "Fanart Shows Muslim Superhero Ms. Marvel Punching Trump in the Face." *The Daily Dot* (December 15, 2015): https://www.dailydot.com/parsec/kamala-khan-marvel-donald-trump-fanart/.

Barthes, Roland. *Image, Music, Text.* Translated by Stephen Heath. New York: Hill and Wang, 1977.

Berlant, Lauren. *Cruel Optimism.* Durham, NC: Duke University Press, 2011.

Bruton, F. Brinley. "Gold Star Families Attack Trump over Comments about Ghazala Khan." *NBC News* (August 1, 2016): https://www.nbcnews.com/politics/2016-election/gold-star-families-attack-trump-over-comments-about-ghazala-khan-n620631.

Carroll, Lauren. "In Context: Donald Trump's Comments on a Database of American Muslims." *Politifact.com* (November 24, 2015): http://www.politifact.com/truth-o-meter/article/2015/nov/24/donald-trumps-comments-database-american-muslims/.

"Comic Heroine Ms. Marvel Saves San Francisco from Anti-Islam Ads." *NBC News* (January 27, 2015): https://www.nbcnews.com/news/asian-america/comic-heroine-ms-marvel-saves-san-francisco-anti-islam-ads-n294571.

Cox, Carolyn. "Kamala Khan Takes a Stand in Teaser Image for Civil War II." *The Mary Sue* (March 10, 2016): https://www.themarysue.com/kamala-khan-captain-marvel/.

Curtis, Edward E. *Muslim Americans in the Military: Centuries of Service.* Bloomington: Indiana University Press, 2016.

Grewal, Zareena. *Islam Is a Foreign Country: American Muslims and the Global Crisis of Authority.* New York: NYU Press, 2013.

Haberman, Maggie, and Richard A. Oppel Jr. "Donald Trump Criticizes Muslim Family of Slain U.S. Soldier, Drawing Ire." *The New York Times* (July 30, 2016): https://www.nytimes.com/2016/07/31/us/politics/donald-trump-khizr-khan-wife-ghazala.html.

Jenkins, Henry. "Introduction: Should We Discipline the Reading of Comics?" *Critical Approaches to Comics: Theories and Methods.* Eds. Matthew J. Smith and Randy Duncan. New York: Routledge, 2012. 1–14.

Johnston, Rich. "When Kamala Khan Punches Donald Trump…" *Bleeding Cool* (December 9, 2015): https://www.bleedingcool.com/2015/12/09/when-kamala-khan-punches-donald-trump/.

Lewis, A. David, and Christine Hoff Kraemer. "Introduction." Lewis and Kraemer, eds. *Graven Images: Religion in Comic Books and Graphic Novels*. New York: Bloomsbury Academic, 2010.

Mamdani, Mahmood. *Good Muslim, Bad Muslim: America, the Cold War, and the Roots of Terror*. New York: Pantheon Books, 2004.

Melrose, Kevin. "Trump May Have Quoted Bane in His Inaugural Speech." *Comic Book Resources, cbr.com* (January 20, 2017): https://www.cbr.com/trump-bane-inaugural-speech/.

Mercia, Dan. "Women Detail Sexual Allegations against Trump." *Cnn.com* (December 12, 2017): http://www.cnn.com/2017/12/11/politics/donald-trump-women-allegations/index.html.

Muaddi, Nadeem. "The Bush-Era Muslim Registry Failed. Yet the U.S. Could Be Trying It Again." *Cnn.com* (December 22, 2016): http://www.cnn.com/2016/11/18/politics/nseers-muslim-database-qa-trnd/index.html.

Romano, Aja. "Muslim American Superhero Kamala Khan Has Become a Real-World Protest Icon." *Vox* (February 2, 2017): https://www.vox.com/culture/2017/2/2/14457384/kamala-khan-captain-america-protest-icon.

Seifert, Mark. "Phil Noto Revised His Civil War II #0 Kamala Khan Cover Art in Reaction to Trump's Immigration Ban." *Bleeding Cool* (January 28, 2017): https://www.bleedingcool.com/2017/01/28/phil-noto-revises-civil-war-ii-0-kamala-khan-ms-marvel-cover-art-reaction-trumps-immigration-ban.

Stevenson, Peter W. "This Section of Trump's Inaugural Address Sounds a Lot Like Bane from *Batman*." *Washington Post* (January 20, 2017): https://www.washingtonpost.com/news/the-fix/wp/2017/01/20/this-section-of-trumps-inaugural-address-sounds-a-lot-like-bane-from-batman/?utm_term=.a98ec5acf604.

Tolentino, Jia. "The Writer behind a Muslim Marvel Superhero on Her Faith in Comics." *The New Yorker* (April 29, 2017): https://www.newyorker.com/culture/persons-of-interest/g-willow-wilsons-american-heroes.

Wiegman, Robyn. *American Anatomies: Theorizing Race and Gender*. Durham, NC: Duke University Press, 1995.

Wilson, G. Willow. Interview with Jana Riess. Festival of Faith and Writing. Grand Rapids, MI. April 12, 2014.

Wilson, G. Willow, and Adrian Alphona. *Ms. Marvel, Vol. 1: No Normal*. New York: Marvel Now!, 2014.

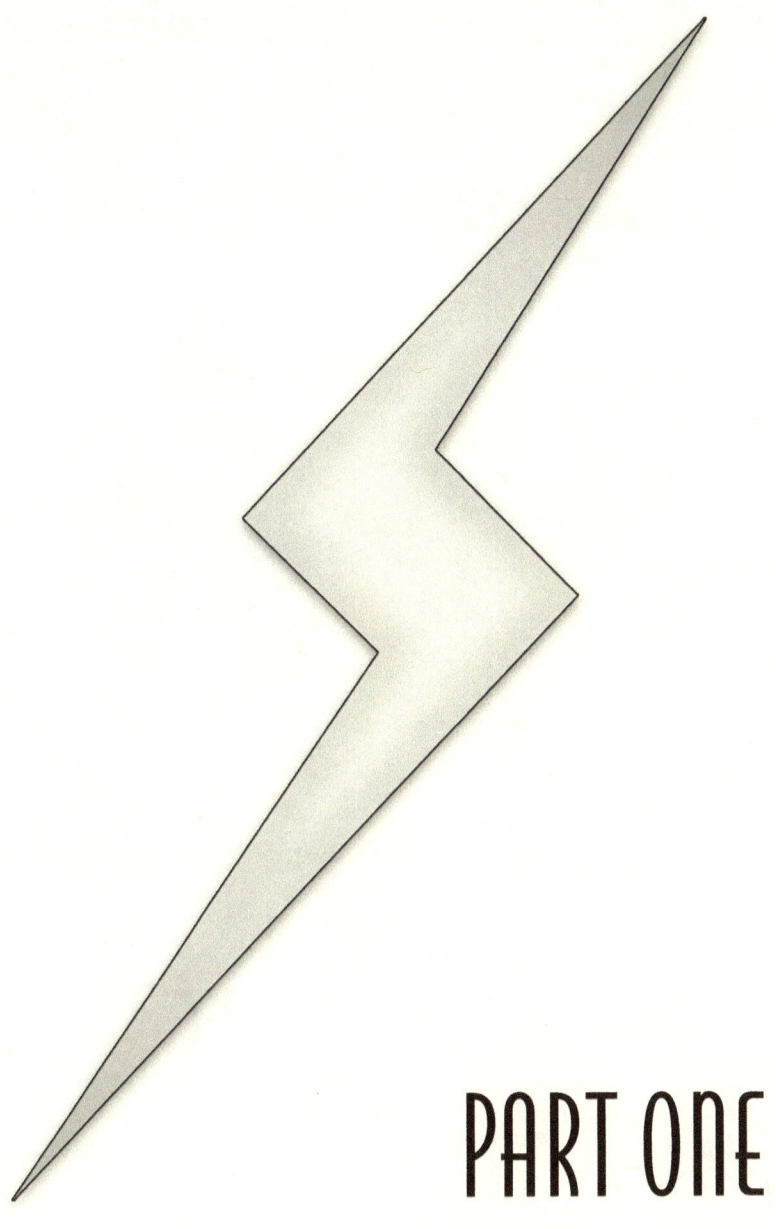

PART ONE

Precursors

MENTORING MS. MARVEL

Marvel's Kamala Khan and the Reconstitution of Carol Danvers

J. RICHARD STEVENS

The phrase "Higher, Further, Faster, More," which adorns t-shirts and merchandise and is the title of the first comic book arc of the 2014 volume of *Captain Marvel*, captures the spirit of Marvel's most successful recent attempt to create an inspiring female superhero figure by again reviving and reconfiguring Carol Danvers, the original Ms. Marvel. The Danvers character has endured several relaunches through the years, but the current series of changes involves nearly every aspect of the character's appearance, history, and even personality. The new Captain Marvel is considered the vanguard of a concerted effort by Marvel to increase the number of female heroes in Marvel's publications to more explicitly address the interests of a rising female readership (Alonso, Armitage).

In 2014, Marvel also launched the third series to be titled *Ms. Marvel*, featuring Kamala Khan as an inclusive and intersectional symbol of female heroism. Taking her name from the original 1977 character, Khan's portrayal represented a convergence of contrasts, a Muslim American teen from New Jersey who initially takes on the form of Danvers, the blonde superheroine from New York.

The 2014 *Ms. Marvel* narrative opens with Khan struggling against conflicting loyalties from her dual identity: the teenage Pakistani American girl who does not wear the *hijab* and cannot eat the sandwich she craves because she does not eat pork; the daughter who seeks parental permission, and violates her parents' rules by sneaking out to a waterfront party to impress her friends.

This act of defiance leads to a transformation when Terrigen Mist envelops her and activates her latent Inhuman powers. As her body transforms, Khan is presented with a psychedelic vision of Carol Danvers and the Avengers. Through dialogue with them, she explores her own standing in multiple communities and considers the gulf between the identity conflicts of her daily existence and her desires for simplicity. She says to Danvers, "I want to be beautiful and awesome and butt-kicking and less complicated. I want to be *you*. Except I would wear the classic, politically incorrect costume and kick butt in giant wedge heels" (Wilson and Alphona "Metamorphosis" 17).

This juxtaposition frames the identity struggle of Kamala Khan: a darker-skinned Pakistani American teen who feels drawn to Western forms of attractiveness, who struggles against both the strictures imposed by her family's culture and the excesses of American-mediated norms. Forced to balance an intricate dance of daily code switching, Khan yearns for simplicity in her identity, a tendency representing the plight of intersectional identities and of millennials in general.

When the vision dissipates, Khan (whose powers include shape shifting) emerges from her cocoon in the image of an earlier "politically incorrect" Carol Danvers Ms. Marvel. She initially uses Danvers's form when employing her shape-altering powers, but she soon fashions a costume from a burkini to make use of her own body during missions (Wilson and Alphona "Past Curfew").

Khan's early adventures include rescuing millennial peers from exploitation, juggling the pressures of school, learning about her new identity as an Inhuman, trying to find peace between her family's home culture and expectations of what it means to be "American," connecting to her new superhero community, enduring the pressures of teenage relationship worries, and navigating the politics of high school.

Generational themes of identity resonate strongly within the comic, and author G. Willow Wilson said she intended *Ms. Marvel* as an anthem to millennials (Wilson, personal interview). This premise becomes most prominent at the conclusion of the first narrative arc, as Ms. Marvel uncovers a plot by a villain called the Inventor, who convinces teens to surrender themselves as living batteries in an effort to reduce their carbon footprint and provide a new energy source to the world. Freeing some teens, Khan begins to challenge their low spirits with rousing dialogue:

> Okay. Real talk time. I get it. I do. The media hates us because we read on our smartphones. The economists hate us because we trade things instead of buying them. (I read that article in The Pedantic Monthly for school the other day.) Just because they're **old** doesn't

make them right. We're not the ones who messed up the economy or the planet. Maybe they do think of us as parasites, but they're not the ones who are gonna have to live with this mess—. (Wilson and Alphona "Generation Why" 2)

Khan gets several opportunities in the text to offer social criticism of intergenerational relations, though issue 10 represents the most concentrated example of such rhetoric. Inspiring her peers to recognize their own individual potential for contribution, they band together in mutual support to defeat the Inventor. Throughout her adventures, Khan's voice serves as a rallying cry for millennials to support one another and to find value from their own generational values. However, this voice still exists within the context of her connections to members of other generations—most prominently her namesake, the original Ms. Marvel, Carol Danvers.

Khan encounters Danvers in issue 16, and the two form an intergenerational bond over their shared superhero identities. Danvers serves as a mentor to the teen superhero. The relationship comes to define both characters and finally provides Danvers with the opportunity to explore her own reconfigured feminism.

Addressing Marvel's Controversies

In 2014, Marvel Studios announced an upcoming film project for the Carol Danvers Captain Marvel. This announcement followed a series of articles and social media postings critical of the fourteen Marvel Studios film portrayals of female characters, including incidents of actors slut shaming a female character (Yamato), continued observations about the lack of any female-led solo film (Brown *The Modern Superhero*, 51), a relative lack of merchandising for female characters (Baker-Whitelaw, Stewart), and general concerns about the trend toward oversexualized presentations of female characters (Gentry).

Marvel Studios struggled with female representation in its first two phases of movie offerings. Part of that struggle likely stems from Disney's gendered conception of Marvel, most prominently on display when Disney purchased Marvel in 2009 to fill a "boy need" (Carlson). However, an additional gender problem exists within the source texts themselves. Though Marvel takes pride in its classic character pantheon of "people with problems," which introduced personal problems to make heroes more relatable to readers, the problems faced by Marvel's female heroes tend toward the kinds of gross mischaracterizations that reinforce negative stereotypes and make film treatments risky. Beyond the commonly observed underrepresentation of female characters in the comics industry at large, the tendency toward revealing costumes, the prominent use of the male gaze, and the problems of gender stereotypes in characterizations indicative across the comics publication spectrum, Marvel heroines suffer from stigmatized personal and social problems such as domestic violence (the Wasp), mental illness (Aurora, Scarlet Witch), experiencing a miscarriage (Invisible Woman), and even rape (Mockingbird). Unfortunately, Carol Danvers suffered a combination of the worst of these treatments.

This chapter reviews the disturbing history of Danvers by tracking the unfortunate editorial decisions Marvel writers made for Danvers over the years. Documenting the turns to redirect the Danvers narrative, this essay analyzes both Ms. Marvel and Captain Marvel as feminist icons Marvel so desperately needs to engage the growing female audience of its film properties, comic books, and (most importantly) merchandise. The two characters' interactions serve to promote both character frames for millennial consumers. Kamala Khan's lack of compromising baggage serves as a touchstone for Danvers, reframing her as an icon worthy of respect through the millennial gaze. The two characters' interactions serve to promote both character frames for millennial consumers.

The Original Ms. Marvel

Far from the feminist characterization that Danvers currently embodies, Captain Marvel began her career as a controversial figure only superficially representing feminist ideals. Created by Roy Thomas and Gene Colan, Carol Danvers originally appeared in *Marvel Super-Heroes*, volume 1, issue 13 (March 1968) as a supporting character to the original (male) Captain Marvel, the alien Mar-Vell. Introduced as head of security, Danvers is initially described as "Man or woman, . . . the finest head of security a missile base could want!" (13). Danvers quickly became a fixture of Captain Marvel's self-titled series (Thomas and Colan "Out of the Holocaust!").

Holding a position normally associated with males gave Danvers a symbolic feminism; however, her real role in the series was to serve as a damsel in distress for Captain Marvel, as she did in issues 1, 7, 9, 10, 13, 14, 16, 17, and 18 of the first volume of *Captain Marvel*. In fact, it is as a damsel in distress in need of rescue that she gets her powers. In *Captain Marvel*, volume 1, issue 18 (Thomas, Kane, Buscema, and Romita), Danvers's genes are fused with Kree genetic material, granting her the powers of flight, invulnerability, strength, and a precognitive "sixth sense," which served as a superhuman form of "women's intuition."[1] Thus, even her origin is tied directly to Captain Marvel, as her powers come from his DNA—Mike Madrid would describe this origin in his 2009 book as the decision by Marvel to "snap off a rib from one of their male characters to create their Eve" (175)—and she dresses in a version of his costume and uses a version of his superhero name.

Danvers first assumed the mantle of Ms. Marvel in the first issue of her self-titled series (Conway, Conway, Buscema, and Sinnott). The "Ms." title served as a direct connection to second-wave feminism (Wheeler), with Danvers battling in her civilian identity for equal pay (White). In her day job, Danvers is the editor of a women's magazine, and she battles with editor J. Jonah Jameson—the same editor with whom *Spider-Man*'s Peter Parker wrangled—for control of the framing of "women's issues."

Within the narrative, Danvers is originally unaware of her adventures as Ms. Marvel; in fact, Danvers transforms during fainting spells and later awakens with no memory of what transpired. Thus, the strength that she exhibits as a modern professional is often undercut by her need to retire from stressful situations to transform, which leads to missed deadlines and unfinished tasks that undermine her position as a strong career woman able to compete in a man's industry. Like many superheroes, her alter-ego adventures explain to the reader the unfairness of such perceptions: her male colleagues, for example, do not suffer the additional burden of representation that her gender imparts. Danvers eventually gains control of her two identities, but her derivative relationship to Captain Marvel (e.g., wearing a version of his costume), the bare midriff of her uniform, the fainting spells, and her inability to "move far from traditionally female roles" (Inness 145) made Danvers's original incarnation a considerably weak feminist icon. She would change her costume in issue 9 (Claremont, Pollard, Sinnott, and Grainger) and eventually be fired from her job.

As a hero, Danvers had solo adventures in her self-titled series, but she also began to consort with the Avengers, a team that she later officially joined (Michelinie and Byrne). While on the Avengers, Danvers inexplicably becomes pregnant and gives birth within hours to a being who rapidly grows into an adult (Shooter et al.). Her "son," a being known as Marcus, explains that he abducted Danvers, used mind control to seduce her, impregnated her with himself, and then wiped her memory before returning her to Earth. Danvers is initially repulsed, but she agrees to accompany Marcus back to his dimension. Marvel had already announced the impending cancelation of the *Ms. Marvel* title, and Danvers's departure was a way to remove her from the pages of the *Avengers*.

This story arc, most notably its thinly veiled rape, drew the ire of several fans and commentators:

> [I]t was rape and obvious rape at that. The writer had to go an extra, knowing step to add that line about mind control. If he'd just left that off, it would have merely been a fanboy romance, where the blonde and buxom heroine is swept off her feet by flowers and candy (no need for romance or love), and readily agrees to anything and everything the hero (or fanboy in clever disguise) wants.
>
> But time went by and NO ONE said anything about the rape! Not one word besides how some readers were so happy that Ms. M had finally found a good man. I wanted to barf. (Strickland)

Another critic was *Ms. Marvel* writer Chris Claremont: "[H]ow callous! How cruel! How unfeeling! Considering that [the Avengers] must have seen Ms. Marvel only a couple of days before, or even a couple of months before. She wasn't pregnant then. How could she be eight months pregnant now?" (qtd. in Sanderson 23).

Claremont effectively erased that episode from Danvers's remembered (in-continuity) character history by having her mind violated by the mutant Rogue in *Avengers v. 1 Annual*, issue 10.[2] Rogue's abilities allowed her to drain and "borrow" the powers of anyone she touched, and, during the fight, she held onto Danvers too long, permanently absorbing her powers and erasing Danvers's memory (Claremont and Golden). Claremont later had Danvers erase all records of the existence of Ms. Marvel (Claremont, Cockrum, and Wiacek), removing all in-continuity record of the rape storyline from Marvel Comics continuity.

Danvers turns to Professor X, telepath and mentor for the X-Men, to recover some of her memories, returning the history of her violation to continuity. She expresses outrage that the Avengers allowed her to depart with her rapist and then joins the X-Men for a series of adventures. Beginning with *Uncanny X-Men*, volume 1, issue 164, she gains cosmic powers and has a series of adventures under the name "Binary" (Claremont and Cockrum).

The 1990s saw Danvers return to her black Ms. Marvel costume, but with the new name "Warbird." She rejoins the Avengers (Busiek and Perez "Too Many Avengers"), but she sees her powers diminished, and she turns to alcohol to cope. Her insecurities mount, and she attacks Tony Stark in a drunken rage (Busiek, Howell, and Chen), harms one of the Inhumans when fighting drunk (Ostrander, Edkin, and Aucoin), and is court-martialed by the Avengers (Busiek and Perez "The Court Martial"). She later endures a judicial hearing on destruction of property caused while intoxicated (Busiek, Immonen, and Grawbadger) and is ordered to rejoin the Avengers to avoid jail time (Busiek and Perez "New Order").

These events produced another stain on the already-strained reception of Ms. Marvel as a second-wave feminist icon.[3] However, beginning in 2006, Marvel writers began a concerted effort to recover the Danvers character from her troubled past. In *The New Avengers*, volume 2, issue 15, Danvers declines an invitation by Captain America to rejoin the Avengers, pledging to him that she intends to reclaim her status and "re-earn my wings as a superhero" before returning to the Avengers (Bendis and Cho 9).

Two months later, the second volume of *Ms. Marvel* premiered. Writer Brian Reed reformulated Danvers as a high-flying adrenaline junkie (Reed and De La Torre) who had suffered a brutal POW experience that ended her flying career and launched her career in intelligence (Reed and Siqueira; Reed and Melo). Visually, the series places Danvers quite literally within the "Bad Girl" frame, complete with the stereotypical "huge, gravity-defying breasts, mile-long legs, perpetually pouty lips, and perfectly coiffed big hair" (Brown *Dangerous Curves*, 55). These markers allowed Danvers to be coded female by the stereotypes of her swimsuit costume and the amount of skin she showed but still fit the recognizably male superhero trope to her core audience: "The comic book industry was so dominated by men for so long and so little attention was paid to the polysemy of comic book texts that most of the differentiation of female characters remained at the visual level; the code, message and way of thinking were clearly male and simply transposed into the mouths and minds of heroines" (Bongco 111).

The series catered to its male audience with revealing presentations of Danvers's anatomy, and the characterization of her personality was more masculine than feminine, a common trait of female superheroes: "[A]ny feminist critic could demonstrate that most of these characters fail to inscribe any specific female qualities: they behave in battle like male heroes with thin waists and silicone breasts" (Reynolds 80). Taken as a whole, the thirty-five-year literary history of Carol Danvers leading up to the emergence of the cinematic Marvel narratives is fraught with uncomfortably gendered texts. Though some symbolic forms of second-wave feminism are apparent within the text, her fainting spells, the derivative origin of her powers, her revealing costume—to say nothing of her instances of memory loss, struggles with alcoholism, and rape—presented significant challenges for film adaptation. The moment reviewers or casual fans turned to the original source material, Danvers's credibility as a feminist symbol would be undermined.

But all that changed in 2012, as the character was reformulated as Captain Marvel, redesigned and brought into a series of tight dialogues with a new Ms. Marvel. Over the next few years, Carol Danvers would appear in four new "Captain Marvel" titles, each adding new elements to her narrative, as the character was slowly reconstructed to fit more recent sensibilities.

Reclaiming Carol Danvers

A new series titled *Captain Marvel* (the seventh Marvel series to be so titled) was released in 2012, with Carol Danvers appearing on the cover in a costume more reminiscent of a military flight suit than spandex. Above the logo appeared the text tagline "Earth's Mightiest Hero."

Even before the first issue, the promotional materials generated strong reactions. In the editorial section of issue 1, the editor printed four submitted fan drawings of the new costume. In the letter column section of issue 2 appeared two strong objections to the new costume by (male) fans (Apfel; Brown, A.). The 2012 series signaled a new approach to the character, one better suited for female readers and fans.

The first issue presented Danvers idolizing Helen Cobb, a pilot who set fifteen speed records in the 1950s and was a member of the Mercury 13 space program before the glass ceiling prevented her selection for spaceflight. Cobb passes away in the issue, and Danvers flies her ashes into space (DeConnick and Soy). Writer Kelly Sue DeConnick had reportedly "pitched Carol as Chuck Yeager," drawing more heavily upon the character's air force background to instill a new spirit in her: "Carol has a similar appeal to me. She's got that thing—that need to faster, further, higher, more . . . always more" (Hudson).

This spirit would be challenged as the series focused on Danvers coming to terms with a growing brain tumor, which forces her to choose between using her powers and preserving her personality.[4] After spending several issues holding her powers in check, Danvers eventually chooses to save New York City by flying into outer space to break her connection to an alien machine (DeConnick and Andrade). As a result of her exertion, Danvers's brain hemorrhages, and she loses her memories.

Due to this injury, Carol Danvers is once again freed from the consequences of her negative publication history (this time her history with alcoholism) through memory loss, and all the trauma and controversial events from her past are pushed aside. DeConnick explained that her goal was to have Danvers rebuild her memories through conversations with a little girl that idolizes her: "She's trying to figure out who she is and how to move forward, recreating everything for herself, and the deepest connection she has at that point is with this little girl. So she starts to relearn her personal history through the eyes of this 8-year-old girl who sees her in the best possible light—that is, what she is trying to be now. That's how she understands herself" (qtd. in Ching). This decision not only gave DeConnick a way to banish the problematic elements of Danvers's past but also provided the chance to bring Danvers into closer alignment with the "Carol Corps" fan base growing around the character. From the earliest announcement of Danvers's transition to Captain Marvel, her new uniform, her authorship by a female writer, and the change in direction had been celebrated by female fans.

As one writer observed: "Carol Danvers isn't suddenly popular after languishing in relative obscurity because she's now Captain Marvel. She's popular because Kelly Sue DeConnick has tapped into a market demographic that's been not only ignored but actively abused by publishers and fans alike" (Rosburg). The final issue of the series culminates in a celebration of fan involvement. As Captain Marvel stands on a podium to receive the key to the city, she is attacked by a gathering of drones, who begin to focus their microwave weaponry upon her. In order to save her, the individuals in the crowd begin to yell, "I am Captain Marvel!" to redirect the targeting systems of the drones and diffuse the beam.[5] Danvers recovers and destroys the remaining drones (DeConnick and Andrade).

Issue 17 is also the second appearance of Kamala Khan, shown pinning up one of Captain Marvel's cards to a bulletin board. (The first appearance was a background cameo in issue 14, the same issue in which Danvers lost her memories). The new Ms. Marvel would premiere just a few short months later, and the relationships between her and Danvers would provide a powerful framework for both characters, as well as their respective fans.

More importantly, this intergenerational dialogue allowed Danvers's (reconstructed) second-wave baby-boomer feminism to interact with Khan's postfeminist millennial attitude. This dialogue is essential to extending Danvers's discourse into spaces accepted by millennial audiences. Danvers and Khan's interaction is important because the kind of postfeminist rhetoric typically employed through millennial discourse "actively draws on and invokes feminism as that which can be taken into account in order to suggest that equality is achieved, in order to install a whole repertoire of meanings which emphasize that it is no longer needed, a spent force" (McRobbie 4). Modern female superheroes tend to consider their forerunners as "Camp Mothers" (Hopkins), appreciating the style but not the substance of the earlier feminist struggles. As Jeffrey Brown explains: "For better or worse, the girl action heroine represents a kind of post-feminist character who operates in a world where earlier feminist concerns are seen as outdated. This is an era in which the media embrace a rhetoric that declares girls are unquestionably empowered. Girls can be anything they want, and they can do anything they want" (*Dangerous Curves* 142).

The retroactive continuity (retcon) adjustments to Danvers's publication history instilled a stronger sense of second-wave feminism just as Khan's adventures were exploring millennial concerns from a postfeminist perspective. Therefore, bringing the two into direct dialogue was essential to establish each as a source of cultural authority.

Mentoring Ms. Marvel

Even before *Ms. Marvel*, volume 3, issue 1 hit store shelves,[6] the announcement that the new Ms. Marvel would be a Muslim teenager drew praise and attention from fans and media outlets alike. The premiere of the 2014 *Ms. Marvel* comic sold out and went into seven printings, a rarity for any comic. The creators and the comic were nominated for various awards, and the first story arc won the 2015 Hugo Award for Best Graphic Story, as well as the 2016 Dragon Award for Best Comic. The first three collected volumes of *Ms. Marvel* debuted on the *New York Times* bestseller list.

Khan's adventures revolved around balancing her high school relationships against her superhero mission, and author G. Willow Wilson explained that she intended *Ms. Marvel* "as a love letter to the millennial audience" (Wilson "Islam in Comics"). According to Wilson, the millennial generation is vastly misunderstood, and she felt driven to tell stories about their experiences both with and against older generations. Kamala Khan and Carol Danvers would begin to interact, establish an intergenerational dialogue, and form a relationship that would inform both characters, even as it also distinguished them from each other.

When Danvers visits Khan in "Last Days, Part Two," she gives her namesake a call to action: "That's what I came here to tell you. The airlifts and the heroes and the money—they're not coming to Jersey City. You're *it*, Ms. Marvel. Today is the day *you* stand up" (Wilson and Alphona 4). Danvers helps Khan with a one-hour mission. She advises her that she cannot save everyone (12) and that she should remember that self-care is essential for a superhero (14). At the conclusion of their brief adventure, Danvers gives Khan a Captain Marvel medallion with a GPS locator ("Last Days, Part Three" 11) and tells her she is proud of Khan (13). The mentor relationship established, Danvers departs for New York to face the end of the universe (and the beginning of the Marvel 2015 Secret Wars event).

Both characters would soon appear in the Secret Wars event within the pages of *A-Force*.[7] Danvers also appeared in *Captain Marvel and the Carol Corps*, a reimagined event in which Danvers leads a group of female pilots on World War II missions. When the Secret Wars event concluded, both Danvers and Khan received new self-titled series with the same writers who had previously been authoring them.

Both new series involved significant components of the Civil War II event storyline. Like the 2006 Civil War event, the hero community was divided over a moral issue—in this case, whether to stop crimes before they happened by using a mutant who had the ability to predict the future. Danvers was the prime mover in favor of using the future intelligence, while Tony Stark (Iron Man) was the primary opponent of the use. This framing established Iron Man and Captain Marvel as the two most influential and important characters in the Marvel Universe (just as Captain America and Iron Man had been the most influential characters in the 2006 Marvel Civil War event).

Even before the Civil War II event, tensions between Danvers and Stark were rising because of Khan's mentorship. Khan joined one of the Avengers teams, and as such had frequent interactions with Iron Man. The fourth volume of *Ms. Marvel* tracked Khan's increasing difficulty juggling school, her superhero mission in Jersey City, and her operational duties as an Avenger, echoing the parallel real-life narrative of millennials who are overcommitted and experience stress trying to balance their many obligations. In issue 6, Khan calls Danvers for help in a difficult situation. Danvers arrives to save the day and then advises Khan to put her school work first and to learn to say no to some of her obligations with the Avengers (Wilson and Leon "Army of One" 14). Iron Man arrives, and he and Danvers have a tense exchange over whom Khan should turn to for help and mentorship.

The competition for mentorship between Iron Man and Captain Marvel closely resembles the struggle for Spider-Man's loyalty in the 2006 Civil War event. In the earlier version, Spider-Man sided with Iron Man against Captain

America but was won over to Captain America's side when his ideals were challenged by Iron Man's actions.

Civil War II repeats this character arc with Khan. In issue 8 of the series, Danvers explains her new program to Khan and convinces Khan to support the enforcement of predicted future crimes (Wilson, Miyazawa, and Alphona "Civil War II"). Initially, Khan is supportive and is even excited to be siding with Danvers as tensions with Stark mount: "How cool was Captain Marvel? She doesn't take any of his sass" (Bendis and Leon "Spider-Man 2" 15). Her mentorship bond leads her to idolize Danvers, and, at first, she blindly supports Danvers's decisions. For Danvers's part, she recognizes the importance of the mentorship and begins to keep her own insecurities from Khan, privately telling Hawkeye:

> [S]he idolizes me. The idea of holding people responsible for things they might've only thought about makes her nervous. Makes me nervous, too. I'm confident we can correct for it. But it's a bump. Thing is, if I admit that to her, and she loses confidence—starts second-guessing our mission in the field—maybe she gets killed. Another death Tony can lay at my feet, next to Rhodey [War Machine] and Bruce [Banner, the Hulk]. This time, he'd be right. (Gage, Gage, and Anka "Lonely at the Top" 12)

Ms. Marvel is put in charge of a team to prevent future calamities (including incarcerating individuals who have not yet broken the law) and progressively begins to doubt the justness of the system. This discontent eventually leads Khan to a confrontation with Danvers, and the two (in the presence of Iron Man) argue about their disagreement. Furious, Danvers ends the conversation: "I trusted you, you have my *name*, you wear my colors—but seeing how far you've gone to make your point, I can see my trust was misplaced" (Wilson, Miyazawa, and Alphona "Civil War II" 13). Danvers then flies away.

Wilson explained in a 2016 lecture that this confrontation had been one of the storytelling goals of the Civil War II event for her. "In life, we eventually outgrow our unexamined trust in mentors. Part of growing up is learning that we don't always agree with those we respect. I think one of the greatest moments of growth can occur when we challenge our elders and mentors and learn to take responsibility for our own ethics" (Wilson "Islam in Comics").

Through this encounter, Khan and Danvers separate. Narratively, the transcendence of the student from the mentor and the establishment of ideological boundaries is a natural stage in a mentoring relationship. In that sense, the parting mirrors the character arc of Spider-Man in *Civil War* (for example, Spider-Man began that arc wearing the "Iron Spider" armor that looked like Iron Man's, and then he transitioned back to his cloth costume when he switched sides). Narratively, Danvers and Khan repeat the Stark and Parker dynamic, complete with hypermasculine posturing and confrontation.

However, in terms of the character arc, the relational effects in *Civil War II* seem quite different. For Khan, the loss is palpable: "Worse than getting punched in the gut. Worse than having my heart broken. Worse than pretty much anything" (Wilson, Miyazawa, and Alphona 13). Khan discards the Captain Marvel medallion, quits the Avengers, and departs for Pakistan to visit family and explore other aspects of her identity. She joins a new team of teenage heroes called the Champions, though she lets slip that one of her driving motives is to prove herself to Danvers (Waid and Ramos 9).

The Resulting Reconstitution of Carol Danvers

Since 2012, Marvel writers have employed a variety of narrative and visual techniques to effectively erase embarrassing historical elements of the Carol Danvers story in preparation for her entry into the Marvel cinematic universe. The new name, the new costume, another memory wipe, the retroactive continuity adjustments to her origin and literary history to enhance her second-wave feminism achievements, her prominent positioning in the Civil War II narrative, her mentorship with the new Ms. Marvel, and the dissolution of that mentorship relationship all worked together to reconfigure the elements embodied in the contemporary Captain Marvel text. Yet another significant retcon occurred in the 2017 preview issue (0) of *The Mighty Captain Marvel*. Within the comic, Danvers's origin is reframed yet again, altering her air force career and intelligence career into a drive toward space. Danvers now appears to be one of the first female astronauts (if not the first), and the text implies it was on a space mission that she received her powers. For the first time, this story is presented without Mar-Vell's presence at all, as if her powers came directly to her in space (Stohl, Laiso, and Rosanas 13). On one page, Carol Danvers's history with Mar-Vell is seemingly erased, and references to this male role in her origin (as well as the damsel-in-distress framing and the "imprinted DNA" explanation for her powers) are wiped from publication history and contemporary continuity.

At the end of her solo series (*The Mighty Captain Marvel* simultaneously launched to replace it), Danvers uncovers and battles—from among her own staff—the self-proclaimed Master of the World. As she fights, she verbally clarifies her understanding of her own leadership and the isolation it brought (which she believes suited her personality) and appears to find renewed purpose through the conflict:

> A leader has to project confidence. Fight for what she believes in. But never stop questioning, wondering how to be better. You take in everything . . . and make your call. You thought isolating me would make me weaker? Buddy, you don't know me too well. All my life I've had to rely on myself, trust my instincts and convictions when others doubted me, and be prepared to back them up. You didn't hurt me with what you did. You gave me what I needed to win. (Gage, Gage, and Silas 11)

This rhetoric frames the likely direction of Marvel's new approach to the character. Danvers prevails and then wrestles with her status as a symbol as she is confronted with a large crowd of adoring fans. She gives a wave to honor their hopes, despite feeling that she does not deserve the praise. She then silently commits to earning their adoration every day (23).

The Civil War II event resolves when the mutant Ulysses, who enables the future profiling, evolves past his humanity and leaves Earth, ending the controversy. Iron Man is critically injured by Danvers in the final conflict, leaving Danvers with increased responsibilities. Danvers is repeatedly told that she is trusted and respected by friends and foes alike, even Iron Man. The series concludes with Danvers being debriefed by President Barack Obama, who exclaims, "You handled all of this, even with the eyes of the world on you, with incredible grace" (Bendis and Marquez 31). He concludes the encounter by calling Danvers the "future of the country" (35).

For a new reader (particularly a member of the Carol Corps), the four new *Captain Marvel* series push into inaccessible archives of unmentioned history, such as the mentions of rape, alcoholism, fainting, dual identities, alien births, and her earliest portrayals as a damsel in distress. Danvers's earliest adventures under the title *Ms. Marvel* can be found in expensive back issues (the 1977 premiere issue of *Ms. Marvel* sells for well over $100 in good condition), the out-of-print Masterworks collection, the out-of-print *Essential* collection, or by subscribing to Marvel Unlimited to access digital back issues. Unlike other 1960s and 1970s heroes, Danvers's historical texts have not been as widely republished since the 2012 relaunch of *Captain Marvel*.

Rather, the four recent series have become the more accessible text for new readers. Even Danvers's connection to the original Captain Marvel fades into a vague conception. Captain Marvel emerges as "Earth's Mightiest Hero," a former astronaut, and increasingly one of the most influential characters in mainstream Marvel continuity. This transition occurred carefully and in stages, as female creators and fans alike participated in an unlikely revival (really a reconstruction) of Marvel's first premiere female superhero—just in time for her cinematic feature film.[8]

Central to this reconfiguration is the mentor relationship with Kamala Khan. The interaction between second-wave feminism and postfeminism proved vital, not just in rendering the concerns of each generation in the terms of the other, but also in normalizing the agency of each character for the growing reading audience. By mostly removing troubling elements from Danvers's past and reframing her status as a feminist icon, Marvel has potentially positioned her to be less relevant to the concerns of millennials. The exchanges with Khan, however, provide rhetoric and positions for articulation that make both characters more accessible to both audiences.

NOTES

1. Marvel writers seemed to think "women's intuition" was a female marker of superheroism. In fact, earlier that decade, the "Femme Force," a group of female S.H.I.E.L.D. agents with extrasensory perceptions, appeared in *Captain America*, volume 1, issue 144 (Friedrich and Romita).

2. This annual, usually cited as the first appearance of the mutant and future X-Man Rogue, was actually the continuation to Claremont's story for *Ms. Marvel*, volume 1, issue 25, which was not published before the series was canceled. That story (and the actual first appearance of Rogue) would finally be printed in 1992 in the pages of *Marvel Super-Heroes*, volume 3, issue 11.

3. See Brown *Dangerous Curves* and D'Amore, "Invisible Girl" and "Accidental Supermom," as well as Emad, Gibson, Madrid, Murray, Robinson, and Stuller.

4. The tumor was predicted to destroy her brain, which would grow back because of her powers, but it would leave her without memories.

5. Many readers will recognize this scene as a technological update of the 1960 Stanley Kubrick film *Spartacus*. –Eds.

6. See our note in the introduction about numbering Kamala Khan's official introduction as Ms. Marvel. While we refer to *No Normal* as volume 1 in our own pieces, we retained the official numbering preserved by individual authors in this collection who chose to use it. –Eds.

7. Although most of the female heroes in *A-Force* were drawn wearing their vintage or classic era costumes, Danvers was one of the few characters to appear in her modern uniform.

8. The end of 2018's *Avengers: Infinity War* film suggested that Danvers would prove a key figure as the franchise continues, and a solo Captain Marvel film is now slated for release. –Eds.

BIBLIOGRAPHY

Alonso, Axel. "Break Out the New." *Comic Book Resources,* March 23, 2012, http://www.cbr.com/break-out-the-new/.

Apfel, Eric. Letter. *Captain Marvel* 7(2), October 2012: 19.

Armitage, Hugh. "Marvel Comics' Axel Alonso Promises More Female-led Titles." *Digital Spy,* March 25, 2012, http://www.digitalspy.com/comics/news/a373026/marvel-comics-axel-alonso-promises-more-female-led-titles.html.

Baker-Whitelaw, Gavia. "Why Is Gamora Missing from 'Guardians of the Galaxy' Merchandise?" *TheDailyDot,* August 6, 2014, http://www.dailydot.com/parsec/fans-notice-lack-of-gamora-merchandise/.

Bendis, Brian Michael, and Frank Cho. *The New Avengers* 1(15), March 2006.

Bendis, Brian Michael, and Nico Leon. *Spider-Man* 2(8), November 2016.

Bendis, Brian Michael, and David Marquez. *Civil War II* 1(8), February 2017.

Bongco, Mila. *Reading Comics: Language, Culture, and the Concept of the Superhero in Comic Books.* New York: Garland, 2000.

Brown, Alan. Letter. *Captain Marvel* 7(2), October 2012: 19.

Brown, Jeffrey A. *The Modern Superhero in Film and Television: Popular Genre and American Culture.* New York: Routledge, 2016.

———. *Dangerous Curves: Action Heroines, Gender, Fetishism, and Popular Culture.* Jackson: University Press of Mississippi, 2011.

Busiek, Kurt, Richard Howell, and Sean Chen. "Bad Moon Rising." *Iron Man* 3(7), August 1998.

Busiek, Kurt, Stuart Immonen, and Wade Grawbadger. "... Under the Cover of Night!" *The Avengers* 3(26), March 2000.

Busiek, Kurt, and George Pérez. "The Court Martial of Carol Danvers." *The Avengers* 3(7), August 1998.

———. "New Order." *The Avengers* 3(27), April 2000.

———. "Too Many Avengers!" *The Avengers* 3(4), May 1998.

Carlson, Nicholas. "Marvel Solves Disney's $50 Billion Boy Problem." *Business Insider,* August 31, 2009, http://www.businessinsider.com/marvel-solves-disneys-50-billion-boy-problem-2009-8.

Ching, Albert. "'Captain Marvel' Returns in a Cosmic Journey to Find Herself." *UpRoxx,* February 16, 2014, http://uproxx.com/hitfix/captain-marvel-returns-in-a-cosmic-journey-to-find-herself/.

Claremont, Chris, and Dave Cockrum. "Binary Star!" *The Uncanny X-Men* 1(164), December 1982.

Claremont, Chris, Dave Cockrum, and Bob Wiacek. "The Life That Late I Led ..." *The Uncanny X-Men* 1(158), June 1982.

Claremont, Chris, and Michael Golden. "By Friends—Betrayed!" *Avengers Annual* 1(10), 1981.

Claremont, Chris, Keith Pollard, Joe Sinnott, and Sam Grainger. "Call Me Death-Bird!" *Ms. Marvel* 1(9), September 1977.

Conway, Gerry, Carla Conway, John Buscema, and Joe Sinnott. "This Woman, This Warrior!" *Ms. Marvel* 1(1), January 1977.

D'Amore, Laura Mattoon. "Invisible Girl's Quest for Visibility: Easy Second Wave Feminism and the Comic Books." *Americana: The Journal of American Popular Culture, 1900–present,* 2008, http://www.americanpopularculture.com/journal/articles/fall_2008/d'amore.htm.
———. "The Accidental Supermom: Superheroines and Maternal Performativity, 1963–1980." *The Journal of Popular Culture* 45(6), 2012: 1226–48.
DeConnick, Kelly Sue, and Filipe Andrade. *Captain Marvel* 7(17), January 2014.
DeConnick, Kelly Sue, and Dexter Soy. *Captain Marvel* 7(1), September 2012.
Emad, Mitra C. "Reading Wonder Woman's Body: Mythologies of Gender and Nation." *Journal of Popular Culture* 39(6), 2006: 954–84.
Friedrich, Gary, and John Romita. "Hydra over All." *Captain America* 1(144), December 1971.
Gage, Christos N., Ruth Fletcher Gage, and Kris Anka. "Lonely at the Top, Part 3." *Captain Marvel* 8(8), October 2016.
Gage, Christos N., Ruth Fletcher Gage, and Thony Silas. "Lonely at the Top, Part 5." *Captain Marvel* 8(10), January 2017.
Gentry, Sage. "The Women of Marvel and Geek Subculture." *Sequart,* July 2, 2015, http://sequart.org/magazine/58745/the-women-of-marvel-and-geek-subculture/.
Gibson, Mel. "Who Does She Think She Is? Female Comic Book Characters, Second-Wave Feminism and Feminist Film Theory." Eds. Mel Gibson, David Huxley, and Joan Ormond, *Superheroes and Identities.* Oxford: Routledge, 2015. 135–46.
Hopkins, Susan. *Girl Heroes: The New Force in Popular Culture.* Melbourne, Australia: Pluto Press, 2002.
Hudson, Laura. "Kelly Sue DeConnick on the Evolution of Carol Danvers to Captain Marvel." *Comics Alliance,* March 19, 2012, http://comicsalliance.com/kelly-sue-deconnick-captain-marvel/.
Inness, Sherrie A. *Tough Girls: Women Warriors and Wonder Women in Popular Culture.* Philadelphia: University of Pennsylvania Press, 1999.
Madrid, Mike. *Supergirls: Fashion, Feminism, Fantasy, and the History of Comic Book Heroines.* Minneapolis: Exterminating Angel, 2009.
McRobbie, Angela. "Notes on Postfeminism and Popular Culture: Bridget Jones and the New Gender Regime." *All About the Girl: Culture, Power, and Identity,* ed. Anita Harris. New York: Routledge, 2004.
Michelinie, David, and John Byrne. "The Redoubtable Return of Crusher Creel!" *The Avengers* 1(183), May 1979.
Murray, Ross. "The Feminine Mystique: Feminism, Sexuality, Motherhood." *Journal of Graphic Novels and Comics* 2(1), 2011: 55–66.
Ostrander, John, Joe Edkin, and Derec Aucoin. "Live Kree or Die! Part 3: Blue Moon." *Quicksilver* 1(10), August 1998.
Reed, Brian, and Adriana Melo. "Secret Agent Danvers Part 2: Vitamin." *Ms. Marvel* 2(32). January 2009.
Reed, Brian, and Paulo Siqueira. "Secret Agent Danvers Part 1: Ascension." *Ms. Marvel* 2(31), December 2008.
Reed, Brian, and Roberto De La Torre. "Best of the Best." *Ms. Marvel* 2(1), May 2006.
Reynolds, Richard. *Super Heroes: A Modern Mythology.* Jackson: University Press of Mississippi, 1992.
Robinson, Lillian S. *Wonder Women: Feminisms and Superheroes.* New York: Routledge, 2004.

Rosburg, Caitlin. "Marvel Learned the Wrong Lessons from the Carol Corps." *The A.V. Club*, 2 April 2015, http://www.avclub.com/article/marvel-learned-wrong-lessons-carol-corps-218003.

Sanderson, Peter, ed. *The X-Men Companion II*. Stamford, CT: Fantagraphics Books, 1982.

Shooter, Jim, George Perez, Bob Layton, David Michelinie, and Dan Green. "The Child Is Father To . . . ?" *The Avengers* 1(200), October 1980.

Stewart, Sara. "Marvel and Its Sexist Superhero Movies Hit a New Low." *New York Post*, May 7, 2015, http://nypost.com/2015/05/07/marvel-and-its-sexist-superhero-movies-hit-a-new-low/.

Stohl, Margaret, Emilio Laiso, and Ramon Rosanas. *The Mighty Captain Marvel* 1(0), February 2017.

Strickland, Carol A. "The Rape of Ms. Marvel." *carolastrickland.com*, January 1980, http://www.carolastrickland.com/comics/msmarvel/index.html.

Stuller, Jennifer K. *Ink-Stained Amazons and Cinematic Warriors: Superwomen in Modern Mythology*. New York: I. B. Tauris, 2010.

Thomas, Roy, and Gene Colan. "Out of the Holocaust—A Hero!" *Captain Marvel* 1(1), May 1968.

———. "Where Stalks the Sentry." *Marvel Superheroes* 1(13), March 1968.

Thomas, Roy, Gil Kane, John Buscema, and John Romita. "Vengeance Is Mine!" *Captain Marvel* 1(18), November 1969.

Waid, Mark, and Humberto Ramos. *Champions* 2(1), December 2016.

Wheeler, Andrew. "Marvel Unveils New Ms. Marvel: A Muslim Pakistani-American Teenager." *Comics Alliance*, 5 November 2013, http://comicsalliance.com/marvel-comics-ms-marvel-g-willow-wilson-alphona-muslim-teen/.

White, Brett. "Marvel Women of the 70s: Ms. Marvel." *Marvel.com*, 9 July 2014, https://news.marvel.com/comics/22834/marvel_women_of_the_70s_ms_marvel/.

Wilson, G. Willow. "Islam in Comics." Public lecture. University of Colorado Boulder, 22 September 2016.

———. Personal interview. University of Colorado Boulder, April 12, 2017.

Wilson, G. Willow, and Adrian Alphona. "Generation Why. Part Three of Four." *Ms. Marvel* 3(10), February 2015.

———. "Last Days, Part Three." *Ms. Marvel* 3(18), November 2015.

———. "Last Days. Part Two." *Ms. Marvel* 3(17), October 2015.

———. "Metamorphosis. Part One of Five." *Ms. Marvel* 3(1), April 2014.

———. "Past Curfew. Part Four of Five." *Ms. Marvel* 3(4), June 2014.

———. "Urban Legend. Part Four of Five." *Ms. Marvel* 3(5), August 2014.

Wilson, G. Willow, and Nico Leon. "Army of One, Part 3 of 3." *Ms. Marvel* 4(6), June 2016.

Wilson, G. Willow, Takeshi Miyazawa, and Adrian Alphona. "Civil War II." *Ms. Marvel* 4(11), November 2016.

———. "Civil War II." *Ms. Marvel* 4(8), August 2016.

Yamato, Jen. "The Avengers' Black Widow Problem: How Marvel Slut-Shamed Their Most Badass Superheroine." *The Daily Beast*, 28 April 2015, http://www.thedailybeast.com/articles/2015/04/28/the-avengers-black-widow-problem-how-marvel-slut-shamed-their-most-badass-superheroine.html.

PLACING MS. MARVEL AND DUST

Marvel Comics, the New York Metro Area, and the "Muslim Problem"

MARTIN LUND

Moustafa Bayoumi writes that "[t]o be a Muslim American today often means to exist in that slightly absurd space between exotic and dangerous and between victim and villain simply because of people's assumptions about you" (15). This dynamic is nothing new. For most of its history and into the present, the United States has defined its relationship with race and ethnicity as problematic; it has grappled with a "problem of the color line," a "negro problem" in different configurations, a "Japanese" and a general "Asian problem," a "Jewish problem," and an "Irish problem," as well as an "immigrant problem," and many more.[1] These "problems" emerge when identity becomes a politically charged issue; constitute a negotiation of cultural and political anxieties (Maira 15–17); and have as a central concern if and how to make room for perceived Others in the polity and body politic. Following 9/11, Islam, Muslims, and their place in America have become a regular focus in American media, research, policy, and everyday life: "In short," writes Bayoumi, "Muslims in America have become a sociological dilemma" (130).[2] Thus, the "Muslim problem" is a prominent issue in the early twenty-first century.[3]

Muslim and Arab stereotypes have been part of the American superhero genre since its beginning,[4] but the industry has escalated such representation since shortly after 9/11; in the years since, an atmosphere of militancy, fear, and paranoia has increasingly permeated the overall output.[5] But Marvel Comics has also introduced a few Muslim characters who have responded more directly, and in radically different ways, to the "Muslim problem" and its discontents. This chapter discusses and compares the two most prominent examples: Dust, a member of the X-Men, and Kamala Khan, the most recent Ms. Marvel. On their own and together, Dust and Ms. Marvel suggest something important about Muslim women and representation in the United States, as well as about how superhero comics use space to frame issues of identity and belonging.

On Marvel's New York, Character, and Belonging

Much has been written in recent years about the supposed relationship between New York City and American comics in general, Marvel in particular.[6] Most such claims rest on several dubious assumptions about the field's history, though there is no room here to explore these issues.[7] More important, and more relevant for the present purpose, is that the claims are based on unsupportable assumptions of a direct relationship between space and representation.[8] When, for example, political scientist Matthew Costello writes that Marvel's use of "the real world"—that is, New York—"create[s] a closer link between the world of the superheroes and the world of the readers," he glosses over the reductive processes involved in what Scott McCloud calls comics' "amplification through simplification" and their accompanying processes of ideological meaning making (Costello 11; McCloud 24–59).[9]

Lost in this type of reading is the understanding that place—especially in representation—is not straightforward. Health and social scientist Cameron Duff has cautioned against reducing place to "a determinate set of points on a map, a simple geographical expression"; rather, it should be thought of as being produced through affect and practice (885).[10] This idea, that place or a sense of place is made rather than independently existent, is important to keep in mind when looking at serialized comics, where recurring places are continually (re)created and (re)defined by numerous artists and writers. As a medium with no stylistic limitations beyond the talent and creativity of creators, comics is perhaps particularly apt at provoking aesthetic and affective responses, using recognizable environments not only as settings but also to reinforce characterizations and to strengthen narrative and emotional resonances. These characteristics, combined with Marvel's longstanding and widely accepted claim to New York City,[11] makes the publisher particularly well suited to the creation of idealized imaginative maps of the city and its surroundings.

Comics' place-making cannot be reduced to stylistic and narrative choices, however. Imaginative representation of place is never merely mimetic of material space, but always a symbolic, selective, and ideologically or affectively informed visual and narrative collage. Representation's claim to real-world space is necessarily normative: it takes a space that exists, reduces it to a few traits, and recreates it in a way that implicitly or explicitly says what the place is supposed to be and who belongs there.[12] These claims are never innocent, and they often promote conservative messages, particularly since the superhero genre has long been centered around a framework that privileges white, heterosexual (and heteronormative) hypermasculinity and related values.[13] Deviations from this standard, like Ms. Marvel and Dust, are challenges to both social realities and representational conventions that can signal changing attitudes, but they do so in an often resistant environment. Thus, for example, Marvel's New York has often been framed to privilege the white middle class, particularly in the supposedly rebellious 1960s, or as in need of progentrification policing in a period of spatial contestation, in series like the 2004–2006 *District X* (Yockey; Lund "X Marks the Spot").

Furthermore, as Duff writes, "[t]o feel connected to place *is to experience a sense of belonging in place* that itself generates resources of immense value in the promotion of health and well-being" (893, emphasis in original). Duff is writing about lived place making, but the idea can also be applied to imaginative place making and its reception, since a represented idea of belonging can affect the well-being of readers who identify with characters placed in that representation. In part because Islam and some of the communities most closely associated with it have been misperceived and misrepresented in American culture, leading to feelings of danger and insecurity, taking ownership of representation has become a more urgent concern in recent years (Abu-Ras and Abu-Bader 235; Bryan 154; Shryock 202–03).[14]

Dust, a Precursor

While the reader of this volume may be familiar with Ms. Marvel, Dust's characterization needs to be addressed at some length before any comparison can be made. In literary critic Shlomith Rimmon-Kenan's definition, character in narrative is a network of character traits that appear in explicit and implicit ways, for which the basic indicators are direct and indirect presentation: the former names the trait explicitly, while the latter embodies the trait but leaves the reader to infer it (59–60).[15] When contextualized, characterizations provide insight into how comics creators structure their work in conscious and unconscious ways and how they address their audiences, which helps clarify what conception of belonging characters embody.

Dust, or Sooraya Qadir, is a *niqab*-wearing Afghan Muslima, created by writer Grant Morrison and artist Ethan van Sciver and introduced in

New X-Men, issue 133 (December 2002).[16] She has since been a recurring cast member in four other series: *New X-Men: Academy X* (issues 1–14 and *Yearbook,* July 2004–December 2005); the spin-off miniseries *New X-Men: Hellions* (July–October 2005); *New X-Men* (volume 2) (issues 20–46, January 2006–March 2008); and *Young X-Men* (issues 1–12, May 2008–May 2009). At the time of writing, aside from Ms. Marvel, Dust is the most frequently-appearing Muslima in Marvel's roster, with 122 appearances.[17] However, as becomes clear from a breakdown of her presence from *New X-Men,* issue 133 through June 2015's *Uncanny X-Men* (volume 3) issue 33, she has remained a peripheral character.

Dust's appearances can be divided into four broad categories: first, she has appeared fifty-four (44 percent) times as "set dressing," seen only in passing (often at the very back in group shots) and without dialogue[18]; second, as a "speaking extra," she has played a minor role and added some dialogue, most of it expository, in forty-one appearances (34 percent); third, she has been given some (mostly slight) characterization in twenty-four comic books (20 percent); and, finally, she has played a leading role in three issues (2 percent). In what follows, I will focus on the appearances in which Dust, at the very least, gets to speak.

Creating Dust

It is sometimes said that Dust was intended as a satire of post-9/11 Islamophobia or, as literary critic Julian Darius writes, "in defiance of anti-Muslim sentiment. Her presentation may not have been perfect, but her inclusion was far ahead of her time" (Darius). However, little satire, defiance, or inclusion is evident in Dust's five *New X-Men* appearances, in which Morrison acknowledges that she was peripheral: "Nothing much happened with her because of 9/11. . . . [T]he real-world situation had become so volatile that I just didn't want to touch her" (DeFalco 235). As a result, all readers knew about Dust after Morrison was that she was Other, a vaguely Orientalist stereotype.

Dust is a mutant and shares with her fellow X-Men a genetic trait that gives her superpowers. Over the years, this genetic difference has been inscribed with an allegorical and ever-changing form of Otherness that has repeatedly (and often counterproductively) been invested with extratextual ideological meanings (Shyminsky; Lund "'X Marks the Spot'"). Although in a general sense Dust is part of the mutant community, she is marginal even within that group. More important to note here, her power is to transform into a malleable cloud of dust. Communications scholars Julie Davis and Robert Westerfelhaus note that Dust's "codename and superpowers indexically connect her to the arid sands of the Arabian and Saharan deserts," despite having "roots in a very different part of the world culturally, ethnically, linguistically, and topographically" (804).[19] Although Afghanistan has large desert areas as well, this point is well-made to the extent that it is suggestive of the lingering power of reductive views of Muslims as primarily Arabs, even among people who might be trying to counter negative representations.

In Dust's first appearance (Morrison et al., issue 133) she is saved from Afghan slavers by the X-Man Wolverine, which situates her in an Orientalist tradition. As comics scholar Fredrik Strömberg has remarked, she is the female "Oriental Other who needs to be rescued by the character with whom Western readers are supposed to identify"; she is veiled, meaning that her rescue adheres even more closely to the specific project of "saving" Muslim women, which was an important alibi for America's invasion of Afghanistan ("Yo, Rag-Head!" 583–84).[20] When next encountered, Dust is being taken to the Xavier Institute, a mutant school in the United States, and further marked as Other when she is told to not be scared by anything she sees when they land (issue 138). When she later tries to warn the X-Men about a new danger, her behavior is called "crazy Jihad!" (issue 146). Although these comments are made by others and can be read as parodic, they are Morrison's only characterization of Dust, and she gets no say herself: her dialogue is limited to the word *turaab*, "dust" in Arabic (issue 133), and asking for help (issue 146), and in her two remaining appearances (issues 149–50), she simply stands silently in the background.

Through her limited characterization, her lack of cultural specificity, and her minimal interaction with the world, Dust conforms to a pattern religion scholars Peter Gottschalk and Gabriel Greenberg have observed about much pop culture representation, where Muslims do not appear in the context of everyday life: "[T]hey appear when the need arises to include a Muslim, and then, shorn of all other identities . . . they stand as only Muslim men or Muslim women, with the built-in expectations about what this means" (144).

Characterizing Dust

Dust's role in writers Nunzio DeFilippis and Christina Weir's *Academy X* is minor; she is a member of the "Hellions," a team of mutants-in-training and the protagonists' main rivals at Xavier's. Other Hellions are given personal character arcs and narrative importance throughout the series, but Dust remains marginal and alien. Out of her fourteen appearances, she provides exposition in one (issue 4), while four of her appearances are as set-dressing (issues 1 [front cover only], 13, 15, and *Yearbook*). The remaining nine are dominated by what can be called "*niqab*-talk,"[21] meaning superficial discourse about her Muslimness.

In almost all *niqab* talk—most commonly an uneven debate between Dust and her roommate, who always gets the final word—Dust is often put on the defensive about her veil. The focus is mostly on "the **modesty** and **protection** it [the veil] affords [her] from the eyes of men" (DeFilippis, Weir, and Henry, issue 2).[22] As a vast body of scholarship shows, modesty is often a reason for veiling, but there are many others, often tied, for example, to pride in Muslim identity and resistance to patriarchy.[23] Dust never goes beyond or expands upon her modesty, which is framed only in negative terms of her hiding her body. Furthermore, few writers take this modesty seriously: in several issues, Dust's *abaya* is made so tight as to counteract any resistance it might otherwise pose to the male gaze,[24] while in others, she is unveiled (Kyle et al., issue 31), shown in her underwear (Kyle et al., issue 27), or completely naked (DeFilippis and Weir, issue 6; Guggenheim at al., issue 5). In some of these situations, Dust is alone with only women, and thus would not be veiled. In others, her skin is shown for cheap laughs. Whatever the reason, however, the writers—many of whom stress Dust's modesty—contrive to put her in situations that are in no way necessary, in order to allow readers, many of whom are male, to voyeuristically gaze at her exposed flesh.[25]

In one important instance, Dust is accused of setting women back fifty years because of her veiling, and she is given no chance for rebuttal (issue 2). Her representation, then, seems rooted in the idea that Western women are more liberated and that their lives are (or should be) desirable to their Others, as evidenced by their "freedom" to dress in more revealing ways; Dust's inability to "understand" this worldview and her refusal to unveil becomes a contrast through which American "civilization" can be elevated.[26] Here, she is embroiled in War on Terror political rhetoric, symbolizing a threat to the "American way of life." Through Dust, Afghanistan is figured as completely Other, and her choice to wear a veil expresses a nonconformity that is represented as implicitly threatening capitalism (as her roommate remarks in issue 6, she can only listen to American pop music when Dust is out) (Zeiger). Dust's remaining characterization figures her as friendly but having little will of her own, a follower (issues 5, 6). This, coupled with more developed characters' thoughts about her ("religious nut" [issue 2]; "big freak" [issue 6]) and her being voted, in traditional Orientalist terms, "Most mysterious" in the Xavier Institute "yearbook," further adds to her Otherness.

Dust's role is slightly expanded in *Hellions*, DeFilippis and Weir's *Academy X* spin-off. Initially, Dust tries to discourage her friends from fighting with airport security and from making a deal with a mysterious stranger who promises to realize their deepest wishes (issues 1 and 2). She overcomes her hesitance off-panel, however, and she is next shown living her own wish of reuniting with her mother in Afghanistan. Their short dialogue focuses on Dust's *niqab* and how she is still wearing it in America. Dust reiterates that it is her choice, and her mother replies that she is lucky to be in a place where she can choose (issue 2). This reinforces Western discourse about veiling in the Muslim world as only and always a form of oppression. It also reproduces a narrative of American exceptionalism that ignores how veiled Muslims in the United States often face invective, discrimination, and persecution because of their choice,[27] which Dust herself has been subject to in DeFilippis and Weir's earlier *niqab* talk.

Numerically, Craig Kyle and Christopher Yost's *New X-Men* (volume 2) looks different. In the twenty-five issues in which she appears, Dust is only set-dressing in three (issues 33, 36, and 41), and there is only one instance of *niqab* talk, in which one character explains to another that what Dust is wearing is not a body-enveloping *burqa*, but a robelike *abaya* with a *niqab* (issue 42). In nine appearances, Dust provides exposition,[28] while more room is given for characterization, which dominates twelve.[29] This characterization, again, is almost exclusively religious: for example, by showing her using words with Islamic connotations (issue 38), praying, or speaking of what Allah demands (issues 24, 26, and 38), and reproducing ideas of Islam as a "demanding and condemning religion," and of veiled Muslim women as passive and submissive (Strömberg "Yo, Rag-Head!" 587).[30]

Other characters' direct presentation of Dust similarly focuses on her religion: a fellow X-Man correctly identifies her as Sunni (issue 22), while the satanic villain Belasco describes her, seemingly correctly, as fearing that she is unworthy of her God's love (issue 39): he calls her "the devout little girl" (issue 41). In addition to her religion, Dust's characterization shows her to be prone to guilt, even over things for which she bears no responsibility (issues 28, 29, and 32); other-directed to the point where she is willing to break her moral tenets to help others (issue 44); and proper or ignorant in a way that is played up for humor (issues 32 and 35). Thus, while she is more frequently characterized in these later appearances, these representations do nothing to make her less Other.

Dust follows a similar, but perhaps initially more promising, pattern in Marc Guggenheim's *Young X-Men*.[31] She is only set-dressing once, when she is turned into glass (issue 3). There is also only one instance of *niqab* talk, when Dust discusses religion with a villain (issue 6). In four of her remaining appearances, she provides exposition (issues 1, 5, 8, and 9), while two issues provide deeper characterization, and three see her in a leading role. In the first characterization, she speaks out against minority self-hatred and gets a personal character arc when she finds out that she is dying due to complications related to having been turned into glass, then back to flesh and blood (issue 7); in the second, she is shown wanting to suffer this death in silence (issue 10).

Dust's first lead appearance gives her an equal part in plot developments (issue 2), while the remaining two put her in a pattern common to women in superhero comics; in a glimpse of the future, Dust is revealed to have become psychotic, setting out to kill the world's few remaining mutants (issues 11 and 12).[32] Here, in addition to ultimately functioning as a vehicle for a male X-Man's redemption—Dust ends her run of regular appearances the way she started it: being saved by a man—she is demonized for her power, by losing control of it and her emotions at the point where she first shows initiative (c.f., Miettinen 136–51). She then starts doubting her place in the X-Men. It is worth noting that, instead of the veil that has been so defining of her, future-Dust wears a top that is more cleavage than cloth, and she poses provocatively, which turns her into one in a long line of fetish-dressed and hypersexualized objects for the male gaze in X-Men comics (Miettinen 142, 146).[33]

Thus, Dust is, in effect, punished by her writer for his questioning her always-marginal role in the team. Deprived of her already thin identity, she is made anathema both to her one developed characteristic and to the one group where she could find belonging, but to which she has only ever half-belonged. At the time of writing, she has not played anything but a passing role in a Marvel comic book since. Dust's publication history has allowed her almost no characterization; if she is anything at all, she is her veil—and, given the veil's treatment by comics writers and artists, even that characterization is debatable. Ultimately, then, Dust functions strictly as an Other: by providing a point of contrast, her inability to understand and embrace Americanness erects a boundary that reifies national identity.

Dust in Place

After 9/11, veiling has become a way for Muslim Americans to claim a certain religious and national identity—"as citizen/subject with particular rights"—by increasing the space in which it is allowed (Moore 248). Thus, veiling is intimately connected to place making and mobility. Similarly, Dust's alien status is deepened through how she is placed; where she is allowed—or not allowed—to go, what spaces she inhabits, and how she is made to move within them, all articulate the limits of her belonging. Her freedom of movement is limited: ninety-one (75 percent) of her appearances place her in mutant spaces, places lacking extratextual referents beyond signifying mutantcy and its generalized Otherness. Most frequently (forty-eight times), she is placed at the Xavier Institute in upstate New York's Westchester County, which has been the X-Men's home since their first appearance. Initially a place where mutant superheroes lived in consumerist comfort when not policing rogue mutants who challenged the status quo, Xavier's has increasingly become a mutant ghetto of sorts. This figuration deepened after the 2005 crossover event "House of M," in which the mutant population was brought to the brink of extinction and the remaining mutants were offered sanctuary in Westchester (Claremont et al.).[34] Dust's second most common place (twenty-eight appearances) is "Utopia," an artificial island off San Francisco, which was grandly established as a mutant "homeland" in 2009 (Fraction et al.).

As far as Dust is concerned, these are "thin" places, "places that have been erased of any local specificity, any unique quality or feature that might enable individuals and groups to actively engage with place, to secure some kind of purchase" (Duff 886). Granted, this "thinness" comes partly from the pace of the action and the size of the cast, but other cast-members of *Academy X*, *New X-Men* (vol. 2), and *Young X-Men* are allowed to invest their bedrooms, coffee shops, and other places with "thickness" by interacting in them and broadening their experience and character in and through them. Conversely, not even in places that are supposed to be welcoming to her as a mutant is Dust granted belonging or agency. For example, her own room at the Xavier Institute, which by any measure should be a sanctuary, is a place of conflict; almost immediately after meeting her roommate in *Academy X*, issue 2, Dust is put on the defensive over her veil in a dynamic that lasts throughout the run. Later, Dust gets a new roommate, who is a bit more welcoming, although here, too, Dust becomes a passive party: Dust is about to act to save a teammate, but X-23 knocks her out and uses her veil as a disguise to bring down the enemy (Kyle et al., issues 26 and 27).[35]

A handful of appearances place Dust outside mutant-only spaces, most often while on a mission, safely shrouded in the hyperbolic unreality of superheroics. In only one location is she not in all-mutant company, on a mission, or fighting an X-Men foe: Afghanistan, where she appeared three times. She is first placed there when she is rescued from slavers (*New X-Men*, issue 133); her second appearance there is when she meets her mother and defends her continued veiling in the United States (*Hellions*, issue 2); and finally, she is recruited to Afghanistan in *Young X-Men*, issue 1, where she is shown fighting America's foes (Morrison et al.; DeFilippis, Weir, and Henry; Guggenheim et al.). As a result, Dust's presence seems "natural" or desirable only in places that are already primed to connote Otherness or Islam-related geopolitics.

As opposed to most other Marvel superheroes of her time, Dust rarely sets foot in New York, which is telling if the city is indeed the center of Marvel's universe. This detail is not surprising: Marvel has rarely peopled its New York in a way reflective of the city's diversity. While the so-called "Marvel Age" began in 1961, it was not until 1965 that the first "incidental" black characters were seen in their comics (Wright 219, 320 n. 76); the first black New Yorker in *X-Men* appeared five years into the series (issue 57, June 1969).[36] Black Panther, Marvel's first black superhero, was introduced in 1966, when he enlisted the Fantastic Four to help rid his African nation of an insidious outside force. Since this storyline was figured in Cold War terms and the character was Americanized, Black Panther could "safely" be placed on the streets of New York afterward, because the adventure had, metaphorically, positively tied him to the Soviet-American ideological struggle over the "Third World" that marked the 1960s (Lee and Kirby, issues 52 and 53).[37] The first black superhero to have his own series was the Blaxploitation-inspired Luke Cage: in June 1972, Cage premiered with an office in Times Square, then regarded as a "virtual Sodom," and thus "safely" beyond the pale of "respectable" society (Goodwin et al.; Patterson 46).[38]

As Marvel's first post-9/11 Muslim superheroine, Dust similarly requires an alibi to enter New York. In two Morrison-penned issues, she is seen briefly along with other X-Men, out of the way in Mutant Town, the city's mutant ghetto (Morrison et al., issues 149–50). During "House of M," when mutants have been granted their deepest desires, Dust's New York presence is not limited to mutant spaces: she navigates the city at large, but this openness is accompanied by her being stripped of what little character she previously had; the "utopian" version of Dust is vocally consumerist and wearing a miniskirt (DeFilippis et al., issues 16–19).[39] Her next return to New York in 2011's "Fear Itself," which allegorizes United States political polarization and culture of fear, is part of a larger pattern of ecumenical gesturing in the event. In a one-page vignette, Dust exemplifies religious conviction as a motivator for positive inter-group relations by protecting a Hasidic family. For the first time, her Otherness is acceptable on New York's streets. Her religion is even presented, through the perceived "extremeness" of a veiled Muslim helping Hasidic Jews, as a social positive: it inspires civility and the creation of "bridging" (or inclusive) social capital rather than particularism and "bonding" (or exclusive) social capital; as she puts it, "faith **without** works is **dead**" (Gage et al., issue 6).[40] In Dust's experience, then, entering New York always comes with a caveat: either stay hidden and surrender your beliefs and traditions, or put them to work.

Ms. Marvel, a Trailblazer

As written by G. Willow Wilson, the Kamala Khan version of Ms. Marvel is almost a polar opposite of Dust. She is Muslim, but absent of the usual stereotypes. Issues of modesty are not addressed in reductive and superficial fashion (Wilson et al., issue 3). Her stories are deeply concerned with her coming to terms with who she is, her new powers, and how to reconcile them with her relatively conservative Pakistani family. As opposed to Dust, Khan always speaks and is always at the center of the action and of the story. When she meets Wolverine, it is not to be rescued, but to cooperate with him on equal footing (issues 6–7). As other articles in this volume discuss, the series also focuses on generational identity (especially issue 10). In contrast to Dust, then, the question for Ms. Marvel is not whether she belongs, but to what extent and how she negotiates a sense of cultural citizenship that is both flexible and multicultural.[41]

Ms. Marvel is not a New Yorker. The first page of *Ms. Marvel*, issue 1 situates the series in "Jersey City. 12 Miles from Manhattan." Indeed, Khan is in New York for only seven panels in the entire series (in issue 16). While this detail is noteworthy, New York's absence does not signal Khan's marginality, the way it seemingly does for Dust. The series even occasionally mocks New York; most notably, when the god Loki comes to Jersey City (issue 12), he is perceived as a "hipster Viking" from Brooklyn, a harbinger of gentrification and a clear signal of the undesirability of one of New York's most visible and supposedly avant-garde cultural fields. Here, New York is clearly not the gold standard that fans, critics, and creators alike have long hailed it as, although the series still pokes fun at New Jersey's occasional inferiority complex.

Second, *Ms. Marvel* celebrates Jersey City in its own right, both narratively and through careful choices of locations and care in representing them "realistically."[42] One should not make too much of this "realism," however; mimeticism in comics often highlights an alienation from the represented world that occurs in imaginative place-making, particularly in works filled with as much accidental, exaggerated comedic detail as *Ms. Marvel*.[43]

Third, after 9/11, Jersey City was one of the New York Metro area's most "suspect" Muslim spaces, becoming both a central focus of FBI investigations and dubbed "Terror Town" by the media (Bryan).[44] With all of these details in mind, the ways Ms. Marvel is placed become even more noteworthy.

Private Places: Sacred and Everyday Muslim Space

As a creative work, *Ms. Marvel* allows readers glimpses of Muslim American private life that other forms of representation cannot (Shryock 206). Almost all places Khan inhabits are "thick" places that, according to Duff, "enhance one's sense of meaning and belonging, forging a series of affective and experiential connections in place"; they invite "'concernful absorption'–a deepening and broadening of the individual's lived experience of place–while supporting various practices of 'personal enrichment'" (Duff 882, 886).

One of Khan's most important private places is her bedroom.[45] This is where much of her broadest characterization happens; it is where she plays her computer games, writes her fan fiction (issue 1), watches Bollywood cinema—which serves as a source of co-identification with other Pakistani Americans (issue 13)—and fantasizes about boys (issue 12). It is, then, a place where she can engage with both American and South Asian culture to fashion a transnational identity,[46] but also a place where she can engage in activities that differentiate her from the capitalism-threatening nonconformity that helped mark Dust as beyond the pale of American national identity.

Then there is the Khan household itself, a nondescript middle-class space that is occasionally infused with ethnoreligious markers like wall-hangings, South Asian foods, and Urdu terms of endearment. When Khan is placed here, in comparison to Dust—who, for a time, effectively was the X-Men franchise's (and, indeed, Marvel Universe's) lone representative of Islam[47]—she is supported by a cast that deepens her characterization, and in its own right diversifies the series' immigrant and Muslim identities. In addition to Khan's *hijab*-wearing Turkish-American Muslim best friend Nakia, there is Khan's father, Yusuf, her mother, Disha, and her pious brother, Aamir, all of whom introduce familial interrelationships of love, care, and frustration.[48] Notably, Aamir is a self-described Salafi (issue 18) who, through his representation as overtly religious, well-versed in American culture, and a teasing big brother who is loving at heart, challenges common associations between Islamist extremist militancy and the traditionalist reformist ideology known as Salafism.[49] In a sense, then, the Khan household is a limited microcosm of US Pakistani Muslim minority, as well as, more broadly, suggestive of the heterogeneity of America's Muslim communities.[50]

Khan is also placed in sacred space, through mosque scenes in which she talks with her imam about helping people (issue 6) and challenges gender segregation with a discourse that suggests that "authentic" Islam—the Islam of its Golden Age—was gender-equal (issue 3). In addition to entering a Muslim feminist discourse here, Khan represents a figuration of Islam that is inherently compatible with progressive, democratic ideals, which has precedents in post-9/11 Muslim American communities and in other American minority histories (Shryock 204; Ewing and Hoyler).[51] Through these "thick" locations, Khan's placement in private spaces provides a middle-classness to her characterization that gives her more mobility within the public sphere.[52]

Public Places: Ms. Marvel's Jersey City

There are three public spaces that are particularly important in placing Khan. The first is the Circle Q, a convenience store where she and Nakia often hang out with their Italian American friend Bruno, who works there. Throughout the series, Circle Q is a place where Khan can learn more about her superpowers and how to navigate them (issues 4 and 5). It is also a multicultural space where she negotiates the push and pull of her Muslim and American identities. This tension can be seen from the very first pages of the series: Khan is torn between the desirable smell of bacon and the principles of *halal*, as well as between Bruno's acceptance (and semi-unrequited love[53]) and the casual Islamophobia of popular white girl Zoe, whose feigned concern that Nakia would be "honor-killed" if she removed her *hijab* is familiar to many young veiled Muslims (issue 1; Ewing and Hoyler 94–95). Circle Q, then, is a place for encounters across group boundaries and, thus, a site for the enactment (and, for the creators, for representation) of the inclusionary and exclusionary practices that are part of the everyday for many South Asian and Muslim youth (Maira 29–31).

A second important public place is Khan's school. Khan's school life is simultaneously banal and infused with personal drama that is never reduced simply to one part of her identity. School is a center for Khan's identity—as a teenager, a friend, a daughter and sister, and a superhero—and a place for her character and interpersonal relationships to develop into depths that after a decade of limited characterization seem unimaginable for Dust, particularly in the final story arc when the school becomes a fortification against apocalyptic events (issues 16–19). Noteworthy is that the school, where values of citizenship are traditionally inculcated, does not primarily try to make American subjects out of ethnoreligious Others like Khan, as has historically been common in the United States.[54] Instead, it develops respectable subjects out of an ethnoracially diverse generational cohort (issues 8 and 11), suggesting that the acceptance of Khan's other identities is, more or less, complete.

Khan's third recurring public place is the streets, which are perhaps the thinnest of her everyday places. She and her friends and family are repeatedly shown mixing with a diverse citizenry; these scenes are often short and humorous, such as the one in issue 16 that shows Khan drowning her romantic sorrows with hot dogs by the waterfront. These scenes must be included here because they are part of the series rather than simple backdrops for battles, as is often the case for Dust (although they are sometimes backdrops, too: cf. issue 14). Thus, Khan's consumption, cross-cultural interaction, acceptance in school, and ability to walk Jersey City's streets without impediment, coupled with the introspective nature of much of her dealings with identity issues, suggests that the issue of belonging is largely—but not exclusively—considered on individual terms.

Double-Placed

Khan was created and written by G. Willow Wilson, a white convert to Islam, and Marvel editor Sana Amanat, a Pakistani American Muslima. Despite the difference in life experience represented by her creators, Khan's struggles as a young Pakistani American Muslima capture the dissenting citizenship of South Asian Muslim American youth, in that they figure "the United States [as] simultaneously a place invested with their parents' desire for economic advancement and security and their own hopes to belong in a new home, and also the site of alienation, discrimination, fear, frustration, and anxiety about belonging" (Maira 37).

Ms. Marvel is unapologetic about its use of ethnoreligious markers such as Urdu words, Quranic verses, and Sufi poetry.[55] But, as has been noted above, Khan's world largely conforms to middle-class standards, which might account in part for its generally warm reception, since this place making helps the series walk a fine line between popular identity politics and "normalization," a strategy that often costs more than it gains for minorities (Anspach, esp. 769). That reviewers have tended toward a "normalizing" reading has been suggested by media scholar Miriam Kent, who notes in a survey of Khan's early reception that what was often stressed was her "relatability"—that she is "just like us"—in a way that cast aside the most particular aspects of the character as "a *specific sort* of outsider in terms of gender, race, religion, and nationality," and instead indicated "almost a fondness for assimilation" (524–25).[56]

Khan is placed as feeling both the outsider—"everybody else gets to be **normal**" (issue 1)—and as feeling at home—for example, in her assertion of belonging at the end of the first story arc: "This is **Jersey City**. We talk loud, we walk fast, and we don't take any disrespect" (issue 5). This simultaneous awareness of belonging and exclusion can be described as a form of double-consciousness, or a sense of being fully American but not quite full participants in American life.[57] This sense is present and developed from the first issue, in the racist undertones in Zoe's comment about Nakia's *hijab*, as well as in her later claim that Khan "smell[s] like curry" (issue 1). Most forcefully, perhaps, it is expressed in Khan's assertion that she is from "Jersey City, not **Karachi!**" (issue 1) and in her fear that the FBI would wiretap her mosque if they found out about her powers (issue 4). Through her actions and through the actions of others, then, Khan comes to represent contemporary South Asian Muslim American youth, "often perceived as not American enough, or as desiring to 'become American' but being 'caught between two worlds,' and thus culturally suspect" (Maira 15).

I want to return here to where this chapter began, with Moustafa Bayoumi's observations that, today, to be a Muslim American often means to exist in the slightly absurd space between exotic and dangerous, victim and villain, simply because of people's expectations. It is also worth noting here that both Dust and Khan are teenagers, who "are generally viewed as the next generation of citizens, who symbolize the cultural and political future of the nation and are invested with adult hopes and fears" (Maira 16). Both characters are workings-through of these situations, albeit with very different perspectives, which likely stem from differences in experience that allow for differences in imagination and empathy, and thus, different results.[58] None of Dust's writers, it seems, could imagine a Muslima who went beyond the fiction of an American national ideal that juxtaposes the Muslim world and its women through a "lack of freedom, lack of education, lack of choice" (Zeiger 271). This stereotype, in turn, is challenged in Khan's character, and the difference is echoed and supported in Khan's and Dust's respective freedom of movement: Dust is perennially peripheral to the New York Metro area, whereas Khan takes center stage in those parts of it she and her writers most care about. Dust and Ms. Marvel show in palpable ways how difficult it can be to negotiate room for identity, as well as to navigate as Muslim women in public American space.

Although Khan is, in this sense, a trailblazer, opening new places up to Muslim representation, her writers might be too optimistic about the belonging that middle classness can confer—an optimism that is particularly clear in Zoe's apology for her Islamophobia at the end of the series (issue 19). Khan was introduced because Marvel executives had noted changing demographics in the comics readership; the gamble to introduce Khan, as well as her retention, are dictated by the market.[59] How long it will last is a different question: when Khan was first announced, American Islamophobia seemed on a slow decline (Council on American-Islamic Relations 41); by the turn of 2016, it was again increasing, as can be seen from a rise in hate crimes and acceptance of presidential candidate and then President Donald Trump's anti-Muslim demagoguery (Downes; Chalabi; Villeda and Chandler). As of this writing, Khan is still welcome in Jersey City, but other voices might yet overpower her and force her off the streets.

NOTES

I want to thank Fredrik Carrasco, Julian Chambliss, Huma Mohibullah, and Jonas Otterbeck for their comments, suggestions, and help in preparing this chapter.

1. See, e.g., Takaki, Roediger, Goldstein (esp. chap. 5), Ignatiev, and Stibili.

2. It seems reasonably clear that Bayoumi is here referencing economist and sociologist Gunnar Myrdal's famous framing of the "Negro problem" as an "American dilemma." Also see Maira. This "problem" did not emerge fully formed after 9/11; throughout the post–World War II period, geopolitical fears of a Muslim "green peril" emerged, and the notion

of an "Islamic threat" grew more common after the Cold War ended. Cf. Said, Esposito, and Gottschalk and Greenberg.

3. "The problem of the twentieth century is the problem of the color-line," sociologist and activist W. E. B. Du Bois once famously wrote, and history proved him right (23). Two decades into the twenty-first century, it is clear that this "problem" is still a lethal fact of American life, and the discussion here of the "Muslim problem" is in no way intended to deny or belittle this fact.

4. Stereotyped Arabs in superhero comics have been around since at least November 1940's *Action Comics* 29, reprinted in Siegel et al., *SC4*.

5. Cf. Nyberg, Lewis, and Johnson.

6. E.g., Jennings, MacDonald and Sanderson, and Bainbridge.

7. Two issues in particular stand out: first, the supposed significance of this "relationship" is never defined or discussed; second, proponents of this connection do not account for the fact that the relationship between real-world space and its depiction is never one of direct reproduction, but of representation.

8. See Lund, "X Marks the Spot" and "NY 101."

9. Also see Lovell, 163–65.

10. See also Wirth-Nesher.

11. Sanderson's *Marvel's Comics Guide to New York City* is perhaps the best example of how Marvel has actively and with relative success tried to make its identification with New York a selling point.

12. C.f. Lund, "X Marks the Spot" and "NY 101."

13. See the survey of superhero characteristics in Yanora 114–17. C.f. Lund, "American Golem."

14. That comics have psychological effects of this kind can be seen, for example, in the strong praise garnered by the mere announcement that a Pakistani-American Muslima named Ms. Marvel was going to be introduced by Marvel. See Jebreal, Janmohamed, and Pervez. Furthermore, as comics historian Bradford Wright notes in *Comic Book Nation*, "Emerging from the shifting interaction of politics, culture, audience tastes, and the economics of publishing, comic books have helped to frame a worldview and define a sense of self for the generations who have grown up with them" (xii).

15. "The first type names the trait by an adjective (e.g. 'he was good–hearted'), an abstract noun ('his goodness knew no bounds'), or possibly some other kind of noun ('she was a real bitch') or part of speech ('he loves only himself'). The second type, on the other hand, does not mention the trait but displays and exemplifies it in various ways, leaving to the reader the task of inferring the quality they imply."

16. There is no pagination in any of the comics cited in this chapter.

17. The only character to come close is Monet St. Croix, who was introduced in 1994 but was retroactively made Muslim only in 2011.

18. It should be noted that Dust is rarely alone in being put in the background in these instances, but it is worth noting that she is often pushed to the side or farthest away in the background. Cf. David, DeLandro, and Davidson; Bendis and Marquez; and the cover of Whedon and Cassaday.

19. See also Haddad (259).

20. Also see Ahmed, Zeiger (271), and Haddad (255). On the importance in the United States of the white masculine hero narrative after 9/11, see Lorber and Faludi.

21. Issues 2, 3, 5, 6, and 14. Issues 16–19 are discussed under the heading "Dust in Place" below.

22. Also c.f. Droogsma (305–7).

23. C.f. the multifaceted reasoning for veiling presented by the women interviewed in Droogsma. Also c.f. Ewing and Hoyler (93–95) and Bryan (152).

24. C.f. DeFilippis and Weir, *Academy X*, issue 14; Kyle et al., *New X-Men*, v. 2, issue 25; cover of DeFilippis, Weir, and Henry, issue 2. Also c.f. Strömberg, "Yo, Rag-Head!" (587).

25. C.f. Ewing and Hoyler: "When even the partial exposure of skin and hair is associated with impiety, forced nudity seems not only shameful but sinful" (86). On readership demographics, Brienza notes that around the time of Dust's regular appearances, up to 90 percent of American superhero comics' readership was male. C.f. Shyminsky, as well as Miettinen (141).

26. See especially Droogsma (306). Also c.f. Haddad (262) and Zeiger (271, 277–78).

27. Haddad, for example, notes that "in an America traumatized by 9/11, many Americans began to identify the *hijab* as the standard of the enemy" (263). See also Moore, Droogsma (303, 308), and Bryan (143–145).

28. Issues 20, 21, 23, 25, 30, 31, 34, 40, and 46.

29. Issues 22, 24, 26, 27, 28, 29, 32, 35, 38, 39, 43, and 44.

30. Also c.f. Ewing and Hoyler (93–95) and Maira (32) for the stereotype of passive Muslim women.

31. Also c.f. Kyle et al., *New X-Men* v. 2.

32. C.f. Miettinen: "Especially females with significant power tend to be demonized, their power often seen as a geopolitical threat to the entire world" (136).

33. Examples of such characters include Emma Frost, Selene, and Mystique.

34. C.f. Lund "X Marks the Spot," 37–38; also c.f. Claremont, Green, and Lopresti.

35. The device of Dust's veil being taken by someone for a disguise was also used by writer Chris Claremont in his *X-Men: The End Book 2*, issue 4 (August 2005) and *Book 3*, issues 1, 2, 4, and 5 (March–July 2006).

36. Also c.f. Thomas et al.

37. C.f. Lund, "The Mutant Problem," n. iv. See also Gaddis (122–28).

38. It should also be noted that Cage's series initially reinforced, or at least elided, racial inequalities in the United States (c.f. Bould, 178–79).

39. See Lund, "X Marks the Spot" (49–51), for another example of a "House of M" spin-off that creates problematic "utopian" ethnoracial consequences from the event premise.

40. C.f. Putnam 22–23; see also Williams 242.

41. For more on these types of cultural citizenship, see Maira: "Cultural citizenship is the 'behaviors, discourses, and practices that give meaning to citizenship as lived experience' in the context of 'an uneven and complex field of structural inequalities and webs of power relations'" (23).

42. C.f. photographer and documentary filmmaker Jack Gordon's side-by-side comparison of a panel from the comic and a picture of the same street corner in the real world (Gordon).

43. C.f. Lund, "NY 101." Furthermore, the creative team takes numerous liberties. In issue 7, for example, when Khan finds herself in the city's sewage system searching with Wolverine for the supervillainous Inventor, a full-page panel features a sewer diagram. The rooms double as panels, and the gutters between show the soil surrounding them, filled with eclectic detritus that includes, among other things, a full dinosaur skeleton, a person-sized sword, and a box sided with question marks borrowed from the Super Mario video game franchise. This type of comedic detail, which is similar to, if somewhat less exaggerated than, the background sight gags that have long been a hallmark of *MAD Magazine*, has as one of its effects a countering of the visuals' "realism": in a very real sense, it turns the cartooned space into a *cartoon*, a humoristic, highly unreal landscape.

44. This stamp has proved resilient, as Donald Trump's remarks of November 2015 about seeing "thousands" of Muslims in Jersey City cheering the attacks on 9/11 suggest.

45. She also spends some time in New Attilan, a superhero-specific place that it is not strictly necessary to discuss here; while it does play into Khan's characterization, it is a minor setting.

46. C.f. Maira, esp. 25–26.

47. There have been other Muslim characters, but most of them have had only a fleeting presence in the comics.

48. E.g. issues 1, 2, 5, and 9.

49. Similar attempts have been made in American media: e.g., see Zhou.

50. For an overview, see Smith. See also the discussion about the early series' possible reproduction of stereotypes about Muslim men in Khoja-Moolji and Niccolini.

51. C.f. Wenger.

52. Perhaps most notable, Khan does not have to work to support her family, which is a common source of alienation among South Asian American Muslim youth. C.f. esp. Maira (26–27), where the role of labor in shaping experiences of difference or exclusion is discussed.

53. This love in itself is a recurring theme: Khan and Bruno both know that a relationship is unlikely, due to their different heritage and the elder Khans' traditionalism.

54. C.f. Roediger (193–95).

55. It is worth pointing out that Khan's Islamic references are of a particular kind. When she references Sufi poet and mystic Rumi (issue 5), for example, she is referencing a poet who has become extremely popular in the United States but has been received in a way framed more by a generalized "spirituality" than as a Muslim thinker. C.f. El-Zein, Seelarbokus, and Ali. (My thanks to Fredrik Carrasco for pointing this out.)

56. Emphasis in original.

57. This concept was introduced by W. E. B. Du Bois in *Souls of Black Folk* (16–17). It has been developed in the sense it is used here, more closely connected with immigrant identity, in such works as Prell (esp. 163–65) and Brodkin.

58. C.f. Michael.

59. C.f. Marvel's publisher Dan Buckley in Wheeler: "We were assessing it qualitatively just from going to [comic-]cons, feedback from social media, the old method of letters, emails. Just through that qualitative data you can sense there's a diversifying of the

readership base. Obviously there's a great impact from what's happening in the mass media when people go to the movies and say, 'Oh this is for me, too.' You've been to cons, and you can see a definite shift in the demographic deliverance there too."

BIBLIOGRAPHY

Abu-Ras, Wahiba, and Soleman H. Abu-Bader. "The Impact of the September 11, 2001: Attacks on the Well-Being of Arab Americans in New York City." *Journal of Muslim Mental Health*, no. 3 (2008): 217–39.

Ahmed, Leila. *A Quiet Revolution: The Veil's Resurgence, from the Middle East to America.* New Haven: Yale University Press, 2011.

Ali, Rozina. "The Erasure of Islam from the Poetry of Rumi." *The New Yorker*, January 5, 2017. http://www.newyorker.com/books/page-turner/the-erasure-of-islam-from-the-poetry-of-rumi.

Anspach, Renee R. "From Stigma to Identity Politics: Political Activism among the Physically Disabled and Former Mental Patients." *Social Science & Medicine. Part A: Medical Psychology & Medical Sociology* 13 (1979): 765–73.

Bainbridge, Jason. "'I Am New York'-Spider-Man, New York City and the Marvel Universe." *Comics and the City*, ed. Jörn Ahrens and Arno Meteling. New York: Continuum, 2010. 163–79.

Bayoumi, Moustafa. *This Muslim American Life: Dispatches from the War on Terror.* New York: New York University Press, 2015.

Bendis, Brian Michael, and David Marquez. *All-New X-Men* 6. New York: Marvel, 2013.

Bould, Mark. "The Ships Landed Long Ago: Afrofuturism and Black SF." *Science Fiction Studies* 34, no. 2 (July 1, 2007): 177–86.

Brienza, Casey. "Men of Wonder: Gender and American Superhero Comics." *University of Cambridge*, November 1, 2011. http://www.cam.ac.uk/research/discussion/men-of-wonder-gender-and-american-superhero-comics.

Brodkin, Karen. *How Jews Became White Folks and What That Says about Race in America.* New Brunswick: Rutgers University Press, 1998.

Bryan, Jennifer L. "Constructing 'the True Islam' in Hostile Times: The Impact of 9/11 on Arab Muslims in Jersey City." *Wounded City: The Social Impact of 9/11*, ed. Nancy Foner. New York: Russell Sage Foundation, 2005. 133–59.

Chalabi, Mona. "How Anti-Muslim Are Americans? Data Points to Extent of Islamophobia." *The Guardian*, December 8, 2015, sec. U.S. news. http://www.theguardian.com/us-news/2015/dec/08/muslims-us-islam-islamophobia-data-polls.

Claremont, Chris, Randy Green, and Aaron Lopresti. *Decimation: House of M—The Day After.* New York: Marvel, 2006.

Costello, Matthew J. *Secret Identity Crisis: Comic Books and the Unmasking of Cold War America.* New York: Continuum, 2009.

Council on American-Islamic Relations. "Legislating Fear: Islamophobia and Its Impact in the United States," 2013. http://www.cair.com/images/islamophobia/Legislating-Fear.pdf.

Darius, Julian. "Grant Morrison's 9/11: New X-Men's 'Ambient Magnetic Fields.'" *Sequart Organization*. Accessed December 22, 2015. http://sequart.org/magazine/43759/grant-morrison-9-11-new-x-men-ambient-magnetic-fields/.

David, Peter Allen, Valentine DeLandro, and Pat Davidson. *Nation X: X-Factor.* New York: Marvel, 2010.

Davis, Julie, and Robert Westerfelhaus. "Finding a Place for a Muslimah Heroine in the Post-9/11 Marvel Universe: New X-Men's Dust." *Feminist Media Studies* 13, no. 5 (2013): 800–9.

DeFalco, Tom. "Grant Morrison." *Comics Creators on X-Men.* London: Titan Books, 2006. 228–39.

DeFilippis, Nunzio, Christina Weir, and Clayton Henry. *New X-Men: Hellions.* New York: Marvel, 2005.

DeFilippis, Nunzio, Christina Weir, Randall Green, Staz Johnson, Michael Ryan, Pagulayan Carlos, Paco Medina, and Aaron Lopresti. *New X-Men: Academy X* 1–19. New York: Marvel, 2005.

Downes, Lawrence. "New Poll Finds Anti-Muslim Sentiment Frighteningly High." *Taking Note.* Accessed January 4, 2016. http://takingnote.blogs.nytimes.com/2015/09/29/new-poll-finds-anti-muslim-sentiment-frighteningly-high/.

Droogsma, Rachel Anderson. "Redefining Hijab: American Muslim Women's Standpoint of Veiling." *Journal of Applied Communication Research* 35, no. 3 (2007): 294–319.

Du Bois, W. E. B. *The Souls of Black Folk: Essays and Sketches.* Fawcett World Library. New York: Fawcett, 1961.

Duff, Cameron. "On the Role of Affect and Practice in the Production of Place." *Environment and Planning D: Society and Space* 2010, no. 28 (2010): 881–95.

El-Zein, Amira. "Spiritual Consumption in the United States: The Rumi Phenomenon." *Islam and Christian-Muslim Relations* 11, no. 1 (March 2000): 71–85. doi:10.1080/095964100111526.

Esposito, John L. *The Islamic Threat: Myth or Reality?* New York: Oxford University Press, 1992.

Ewing, Katherine Pratt, and Marguerite Hoyler. "Being Muslim and American: South Asian Muslim Youth and the War on Terror." *Being and Belonging: Muslims in the United States since 9/11,* ed. Katherine Pratt Ewing. New York: Russell Sage Foundation, 2008. 80–103.

Faludi, Susan. *The Terror Dream: Fear and Fantasy in Post-9 11 America.* 1st ed. New York: Metropolitan Books, 2007.

Fraction, Matt, Mark Silverstri, Mike Deodato Jr., and Luke Ross. *Dark Avengers/Uncanny X-Men: Utopia.* New York: Marvel Comics, 2009.

Gaddis, John Lewis. *The Cold War: A New History.* New York: Penguin, 2005.

Gage, Christos, Mike Mayhew, Rain Beredo, Peter Milligan, Elia Bonetti, Fred Van Lente, and Alessandro Vitti. *Fear Itself: The Home Front.* New York: Marvel, 2012.

Goldstein, Eric L. *The Price of Whiteness.* Princeton: Princeton University Press, 2006.

Goodwin, Archie, John Romita Sr., Roy Thomas, and George Tuska. *Luke Cage, Hero for Hire.* New York: Marvel, 1972.

Gordon, Jack. "Love the Impeccably Researched #JerseyCity Locations in #MsMarvel." *Twitter,* November 14, 2015, 1:56 AM.

Gottschalk, Peter, and Gabriel Greenberg. *Islamophobia: Making Muslims the Enemy.* Lanham: Rowman & Littlefield, 2008.

Guggenheim, Marc, Yanick Paquette, Ben Oliver, Rafa Sandoval, and Daniel Acuña. *Young X-Men.* New York: Marvel, 2008–2009.

Haddad, Yvonne Yazbeck. "The Post-9/11 'Hijab' as Icon." *Sociology of Religion* 68, no. 3 (2007): 253–67.

Ignatiev, Noel. *How the Irish Became White.* Taylor & Francis, 2008.
Janmohamed, Shelina. "Hallelujah! Even Muslim Women Can Now Be Superheroes." *The Telegraph,* November 6, 2013. http://www.telegraph.co.uk/women/womens-life/10430505/Even-Muslim-women-can-be-superheroes.-Hallelujah.html.
Jebreal, Rula. "Meet the Muslim Ms. Marvel: Kamala Khan's Fight against Stereotypes." *The Daily Beast,* November 8, 2013. http://www.thedailybeast.com/articles/2013/11/08/meet-the-muslim-ms-marvel-kamala-khan-s-fight-against-stereotypes.html.
Jennings, Dana. "New York Action Hero." *The New York Times,* November 23, 2003, sec. N.Y. / Region. http://www.nytimes.com/2003/11/23/nyregion/new-york-action-hero.html.
Johnson, Jeffrey K. "Terrified Protectors: The Early Twenty-First Century Fear Narrative in Comic Book Superhero Stories." *Americana: The Journal of American Popular Culture (1900-Present)* 10, no. 2 (Fall 2011). http://www.americanpopularculture.com/journal/articles/fall_2011/johnson.htm.
Kent, Miriam. "Unveiling Marvels: Ms. Marvel and the Reception of the New Muslim Superheroine." *Feminist Media Studies* 15, no. 3 (2015): 522–27.
Khoja-Moolji, Shenila S., and Alyssa D. Niccolini. "Comics as Public Pedagogy: Reading Muslim Masculinities through Muslim Femininities in *Ms. Marvel*." *Girlhood Studies* 8, no. 3 (2015): 23–39.
Kyle, Craig, Christopher Yost, Mark Brooks, Paul Pelletier, Paco Medina, Duncan Rouleau, Mike Norton, Niko Henrichon, Skottie Young, and Humberto Ramos. *New X-Men* 2, nos. 20–46. New York: Marvel, 2006.
Lee, Stan, and Jack Kirby. *Essential Fantastic Four.* Vol. 3. New York: Marvel, 2007.
Lewis, A. David. "The Militarism of American Superheroes after 9/11." *Comic Books and American Cultural History,* ed. Matthew J. Pustz. New York: Continuum, 2012. 223–36.
Lorber, Judith. "Heroes, Warriors, and *Burqas*: A Feminist Sociologist's Reflections on September 11." *Sociological Forum* 17, no. 3 (2002): 377–96.
Lovell, Jarret. "Step Aside, Superman . . . This Is a Job for [Captain] America! Comic Books and Superheroes Post September 11." *Media Representations of September 11,* eds. Steven Chermak, Frankie Y. Bailey, and Michelle Brown. Westport: Praeger, 2003. 161–73.
Lund, Martin. "American Golem—Reading America through Super New-Dealers and the 'Melting Pot.'" *Comic Books and American Cultural History,* ed. Matthew J. Pustz. New York: Continuum, 2012. 79–93.
———. "The Mutant Problem: *X-Men,* Confirmation Bias, and the Methodology of Comics and Identity." *European Journal of American Studies* 10, no. 2 (2015). http://ejas.revues.org/10890.
———. "'NY 101': New York City according to Brian Wood." *International Journal of Comic Art,* in production.
———. "'X Marks the Spot': Urban Dystopia, Slum Voyeurism and Failures of Identity in District X." *Journal of Urban Cultural Studies* 2, nos. 1–2 (2015): 34–56.
MacDonald, Heidi, and Peter Sanderson. "New York Is Comics Country." *PublishersWeekly.com,* January 27, 2006. http://www.publishersweekly.com/pw/print/20060130/2746-new-york-is-comics-country.html.
Maira, Sunaina. "Citizenship, Dissent, Empire: South Asian Muslim Immigrant Youth." *Being and Belonging: Muslims in the United States since 9/11,* ed. Katherine Pratt Ewing. New York: Russell Sage Foundation, 2008. 15–46.

McCloud, Scott. *Understanding Comics: The Invisible Art.* New York: Harper Paperbacks, 1993.
Michael, John. *Identity and the Failure of America: From Thomas Jefferson to the War on Terror.* Minneapolis: University of Minnesota Press, 2008.
Miettinen, Mervi. "Superhero Comics and the Popular Geopolitics of American Identity." Licentiate thesis, University of Tampere, 2011.
Moore, Kathleen M. "Visible through the Veil: The Regulation of Islam in American Law." *Sociology of Religion* 68, no. 3 (2007): 237–51.
Morrison, Grant, Ethan van Sciver, Keron Grant, Frank Quitely, Phil Jimenez, and Chris Bachalo. *New X-Men.* 133–50. New York: Marvel Comics, 2001-2.
Myrdal, Gunnar. *An American Dilemma: The Negro Problem and Modern Democracy.* New York: Harper & Brothers, 1944.
Nyberg, Amy Kiste. "Of Heroes and Superheroes." *Media Representations of September 11,* eds. Steven Chermak, Frankie Y. Bailey, and Michelle Brown. Westport, CT: Praeger, 2003. 175–85.
Patterson, James T. *Restless Giant: The United States from Watergate to Bush v. Gore.* New York: Oxford University Press, 2005.
Pervez, Sabbiyah. "Why We All Should Marvel at This Muslim Superhero." *The Independent,* November 14, 2013. http://www.independent.co.uk/voices/comment/why-we-all-should-marvel-at-this-muslim-superhero-8932359.html.
Prell, Riv-Ellen. *Fighting to Become Americans: Jews, Gender, and the Anxiety of Assimilation.* Boston: Beacon, 1999.
Putnam, Robert D. *Bowling Alone: The Collapse and Revival of American Community.* New York: Simon & Schuster, 2000.
Rimmon-Kenan, Shlomith. *Narrative Fiction: Contemporary Poetics.* 2nd ed. London & New York: Routledge, 2002.
Roediger, David R. *Working toward Whiteness: How America's Immigrants Became White. The Strange Journey from Ellis Island to the Suburbs.* New York: Basic Books, 2005.
Said, Edward W. *Covering Islam: How the Media and the Experts Determine How We See the Rest of the World.* New York: Pantheon Books, 1981.
Sanderson, Peter. *The Marvel Comics Guide to New York City.* New York: Pocket Books, 2007.
Seelarbokus, B. Chenaz. "Thoroughly Muslim Mystic: Rewriting Rumi in America." *Muslims and American Popular Culture,* eds. Iraj Omidvar and Anne R. Richards, 1. Santa Barbara: Praeger, 2014. 267–87.
Shryock, Andrew. "Epilogue: On Discipline and Inclusion." *Being and Belonging: Muslims in the United States since 9/11,* ed. Katherine Pratt Ewing. New York: Russell Sage Foundation, 2008. 200–7.
Shyminsky, Neil. "Mutant Readers, Reading Mutants: Appropriation, Assimilation, and the X-Men." *International Journal of Comic Art* 8, no. 2 (Fall 2006): 387–405.
Siegel, Jerry, Joe Shuster, Wayne Boring, and Jack Burnley. *Superman Chronicles: Volume Four.* New York: DC Comics, 2008.
Smith, Jane I. *Islam in America.* 2nd ed. Columbia Contemporary American Religion Series. New York: Columbia University Press, 2010.
Stibili, Edward C. *What Can Be Done to Help Them? The Italian Saint Raphael Society, 1887-1923.* New York: Center for Migration Studies, 2003.

Strömberg, Fredrik. *Black Images in the Comics: A Visual History*. 2nd ed. Seattle: Fantagraphics, 2012.

———. "'Yo, Rag-Head!': Arab and Muslim Superheroes in American Comic Books after 9/11." *Amerikastudien* 56, no. 4 (2011): 573–601.

Takaki, Ronald T. *A Different Mirror: A History of Multicultural America*. New York: Back Bay Books/Little, Brown, 2008.

Thomas, Roy, Arnold Drake, Dennis O'Neil, Don Heck, Werner Roth, Neal Adams, Sal Buscema, Vince Colletta, Sam Grainger, and Tom Palmer. *Essential Classic X-Men* 3. New York: Marvel, 2009.

Villeda, Ray, and John Chandler. "Man Yells He Wants to 'Kill Muslims,' Attacks Store Owner: Victim." *NBC New York*, December 10, 2015. http://www.nbcnewyork.com/news/local/Muslim-Store-Owner-Assault-Queens-New-York-City-Bias-Attack-361354111.html.

Wenger, Beth S. *History Lessons: The Creation of American Jewish Heritage*. Princeton: Princeton University Press, 2010.

Whedon, Joss, and John Cassaday. *Giant-Size Astonishing X-Men*. New York: Marvel, 2008.

Wheeler, Andrew. "The Books Are Selling: Marvel Publisher Dan Buckley on the Company's Gamble with Diversity." *Comics Alliance*, January 20, 2015. http://comicsalliance.com/marvel-publisher-dan-buckley-diversity/.

Williams, Rhys H. "Civil Religion and the Cultural Politics of National Identity in Obama's America." *Journal for the Scientific Study of Religion* 52, no. 2 (June 1, 2013): 239–57. doi:10.1111/jssr.12032.

Wilson, G. Willow, Adrian Alphona, Jake Wyatt, Elmo Bondoc, and Takeshi Miyazawa. *Ms. Marvel* 1–19. New York: Marvel, 2014.

Wirth-Nesher, Hana. *City Codes: Reading the Modern Urban Novel*. Cambridge & New York: Cambridge University Press, 1996.

Wright, Bradford. *Comic Book Nation: The Transformation of Youth Culture in America*. Baltimore: Johns Hopkins University Press, 2001.

Yanora, Mercedes. "Marked by Foreign Policy: Muslim Superheroes and Their Quest for Authenticity." *Muslim Superheroes: Comics, Islam, and Representation*, eds. A. David Lewis and Martin Lund. Boston: Ilex Foundation, 2017. 110–33.

Yockey, Matthew. "This Island Manhattan: New York City and the Space Race in *The Fantastic Four*." *Iowa Journal of Cultural Studies* 6, no. 1 (Spring 2005): 58–79.

Zeiger, Dinah. "That (Afghan) Girl! Ideology Unveiled in *National Geographic*." *Veil: Women Writers on Its History, Lore, and Politics*, ed. Jennifer Heath. Berkeley: University of California Press, 2008.

Zhou, Steven. "'Salafi' Does Not Equal 'Terrorist': Stop Assuming All Conservative Muslims Are Violent Extremists." *Salon*, December 21, 2015. http://www.salon.com/2015/12/21/salafi_does_not_equal_terrorist_stop_assuming_all_conservative_muslims_are_violent_extremists/.

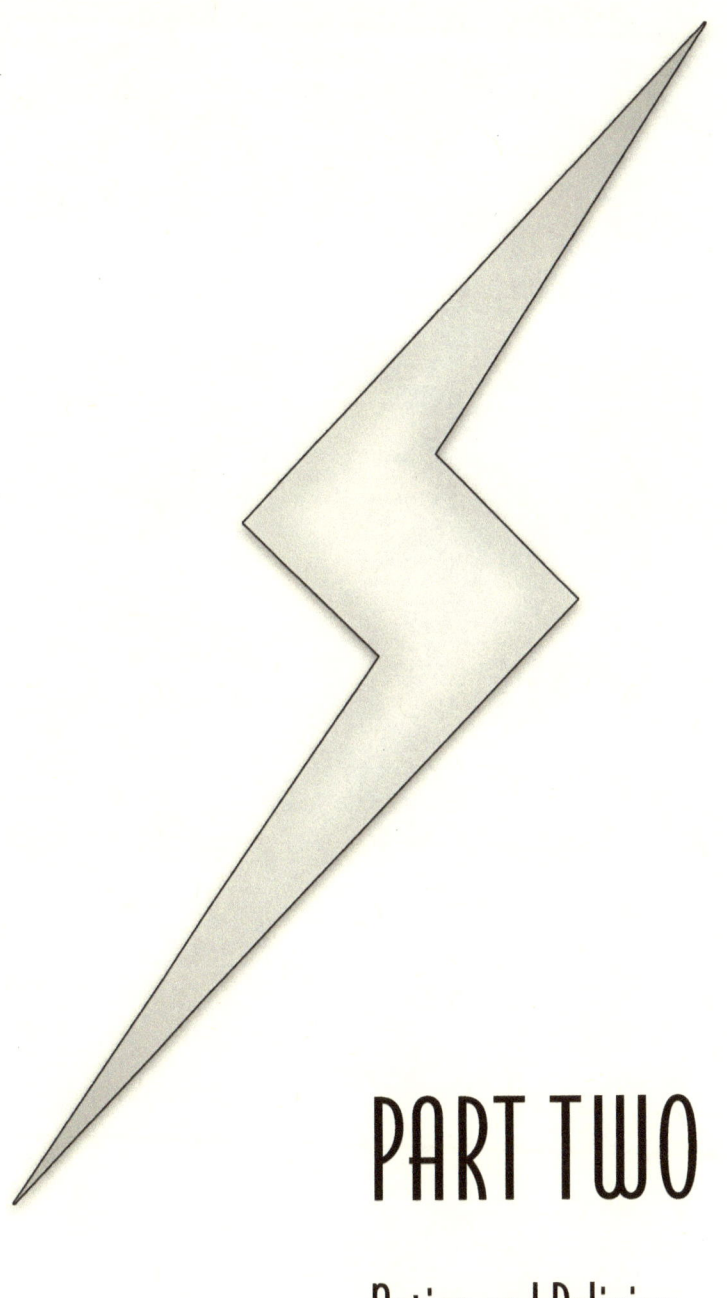

PART TWO

Nation and Religion, Identity and Community

MS. MARVEL IS AN IMMIGRANT

HUSSEIN RASHID

Kamala Khan, the new Ms. Marvel, is a hero who is often described as a Muslim superhero. But her official description mentions more than her religion, explaining that her family is from Pakistan, that she is a teenager, and that she is from New Jersey. In other words, she is clearly a multi-identified individual. Unlike a Peter Parker, none of her characteristics makes her "normal," aptly earning the title of her first collected volume, *No Normal*. By "normal," I mean the "all-American" ideal of the white male, often read as Christian, and at least middle class. This conception of what it means to be American is enshrined in the founding documents of the United States, which privilege race, class, and gender explicitly and establish norms around religious belonging.

Khan is not alone in being "not normal." The way she exhibits her second-generation identity is a particular case study in how immigrants of any generation, unless phenotypically white, are not normal. The reality is that her struggles and demeanor in that immigrant context are perfectly normal and expected. From a sociological perspective, she walks the line between straight-line assimilation theory (the melting-pot model) and integration theory (the mosaic model) of belonging.

The use of language, food, and webs of familial obligations are familiar sites of contestation in the struggle to belong, in both assimilation or integration models. We see all of these markers represented in Khan's story. However, her appearance, which includes more than her clothes, contains important signifiers for her struggle to be part of an "American normal." As a polymorph, an individual who has the ability to change her physical characteristics, clothing becomes only one layer of meaning for her. Her very body represents her conception of being "American."

The discussion of Khan's immigrant nature helps ground us in understanding the socially transformative work that the *Ms. Marvel* series is doing. While there is arguably work being done by the comic through para-social contact (Charlton; Horton; Pettigrew and Tropp; Schiappa, Gregg and Hewes, "Parasocial"), the stories also mimic the real social transformation performed by immigrants. The stories of immigrants are often invisible to members of the host nation, so *Ms. Marvel* serves to make a subset of those stories visible.

The integration of a marginalized community into the cultural center is not unidirectional, but dialogic; both the center and the margin change. The mechanism for this change is the process of hybridity, but that process cannot be fully understood without an engagement with how the dominant society is marginalizing Khan's various identifications and how she is being written in response to that marginalization. Therefore, I argue that in looking at how Kamala Khan, rather than Ms. Marvel, navigates the competing pulls of her identity, we can more clearly see how the hybridity process functions and the changes it makes. Khan's individual struggles open up doors to understanding communal dynamics. We can say that Khan is a superhero who is Muslim, but not that she is necessarily a Muslim superhero.

South Asian Immigration and Whiteness

In many ways, it is Khan's ethnic identity that is deeply contested in the series, more than her religious identity. While it is true that Muslims are a highly racialized religious group, with South Asian and Arab bodies conflated with Muslim bodies, Khan's story does not seem to play into this elision. Rather, the series demonstrates a wide variety of different ethnicities as Muslim and focuses on Khan's particular Pakistani identity as something distinct from, but related to, her religious identity. Therefore, while her religion is important, it stands in relationship to her ethnic identity and is inflected by the place of that ethnicity in America's social hierarchy.

The story of South Asian immigration in the United States switches from de facto acceptance, to official rejection, to official acceptance, without ever creating or sustaining a social acceptance. The question of social acceptance was further aggravated after the attacks on the United States on September 11, 2001. We can categorize South Asian immigration into three waves. The first was from 1819 through 1914, which was a period of migrant labor. This wave consisted mostly of male agricultural workers, arriving on the West Coast. For various reasons related to questions of race and citizenship, this wave did not create a sustained community that is politically distinct today. However, it was during this time that the US government established laws concerning the immigration of Asians to the country, thus, contributing to American stereotypes of South Asians that were developing at this time.

The first immigration law passed in the United States was in 1790. It linked citizenship through naturalization to the category of "free white person" (Kim 33). This exclusion from citizenship eventually transformed into a ban on immigration. Although initially targeting Chinese and Japanese immigration, de facto limits to South Asian immigration began in 1910, and formal exclusion of South Asians began in 1917.

The issue of citizenship was more convoluted. The initial intent of the phrase "free white person" seems to be non–enslaved and non–Native American, the only other possible categories of human beyond white in 1790s America. In 1922, Takao Ozawa, a Japanese immigrant, was denied citizenship. The US Supreme Court ruled that "white" means "Caucasian," not just not nonblack or non–Native American. Bhagat Singh Thind, a South Asian immigrant, had applied for citizenship after he served in the US Army in World War I, believing that since Indians are Aryan, he was Caucasian, as the terms were treated synonymously. The US Supreme Court ruled later, in 1923, that he could not become a citizen. According to their ruling, when they used "Caucasian," they meant it in the popular sense of having white skin. Both these rulings retroactively stripped citizenship from members of groups who already had citizenship. Following these cases, the US Congress passed legislation that prohibited immigration for anyone ineligible for citizenship. Indians eventually became eligible for citizenship, and the government slightly eased immigration restrictions in 1946. However, Indian immigration numbers were minuscule and were incapable of generating a large self-sustaining community.

The second wave came after the Immigration and Nationality Act of 1965, which had a profound impact on South Asian immigration to the United States. Because the law expressed a preference for immigrants in skilled and professional jobs, the majority of South Asians immigrating between 1965 and 1986 were highly educated. The third wave arrived after the Immigration Reform and Control Act of 1986 was passed. The act granted amnesty to undocumented migrants in the United States, allowed for family sponsorship of new immigrants, and eased the preferential selection of skilled and professional labor. All these factors changed the demographic composition of the South Asian American community.

With each successive wave of migration, there were different patterns for integrating into the American mainstream related to "whiteness." The use of "whiteness" here is not a reference to phenotype, but to power structures, which in the American context are connected to race. In the first wave of migration, immigrants were stripped of their citizenship, their property, and their ability to integrate in any capacity into the dominant American culture. The argument in the Thind Case connected being Aryan and Caucasian, so that Indians could become US citizens. This argument was one that equated Indian with "white" as a way to get citizenship, while reinforcing narratives of what "American" means through racial power structures.

The second wave, due to preferential selection, had a relatively high economic status and was able to lay a stronger claim to "whiteness." Economic privilege allowed for choices in how to participate in the dominant society—choices that may not have been available to people from lower classes (Karst 411). For example, many of these immigrants came during a period of immigration in America conceived of as a "melting pot," where immigrants would surrender part of their difference to become "American." To participate in this whiteness meant that these immigrants had to ignore the directed racism of groups like the Dotbusters, who targeted South Asians (Prashad 87). The most well-known Dotbuster attack was on Navroze Mody, who died four days after he was assaulted, in September 1987. The attack took place in Jersey City, the home of the fictional Kamala Khan. One of the dominant ways this racism was rationalized by immigrants was to hearken back to the arguments from the early part of the century: racists do not know that South Asians are the true Aryans (Prashad 93). By the late 1970s, the melting-pot model of assimilation was changing to a mosaic model of integration, whereby immigrants could maintain markers of ethnic identity. It was in this cultural environment that the third wave of South Asian immigrants arrived.

The racial dynamic of this period was complicated by the rise of the "model minority," a term that described Asian Americans as economically successful and was used to further marginalize African Americans, who remained pushed down to the bottom of the American racial ladder (Petersen; Prashad 169–70). South Asian Americans of the third wave came through family reunification, and because many of them were not as economically well positioned as their predecessors, they were more racialized. The second-generation of both waves were more conscious of the racial positioning and adopted more integrative practices, which allowed them to exert their own ethnic identities in an American context.

The post-9/11 period further demonstrated the precarity of whiteness for South Asian immigrants, as they were subject to increased national security interest (Maira 4). Ethnic studies scholar Sunaina Maira argues that citizenship and cultural citizenship, "everyday understandings of belonging and exclusion," are distinct but related categories and that cultural citizenship is tied intimately to popular culture and locality (Maira 10–11)—although earlier generations of immigrants had to contend with discrimination and exclusion based on phenotype, and often that racism was conflated with religious identity. Muslim subjects—in particular South Asians and Arabs who, because of stereotypes and racism, were more readily read as Muslim—were told that Islam and America were competing ideologies (Maira 10). The result for South Asian immigrants was a need to move beyond straight-line assimilation theory and look at other types of integration.

The practice of a segmented assimilation, which recognizes that integration into the American narrative is not bound to whiteness, allows connections and alliances with other marginalized communities. The result is an awareness of South Asian Americans belonging to a diverse American society with a history of ongoing racism, and it is in this context that Kamala Khan functions.

Ms. Marvel's Performance

Based on analysis by Sika A. Dagbovie-Mullins and Eric Berlatsky in this volume,[1] we know that Khan was born in the late 1990s. As a result, we expect her to belong to a sociological pattern of segmented assimilation, where she associates with other marginalized groups. The diversity of her friends hints at this pattern of adaptation. We see that she does not jettison her parental languages, and she does not shy away from expressing her religiosity in public. Yet she also exhibits many of the markers of a second-generation individual within the straight-line model, an earlier model of assimilation. She does avoid wearing clothing marking her Pakistani descent, and she does feel the need to distance herself from her parents' Pakistani culture. The latter impulse may also be part of adolescence, but the constant reference to their "unAmerican" way of doing things makes her actions also fit comfortably into a second-wave, second-generation paradigm of assimilation.

We first meet Khan at the Circle Q, a neighborhood convenience store where she is looking at an "Easy Greasy BLT [bacon, lettuce, and tomato]" sandwich. Muslim dietary laws forbid the consumption of swine, except in exigent circumstances. As she looks at the sandwich, she says "delicious, delicious infidel meat . . .," performing her Islam in a public space and in front of her non-Muslim friend Bruno (Wilson and Alphona, v. 1, i. 1). This performance indicates that Khan is comfortable in revealing parts of herself in public and that there is a level of understanding among her friends who are present. There is a familiarity that speaks to an intimacy among her friends.

Also with Khan and Bruno is Nakia, their friend of Turkish descent, who chooses to wear a *hijab*. As they are talking at the Circle Q, popular girl Zoe and her boyfriend, Josh, enter the store. Bruno describes Zoe as a "concern troll," who, as Nakia says, "[is] only nice to be mean" (ibid.). Zoe questions if Nakia is wearing the *hijab* by choice and if Nakia will suffer an "honor killing" if she removes it. Zoe offers an explicit critique of Islam, Khan's religion, based on stereotypes and violence. All these characters go to the same school, which means that Zoe is aware of Khan's and Nakia's religion and has had the opportunity to talk to them about it (Kent 525). Zoe frames her dominance through feigned empathy, disrupting the idyll of Khan's performance. There is a shift in tenor across the pages as we are introduced to these characters in Khan's life. The shift demonstrates the different worlds in which Khan exists: she can perform aspects of her identity, but she has to be aware of her audience. While audience awareness is not unique to Khan, to understand the tensions in her life, we have to look at how her performance changes in different circumstances. For example, after Zoe makes her comments and leaves the Circle Q, Khan says, "[B]ut she's so nice. . . . [S]he's so adorable and happy." Khan then says there's no chance of she herself "becoming blonde and popular." As a result of this exchange, we can read Zoe as someone Khan wants to be like. Zoe is the "normal" standard who, seemingly, can always be who she wants to be, in any situation. Ultimately, this is Khan's desire, to perform her identities as she wants, regardless of the views of other people.

As a teenage girl born in New Jersey to parents who emigrated from Pakistan, Khan exists in a doubly liminal space: through her age and her cultural referents (Maira 15–16). Religion and/as culture are important to her family. As we see Khan in her home setting, she is writing fanfic about the Avengers, a group she clearly admires. Her older brother, Aamir, who shows his devotion to Islam through dress, language, and public praxis, is vocalizing a prayer of thanks for the food, which remains untranslated.[2] In the next panel, her mother walks in front of a piece of framed artwork on the wall (figure 2.1). The artwork she obscures seems to be "Allah" in Arabic calligraphy. (The word has a recognizable shape الله, and there are popular forms of design of the calligraphy in American Muslim homes that seem to match up with what is visible.) In the same panel, her father is reading an English-language paper that is most likely meant to represent the "ethnic press" of the area. The paper is called *Jersey Akhbar* (*Jersey News*), and

Figure 2.1 Wilson and Alphona, *No Normal*

the back page has an ad for a restaurant, which says "Eat Now! Radoslav's Chicken Salan" (figure 2.1).³ The word *salan* is Urdu for food in a sauce or broth, what would be considered a "curry" in English. However, Radoslav is an eastern European name, so the ad signifies the ubiquitousness of South Asian food and perhaps the mixing of immigrant/marginalized communities.

Gender-based, heteronormative expectations, such as mixing with boys, checking in with parents, and "acceptable" activities, also play a role in Khan's construction of self. Yet, while initially indexed as Pakistani or Muslim in her familial restrictions, there is nothing out of the ordinary in her father's admonitions from the perspective of a patriarchal American parental figure (Reyns-Chikuma and Lorenz 80). As they sit at the dinner table, Khan asks her father if she can go to a party that night, and he refuses. The conversation continues:

> KHAN: Come on, Abu [father]! I'm **sixteen**! I promise I won't do anything **stupid**! Don't you trust me?!
> ABU: Of course I trust **you** *beti* [dear]. But it's not safe for a young girl to be out late at night with strange boys, **drinking** God knows what and thinking God knows what.

One could read Abu's references to God as either a common figure of speech or a religious admonishment. The ways in which readers index knowledge of Abu's religion and his immigrant status to his statement dramatically impact the way the text is received. However, as much as possible, I will treat statements as uninflected by religion or immigrant status, unless no other reading is possible. The struggle of Khan's belonging is informed by her familial situation but determined by the power structures outside of that setting.

The way Khan chooses to present herself at various times during the discovery of her powers reveals her struggle with "normalcy" and belonging. The visible manifestations of her sense of self signal a struggle of belonging to an American narrative. This struggle also results in a moral injury to herself. (A moral injury is the performance of actions contrary to one's notion of self, which is dependent not just on individual will, but on structures of authority that condition these actions [Kinghorn 57].) After her father prohibits her from going to the party, Khan sneaks out of her house to go anyway, in order to prove she's "normal." As she struggles with whether to go to the party or not, she thinks "everybody else gets to be **normal**. Why can't I?" (Wilson and Alphona, v. 1, i. 1). Earlier in the day, when Zoe highlighted Khan's "Otherness" via Islam, she focused on some of the gender-based expectations that Khan may experience. Although Zoe's comments are based on stereotypes, they are stereotypes that the reader may have, and they affect the way in which Abu's comments are read. Khan does act against her parents' expectations, and at least some part of her beliefs, to satisfy a competing interest of "fitting in." We are pushed to reading the exchange as based in religion or Pakistani culture, but there is nothing intrinsic in Abu's statements that would lead us to that reading. Such an interpretation could also very easily emerge from the patriarchal culture of the United States. Khan engages with her guilt over her actions, demonstrating an internal discomfort, even as she willingly chooses her actions.

After this party, Khan's powers as a polymorph, or shapeshifter, manifest. At the end of the first issue, Khan is transformed by a Terrigen Mist, and she begins to hallucinate a conversation with Captain America, Iron Man, and Captain Marvel, her heroic idol, also known as Carol Danvers. Khan explains why she snuck out to a party her parents forbade her to go to: "I grew up here! I'm from Jersey City, not Karachi!" When Danvers, in Khan's hallucination, asks Khan who she wants to be, she replies, "I want to be beautiful and awesome and butt-kicking and less complicated. I want to be you. Except I would wear the classic, politically incorrect costume."

Danvers then promises her a "reboot," but she says that "it's not going to turn out the way you think." We end with Khan morphed into Danvers, asking, "[I]s it too late to change my mind?" In this short sequence, which covers eight panels over four pages, Khan outlines the tensions in her life and how she sees a successful resolution emerging, as well as an awareness that she may have wished upon the Monkey's Paw.[4]

The obvious, initial tension rests between Khan and her parents. At a basic level, this is the reaction of a teenager. There may be a gender issue at play—a young girl not being allowed to go to a party by herself—but nothing initially marks this tension as an immigrant issue. It is only when Khan begins to explain the situation that she brings her parents' point of origin into the discussion. Khan understands the issue as an immigrant issue, but as readers who know we have been guided to a similar understanding, we can ask whether she is conditioned to think this way by external factors. By having one point of difference, everything Khan does is projected as different, even if that difference is not objectively true.

The rest of the conversation happens in the shadow of the declaration of difference: "I'm . . . not [from] Karachi!" Her peers see her as from "there," and her parents fear her belonging "here." Khan does not dismiss her parents completely, but she places herself in Jersey City. As a result, her sense of beauty is shaped by the stereotypical all-American ideal of Carol Danvers. Khan's belief that she is not beautiful exists despite the fact that Bruno, a white classmate, has a crush on her, of which she seems to be unaware. Bruno's crush signals both that Khan is beautiful and that there are many definitions of American beauty.

Khan further sees beauty as something that needs to be sexualized. She wants Danvers's old "politically incorrect" costume, with a (p)leather look, high heels on thigh-high boots, and significantly more flesh revealed than with Danvers's current costume. Danvers warns Khan that this identity is not what she thinks it will be, but the wish is granted, and Khan immediately realizes that Danvers was right.

In the second issue, Khan, as she looks at her new form, thinks to herself, "This is what I asked for, right? So why don't I feel strong and confident and beautiful? Why do I just feel freaked out and underdressed?" She is beginning to realize that that "American girl" is not who she is either (Landis 35). At the same time, when she hears the voice of Zoe—the classmate who was concern trolling her earlier—in danger, she reflexively turns into Danvers again, because she has "to be someone else. Someone cool." She describes her transformation upon hearing Zoe's voice as a "reflex," a "fake smile," because she feels uncomfortable in Zoe's presence. Her initial transformation is into the current Captain Marvel costume, but when she decides to save Zoe, she morphs into Danvers's Ms. Marvel costume. Her first instinct for comfort is the less sexualized, more controlled version of her hero, but as she comes out of hiding to perform a rescue, she switches to the sexualized presentation of her hero. Her intellectual understanding of what is practical and comforting to her and her social conditioning of what look would make her popular are coming into conflict (Reyns-Chikuma and Lorenz 82; Kent 525). By reflexively taking the form of her idol, Carol Danvers, the former Ms. Marvel and an almost archetypal representation of the American mainstream, Khan literally embodies the multiple pulls on her sense of self through appearance and action. Khan decides to save Zoe's life after remembering a verse from the Qur'an her father taught her.[5] Her guiding spiritual text is the Qur'an, and the verse acknowledges the relationship between Muslims and Jews. A similar passage to the one quoted in the comic is found in the Babylonian Talmud.

At Khan's time of stress, she may wish to look like those around her, but she goes back to the teachings of her parents and her faith. The push-pull forces on her identity continue to exert themselves. After spending some time in her idol's skin, she realizes that that identity is not hers either. After the heroic save, Khan thinks to herself, "I always thought that if I had amazing hair, if I could pull off great boots, if I could fly—that would make me feel strong. That would make me happy. But the hair gets in my face. The boots pinch . . . and this leotard is giving me an epic wedgie" (Wilson and Alphona v.1, i. 2). The adopted persona is uncomfortable, and solves none of what is really bothering her.

Khan's next full-body transformation happens in the third issue. She is losing control of her powers while in school, and she runs into the locker room to hide. She attempts to regain control of her powers and is moderately successful in maintaining the size of her body. When she tries to turn into someone other than Carol Danvers, she becomes her mother, although she says she was aiming for pop singer Taylor Swift.

Khan's conscious desire is still to turn to stereotypical standards of American beauty. However, in a time of stress, she once more turns into a personal hero, this time her mother. Carol Danvers and her Ammi are the two older women who have influenced Khan the most and who provide comfort to her in different ways. In the two figures she morphs into, we read the pulls on who she is/wants to be. While Danvers is her hero, she is also the epitome of America for Khan. At the same time, Khan cannot escape the obligations and teachings of her family, who have sacrificed for her success.

Khan, as a second-generation immigrant, would normally feel three pulls on her identity: her parents, the dominant culture surrounding her, and her peer group. Because her religion is a salient point in her characterization, it becomes another pole around which she can attempt to craft her own identity. In this situation of competing allegiances, it would be easy for Khan to suffer from moral injury. In sneaking out to the party, we believe that Khan will suffer from a moral injury. Her transformation to Danvers suggests to the reader that she will jettison parts of her identity in order to participate in a dominant culture. However, in remembering religious teachings as transmitted by her father, she seeks to constitute herself as an American hero with multiple identifications. She is struggling to avoid that moral injury.

This navigation of multiple identifications to constitute something new is a hybridizing process. However, while the broad patterns of hybridization are fairly consistent, it is particularities of each instance that help us understand how Khan operates in her own specific hybridizing environment and what it is she symbolizes and is creating.

What Does the Hybrid Do?

Khan is situated in a metaphoric diaspora (Levy and Weingrod 7, 17). She has no desire to return to her parents' homeland of Pakistan, but she maintains an awareness of, and connection to, Pakistan. Her home, as she clearly articulated during her superhero transformation, is Jersey City. By virtue of having this diaspora consciousness, she rejects assimilation into the dominant cultural forms, without rejecting her host society. The result is that Khan is attempting to redefine how we conceive of the mainstream (Brah 210).

Many other essays in this volume deal with Khan and her fictional world through the lens of hybrid products.[6] My interest is more in the process than the product. That process is determined by the power structures of race and place, as well as time. It is also linked to an audience, presumably the readers of the series. Therefore, we must understand both the premises of hybridity and the potential process through which mass media may effect social change.

Russian theorist Mikhail Bakhtin argues for a dialogic where multiple meanings of a language can exist simultaneously (Bakhtin 426). Unlike the Hegelian dialectic, there is no need to push toward a resolution of thesis and antithesis. Competing ideas are in relation to one another and exist in a state of harmony, until a rupture occurs, which catalyzes a transformation of that relationship (Kristeva and Moi 58). The coexistence of multiple meanings of language, or the contact among different languages, is called *heteroglossia*. Languages can mix, but the relationship is inherently unequal. As Bakhtin says of the hybrid construction that comes out of heteroglossia,

> Languages that are crossed in it [the hybrid construction] relate to each other as do rejoinders in a dialogue; there is an argument between languages, an argument between styles of language. But it is

not a dialogue in a narrative sense, nor in the abstract sense; rather it is a dialogue between points of view, each with its own concrete language that cannot be translated into the other. (Bakhtin 75–76)

In this meeting of languages, it is possible that the dominant language can incorporate the weaker language without losing its character (Saussure 194). Bakhtin's view, an alternative to this incorporation, is that the dominant language is so changed that it becomes something new and enters into a new relationship with a different language. What is more likely is that both languages constantly change each other, redefining what is "normal."

While Bakhtin is interested in languages, his work is adaptable to culture as well. Cultural theorist Homi Bhabha argues that it is in the meeting of cultural systems and the ways that the meeting is negotiated that a new culture is generated (Bhabha 38). We can understand that productive, generative space in the hyphen of American racial and ethnic identity labels like "South Asian–American." The hyphen represents that space where the South Asian and American cultural systems come into contact and create something new.

What Is the "New" of Kamala Khan?

However, in this construction, the power dynamic is also visible. "South Asian" and "American" are presented as irreducible entities that cannot be merged. No matter how many generations descendants of immigrants have been in the United States, phenotypically darker-skinned people are always portrayed as "immigrants." Culturally, "American" privileges the definition tied to legal citizenship from the founding of the country: free white person. Therefore, while the hyphen is a generative space, it is also the point at which the heteroglot relationship is fixed. At the same time, Bakhtin argues that there needs to be a rupture to create a new relationship, which becomes a new composite language. Sociologists Richard Alba and Victor Nee, mirroring the idea of the rupture, argue that when immigrants change the dominant culture, a new "composite culture" is created (Alba and Nee 10).

Kamala Khan, as a character, is embedded in a very particular set of power dynamics. She is located in New Jersey, across the river from New York, and can see the Manhattan skyline from parts of Jersey City. She is the child of immigrants, living in a multiethnic and multiracial neighborhood. While she seems to live in a comfortable environment from an economic perspective, it is not clear what the broader economic class of her fictional city is within the run of comics we are investigating. Her parents come from Pakistan, and express different levels of religiosity in public. We have to be conscious of how Khan, as a post-9/11 young adult near New York City, is negotiating her space.

Khan's initial transformation into Carol Danvers does not provide the moment of rupture. It reinscribes the categories that already exist—white and not white, American and South Asian—and submits to the dominant power. By integrating the various parts of her identity, Khan maintains the existing relationship of power. However, slowly, over the course of the series, we see Khan offering a disruptive experience. She adapts her burkini, a piece of modest dress that she views negatively, into her superhero costume. She integrates the *dupatta*, a type of scarf worn by South Asian women, into her both her civilian and hero outfits.[7] These visual cues signal that the definition of "American" dress is broadening. Bruno is the only one of her friend circle whom she tells about her secret identity. Aamir becomes engaged to an African American Muslim later in the series. These social connections are more powerful indicators than dress of a changing social dynamic. They signify the changing nature of social networks, with Khan being the center of friends and family of Pakistan, Turkish, Italian, and African American heritages.

The reader sees all of these shifts in what is normal for Khan's world. In addition, they are met with a language, Urdu, that is sometimes glossed and sometimes not. The metonymic gap serves as invitation to the reader to make sense from context and enter into a conversation with the text. Other text, such as the prayer of thanks that Aamir offers in Arabic, remains totally untranslated, and readers are expected to treat it as normal, even if they do not recognize that Arabic is not a national language of Pakistan. While readers may not understand every reference, Khan, as a cultural object, still generates an affective response in the audience.

The basic mechanism of social change is derived from parasocial contact hypothesis (PCH), which argues that media can produce a sense of dissonance within a consumer that can create an attitude change (Schiappa, Gregg, and Hewes, "Parasocial Contact," 94). This attitude change is the rupture expected from heteroglossia. Although PCH emerges in the context of TV, comics offer a similar structure of serialized storytelling. The result is that the consumer is more inclined to identify with the characters (Schiappa, Gregg, and Hewes, "Can One TV Show," 20). If stories of difference and integration are organically told as part of the story as a whole, rather than as the dominant story, audiences are more receptive to the vision offered by the story (Bell 134, 138, 149). As a result, the fact that we see Abu reading an ethnic paper or Ammi walking in front of a piece of calligraphy seems to function to allow the reader to make sense of the composite culture of the house.

If the hybrid is an ongoing process, because of the dialogic of power and belonging, we expect the story to adapt to address the new ways in which power systems seek to exclude difference from cultural citizenship. The hybrid product of Khan calling her father "Abu" will not always be sufficient to effect change. We see some of that shift happening within the first pages of Ms. Marvel. When Zoe asks Nakia if she will suffer an honor killing, we as readers are aware of the rhetoric around Muslim women needing saving (c.f., Abu-Lughod). Nakia's dismissal of Zoe's concern is also for the benefit of the reader, who is also being told that this story of weak, abused Muslim women is not actually the story of Muslim women. We quickly understand that the concern of the teenage Muslim women of Jersey City are the concerns of teenagers in general: what to eat, what to wear, who to hang out with, and what to do for fun. Although a full analysis of later Kamala Khan stories is outside the scope of this anthology, we see the series delve into Khan's relationship and connection to South Asia, which continues to push the dialogic, as readers become integrated into Khan's New Jersey identification.

Representing the Real World

This social transformation we experience as readers is a demonstration of PCH. In addition, the Khan story is representative of how quotidian interactions affect relationships and notions of belonging in real life (c.f., Allport). Some critics remain concerned, however, that simply consuming South Asian "products" like *Ms. Marvel* can result in a focus on the product, over the process and power dynamics that produced the product (Hutnyk 38, 102). The result is that the acceptance of the product does not make the producers any more real and may make the producers seem more abstract to the consumers (Kalra 23).

While the commodification of cultures of marginalized communities is an important concern, it does not negate the ways in which social contact effects change. For example, "Radoslav's Chicken Salan" is both a marker of potential segmented assimilation and the recognition that societal norms shift as a result of integration. When Khan describes the BLT at the Circle Q as "delicious, delicious infidel meat," not only does her non-Muslim, non-Pakistani friend Bruno understand the context of the comment, but he is also able to respond in a way that indicates more than a surface understanding. He says, "[E]ither eat the bacon or stick to your principles." His retort demonstrates that he knows that, for Khan, not eating the bacon is truly a matter of principle, not just something that she is mimicking from her parents. He forces her to confront what is important to her, and that knowledge comes from connection and transformation. Khan accepts the chiding because their relationship is one of mutual change and acceptance.

These two examples that illustrate social and personal transformation are the most obvious ones in the first collection of Ms. Marvel. While there are more detailed and sustained examples in later Ms. Marvel stories that demonstrate similar points, these two points early in Khan's story reveal the details of her world and determine how the hybrid is generated: for Khan, through food and dress, as well as through the pressure of her race, religion, and gender, and the status of her parents as immigrants.

Conclusion

In order to fully understand Kamala Khan as an immigrant, we need to understand the sociology that defines her sense of belonging within the dominant American narrative and how she may change that narrative to integrate herself into it. The result is a hybrid process, which gives us further insight into the sociology of immigrants and the social change they are making—which, in turn, alters the hybrid process. This loop is the diachronic approach to understanding how hybridization and social change happen in society, as opposed to the synchronic approach, which focuses on the hybrid product.

This sort of investigation offers an important way to understand and think about the work that Ms. Marvel is doing in and with the real world. It also demonstrates the need for a religious literacy that does not overdetermine the role of religion. Khan is Muslim, which is a necessary part of understanding her as a character. But she is defined by her ethnicity, her parents' point of origin, her class, her gender, her sexuality, and the environment in which she lives. To read her as a Muslim superhero, instead of as a superhero who is Muslim, flattens her character and misses the ways in which she is doing important cultural work (Yanora 127; Pumphrey 792).[8]

In fact, religious literacy is dependent on this very type of cultural study. Religion does not exist separately from the lived realities of people, so to understand how religion functions, we need to understand their material conditions. Shifting to this sort of methodology moves us from doing a type of theological work, to understanding religion as a performed and lived tradition (During 1; King 53; Moore 79–80).

Khan is not a Muslim in an abstract sense. She is a living character who interacts with her faith as her situation demands. She is a Muslim of South Asian descent whose parents were immigrants to the United States. Understanding her ethnic and racial situation is as important as—if not more important than—her religion when comprehending what she experiences in the world. She lives in a multiethnic environment and sees the world through the lens of those who need help and whom she can help. Her allies and accomplices come from all the walks of life that make up Jersey City. She cannot escape the history of the attacks on New York City, but that history does not curtail her potential.

All of these histories and identifications help to develop Khan's identity. She, in turn, interacts with her wider world and the real-world audience of Ms. Marvel. It is the dialogic of all these relationships that invites the reader into her world and offers a rupture that helps the reader see the world in a new way. When Khan saves Zoe from drowning, it is the Muslim who does the saving of a white person, not the other way around. This moment is a moment of rupture. Expectations are inverted (Yanora 127).

The more nuanced Khan is as a character, the more the reader has to understand about her reality and to reflect on the structures of the real world. As G. Willow Wilson has argued, it is not diversity for the sake of diversity that brings people to this series, but particularity (Triece and Lacy 3).[9] By remembering that Khan is an immigrant, we are rewarded with a deft handling of a character who allows us to see all of her, not just one facet.

NOTES

1. See "The Only Nerdy Pakistani-American Slash-Inhuman in the Entire Universe," in part 2 of this book.

2. The comic text is: "Allahoma batik lana fima razaqtana waqina ath—" (Wilson, *Ms. Marvel: No Normal*, v. 1, i. 1). The full prayer is most likely:

اللهم بارك فيما رزقتنا و عذاب النار بسم الله

Allahuma bārik fīmā razaqtanā ʿadhāb an-nār bismillah.
Oh God, bless the food you have provided and protect us from Hellfire. In the name of God.

3. See Dagbovie-Mullins and Berlatsky in this book for reference to a "Radoslav's Vietnamese grocery." If connected to Radoslav's chicken curry, this restaurant/grocery is hybridity run amok to a late-capitalist conclusion.

4. Supernatural "three wishes" short story by W. W. Jacobs, first published in 1902.

5. As quoted in the comic, the selection is, "Whoever kills one person, it is as if he has killed all mankind—and whoever **saves** one person, it is as if he has **saved all of mankind**." The full verse of 5:32, using Ali Quli Qarai's translation, follows: "That is why We decreed for the Children of Israel that whoever kills a soul, without [its being guilty of] manslaughter or corruption on the earth, is as though he had killed all mankind, and whoever saves a life is as though he had saved all mankind. Our apostles certainly brought them manifest signs, yet even after that many of them commit excesses on the earth."

6. See chapters in this book by Baldanzi and Dagbovie-Mullins/Berlatsky.

7. See Peterson in this volume for a more in-depth discussion of Khan's sartorial choices.

8. For a reading of a more "Muslim" character, see Davis and Westerfelhaus.

9. Also see Baldanzi, in this volume.

BIBLIOGRAPHY

Abu-Lughod, Lila. *Do Muslim Women Need Saving?* Cambridge: Harvard University Press, 2013.

Adorno, Theodor W. *The Culture Industry: Selected Essays on Mass Culture*. New York: Routledge, 2001.

Alba, Richard, and Victor Nee. *Remaking the American Mainstream: Assimilation and Contemporary Immigration*. Cambridge: Harvard University Press, 2003.

Allport, Gordon W. *The Nature of Prejudice*. Reading, MA: Addison-Wesley, 1979.

Bakhtin, M. M. *The Dialogic Imagination: Four Essays*. Austin: University of Texas Press, 1981.

Bell, Carole V. "Talking Racial Politics Online." *Parasocial Politics: Audiences, Pop Culture, and Politics*. Ed. Jason Zenor. Lanham, MD: Lexington Books, 2014. 133–52.

Bhabha, Homi K. *The Location of Culture*. New York: Routledge, 1994.

Brah, Avtar. *Cartographies of Diaspora: Contesting Identities*. New York: Routledge, 1996.

Charlton, Michael. "'Para-Social Interaction'—Social Interaction as a Matter of Fact?" *Communications* 26, no. 4 (2001): 499–507.

Davis, Julie, and Robert Westerfelhaus. "Finding a Place for a Muslimah Heroine in the Post-9/11 Marvel Universe: New X-Men's Dust." *Feminist Media Studies* 13, no. 5 (2013): 800–9.

During, Simon. *Cultural Studies: A Critical Introduction*. London; New York: Routledge, 2005.

Horton, Donald and R. Richard Wohl. "Mass Communication and Para-Social Interaction: Observations on Intimacy at a Distance." *Psychiatry* (1956): 215–29.

Hutnyk, John. *Critique of Exotica: Music, Politics, and the Culture Industry*. London; Sterling, VA: Pluto, 2000.

Kalra, Virinder S. "The Political Economy of the Samosa." *South Asia Research* 24, no. 1 (2004): 21–36.

Karst, Kenneth L. "Paths to Belonging: The Constitution and Cultural Identity." *Critical White Studies: Looking behind the Mirror*. Eds. Richard Delgado and Jean Stefancic. Philadelphia, PA: Temple University Press, 1997. 407–13.

Kent, Miriam. "Unveiling Marvels: And the Reception of the New Muslim Superheroine." *Feminist Media Studies* 15, no. 3 (2014): 522–27.

Kim, Hyung-chan. *A Legal History of Asian Americans, 1790–1990*. Westport, CT: Greenwood, 1994.

King, Richard. *Orientalism and Religion: Post-Colonial Theory, India and the Mystic East.* London; New York: Routledge, 1999.

Kinghorn, Warren. "Combat Trauma and Moral Fragmentation: A Theological Account of Moral Injury." *Journal of the Society of Christian Ethics* 32, no. 2 (2012): 57–74.

Kristeva, Julia, and Toril Moi. *The Kristeva Reader.* New York: Columbia University Press, 1986.

Landis, Winona. "Diasporic (Dis)identification: The Participatory Fandom of Ms. Marvel." *South Asian Popular Culture* 14, nos. 1–2 (2016): 33–47.

Levy, André, and Alex Weingrod. "On Homelands and Diasporas: An Introduction." *Homelands and Diasporas: Holy Lands and Other Places.* Eds. André Levy and Alex Weingrod. Stanford, CA: Stanford University Press, 2005. 3–28.

Maira, Sunaina. *Missing: Youth, Citizenship, and Empire After 9/11.* Durham: Duke University Press, 2009.

Moore, Diane L. *Overcoming Religious Illiteracy: A Cultural Studies Approach to the Study of Religion in Secondary Education.* New York: Palgrave Macmillan, 2007.

Petersen, William. "Success Story, Japanese American Style." *New York Times Magazine*, January 9, 1966.

Pettigrew, Thomas F., and Linda R. Tropp. "Allport's Intergroup Contact Hypothesis: Its History and Influence." *On the Nature of Prejudice: Fifty Years after Allport.* Eds. John F. Dovidio, Peter Samuel Glick, and Laurie A. Rudman. Malden, MA: Blackwell, 2005. 262–77.

Prashad, Vijay. *The Karma of Brown Folk.* Minneapolis: University of Minnesota Press, 2000.

Pumphrey, Nicholaus Benjamin. "Avenger, Mutant, or Allah: A Short Evolution of the Depiction of Muslims in Marvel Comics." *The Muslim World* 106, no. 4 (2016): 781–94.

Reyns-Chikuma, Chris, and Désirée Lorenz. "Kamala Khan's Superhero Burkini: Negotiating an Autonomous Position between Patriarchal Islamism, French Secularism, and Feminism." *Muslim Superheroes: Comics, Islam, and Representation.* Eds. A. David Lewis and Martin Lund. Boston, MA: Ilex Foundation, 2017. 63–87.

Saussure, Ferdinand de. *Course in General Linguistics.* Translated by Roy Harris. LaSalle, IL: Open Court, 1986.

Schiappa, Edward, Peter B. Gregg, and Dean E. Hewes. "Can One TV Show Make a Difference? Will & Grace and the Parasocial Contact Hypothesis." *Journal of Homosexuality* 51, no. 4 (2006): 15–37.

———. "The Parasocial Contact Hypothesis." *Communication Monographs* 72, no. 1 (2005): 92–115.

Triece, Mary Eleanor, and Michael G. Lacy. "Introduction: Gramsci, Race, and Communication Studies." *Race and Hegemonic Struggle in the United States: Pop Culture, Politics, and Protest.* Eds. Michael G. Lacy and Mary Eleanor Triece. Madison, NJ: Fairleigh Dickinson University Press, 2014. 1–15.

Wanner, Kevin. "'And, Erm, Religious Stuff'": Islam, Liberalism, and the Limits of Tolerance in Stories of Faiza Hussain." *Muslim Superheroes: Comics, Islam, and Representation.* Eds. A. David Lewis and Martin Lund. Boston, MA: Ilex Foundation, 2017. 40–62.

Wilson, G. Willow, Adrian Alphona, et al. *Ms. Marvel: No Normal.* New York: Marvel Comics, 2014.

Yanora, Mercedes. "Marked by Foreign Policy: Muslim Superheroes and the Quest for Authenticity." *Muslim Superheroes: Comics, Islam, and Representation.* Eds. A. David Lewis and Martin Lund. Boston, MA: Ilex Foundation, 2017. 110–32.

"THE ONLY NERDY PAKISTANI-AMERICAN-SLASH-INHUMAN IN THE ENTIRE UNIVERSE"

Postracialism and Politics in the New *Ms. Marvel*

SIKA A. DAGBOVIE-MULLINS AND ERIC BERLATSKY

Hybridity to the Rescue

In Danzy Senna's novel *Caucasia* (1998), black/white mixed-race protagonist Birdie Lee plays "Elemeno," a made-up game, with her sister, Cole: "The Elemenos . . . could turn not just from black to white, but from brown to yellow to purple to green, and back again. [Cole] said they were a shifting people, constantly changing their form, color, pattern, in a quest for invisibility . . . less a game of make-believe than a fight for the survival of their species" (Senna 7). Birdie, too, becomes a shapeshifter in the novel when she passes for both black and white, her face prompting strangers to believe she is a range of ethnicities from Sicilian to Pakistani. Cole's description of Elemeno ("a place and a people") reads like a creation of superhero comic books, and there are at least two references to comics in *Caucasia*. First, Birdie mentions that she and Cole read them as children and, seemingly envious of the Elemenos, Cole "had ordered Sea Monkeys and love potions from the backs of our comic books, believing that the invisible might exist" (242). Later, when Birdie is passing for white, she laughs at the racist, gross misrepresentation of Africans in her white friend's *Tintin in the Congo* comic book. These brief references are related to one of the novel's thematic concerns: the simultaneous "escapability" and inescapability of race and identity. As a teenager who is frequently passing for someone else, Birdie Lee is remarkably similar to literal comic book shapeshifter Kamala Khan/Ms. Marvel, who also experiences identity as both fixed and fluid. Once Khan accepts her nonhuman ancestry and superpowers, she muses, "This isn't a costume—it's a parallel life" (Wilson, Wyatt, and Alphona 11).[1]

Both Khan and *Caucasia*'s Birdie seek belonging and acceptance from others, but they eventually learn to accept themselves the way they are. In a nod to public-service announcements encouraging adolescent self-confidence, Khan realizes, "I'm here to be the best version of Kamala" (5). Yet, initially, both girls long to look like someone else (Birdie yearns for blackness, while, at the outset, Khan wants to look like the "original" Ms. Marvel, Caucasian blond Carol Danvers) and both struggle to please their fathers. When Birdie is mistaken for Pakistani on an airplane, her self-identification as a biracial American registers a profound disappointment in her fellow passenger who "had been homesick and had seen his home in [her] face" (379). This moment parallels Khan's experiences with her parents, who mourn what they see as her increasingly diluted "Pakistaniness." In short, both girls resent the racial and/or cultural expectations placed on them. We draw on this perhaps unlikely comparison to underscore Khan's role as a symbolic mulatta passer in the most recent iterations of *Ms. Marvel*.[2] As a Muslim Pakistani American whose parents are immigrants, Khan occupies a neither/nor position familiar both in American "mulatto" literature and in postcolonial immigrant literature, wherein the mixed-race character is frequently marginalized, alienated, and Other. The earliest issues in the series particularly underscore her liminality: Khan is American and Pakistani, human and Inhuman, brown and white. In one crucial scene, she visually transforms into a copy of the "original" Carol Danvers Ms. Marvel (albeit in her contemporary "Captain Marvel" uniform) before resuming her own "brown" appearance.

Soon enough, Khan learns from Queen Medusa that she is Inhuman, as defined by fifty years of Marvel comics continuity: "Long ago, one of your human ancestors was genetically altered by the *Kree*—an alien race. That genetic legacy has been passed down through the generations—to *you*" (9). Khan's genetic aberration recalls LeiLani Nishime's argument about cyborgs whose indeterminate status as human/machine suggests they "must be read as a powerful metaphor for the historical bogeyman of contamination—racial mixing" (34). Like the monster, alien, and cyborg, Khan's human/Inhuman mix invites us to consider how the mulatta trope operates in the comic. Yet, if Khan's storyline recalls the mulatta archetype, what is to be made of the comic's racial politics and what has been described as its assimilation fantasy? First, let us address our decision to analyze Khan as a symbolic "mulatta" rather than specifically Eurasian. Alexander Cho explains that the Eurasian archetype mirrors the tragic mulatto in American fiction:

> The figure of the Eurasian has a long history in popular culture, often used as a parable for the tragic perils of miscegenation, carrying an implicit imperative to shore up the boundaries of race. Recurring frequently in English-language fiction in the late nineteenth and early twentieth centuries, Eurasian characters act as dangerous figures, close enough to both races to understand them intimately but never ultimately aligned with either one. The Eurasian characters usually yearn to obtain full whiteness but never can, and often end up dying by the narrative's end. (481)

Thus, Khan presents a kind of danger in that she cannot be Pakistani in the same way her parents are, but she is also too ethnic to be considered American. Yet we are more interested in the effects of Khan representing a postracial "super"-multiraciality,[3] a racial positioning that is inextricably connected to how Barack Obama's black/white mixed-race identity came to embody the Great Mixed-Race Hope at various times during his campaign and presidency. Aimee Carrillo Rowe's assessment of Obama also pertains to Kamala Khan: "The cultural production of Obama remains caught in postracialism's color-blind discursive and affective economies; race is simultaneously evoked and elided" (Carrillo Rowe 231). Similarly, in the case of Kamala Khan/Ms. Marvel, Khan's Pakistani/Muslim heritage *and* her symbolic mixed race are constantly emphasized, while racial politics are simultaneously ignored or elided.

Ralina Joseph explains that "[m]ixed-race African Americans from 1998 to 2008 have crystallized the two-sided stereotype of the new millennium mulatta and the exceptional multiracial" (5). She asserts, "In order to avoid being the 'new millennium mulatta' who is always divided, alone, and uncomfortable ... popular images suggest that one must become the 'exceptional multiracial' who is the unifying, post-racial, U.S. ideal" (4). Before Khan is exposed to the green Terrigen Mist, she represents various aspects of the new millennium mulatta as her teen angst is grounded in feeling alienated and confused. She laments, "I don't know what I'm supposed to be" (1). Once Khan gains her superpowers and shapeshifting abilities, she comes to represent the exceptional multiracial, a post-9/11 brown Muslim who is celebrated, not maligned. In fact, Khan's very name symbolizes her supermultiraciality. As her father tells her, "It's a special name. Kamal means perfection in Arabic. ... That's why we gave you your name. You don't have to be someone else to impress anybody. You are perfect just the way you are" (5). Joseph's elucidation of multiracial blackness is instructive here:

> To be more specific about the terms of this binary, on the one hand, multiracial blackness is disdained for its imagined primordially raced nature, with its tragic mulatta lineage. On the other hand, multiracial blackness is desired for its imagined transcendent quality, where it is ahistorically divorced from racism and sexism in the United States with its troubling history of chattel slavery, Jim Crow racism, and entrenched misogyny. (4)

Khan, then, symbolically represents two sides of a "multiracial brownness." Her first name both announces her ethnic difference and symbolizes the valorization of mixedness. To borrow from Joseph, Khan's "raced nature" marks her as tragically un-American and divided. However, Khan obtains a kind of "transcendent quality" as Ms. Marvel in that she is brown enough to be Other yet devoid of, or resistant to, historical or political narratives that would make her less palatable.[4]

An analysis of the first and only time Khan deliberately shifts into Carol Danvers's shape and then morphs back into Khan offers insight into how the series positions her supermultiraciality as transcendent. Michele Elam explains that, increasingly, pop culture and "the social sciences are more likely to reinscribe subtly onto the mixed-race person . . . [the narrative] of the American Adam who embodies values such as individualism, iconoclasm, and free will." She continues, "Once represented as an outcast, the mixed-race person is more often portrayed as a trailblazer" (10). Such descriptions mirror Khan's characterization as an independently minded teenager who, for example, willfully disobeys her parents and boldly questions Sheikh Abdullah regarding gendered religious practices at the mosque. After Khan rebukes her love interest, Kamran, for bringing her somewhere against her wishes, he tells her, "You got in my car of your own free will," highlighting her autonomy. In this, Khan/Ms. Marvel is the Pakistani American Adamina whose symbolic racial split recalls the mixed-race outcast-turned-hero trope.

Khan changes into her costume (and turns into the blond version of Ms. Marvel for the last time) at the corner store Circle Q,[5] a place whose very name reads like a directive often found on questionnaires and surveys where one is asked to "circle" one's race/ethnicity. As John White notes, "In 2006 . . . the Department of Education finally allowed students to circle more than one racial category on its surveys" (58). "Q" becomes a mark of racial Otherness—it both connotes uncertainty and indeterminacy and speaks to how mixed-race people have been positioned as questions. As Emily Raboteau's black/white protagonist in *The Professor's Daughter* (2005) asserts, "I remain a question mark. When people ask me what I am, which is not an everyday question, but one I get asked every day, I want to tell them about [my brother] Bernie. I don't, of course. I just tell them what color my parents are, which is to say, my father is black and my mother is white" (2). Khan's shapeshifting in the Circle Q, then, represents racial ambiguity. When she enters the store, she thinks she is witnessing a serious robbery and deliberately morphs into an Anglo Ms. Marvel in order to attack Victor, Bruno's masked brother, who appears to be robbing the store. During this scene, Khan becomes a question mark: is she Kamala Khan or Carol Danvers? Is she brown or white? Because "everybody's expecting Ms. Marvel. Ms. Marvel with the hair and the spandex and the Avengers swag. Not a sixteen-year-old brown girl with a 9 pm curfew," Khan temporarily becomes that (white) racial expectation (3). After she is shot, she turns back into her "regular self" and heals, quickly learning that she cannot properly recover when "shapeshifting." Fittingly, Bruno then hands her a "Coma Chameleon" sleep mask so she can disguise herself. The faux sleep mask brand employs a different mixed-race metaphor—that of the racial chameleon embodied by *Caucasia*'s description of the Elemenos.[6] The "chameleon" label was often applied to Obama for his "postracial" appeal. For instance, Paul Street argues that Obama's campaign messages were delivered in a "chameleon-like style" in order to appeal to various audiences (xxxi). Ironically, in the 2009 story "Spidey Meets the President," longtime Spider-Man villain the Chameleon attempts to usurp Obama's presidency during his inauguration (Wells and Nauck).

The Circle Q soon becomes Khan's secret headquarters ("Some people hide out in space stations. I get a Circle Q"), the place where she changes into her costume to protect New Jersey from evil (Wilson and Alphona, *All New Marvel Now! Point One* 1). It is important to mention in this context that the corner store is a space that sells multiethnic fare, including Caribbean coco bread and patties, Indian samosas, "Asian River Water," "Bruce Lee's Wataaa," and quintessentially American sandwiches and junk food like BLTs and Slurpees (depicted here as "Squishees"). Next door is a presumably Caribbean bookstore named "Books An' Ting, Ting An' Books" and nearby is Radoslav's Vietnamese grocery (figure 3 1). The main employee of the Circle Q is Bruno Carrelli, a second-generation Italian American. The series' first scene takes place at the store, where students from Coles High School, another hybrid space that comes to represent the exaggerated promise of postracialism, hang out (1). On the second page, Khan and her Turkish American friend, Nakia, are joined in the store by Josh, a white football player, and Zoe, a blond "mean girl" wearing a T-shirt that reads "Bonita." The point is that the Circle Q at

Figure 3.1 Wilson and Alphona, *No Normal*

least superficially represents urban cultural hybridity and multiculturalism. When Loki, the "Viking hipster," enters the Circle Q looking for Khan, Bruno and his brother position themselves in opposition to what they assume is upper-class whiteness: "Probably one of those Williamsburg trust fund kids. They all dress like Martians. They're coming, man. Gentrification. Next year it'll be Viking dudes from here to Newark Ave" (12). This is a particularly interesting comment as it positions the Circle Q and its surrounding area as a hybrid space untouched by a particular racialized narrative of wealthy white infiltration. Gregory Stephens's elucidation of racial frontiers helps situate the Circle Q as a space that exists "in a liminal zone between racial, and postracial, definitions of identity and community." Here we are thinking of how the store operates as both Khan's hideout, where she changes into a postracial superhero, and the store's various multiethnic/multiracial signs.

Stephens continues: "[T]he residents of this contested space are often a 'new people' with a 'new culture.' The people and their cultures sometimes transcend the descriptive power of racial language, even if they cannot escape the structuring power of racial history" (14).

Over the course of the series, Khan's high school comes to resemble the Circle Q both in terms of its diversity and because it represents a safe space for Khan and her shape shifting. As the final issues unfold, New York City is under attack, and the end of the world is approaching. Everything is in chaos, and we see Bruno and Victor trying to protect the ransacked Circle Q from further looting. Khan tells them to "stock up on food and head to the school" (16). A few pages later, students are working together to protect the high school. While ethnic divides and teenage cliques are not completely erased (Bruno praises Josh's "hustle—for a meathead," and Josh offensively responds, "You're not so bad for a geeky guido"), the two are able to fight off looters with the help of a protective spell the "hipster-viking-magician dude" has placed on Coles. In short, racial and ethnic hierarchies and tensions at least momentarily disappear (and even Loki no longer connotes white gentrification) as the students work in harmony. Zoe even apologizes to Khan for saying "really stupid things . . . [including] that stuff about curry and you getting locked up on the weekends" (19). Most notably, the series' last few pages show a communal dance party announced by Josh: "There is only one way to face the end of the world in New Jersey—with a dance party" (19). It is worth noting that there are two other dance parties in the series: early on, Khan attends her cousin's Mehndi (which appears to be all Pakistani), where she argues with her mother (Wilson, *All-New Marvel Now! Point One* 1), and, later, Loki interrupts the Valentine's Day dance by spiking the punch with truth-telling serum (12). In both instances, Khan is arguing or fighting with someone about belonging: at the Mehndi, Khan complains about her mother's narrow and unrealistic expectations that she be "a perfect little Muslim girl," while at the school dance, Khan-as-Ms. Marvel identifies Loki as an outsider ("This guy is **not** in high school"). These dances contrast with the multicultural end-of-the-world dance party, where everyone dances together, and then they collectively perform a presumably traditional Bollywood dance. In a nod to Homi Bhabha's assertion that "all forms of culture are continually in a process of hybridity" and that hybridity "enables other positions to emerge," Khan's friend Nakia teaches Zoe the proper ethnic dance moves ("The Third Space" 211).

Both the Circle Q and Coles High School represent what Homi Bhabha labels a theoretical "third space," a postcolonial condition wherein hierarchies and binaries are disrupted: "It is the Third Space, though unrepresentable in itself, which constitutes the discourse conditions of enunciation that ensure that the meaning and symbols of culture have no primordial unity or fixity; that even the same signs can be appropriated, translated, rehistoricized and read anew" (*Location of Culture* 55). Indeed, both places symbolize a particular kind of "postracial" ambiguity wherein cultures collide but do not clash.[7] Multiple scholars have cited Bhabha's third space to explore representations of mixed-race identity, given its liminality and resistance to fixedness. Khan occupies an in-between position in both her work and school spaces. It is also important to note that her outfit in the last pages of the series signals her liminality. After saving her brother, Aamir, from the Inhuman villain Kamran, she returns to Coles with Carol Danvers (now known as Captain Marvel). Danvers gives Khan her star and lightning bolt necklace, and when Khan reenters the school, she is wearing jeans and a blue-and-white jacket with Ms. Marvel's signature yellow lightning bolt on the front. While her jacket could simply give the impression that Khan is Ms. Marvel's fangirl, it also has the potential to "out" her as Ms. Marvel (though no characters mention this). In other words, Khan is again Khan and Ms. Marvel, human and Inhuman in a hybrid space. Mark Christian's critique of Bhabha's theory with regards to mixed-race identity is thus applicable:

> A problem with Bhabha's analysis is in the way we can simply create something "new" from two histories. It really is ahistorical in perspective.... In theory Bhabha may well have touched on something worth considering, but when put to the acid test of the social world it fails. Of course history and culture is dynamic and ever-changing, but the pattern of framework of oppression and social exclusion can often remain a constant. (Christian 308)

Although the series positions Khan, the Circle Q, and Coles High School as postracial, transcendent, and multiracial/multicultural, it does so at the risk of being ahistorical and apolitical.

Postracial, Postpolitical

Kamala Khan is one of many examples in contemporary superhero comics both of an increased attention to the representation of people of color, and of a potentially ahistorical/apolitical postracialism. There can be little doubt that the recent infusion of racial and gender diversity into contemporary "mainstream" superhero comics, including but not limited to multiracial heroes, is preferable to the longstanding unquestioned delivery of predominantly white male superheroes to a presumptive white-male readership.[8] In this, *Ms. Marvel* is only one of the most prominent examples, accompanied by the black Latino Spider-Man, Miles Morales, the female Thor, the African American Captain America, a revisited Squirrel Girl, the Asian American Hulk, the African American Moon Girl, and revamped titles for characters like Batgirl, Black Canary, Iron Man, and Cyborg, among others. In many, if not all, of these new and/or revived heroes, however, it is worth asking to what extent this celebrated diversity is significantly linked to the quest for political and social equality and to what extent "the structuring power of racial history" (Stephens 14) is even visible enough to be contested. As we have discussed, Ms. Marvel's metaphorical mixed-racedness serves to place her in the vicinity of the postracial or in the lineage of the "multicultural" that preceded it, a vision of the world (or at least the nation) wherein race no longer has political significance, but is instead merely a signifier of, in the words of Chandra Mohanty, "harmonious, empty pluralism" (193). Like Gregory Stephens, Mohanty argues that in the "multicultural" vision of race, "[d]ifference [is] seen as benign variation (diversity) . . . rather than as conflict, struggle, or the threat of disruption, bypass[ing] power as well as history" (193).

On one level, *Ms. Marvel* is inevitably political, and progressively so. Simply by choosing a Pakistani American Muslim superhero, the creators of the comic tacitly resist *some* conventional Muslim stereotypes, rejecting the notion that "All Muslims are terrorists" or that Muslims cannot fit into "mainstream" American society or represent its values. Khan's adventures in teen romance, computer games, and conflict with her teachers make her a "normal" American teen, regardless of her race or religion. No doubt, this portrayal supplies a potential role model for girls in similar circumstances, while also providing white America with a vision of a Muslim heroine who is "just like us," thus combating invidious stereotypes of the "dangerous" and/or inexplicable "Other." At the same time, the political facts of being a Muslim and/or South Asian in America, and particularly in Jersey City, are either underplayed or ignored throughout Khan's first *Ms. Marvel* series.

Kamala Khan is sixteen years old when the series opens, circa 2014. Some elementary math indicates that Khan was born in 1998, making her three years old, or thereabouts, when the events of September 11, 2001, took place. These events, and particularly the response to them, had an incalculable impact on Arabs and/or Muslims (and those who could plausibly be mistaken for Arabs and/or Muslims) throughout the United States, particularly in and around New York City. Not only were New Jersey Muslims subjected to the dramatically increased levels of surveillance, harassment, and police profiling authorized by the federal PATRIOT Act, but they were also faced with more local versions of the same problem. In 2012, New Jersey Muslims filed a federal lawsuit, *Hassan vs. City of New York*, against the New York City Police Department (NYPD) for undertaking unlawful surveillance of Muslim neighborhoods in and around the city, including and especially in New Jersey. The NYPD, in the aftermath of 9/11, from at least 2003 through 2012, sent plainclothes policemen to "[infiltrate] Muslim student groups and mosques, [to track] the activities of Muslims and [to] buil[d] files on people" (Weiser). The suit, filed in Newark, accused the NYPD of making religious belief a "proxy for criminality" and of "religious profiling" (Weiser). The case was dismissed (before being reinstated by an Appeals Court) by a US District Court in February 2014 (Weiser), the very same month that the first issue of Khan's *Ms. Marvel* became available. Meanwhile, from 2004 through 2013, the majority of Khan's fictional life, the US military was carrying out thousands of unmanned drone strikes in Northwest Pakistan, with the intention of killing known terrorists, but with a resultant wide swath of (still contested) collateral damage to civilians. Even the US Special Forces' killing of Osama Bin Laden in Pakistan in 2011 did not halt the strikes or the civilian deaths.

Even more recently, Jersey City found its way into the presidential election news when candidate/rabble-rouser Donald Trump declared that "thousands of [Jersey City] Muslims were cheering" when the World Trade Center towers fell. This provocative and unsubstantiated proclamation came as partial justification of Trump's support of the continued surveillance of "certain" US mosques, signaling a doubling down on racist and xenophobic policies that violate the rights of American citizens (Johnson).[9] Given the degree to which the New York City area, New Jersey, and specifically Jersey City have proven to be an epicenter for political and social conflict surrounding racial and religious matters post-9/11, it is no surprise that *Ms. Marvel*, the first mainstream comic devoted to a Muslim superhero's adventures, is set there. What is surprising is the degree to which these events are either downplayed or avoided entirely in the comic itself, in favor of a version of the utopian multiraciality discussed above.

In *Are We All Postracial Yet?*, David Theo Goldberg notes that despite our purportedly postracial world, "not a day goes by without more or less contentious, often demeaning public reference to some . . . aspect of black, Latino, Muslim, or Palestinian life" (53). Our recounting of some of the most obvious of these incidents referring specifically to New Jersey Muslims is, then, simply a scratching of the surface, but *Ms. Marvel* rarely approaches even this low-hanging fruit, and it does so only allusively or through problematic metaphors. Drone strikes in Pakistan, for instance, are never mentioned at all, as if Pakistani American immigrants would have no connection to or interest in events that connect their adoptive homeland with their nation of origin. Likewise, when the police appear, they are typically depicted as helpful and reliable, rather than as authorized perpetrators of surveillance, harassment, or mistreatment. This is despite the fact that nearly half of all Americans believe that law enforcement "*ought* to profile Arab and Muslim Americans" and that 90 percent of those citizens pulled over and searched by the police are black or brown (Goldberg 62). Though Khan does, at one point (in the Circle Q), choose not to call the police and thinks briefly about potential surveillance by the NSA (4), these are fleeting moments that are less than integral to Khan's life or to Ms. Marvel's story as a superhero. Instead, despite Bakirathi Mani's argument that "[a]ny contemporary examination of South Asian identity and community necessarily contends with the altered racial and political landscape of the United States after September 11, 2001, particularly in terms of its implications for Muslim South Asians" (20), *Ms. Marvel* largely avoids actions, thoughts, and controversies that might render it overly, or overtly, political.

Ms. Marvel's efforts to deliver a utopian multiraciality actually move it away from considering race, religion, and ethnicity as political issues, inflected with power dynamics and influenced by state hegemony. In Goldberg's account, this representation is not only a problematic oversight but also potentially collaborates with the neoliberal discourse known as "colorblindness" (or postracialism), which rationalizes the repealing of affirmative action and resistance to antiracist social movements by suggesting that such movements are not necessary in a new world devoid of racial divisions (74). "Postraciality . . . conceals within its conceptual erasure of race the driving mode of racist articulation. Racisms dis-appear behind the formal deletion of racial classification, state regulation, and legal refusal of racial definition. . . . Racisms proliferate in the wake of the supposed death of race" (Goldberg 70).

Thus, as part of her metaphorical multiraciality, Khan is portrayed both as *racialized* and as *deracialized*. By skirting, or avoiding, mention of drone strikes, police surveillance, Trumped-up controversies, and the like, *Ms. Marvel* can be read as *politically* deracialized, even as Khan herself is *culturally*

Figure 3.2 Wilson and Alphona, *No Normal*

racialized through an emphasis on familiar immigrant tropes, including those specific to South Asianness.

When we first meet Khan, she feels like an outsider because of her strict Muslim parents. She is not allowed to date, drink, or stay out late. She is teased by her less-sensitive white classmates because she looks and acts differently than they do (figure 3.2).

She is shown getting religious instruction at the mosque, and the threat of a more-or-less arranged marriage is mentioned with some frequency. These details serve to "racialize" Khan as specifically South Asian. Indeed, there is no cultural trait associated more with South Asianness than the "arranged marriage," as Shilpa Davé discusses in relationship to American television. The continued references to a "handsome rich guy from Karachi" waiting in Khan's future (14) draw *Ms. Marvel* firmly into this trope, more typically associated with Hindu Indians than with Pakistani Muslims.

As Davé notes, and consistent with our account of Khan's multiraciality, South Asians have been identified with several different racial categories during American history. Once considered "Caucasian," South Asian immigrants have since been classified as "nonwhite," "other," and, finally, as an "Asian-American minority group" (262). Within the more contemporary rhetoric of postracialism, Davé argues that "the representation of South Asian Americans as foreign immigrants with distinctive cultural practices and characteristics is an example of how race is discussed in a supposed post-race world—cultural difference is emphasized over racial difference" (262). We would amend this reading, in *Ms. Marvel*'s case, to suggest that cultural difference is emphasized over political circumstances, allowing readers to be educated in the former without being uncomfortably confronted with the latter.

Just as these immigrant tropes serve to racialize Khan, they also serve to place her in a context outside of the immediate political one. In doing so, they allow for seeming differences between races to actually function as covert similarities. This becomes clearest when Khan's best friend and potential love interest, Bruno, discusses his hopes for romance with Khan's brother, Aamir. In this conversation, Bruno discusses how his Catholic Italian background is more *like* Khan's Muslim Pakistani heritage than different from it. He notes how his grandmother is "crazy religious" like Aamir and how his grandparents were, like the Khans, unwelcome immigrants to the United States He asserts, "I know where you guys are coming from, 'cause I've been there," effectively erasing racial and religious divisions. Aamir responds by saying, "I'm not saying you're not a good guy. But my parents expect Kamala to marry someone like us" (14). Bruno's argument, of course, has already focused on the ways in which he *is* "like the Khans" rather than on simply being a "good guy," but Aamir has trouble seeing the similarities between them. By staging this encounter, it seems that *Ms. Marvel* wants us to see what Aamir does not, emphasizing historical parallels in waves of immigration, rather than highlighting twenty-first-century social and political differences. Not surprisingly, the comic, like both Bruno and Aamir, never draws attention to the ways in which Bruno elides the differences between himself and his grandparents (the people who are actually immigrants and "crazy-religious") and the difference between the frequently persecuted Italian American immigrant community of the early part of the twentieth century and the largely integrated and assimilated twenty-first-century Italian Americanness that Bruno himself represents. That is, the implication made by Bruno and *Ms. Marvel* itself is that "race" does not matter because all immigrants are, more or less, alike, regardless of generation or country of origin. In actuality, as Goldberg discusses, historical assimilation into "racelessness" is hardly an innocent process, as previously "raced" or marginalized communities (like Italian Americans) have historically gained power in and access to the hegemonic culture by acceding to the "common logics defined by dominant—namely white—interests" (18). In their effort to forge a connection between two individuals, neither Bruno nor the *Ms. Marvel* series writ large acknowledges this historical process (though it is certainly possible for such a connection to be forged with full acknowledgment).

Likewise, while some of the specifics of Khan's treatment at school may be associated with her South Asianness, other elements are frequently depicted as universals of teen experience. Popular cultural representations of high schoolers often show them feeling "different" or worrying that they are not part of the "in-crowd." Likewise, parents are often depicted as being "too strict," and popular culture teens often complain that they are not allowed to stay out late enough. These high schoolers also inevitably feel put upon by at least some of their teachers. While Khan's "problems" have some roots in her ethnic, religious, and cultural background, most have easy analogues in the depictions of other teens, regardless of their backgrounds, and indeed have been staples of storylines involving Marvel's most popular hero, Peter Parker, Spider-Man, since his debut in 1962, a parallel acknowledged by critics, commenters, and fans alike (see, for instance, Adlakha). On the other hand, conflicts that focus on disparities of political or economic power between racial and ethnic groups or on harassment and persecution by authority figures based on race and ethnicity do not make appearances.

The closest *Ms. Marvel* comes to tackling post-9/11 politics is metaphorically, through its depiction of a group of militant radical Inhumans. After discovering her own "Inhumanity," Khan develops a crush on Kamran, the Pakistani son of family friends—whom, we discover, is also Inhuman and, Khan later learns, a member of the militant Inhumans. Through Kamran and the militant group, *Ms. Marvel* provides a metaphorical equivalent to ISIS, Al-Qaeda, or the fundamentalist radical Islamic group of your choice. Upon hearing of the group's plan to take over Earth, Khan responds, "It's always the same. There's always that one group of people who think they have special permission to terrorize anybody who disagrees with them. And then everybody else who looks like them suffers" (13). This speech does, of course, allude to the political situation of Muslims, Arabs, and South Asians in America, persecuted for simply "looking like" a stereotypical notion of a terrorist's appearance. At the same time, there is an effacement of the actual political motivations of said terrorists and the process by which US neoimperialism abroad and persecution of minorities at home often leads to the radicalization of Islamic youth. Though the militant Inhumans are clearly the comics' stand-in for radical Islam, their simplistic motivations (or lack thereof) are suitable only for superhero comics (or, to be fair, movies or television). Because of their "genetic superiority" and superpowers, they wish to rule the world, and no longer have to protect or support their inferior human brethren. That is, whereas radical Islam and the terrorism associated with it largely represent a disempowered response to the global political and economic super*power* of the United States and its global allies, the Inhuman radicals exert superpowers to achieve their own global dominance.

Likewise, when Khan asserts that the Inhuman radicals are simply a group who "think they have permission to terrorize," she reduces the problem of global terrorism to one of simplistic choices made by subsets of individuals. In this assertion, both Khan and the comic writ large set up a dynamic whereby good Inhumans (Khan and Queen Medusa) battle bad Inhumans (Kamran, Kaboom, and their leader, Lineage). Good Inhumans are those who protect humanity and the status quo, while the bad Inhumans are those who want radical change, to overthrow humanity, and to establish a "New World Order." This formulation repeats, at only a slight remove, the familiar trope of "good Arab vs. bad Arab" as discussed by Evelyn Alsultany in relation to US television drama. In these shows, good Arabs (or good Muslims) not only are *not* terrorists but are most frequently counterterrorists, who not only love America, its freedoms, and its free markets, but who also use their skills to retain the status quo. Bad Arabs (or bad Muslims) are, by definition, terrorists. The inclusion of both "good" and "bad" Arabs is identified by Alsultany as "Strategy One" for continuing to depict Muslims as the enemy Other, while formally gesturing to not doing so. As Mahmood Mamdani argues, the result of such a strategy is to suggest that "all Muslims are assumed to be bad until they perform and prove their allegiance to the United States" (quoted in Alsultany 150).[10] While representations of Muslims in *Ms. Marvel* are a good deal more diverse than that, often breaking out of what Alsultany calls the "good/bad Muslim dichotomy," the *Ms. Marvel* storyline centering on the radical Inhumans delivers these familiar and problematic divisions (Alsultany 150).

Like the heroes of the television programs Alsultany examines, and as is typically the case in superhero narratives, Khan, as hero, protects the status quo, but the value of the status quo that she protects is itself rarely questioned. Why would Muslim immigrants to America wish to retain a status quo in which their own supposed freedoms are curtailed and surveilled, where their rights to privacy are violated, and where they are presumptive criminals based on their religious beliefs, whose presumptive villainy is politicized for electoral purposes? It is all but impossible for the Inhumans in *Ms. Marvel* to voice these concerns because, though they are stand-ins for Muslim radicals, they are not, for the most part, Muslim, nor can they be profiled by police or by superheroes on the basis of their appearance. Rather, while they do function as a loose metaphor for Muslim persecution and the response to it, they are simultaneously a multiracial group of generic supervillains, a fact that removes the storyline from its political relevance, even as it elsewhere asserts it. Indeed, by removing militant radicalism from any coherent real-world group, the comic further overemphasizes the role individual choice has in such matters.[11]

In fact, Kamran seeks to exploit real Muslim grievances for the purposes of recruiting Aamir to the radical Inhumans—though, not surprisingly, those grievances are never specifically enumerated. He argues to Khan, "You think some little part of Aamir isn't angry? Looking like he does, believing what he does . . . you think he doesn't wish he could live in a world where *he* gets to make the rules?" (16). Here again, however, the comic quickly emphasizes that being "good" versus being "bad" is simply a matter of choice, with Aamir predictably choosing "good" with no further interrogation of what constitutes either end of the ideological spectrum, or to what extent "goodness" itself arises from social definitions and political and economic circumstances. In this reading, the comic collaborates with a neoliberal postracialist discourse that, as Goldberg asserts, "renders individuals solely accountable for their own actions and expressions, not for their groups" (35).

In *Ms. Marvel*, then, Islamophobia, since it is never structural but a matter of individual choice, can be easily overcome without structural, political, or social resistance. Amazingly, the character who displays the most anti-Muslim antipathy is Zoe, who in the early pages of the series, as noted above, mocks Khan because she cannot stay out late at parties and because she eats curry. As the series draws to a close, not only does Zoe apologize, but she also admits that her cruelty to Khan was a result of purely personal (and purely high school) issues. She is jealous of Khan. Despite being the "popular (white) girl," she feels that everyone hates her. Like Khan, she "wants to be better" and makes the individual decision to do so by putting xenophobia behind her (19). Here, it is not the idea that individuals can change their views on such matters that seems problematic, but rather that the neoliberal reduction of racism to personal competition serves, again, to suggest that more endemic structural divisions either do not exist or can be easily overcome.

Personal accountability to the point of libertarianism, or even Ayn Randian objectivism, has long been a mainstay of superhero comics, dating back to at least Spider-Man's catchphrase, "With great power comes great responsibility," in a debut drawn by cocreator and subsequent Randian, Steve Ditko (Young). Spider-Man speaks of the responsibility of one man to do the best he can to fight crime and combat evil—not, for instance, of the responsibility a powerful nation owes its citizens and citizens of the world. Though *Ms. Marvel* hardly adheres to such extremes of individualism, the community it imagines, first in the Circle Q, and later as an oasis in the face of apocalypse at Khan's high school, is a community wherein people band together not to fight for racial justice, but rather to preserve a postracial utopia in Jersey City or a status quo that has never existed in the real world. In doing so, while it provides a glimpse of a heartening world in which actual racial divisions matter little, it papers over real structural divisions that continue to prevent such a world from emerging.

Coda: Complications of/and Intentions

Over the course of this essay, we have almost completely avoided reference to *Ms. Marvel's* creators or their intentions in the creation of Kamala Khan, a character whose story is clearly designed to challenge problematic racial, ethnic, and religious stereotypes, but which, at the same time, manages to avoid some of the more controversial or divisive elements of racial politics. Rather than some latter-day allegiance to the excesses of New Criticism, our avoidance of intentionality originates in the difficulty of precisely locating the author of these stories, as is often the case in superhero comics published by corporate entities like DC Comics, Inc. (owned, ultimately, by Warner Bros. Entertainment) or, in this case, Marvel Entertainment, LLC (owned by the Walt Disney Company). Khan was created through a conversation between Marvel editors Sana Amanat (herself a Muslim) and Stephen Wacker, though neither Amanat nor Wacker has actually written any of the stories in Khan's *Ms. Marvel* series (Gustines). These stories have been written exclusively by G. Willow Wilson, a convert to Islam, known not only for her comics work (including the graphic novel *Cairo* and the DC/Vertigo series *Air*), but also for her journalism, her prose memoir, *The Butterfly Mosque,* and her novel, *Alif, The Unseen*. While the art for the first few issues of *Ms. Marvel* comes from the pen of Adrian Alphona, various other artists, including Takeshi Miyazawa, have taken over for several issues at a time.

All of which is to say that while Wilson is the figure most often cited as the creative force behind *Ms. Marvel,* the comic is, in fact, the product of a creative process that involves not only multiple people but also a huge multibillion-dollar corporation that owns the "intellectual properties" that are Ms. Marvel and Kamala Khan. This multiple and complicated authorship may help to explain some of the discrepancies between the postracial qualities of *Ms. Marvel* and some of Wilson's other work, which is significantly more political in orientation.

The Butterfly Mosque, for example, takes on discrimination against Muslims in the United States in a decidedly more direct fashion than anything we find in *Ms. Marvel* itself, despite the fact that most of the book takes place in Egypt. The memoir relates the processes by which Wilson, a white woman from Colorado (though born in New Jersey), becomes interested in Islam, her slow conversion to the religion, her move to Egypt to teach English and become a journalist, and her love affair and eventual marriage to an Egyptian Sufi Muslim man. In the book, Wilson discusses Western misconceptions about the Islamic treatment of women (80–81, 259–63); the ways in which

Western global economic dominance, moral relativism, and unalloyed materialism combine to create resentment and anger in some Muslims (135–36); the relative flexibility of Islamic doctrine (159–61); the politics surrounding the discourse of academic Orientalism (273–76); and the way in which she and her friends are interrogated and placed under surveillance by the FBI because of her conversion to Islam and a subsequent planned trip to Iran (174–76). In the last of these, Wilson can hardly be accused of ignoring the ways in which Muslims and people of color have been persecuted in the United States, as she herself, while also expressing fears of "Islamophobia" on behalf of her husband, is racialized by her religious affiliation and is placed on the FBI's watch list (273). While *The Butterfly Mosque* is a memoir more than a sophisticated examination of East/West politics, it certainly acknowledges the relationship of politics, religion, race, and gender, and it probes them to a degree rarely, if ever, approached in *Ms. Marvel*. Though there are, no doubt, many reasons for this discrepancy, one of them is almost certainly the multiple and corporate authorship of the series.

For example, as the apocalyptic concluding event to the *Ms. Marvel* series hovers over the Marvel Universe's version of Manhattan, Khan's father voices a fear of "another attack" (16). It is unclear, when he utters these words, if he fears another terrorist attack like that of 9/11 either for fear of terrorism itself or for the backlash likely to be visited upon his community. Alternatively, perhaps he fears "another alien attack" on the Marvel Universe's New York City, whether by Galactus (Lee and Kirby, circa 1964) or by Loki and a cybernetic alien race (*Avengers*, Marvel Cinematic Universe, circa 2012). Here, a political reading is available to the reader who wants one, while a "nerdier" reading inflected with the absurd continuity of a more than fifty-year-old storyworld is also available, should the reader wish to avoid harsh political realities. To the dedicated reader of Wilson's memoir, or for readers old enough to recall 9/11 vividly, the political reading seems unavoidable, but it is the apolitical reading of the elder Khan's comments that the comic eventually embraces, as the events in New York City have no reference to the daily lives of real New Yorkers (or residents of Jersey City). Instead, the "end of the world" that occurs in the final issue of *Ms. Marvel* is simply a joining together of multiple comic book universes (Earth-616 and the Ultimate Universe, to the initiated), an event only intelligible to longtime readers of shared-universe continuity comics, which ultimately functions as marketing for Disney[12] (and as an excuse for a new number 1 issue of *Ms. Marvel*, sure to sell more copies than what would have been issue 20).

This example indicates the ways in which corporate authorship influences the social and political meanings of superhero comics as a whole and *Ms. Marvel* in particular. Nearly all of Marvel's comics summarily came to a temporary end in (more or less) the same month in 2015, in order to merge multiple narrative continuities. Neither G. Willow Wilson nor her collaborators had any choice but to incorporate this "end of [a] world" into their ongoing storylines. That Wilson and colleagues were able to integrate this "earth-shattering" science-fictional event into the more street-level concerns of Kamala Khan and her supporting cast at all is a credit to their skill in operating within a fairly limited radius. While Wilson and her collaborators can use the event as a metaphor for fears of another terrorist attack and even for an engagement with the fear of race-based rioting in a post–Ferguson, Missouri, world, the creators ultimately do not have the power, nor the legal right, to decide what the ultimate threat to Kamala Khan, or to the Marvel Universe(s) writ large, will be. All of which is to say, there is a limit to how political, or how controversial, corporate superhero comics can, or will, be when the "larger storyline" of the entire universe is controlled by a company whose interests in Ms. Marvel are ultimately not in seeing her as a person, or as a role model, or as a representative for racial, religious, or political concerns, but as an intellectual/economic property to be exploited not only in comics but also in merchandise and (potentially) on the silver screen. The joining of the Marvel and Ultimate Universes also has little, if anything, to do with storytelling, and more to do with economics, and the corporate hope that the streamlined universe will be more marketable (and perhaps more congruent with the Marvel Cinematic Universe).

Even with all of that said, it is fair to claim that at least a portion of the postracial optimism in *Ms. Marvel* is consistent both with G. Willow Wilson's authorial persona and with her public statements. As a white Western woman who converted to Islam and wears the *hijab*, who grew up principally in Colorado, but who lived for several years in Egypt, it is not too far of a stretch to suggest that she, like Khan, is a hybrid subject of both West and East, of "Judeo-Christianity" and Islam, and even of brown and white, insofar as Islam is so often racialized in contemporary Western culture. Her memoir provides a kind of inverted mirror to Khan's story, with Wilson traveling to Egypt as a Westerner and having substantial difficulties in "fitting in" to a principally Islamic culture, just as Khan (though born in the United States) has trouble fitting in in the West. Wilson's hybridity and her union with Omar, her husband, makes her, like Khan, a potential avatar for the purportedly transcendent potential of a postrace world, beyond the divisive politics of race and/or religion.

As Wilson herself notes in a 2011 interview, her own metaphorical hybridity is even more literally embodied in her mixed-race children, whom she links to Khan:

> And the year my older daughter was born, 2011, was the first year that the majority of the babies born in the U.S. were non-white. The entire makeup of the United States is starting to change. There is more fluidity. There are many more people now who are the children of multi-racial, multi-ethnic families. We are starting to grapple as a nation with this idea of fluidity. In more than one way, this is a character whose time has come. (Hudson)

In this quotation, Wilson deploys the familiar metaphor of children as "the future," and, in this case, they, like Kamala Khan herself, represent a utopian fluidity, in which the race of individuals is so difficult to pin down that the familiar black/white binary divisions that lead to social and political oppression must necessarily dissolve. Certainly, a vision of a postracial *future* in which neither African Americans nor Muslims (nor any other marginalized community) need worry about hegemonic oppression is a vision with which it is hard to quarrel. At the same time, to represent our current society, whether in a convenience store or a New Jersey high school, as if such a future has already been achieved, is both misleading and potentially dangerous.

While we are both fans of Khan's *Ms. Marvel* and find value in it, both narrative and political, we believe it is also important to acknowledge the limits of the postracialist discourse in which it partakes. Likewise, *Ms. Marvel*'s imbrication in a corporate-owned narrative universe limits its future potential in commenting upon and intervening in contemporary racial politics. Khan's popularity, while heartening, also makes any substantive deviation from her current status quo unlikely. If Marvel Entertainment, LLC, is to make racial diversity profitable, they are more likely to continue to do so within a utopian multicultural "third space," than within the hierarchical relationship of oppression that more accurately describes US race relations in the past, present, and foreseeable future.

NOTES

1. Parenthetical citations of the *Ms. Marvel* series refer to the original issue numbers of the floppy/pamphlet/magazine style-comics, even though our bibliography lists the paperback collections. For convenience, each bibliographic entry for the paperbacks lists the

numbers of the issues included, which can then be referenced back to our citations. The magazine issue numbers double as chapter numbers in the paperbacks. Unfortunately, issue/chapter numbers are as precise as we can be for citation purposes, as the collections are not paginated. The four books listed collect the third series entitled *Ms. Marvel* published by Marvel. The first two featured the original (white, blond-haired, blue-eyed) Ms. Marvel, Carol Danvers, and ran from 1977 through 1979 and 2006 through 2010. Volume 3, featuring Kamala Khan, ran only for the nineteen issues discussed in this essay, though it was immediately followed by a fourth series, launched in 2016, also featuring Khan and with (more or less) the same creative team. The fourth series was completed after thirty-eight issues in early 2019 and replaced by *The Magnificent Ms. Marvel* with a new creative team.

2. As José Aláníz notes (*Death, Disability, and the Superhero*), the superhero-as-passer trope has been analyzed by scholars such as Jules Feiffer, Danny Fingeroth, Scott Bukatman, and Jason Bainbridge.

3. Noah Berlatsky maintains that, for Khan, "flexibility is a strength. Kamala is a superhero because she's both Muslim and American at once. Her power is to be many things, and to change without losing herself" (N. Berlatsky).

4. It is worth mentioning that the first supervillain introduced in the series is also clearly a metaphor for mixedness, though less clearly racialized. The Inventor (first appearing in issue/chapter 5) is a clone of Thomas Edison accidentally mixed with the DNA of a pet cockatiel by a "mad scientist" named Knox. Thus, the Inventor is a mix of human and bird, dead and living, inventor and invented. Despite the series' devotion to the idea of a utopian "good" multiraciality, this character also betrays some anxiety about the dangerous "evil" possibilities of mixedness, albeit in a humorous register.

5. Circle Q references Circle K, a chain of convenience stores throughout the United States (four of which are in New Jersey).

6. For example, consider the following scholarly works: *Multifaceted Identity of Interethnic Young People: Chameleon Identities* (Choudhry) and "Chameleon Changes: An Exploration of Racial Identity Themes of Multiracial People" (Milville et al.).

7. It is useful to contrast Bhabha's notion of a "third space" with Mary Louise Pratt's term "contact zone," a term used to "refer to social spaces where cultures, meet, clash and grapple with each other, often in contexts of highly asymmetrical relations of power, such as colonialism, slavery, or their aftermaths as they are lived out in many parts of the world today" (34).

8. This is not to say that people of color have gone unrepresented in "mainstream" superhero comics until recently. Rather, periodic attempts have been made to launch superheroes of color in supporting roles, as part of superhero teams, and in their own comics, with varying degrees of commitment and success since the 1960s. The record of employment of people of color (and women) in creative roles at major comics companies has been spotty at best, however, perhaps accounting for some of the historical (and more current) failures in representation. For useful histories of superheroes of color in the mainstream American comics industry, see Brown (15–26) and Nama.

9. Trump's subsequent election has obviously only led to more overt expressions of racism and xenophobia. Trump's remarks about Jersey City Muslims on the campaign trail were, of course, predictive of the now infamous "Muslim Ban" of January 2017.

10. This dynamic is also familiar from fifty years of *X-Men* comics (and twenty years of films), wherein good mutants (led by Professor X) battle bad mutants (led by Magneto), often as a transparent metaphor for race relations, the civil rights movement, and/or the gay rights movement (see DiPaolo 219–47).

11. Here, too, the dynamic is similar to 1960s *X-Men* comics, wherein Marvel-universe mutants are used as a completely deracinated metaphor for racial conflict, despite the fact that all of the original X-Men and their enemies are white.

12. See E. Berlatsky for an extended argument about the ways in which the "multiple universe" model of continuity comics is potentially antithetical to diverse racial representation.

BIBLIOGRAPHY

Adlakha, Siddhant. "Power and Responsibility: Why *Ms. Marvel* Matters." *Birth Movies Death*. March 17, 2015. Accessed May 12, 2016. Web. http://birthmoviesdeath.com/2015/03/17/power-responsibility-why-ms.-marvel-matters.

Alaniz José. *Death, Disability, and the Superhero: The Silver Age and Beyond*. Jackson: University Press of Mississippi, 2014. Print.

Alsultany, Evelyn. "Representations of Arabs and Muslims in Post-9/11 Television Dramas." *The Colorblind Screen: Television in Post-Racial America*. Eds. Sarah Nilsen and Sarah E. Turner. New York: New York University Press, 2014. 140–66. Web.

The Avengers. Dir. Joss Whedon. Perf. Robert Downey Jr., Chris Evans, Mark Ruffalo, Chris Hemsworth, Scarlett Johansson. Marvel Studios/Paramount, 2012. Film.

Berlatsky, Eric. "We Are Who We Choose to Be: Sadistic Choices, Forking Paths, and the Rejection of Social and Narrative Progress in Superhero Comics and Films." *The Hooded Utilitarian*. April 29, 2014. Accessed May 11, 2016. Web. http://www.hoodedutilitarian.com/2015/04/we-are-who-we-choose-to-be-sadistic-choices-forking-paths-and-the-rejection-of-social-and-narrative-progress-in-superhero-comics-and-films/.

Berlatsky, Noah. "What Makes the Muslim Ms. Marvel Awesome: She's Just Like Everyone." *The Atlantic*. March 20, 2014. Accessed May 11, 2016. Web. http://www.theatlantic.com/entertainment/archive/2014/03/what-makes-the-muslim-em-ms-marvel-em-awesome-shes-just-like-everyone/284517/.

Bhabha, Homi K. *Location of Culture*. London: Routledge, 1994. Print.

———. "The Third Space: Interview with Homi K. Bhabha." *Identity, Community, Culture, Difference*. Ed. Jonathan Rutherford. London: Lawrence and Wishart, 1990. 207–21. Print.

Brown, Jeffrey A. *Black Superheroes, Milestone Comics, and Their Fans*. Jackson: University Press of Mississippi, 2001. Print.

Carrillo Rowe, Aimee. "For the Love of Obama: Race, Nation and the Politics of Relation." *The Obama Effect: Multidisciplinary Renderings of the 2008 Campaign*. Eds. Heather E. Harris, Kimberly R. Moffitt, Catherine R. Squires. New York: State University of New York Press, 2010. 221–32. Print.

Cho, Alexander. "Eurasian" in *Multicultural America: A Multimedia Encyclopedia*. Ed. Carlos E. Cortés. Thousand Oaks: Sage, 2013. 480–81. Print.

Choudhry, Sultana. *Multifaceted Identity of Interethnic Young People: Chameleon Identities*. Burlington: Ashgate, 2010.

Christian, Mark. "Assessing Multiracial Identity." *"Mixed Race" Studies: A Reader.* Ed. Jayne O. Ifekwunigwe. New York: Routledge, 2004. 303–12. Print.
Davé, Shilpa. "Matchmakers and Cultural Compatibility: Arranged Marriage, South Asians, and Racial Narratives on American Television." *The Colorblind Screen: Television in Post-Racial America.* Eds. Sarah Nilsen and Sarah E. Turner. New York: New York University Press, 2014. 261–84. Print.
DiPaolo, Marc. *War, Politics, and Superheroes: Ethics and Propaganda in Comics and Film.* Jefferson, NC: McFarland, 2011.
Elam, Michele. *The Souls of Mixed Folk: Race, Politics, and Aesthetics in the New Millennium.* Stanford: Stanford University Press, 2011. Print.
Goldberg, David Theo. *Are We All Postracial Yet?* Malden, MA: Polity, 2015. Print.
Gustines, George. "Mighty, Muslim, and Leaping off the Page: Marvel Comics Introducing a Muslim Girl Superhero." *The New York Times.* November 5, 2013. Accessed May 16, 2016. Web. http://www.nytimes.com/2013/11/06/books/marvel-comics-introducing-a-muslim-girl-superhero.html.
Hudson, Laura. "First Look at the New Ms. Marvel, a 16-Year-Old Muslim Superhero." Interview of G. Willow Wilson. January 7, 2014. *Wired.* Accessed May 17, 2016. Web. http://www.wired.com/2014/01/ms-marvel-muslim-superheroine/.
Johnson, Brent. "Trump: 'Thousands' in Jersey City Cheered on 9/11 (Video)." *NJ.Com.* November 22, 2015. Updated November 23, 2015. Accessed March 10, 2016. Web. http://www.nj.com/politics/index.ssf/2015/11/trump_thousands_in_jersey_city_cheered_on_911.html.
Joseph, Ralina L. *Transcending Blackness: From the New Millennium Mulatta to the Exceptional Multiracial.* Durham: Duke University Press, 2013. Print.
Lee, Stan, and Jack Kirby. "The Coming of Galactus." *Marvel Visionaries: Jack Kirby.* New York: Marvel Comics, 2004. Print. Reprinted from *Fantastic Four* 1, no. 48 (1964).
Mani, Bakirathi. *Aspiring to Home: South Asians in America.* Redwood City, CA: Stanford University Press, 2012. Print.
Milville, Marie L., Madonna G. Constantine, Matthew F. Baysden, and Gloria So-Lloyd. "Chameleon Changes: An Exploration of Racial Identity Themes of Multiracial People." *Journal of Counseling Psychology* 52, no. 4 (2005): 507–516. Print.
Mohanty, Chandra Talpade. *Feminism without Borders: Decolonizing Theory, Practicing Solidarity.* Durham: Duke University Press, 2003. Print.
Nama, Adilifu. *Super Black: American Pop Culture and Black Superheroes.* Austin: University of Texas Press, 2011. Print.
Nishime, LeiLani. "The Mulatto Cyborg: Imagining a Multiracial Future." *Cinema Journal* 44, no. 2 (2005): 34–49. Print.
Pratt, Mary Louise. "Arts of the Contact Zone." *Profession* (1991): 33–40.
Raboteau, Emily. *The Professor's Daughter.* New York: Picador, 2005. Print.
Senna, Danzy. *Caucasia.* New York: Riverhead Books 1998. Print.
Stephens, Gregory. *On Racial Frontiers: The New Culture of Frederick Douglass, Ralph Ellison, and Bob Marley.* Cambridge, UK: Cambridge University Press, 1999. Print.
Street, Paul. *Barack Obama and the Future of American Politics.* New York: Routledge, 2016. Print.

Weiser, Benjamin. "Lawsuit over New York Police Surveillance of Muslims Is Revived." *The New York Times*. October 13, 2015. Accessed March 10, 2016. Web. http://www.nytimes.com/2015/10/14/nyregion/appeals-court-reinstates-lawsuit-over-police-surveillance-of-muslims.html?_r=0.

Wells, Zeb, and Todd Nauck. "Spidey Meets the President." *Amazing Spider-Man* 2, no. 583 (March 2009): 36–40.

White, John Kenneth. *Barack Obama's America: How New Conceptions of Race, Family, and Religion Ended the Reagan Era*. Ann Arbor: University of Michigan Press, 2009. Print.

Wilson, G. Willow. *The Butterfly Mosque*. New York: Grove, 2010. Print.

Wilson, G. Willow, and Adrian Alphona. *Ms. Marvel: No Normal*. New York: Marvel Worldwide, 2014. Reprints *Ms. Marvel* 3, nos. 1–5, and *All-New Marvel Now! Point One*, no. 1. Print.

Wilson, G. Willow, Adrian Alphona, Dan Slott, and Christos Gage. *Ms. Marvel: Last Days*. New York: Marvel Worldwide 2015. Reprints *Ms. Marvel* 3, nos. 16–19, and *Amazing Spider-Man* 3, nos. 7–8. Print.

Wilson, G. Willow, Jacob Wyatt, and Adrian Alphona. *Ms. Marvel: Generation Why*. New York: Marvel Worldwide, 2015. Reprints *Ms. Marvel* 3, nos. 6–11. Print.

Wilson, G. Willow, Mark Waid, Elmo Bondoc, and Takeshi Miyazawa. *Ms. Marvel: Crushed*. New York: Marvel Worldwide, 2015. Reprints *Ms. Marvel* 3, nos. 12–15, and *S.H.I.E.L.D.* no. 2. Print.

Young, Thom. "Ditko Shrugged." *Comics Bulletin*. 4 parts. 1 January 1, 2004. Accessed May 16, 2016. Web. http://comicsbulletin.com/ditko-shrugged-part-1-ayn-rands-influence-steve-ditkos-craft-commerce-and-creeper/.

"I WOULD RATHER BE A CYBORG"

Both/And Technoculture and the New *Ms. Marvel*

JESSICA BALDANZI

> There can be an elsewhere, not as a utopian fantasy or relativist escape, but an elsewhere born out of the hard (and sometimes joyful) work of getting on together in a kin group that includes cyborgs and goddesses working for earthly survival. (3)
> —DONNA HARAWAY, *THE HARAWAY READER* (2004)

Kamala Khan, the new Ms. Marvel, sits comfortably within her tech-savvy generation. Khan's immersion in teen technoculture is deep: she is an avid gamer and posts superhero fan fiction online. This new Ms. Marvel's first major trial as a superhero, in fact, is to battle a villain named the Inventor, who is bent on turning some of her fellow area teens into human batteries: inert biotechnological masses, rather than the positive, possibility-filled cyborgs Donna Haraway first defined in her 1984 "Cyborg Manifesto." The Inventor, a human-cockatiel hybrid lab accident, capitalizes on rhetoric that criticizes teens' technocultural connectedness as not only a waste of time but also a drag on societal resources. "The young are seen as a political burden, a public nuisance," he squawks, in one of those extended diatribes for which comic book villains are notorious: "They are not considered worth educating or protecting. They are called parasites, leeches, brats, spawn—If you used these words to describe any minority but children, it would quite understandably be considered hate speech. We are simply taking this loathing to its logical conclusion" (Wilson et al., *Generation Why*).[1]

Such rhetoric, of course, *has* been used against recent immigrants—most notably by our current president, Donald Trump, who echoed the Nazi regime's language of "vermin" by tweeting that recent illegal immigrants threaten to "infest" the United States.[2] Even conservative commentators have raised the alarm that talk of "infestation" against large groups of people, as well as calling such groups "animals," could pave the way not just for injustice, but also for violence. As a Muslim teen, Khan is double-targeted by negative societal rhetoric—and as a woman, perhaps triple-targeted. Khan and the rest of her generation already feel buffeted by global and societal forces, trying to fit in and find a way forward but often tying themselves into knots as they internalize rhetoric like the Inventor's. Khan, however, translates this identity confusion—this desire to shapeshift in answer to societal invective—into a superpower, thus providing her generation with imaginative possibilities for positive change. The internal element of Khan's superpower is crucial: despite the generational, religious, gendered, cultural, and "super" elements of her identity that might serve to marginalize her, by the end of the first story arc, she is not simply a language-based "code-switcher," shifting linguistic registers as she tries to fit in and please everyone. Instead, Khan breaks down, connects, and channels potentially restrictive identity checkboxes into active, polymorph powers.

Even though Haraway's "Cyborg Manifesto" is now over thirty years old, it still sounds cutting edge in its ability to negotiate and reimagine the types of restrictive categories that work to paralyze Khan and her fellow Jersey City high school students. Haraway especially attacks dichotomies that serve to divide people rather than to forge community. Yet she also creates a dichotomy of her own in this essay, by closing with the famous line, "I would rather be a cyborg than a goddess" (CM 316). Her use of the word "goddess" here serves to critique a branch of feminism that privileges, "worships," and often essentializes bodies over technologies. Yet "There is nothing about being 'female' that naturally binds women," she asserts.

> There is not even such a state as "being" female, itself a highly complex category constructed in contested sexual scientific discourses and other social practices.... The recent history for much of the US left and US feminism has been a response to this kind of crisis by endless splitting and searches for a new essential unity. But there has also been a growing recognition of another response through coalition—affinity, not identity. (295–96)

For Haraway, representations of "goddesses" tend to limit and restrict, to jeopardize that potential affinity by overlaying rules and boundaries derived from old, patriarchal texts onto female bodies. At this stage in Haraway's theoretical development, a "goddess" represents a woman whose gendered "religion" constitutes too much of her identity, making her overly invested in her boundaries between other groups rather than her similarities among potential allies.

From Haraway's 1984 perspective, Khan's status as a practicing Muslim might also seem to limit her, to place restrictions on her "cyborg" qualities. Khan, however, represents a productive challenge to Haraway's early view of religion—whether gendered or more broadly defined—as restrictive. In Khan's case, her cyborg, superhero status not only exists alongside, but actually relies on, her active yet questioning Muslim faith. As many essays about Khan have discussed, her superhero identity especially harnesses the moral structure of her faith toward positive action.[3]

Thankfully, Haraway has complicated her more recent work to look for "affinity" across multiple traditional boundaries rather than to divide into dichotomies: not just cyborg/goddess and human/machine, but also human/animal, as well as many dichotomies that do not include humans at all. As the epigraph at the start of this essay suggests, Haraway has revised her original manifesto to be less restrictive, welcoming the "goddess" back into her community of resistance. As she also notes in many of her later works, any strongly held cultural belief can take on religious-sounding rhetoric that proves just as restrictive, and can be just as damaging, as the rhetoric of traditional religion. Although technological advocates, for example, like to see themselves as logic-driven, free of the rhetoric of gods and goddesses and essentialism, discourse around the advent of biotechnology and many other new major technologies in the 90s and beyond suggests otherwise. In her 1997 book *Modest Witness*, Haraway observes how "the 'human genome' in biotechnical narratives regularly functions as a figure in a salvation drama that promises the fulfillment and restoration of human nature" (44). Similarly, in her newest work, *Staying with the Trouble* (2016), she notes two repeated and inadequate responses to global and societal "trouble": the standard human belief that "God will come to the rescue of his disobedient but ever hopeful children" and a more secular "comic faith in technofixes" that nevertheless takes on a religious tone (3). "In the face of such touching silliness about technofixes (or techno-apocalypses)," she writes, "sometimes it is hard to remember that it remains important to embrace situated technical projects and their people" (3)—to break down boundaries and categories to focus instead on local affinities, local communities, in which realistic progress can take place. To help with such progress, this new Ms. Marvel translates the basic ethics of the Muslim faith to the basic ethics of traditional US superheroes, a language that most Americans can more easily understand.[4] As A. David Lewis and Christine Hoff Kraemer argue in their introduction to *Graven Images,* "Particularly in light of Americans' increasing detachment from mainline churches, the religious explorations taking place in and around popular culture products should be taken seriously as one of the ways Americans express their religiosity" (3–4).

Shapeshifting Kamala Khan, then, represents one of Haraway's "situated technical projects," as she takes charge of her hometown, Jersey City, which has been passed over by high-profile superheroes and government figures alike in favor of its resource-hungry neighbor, New York City.[5] *Ms. Marvel* writer and cocreator G. Willow Wilson cites Khan's community rootedness as the source of her popularity: "It's not 'diversity' that draws those elusive untapped audiences, it's *particularity*" ("Diversity in Comics, Part II"). Ms. Marvel speaks from and to a very complicated version of her faith as well, largely because she was created by two Muslim women, Wilson and Marvel editor Sana Amanat—and Amanat, like Khan, grew up Muslim in the United States.[6] This specificity of a foreign-seeming, often oversimplified religion proves especially powerful in the visual medium of comics. Oversimplification and stereotyping—whether of a location, generation, gender, race, religion, or other category—encourage a debilitating passivity, but as Derek Parker Royal argues, "comics are well suited to dismantle those very assumptions that problematize ethnic representation, especially as they find form in visual language. They can do this by particularizing the general, thereby undermining any attempts at subjective erasure through universalization" (qtd. in Aldama 19). A. David Lewis further asserts in *American Comics, Literary Theory, and Religion* that such complication can lead not only to better understanding but also to heightened compassion: "[H]omogenizing oneness has dominated religious and secular Western culture, popular culture very much included, . . . [but] if we recognize that we've all got a number of factions and facets *within* ourselves, then we're likelier to accept differences *between* [us and] others" (3). The new Ms. Marvel, in her rich and productive "cyborg" breakdown of codes, categories, and dichotomies, illustrates how to maintain both the critical gaze and the myriad particularity—an internal but not generalized or essentialized "diversity"—necessary to create community and take action in the face of otherwise paralyzing local, national, and global challenges and crises.

A Shapeshifting Definition of the Cyborg

In her 2003 essay "Cyborgs to Companion Species," Haraway takes a few steps back from the linguistic and ideological play of her manifesto to scrutinize the origin story of the term "cyborg." Haraway devotees have exploded the definition of the cyborg to fit so many theoretical contexts and purposes that she finds it important to pull back and remind her readers of the term's roots. Although Haraway clearly advocates for the type of productive storytelling that spins out a concept like the cyborg—and that might spin a new and dynamic character like Kamala Khan out of Carol Danvers, the former Ms. Marvel—when it comes to technology, spiraling too far from the original term risks watering down the intellectual and real-world work that a productive application of cyborg ideology can accomplish.

"Cyborg," according to Haraway, was "coined by Manfred Clynes and Nathan Kline in 1960 to refer to the enhanced man who could survive in extraterrestrial environments" (*HR* 299). Clynes and Kline defined cyborgs as "self-regulating man-machine systems," and the two authors emphasized how "the machine and the organism are each communication systems joined in a symbiosis that transforms both" (ibid.). Haraway notes how this original cyborg seems stuck in time, "a technohumanist figure of the Cold War and the heyday of the space race" (ibid.).[7] Yet such a technological "symbiosis" is not just a Cold War concept: it well describes Kamala Khan and her friends, all working to breathe and survive from within their own shifting, technologically-defined atmosphere without the benefit of metaphorical spacesuits. Whether or not that environment is defined as "extraterrestrial," Ms. Marvel's use of technology is clearly internalized, embodied—partly because of her inherent superpowers and the (alien) "Terrigen Mist" that triggers them, but also because of her generational relationship to technology.

Khan's forays with her first villain play with the idea of this technological internalization. She may be able to "embiggen" her body—especially, in classic superhero form, her fists—to defeat supervillains, but her first challenge, an armored bot sent by the Inventor, needs to be destroyed from the inside. Highlighting Haraway's emphasis on cyborg "communication systems" in action, however, Khan contacts her sidekick Bruno via cell phone before she enters the bot. Bruno likewise uses the GPS coordinates of Khan's phone to call for police backup. These millennial characters see technological tools as personal and individual—practically internalized parts of themselves—but the massive external tech systems working behind the scenes of their "personal" contact remain invisible to them. "[C]ommunications sciences and

Figure 4.1 Charlie Chaplin, still from *Modern Times* (1936)

modern biologies are constructed by a common move," writes Haraway in her original manifesto, "*the translation of the world into a problem of coding, a search for a common language in which all resistance to instrumental control disappears and all heterogeneity can be submitted to disassembly, reassembly, investment and exchange*" (CM 302, italics in original). Current technoculture translates this non-disruptive "coding" into the search for the perfect algorithm—and in keeping with the militaristic roots of such technology, that code is not only binary and dichotomous but secret as well, oversimplifying our stories and identities with no recourse for nuanced challenge or revision.[8] Such invisible, top-down technology restricts individual possibilities for creating and maintaining positive, productive, and accessible communication systems.

The hard-wired technology of the Inventor's destructive bot proves both visible and vulnerable, however, though still not particularly fun to fight. Khan uses her shapeshifting power to shrink down and crawl into the mechanism. "I have to think small," narrates Khan. "If I can't beat the megabot from the outside . . . maybe I can fight it from the inside" (*Generation Why* issue 11, 10), she speculates. In a nod to Charlie Chaplin, Adrian Alphona draws Khan being sucked into the bot's gears, a visual echo of Chaplin's protagonist in the 1936 film *Modern Times* (figures 4.1, 4.2).

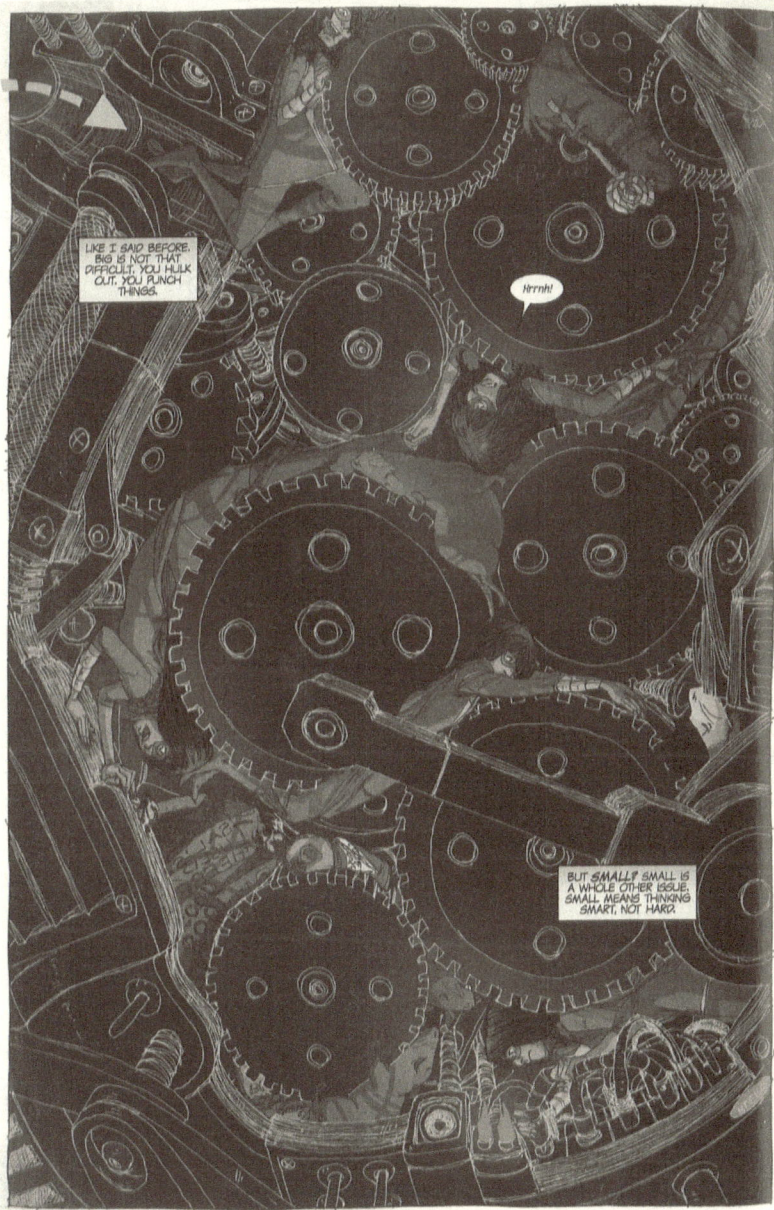

Figure 4.2 Wilson, Alphona, and Wyatt, *Generation Why*

Chaplin's hapless hero is trapped by technology supposedly created to make his job easier, but really designed to increase corporate profit. Khan succeeds in taking down this bot, but Alphona does not let the reader off the hook for complicity in its own technological entrapment: an earlier bot that crashes into Khan's high school classroom sports a "Free Wi-Fi" label (*Generation Why* issue 8, 20).

Although his battle bots seem clunky,[9] the Inventor's scheme holds more insidious elements, mainly his exploitation of teens'—as well as modern culture's—systemic self-entrapment. The Inventor turns teens' internalization of technology against them by using their bodies as batteries to feed his machines: he offers them a slapdash "technofix" rather than a real solution. As Khan tries to "save" these human batteries, she discovers that they have willingly put themselves in this situation: like her, they have internalized technology, but unlike her, they enter their bots not to destroy them but to "help" them by feeding their systems. When Khan tries to save Bruno's wayward brother, Vick, for example, he protests, "Nnno—stop—. . . I'm p-part of it now—I'm giving back" (*Generation Why* issue 8, 14). Not only has the Inventor exploited these teens' oversimplified interpretations of technology and society—in their hunger for some form of purpose, rather than questioning and redefining the Inventor's logic, they see themselves as *either* batteries or teens—but he has also isolated them, put them into pods that feed his structures of power rather than each other and their community. The teens' individual pods hark back to that solo astronaut space-race age, built on the Cold War dichotomy of US versus Russia relations.[10] These negative versions of cyborgs are overindividualized, inflexible, and resistant to change—which, fortunately for Ms. Marvel, also makes them vulnerable.[11]

Khan's real power as a generational savior is not so much in her fists as in her means of reframing the story, as she demonstrates in a pep talk to her fellow teens after they all defeat the Inventor. "What we did here today—we proved them wrong, guys. We're not a generation of phone-wielding losers. We took down the Inventor because we stuck together. And we've gotta keep sticking together. We need to be able to count on each other—no matter what" (*Generation Why* issue 11, 21). One of Haraway's most-cited lines argues that "[c]yborg writing is about the power to survive, not on the basis of original innocence, but on the basis of seizing the tools to mark the world that marked them as other" (CM 311).[12] These cyborg youth, these potentially "phone-wielding losers," have seized and harnessed their technology with the help of Ms. Marvel, subverting both the old-fashioned machinery, with its crushing gears and levers, and the destructive and dividing cultural stereotypes that attempted to mark them as useless.

Khan's internal narration in this scene, which runs parallel to her speech, suggests that her assurance is grounded in generational discourse that aims to bridge rather than restrict: "Man, I sound like my dad. Stay involved. Work hard. Have goals. But you know what? Abu [Dad] is right sometimes" (*Generation Why* issue 11, 21). To defeat the Inventor, Khan specifically draws on what she has learned from her family—especially her Qur'an-quoting father—grounding her "cyborg" pep talk with a more complex foundation. Khan succeeds in saving these teens not simply because she is tech-connected, but more deeply because she embraces complication, refusing the fantasy of the simple, overly broad solution, in addition to the fantasy of a simple identity. "Cyborg writing must not be about the Fall," Haraway argues, "the imagination of a once-upon-a-time wholeness before language, before writing, before Man (CM 311)." Haraway here suggests that religious discourse is atavistic, retributive, sexist, and nostalgic. The "original innocence" that Khan faces here, however, is not religious patriarchy as much as "original" technology. "Do you really think your generation is going to produce innovators of my caliber?" asks the Inventor, standing atop his bot before it collapses. The Inventor's origin story, tied to old, creaky, and overly individualistic technology, is the real dead end.

Clearly, Khan's power to defeat the Inventor was gathered from multiple sources, especially from her diverse community—including Lockjaw, the Inhuman bulldog, who breaks Khan out of the bot's ruthlessly mechanical gears. "I have come to see cyborgs as junior siblings in the much bigger, queer family of companion species" (CCS 300), writes Haraway in "Cyborgs to Companion Species." "Unfairly," she admits, "I will risk alienating my old doppelganger, the cyborg, in order to try to convince my colleagues and comrades that dogs might be better guides through the thickets of technobiopolitics in the Third Millennium of the Current Era" (CCS 298). Lockjaw is not just a dog, however; he is also an Inhuman, a category that puts him on equal footing with Khan rather than marginalizing him as a mere canine sidekick. "The literalized figure of companion species invites 'intersectional analysis' of key themes," writes Haraway, prefiguring the main issues that also drive the plot in the next two collected *Ms. Marvel* trades: "breeds and the history of eugenics; technology and the organic body; histories of class, race, gender, and nation" (CCS 317).

What does it mean, after all, to declare a first-generation Muslim teen "Inhuman"? It depends on the speaker, of course: G. Willow Wilson or President

Trump? Donna Haraway or a corporate Marvel executive, claiming that "diversity" is not profitable?[13] Are the goals of a category's creator more geared toward "affinity" or "identity," per Haraway's initial critique of goddesses (CM 295–96)? Interrogating the category "Inhuman" alongside its lowercase, adjectival descriptor helps make sense of a society—and a story—in the process of accruing increasingly messy and overlapping labels: not simply cyborg or goddess, but not simply human, mutant, or canine either.

Fear of the Inhuman Cyborg

In *Islam Is a Foreign Country,* Zareena Grewal sums up what she sees as a dominant attitude in the United States toward Muslim culture: "[I]n the West, we have culture, but in the East, their culture has them. Our culture is creative, heterogeneous, and constantly evolving, while Muslim culture is constructed as empty habit, monolithic, mindless conformity to lifeless customs and mummified rules in ancient texts" (18).[14] Our national claims to religious freedom have proved more of a challenge to uphold than we would like to admit. Haraway is not the only academic who has proved allergic, at least initially, to religion; US society has traditionally ostracized any unfamiliar religion, especially if it employs clothing as a visual marker of faith. (Recall, among many other and much older examples, fears of the influx of Catholic Irish and Italian Americans, who posed a threat because they might value commands from the pope ahead of the best interests of their new nation.) *Ms. Marvel* fans, however, know better than to heed oversimplifications handed down from the upper echelons of our current political culture. Khan's fans witness her challenging her faith, negotiating her own path through her religion, while also learning from her parents, her imam, and her conservative brother.[15] Khan's version of her religion evolves with questioning and resistance, much like progressive American Christianity continues to evolve—to shapeshift in response to the impossible contortions that assimilation attempts to demand from its citizens.[16]

Crushed, the third trade volume of *Ms. Marvel*, addresses a similar anxiety about religion, inheritance, and citizenship by beginning with Loki, trickster brother of Nordic god Thor, being sent by his mother to Jersey City as punishment. Thor and Loki's mother, Frigga, is a genuine "goddess" of Asgard, representing a throwback to pre-Christian myth. As Ms. Marvel's identity continues to develop in this story arc, questions of gods, goddesses, and "royalty" are complicated by the question of Inhuman inheritance. Much like Thor and Loki were taken in by Asgardian royalty—Thor is adopted, and Loki is a foster child—Khan has been taken in by Inhuman royalty, Queen Medusa.[17] Unlike Loki and Thor, however, whose blood and inheritance are not "pure," Khan's inherent, genetic, "rightful" connection to Queen Medusa and other Inhumans was revealed when she was exposed to a "Terrigen Mist."

According to Marvel comics lore, Inhumans are descended from human subjects on which the Kree, a militaristic alien race, performed experiments. Initially created to serve the Kree, Inhumans have a fascinating and disturbing history of both perpetrating eugenically based enslavement and being enslaved themselves. Inhumans also raise issues of genetics and inheritance: Khan's powers are inborn, yet they need to be triggered to be expressed. This complicated history might explain why, when Khan first passes out in the Terrigen Mist that reveals her powers along with the powers of a large group of other unwitting Inhumans, she says that the Mist "doesn't . . . have a smell, really, but if it did, it would smell like . . . secrets" (*No Normal* issue 2, 2–3). "There is no innocence in these kin stories," writes Haraway in her latest book, "and the accountabilities are extensive and permanently unfinished" (*ST* 114). Of course, the history of assimilation, especially in the United States, is rife with casualties and consequences, especially the cyclical hazing of its newest arrivals, as well as its indigenous population.

Khan's Inhuman status also suggests a fascinating metaphorical analogue to the unpredictable, potentially volatile "alien" or immigrant prior to the process of assimilation, a figure too often characterized as lowercase inhuman—or less than human—within our embattled national borders. Khan's story as a member of a recent immigrant family also parallels the "privilege" of superpowers with the privilege of US citizenship—after all, seminal superhero Superman was an "alien" too, conferred upstanding and unassailable Midwestern values, as well as an accepted traditional religion (Methodist), by his adoptive parents.[18] Yet such "privilege" is rarely as simple or incontrovertible as it might look.

As an alien, Superman was always trying to prove his citizenship and his "right" to it, which some critics have read as a motivation for his over-the-top masculinity (Singer; Lund). His anxious, hypermasculine performance reflects the anxiety of his creators, young descendants of Jewish immigrants who often felt like outsiders as they grew up in the Midwest. Superman's fraught persona, then, has become the foundation on which subsequent superheroes have been built. As José Alaniz writes in *Death, Disability and the Superhero*, building on the analysis of Christopher Murray, "stories fundamentally predicated on split-consciousness and proliferating selves—reflective of American paradoxes regarding freedom, racial/ethnic passing, assimilation, and 'dual citizenship'—render the genre a modern, open-ended psychodrama of masculine identity and the nation" (Alaniz 13; Murray). Ms. Marvel is a woman, of course, so this split consciousness plays out differently, but as comics creator Gene Luen Yang, the son of Chinese immigrants, wrote of his 2015 version of Superman, gender does not erase this main struggle between ancestry and the present: "Something that children of immigrants have to do when they get older is learn to integrate [their] two identities into a single whole" ("A History of Superman"). As Arjana observes of the X-Men, "Like Kamala, the 'mutant' status of the X-Men is about social inclusion—of Jews, queers, immigrants, and Muslims" (58). Arjana quotes creator Stan Lee, who recalls, "I wanted to spotlight a group of innocent people who were feared and shunned and later [hated] and persecuted" (Martin),[19] then notes, "This is, of course, an apt description of the status of American Muslims in the age of Islamophobia" (Arjana 58). Current dominant political rhetoric, I would add, also represents American Muslims and other recent immigrants as "inhuman" with a lowercase "i."

The complicated "privilege" of superpowers—along with the privilege of citizenship—can always, of course, be turned to negative uses, especially by figures who still feel ostracized. Loki, a consummate outsider and trickster figure, initially wreaks havoc at a Valentine's Day dance at Khan's high school by spiking the punch with truth serum—which, predictably, incites arguments and a brawl on the dance floor. When Khan dons her costume and confronts Loki as Ms. Marvel, Loki—now under the influence of his own truth serum—admits that he was sent by his mom to be sure the Inventor had been defused as a threat. "You really wanna help?" asks Khan. "Use your sparkly green power to keep this school from getting trashed by robots again" (*Crushed* issue 12, 19). Loki ultimately proves an ally by putting a charm on the school that protects it not just from robots but also from "anything short of an ice giant" (ibid.) for the rest of the story arc. His trickster and outsider identity is one of the many "oddkin" forces—as Haraway terms such nontraditional, ill-categorizable figures, in her most recent book (*ST* 4)—who help Khan's Jersey City community defend itself long-term.

Khan's next major villain, the not-so-subtly-named Lineage, poses threats that prove more "biological" than the machine-based assaults of the Inventor—yet technology, biotechnology, humanity, and complicity remain central to Khan's story as she matures into her superhero role. This second story arc continues to explore bodily boundaries—"Why should our bodies end at the skin?" Haraway asks in her manifesto (CM 314)—but extends these questions beyond machine technology and into inborn, even "royal" superhero traits. The boundary between internal and external becomes blurred even further when Khan is adopted by Queen Medusa and her Inhuman "tribe." As Khan narrates at the start of this collected trade, while she trains in a voice-activated virtual battle room "at the swank gym facilities of [her] Inhuman cousins across the river," "Lemme tell you: I thought Pakistani family stuff was big and complicated. But Inhuman family stuff? Big and complicated plus superpowers and intergalactic travel" (*Crushed* issue 13, 1).

What "complicates" Khan's life most in this story arc, however, even before she meets Lineage, is a moment when the dividing line between the "Pakistani family stuff" and the "Inhuman family stuff" breaks down: her parents try to set her up with Kamran, the son of Pakistani family friends. Khan initially resists—after all, she is an American teen steeped in the idea of romantic love—until she discovers that, despite the looming cultural threat of arranged marriage, she actually likes Kamran, and they have a lot in common. Their shared outlook seems—and becomes—too good to be true when Khan discovers that Kamran is Inhuman, too. Kamran turns out to be the bad type of Inhuman, a henchman for Lineage. Bent on turning his Inhuman power and privilege to negative—restrictive, exclusive, and even exterminatory—ends, Lineage's rhetoric (as his name suggests) echoes eugenic ideology. Kamran, via Lineage, is driven by a desire to enforce Inhuman sameness rather than encourage positive, inclusive, and complicated difference. As Heather Swanson notes in *Arts of Living on a Damaged Planet*, however, "the monstrosity of monocultures depends on the very multispecies relations that it denies" (M6), which will ultimately bring the downfall of Kamran as well as his insidious boss.

Until then, however, Kamran uses his Pakistani and family connections to employ specialized, gendered ammunition that makes Khan question herself, her powers, and her very purpose. Kamran offers Khan a ride on her way to school but takes her to Lineage instead, insisting that since her "destiny is a lot bigger than homework and quizzes," she should "take her rightful place with the rest of her Inhuman family" (*Crushed* issue 14, 13–15). When Khan refuses to join the "dark side" of the Inhumans, Kamran reverts to patriarchal tactics that "blame the victim": he preys on her guilt, chiding, "You got in my car of your own free will. As far as anybody knows, you chose to be here. You put yourself in this situation" (*Crushed* issue 15, 1).

This cultural and especially gender-based assault on Khan's Inhuman powers enacts a physical effect. She drops to her knees, overcome by self-implicating questions: "Is he right? Is this my fault? Is this what I deserve?"

Figure 4.3 Wilson, Miyazawa, and Bondoc, *Crushed*

(*Crushed* issue 15, 2). What happens when those same pressures that create the extreme masculinity of the traditional male superhero visit themselves upon a female superhero? Rather than playing out Alaniz's "psychodrama of masculine identity and the nation" mentioned above, Khan as a female superhero falls prey to the nation's patriarchal roots, and the resulting "psychodrama" plays out within her, felling her very body.[20]

Khan finds help outside of both her Pakistani family and her new Inhuman family by again using her phone to call her friend Bruno—who, ironically, cites a "family emergency" as he receives the alert and dashes out of his chemistry class (*Crushed* issue 15, 4). Much like last time, Bruno uses GPS technology to locate Khan. Also like last time, the art—this time drawn by Miyazawa—makes a historical pop culture connection, extending a visual bridge to yet another tribe or "family": the nerdy fangirl family so foundational to Khan's character construction in the first story arc. As Bruno runs toward the docks to reach Khan, he verbally pulls up her coordinates from his Siri parody "Sheri," telling her, "Open app 'Find My Homie'" (*Crushed* issue 15, 6). When Bruno barrels around a city corner, he runs between two classic *Star Trek* characters: Leonard Nimoy's Spock, looking on with a small grin, and Nichelle Nichols's Lieutenant Uhura (figure 4.3).[21]

As with Alphona's earlier Charlie Chaplin reference, Miyazawa's visuals time travel, jumping technological eras to challenge the attentive reader. "Retrieve GPS data for contact 'Kamala Khan!'" shouts Bruno, his phone flat in his hand in an echo of those silver clamshell *Star Trek* transmitters—a technology that seemed impossible in the real-world 1960s, when the original series aired. As Haraway has noted, cyborgs themselves were newly defined in this decade as well, just entering the cultural conversation and still more imaginary than real. Bruno is also called in as an anti-Lineage of sorts,[22] a character of motley background, an insider within Khan's generational, Jersey City, and even recent American immigrant "families." However, Bruno remains an outsider when it comes to Khan's Pakistani and Inhuman communities.

Pairing this rescue scene with the Chaplinesque scene from the first story arc forges connections between "families," generations, and technologies, re-emphasizing, as Haraway argues, that the original goal of cyborg technology is communication—and also emphasizing that such communication is at its most productive and positive when local and situated. In this second crisis moment, Khan again brings technology down from the inside, though a bit less literally: rather than shrinking down to enter a robot and pull internal wires, she lures her new villain's henchwoman into the same training room from the start of the story arc and asks the "creepy computer voice" to run one of her practice modules (*Crushed* issue 15, 9). The voice might be "creepy," but Khan, who has been training for battle under Queen Medusa, has become familiar, even intimate, with that digital voice. "That's how you level up," she remarks as she escapes, leaving the henchwoman trapped.

Khan's success in this scene is based not merely on a savvy knowledge of teen tech and gaming culture but also on systemic, locational tech knowledge: this is Queen Medusa's training room, and despite Lineage's small rebellion, Medusa remains in control of the infrastructure in this sector of New Attilan. Nevertheless, the broader technological web that Bruno used to locate Khan remains unquestioned, even sanctioned by the presence of the friendly neighborhood Star Trek characters. As technology and gender studies scholar Lauren Wilcox argues, such technological structures need constant pressure and questioning, because they represent "a form of embodiment that reworks and undermines essentialist notions of culture and nature, biology and technology." Such a subversion is clearly positive, of course, but comes at a price, because this destruction of essentialism is so "often but not necessarily [employed] in the service of projects of domination" (Wilcox 15). Postcolonial theorists also highlight this precarious balance, asserting, as does Reina

Lewis, that "imperialist values frequently structur[ed] even the terms of those who opposed it" (13). Lewis further argues that "A disinvestment in one set of values is counterbalanced by an overinvestment in another" (22), which creates systems that breed continued imbalance rather than social justice.

The villainous Lineage attempts to exploit and perpetuate imbalanced systems by advancing his clearly sinister eugenic goals. Lineage initially tries to recruit Khan—and later her brother, Aamir—by citing the potential advantages her Inhuman status affords. "You're a very powerful Inhuman, kid," he says, his finger beneath her chin. "You deserve to forge your own path, not take orders from a big dog [Lockjaw] and a queen on a power trip [Medusa]" (*Crushed* issue 15, 2). Lineage's crudely expressed desire to exploit Inhuman powers foregrounds the complications behind power and privilege within US society: as Spider-Man taught many comics fans, with great power comes great responsibility, but when characters refuse to take on that responsibility, that "great power" can easily turn dark. Kamran is likewise privileged despite his status as a recent immigrant: when he tries to recruit Khan's brother, Aamir ridicules Kamran's cushy lifestyle as he rejects the invitation: "What is this 'we' thing, private-school boy?" Aamir snaps (*Last Days* issue 18, 5). Kamran, by aligning with Lineage, uses his power to maintain and protect rather than share his privilege. "You know what your problem is, Kamala?" Kamran asks. "You try to fight the chaos instead of turning it to your advantage" (*Last Days* issue 16, 11). Kamran's words again trigger a bodily reaction in Khan, when he tells her to "be a good girl and take care of your parents"—whom he just lulled to sleep in their own house while Khan was out battling the chaos of an approaching apocalypse. "If you'd [taken care of them] in the first place, like you're supposed to, maybe you wouldn't be in this situation right now" (ibid.), he sneers, again felling Khan. "He knows exactly how to hurt me," she narrates from the floor, where she has collapsed. Khan remains battered with insecurity for the rest of the issue, questioning her ability to protect not only her family but also her friends, her school, and her community.

How else besides shapeshifting is Khan supposed to manage these distinct but connected elements of her identity? Complicated pressures battle beneath her skin, while, from the outside, her skin is prone to sparking negative responses within a dominant society unsympathetic to outsiders. A superpower like shapeshifting seems like a "normal" enough response, especially when Khan's gendered body faces pressures traditional male superheroes have tended to steel themselves against and even fly away from. Combine fears of youth culture with the aforementioned fears of unfamiliar religious cultures, and dominant US anxiety reaches a potentially lethal level, confronted with American Muslim youth perceived as "deeply religious and politically disaffected" (Grewal 7). Yet there are better ways to look at religious commitment, supposedly advocated in the very origins of our nation. "Perhaps it is [the] idealism [of American Muslim youth] that is most radical," Grewal theorizes, "the persistence with which they desire a home" (7)—in other words, all these Muslim youth are really asking for is a situated location of their own.

"Both Perspectives at Once": Forging Apocalyptic Affinities

Khan's tussle with Lineage also clarifies that although eugenic goals, based on bodily reproduction, must be situated within individual bodies, the solutions to their defeat lie in control of the surrounding location and its networks. Khan failed to defeat the Inventor until she fully owned her superhero role and claimed Jersey City as her territory—an important step in building her superhero identity, according to Peter Coogan, who notes that "Superheroes actively seek to protect their communities by preventing harm to all people and by seeking to right wrongs committed by criminals and other villains" (92, fn. 1). "This is my city. My home," Khan declares to Wolverine, when he suggests that she step aside to let him handle the Inventor. "I know [this city] inside and out. If the Inventor messes with Jersey City, he messes with me. I can handle this" (*Generation Why* issue 7, 17).

Finally, in the face of looming apocalypse in the fourth collected trade, *Last Days*, Ms. Marvel's third major crisis in these early volumes of her story, it takes both a protected location—the Loki-charmed gym at Khan's high school—and a mentor better equipped than Wolverine to help her battle the psychological threat of her gender-specific guilt. When Jersey City becomes too locationally diffuse for Khan to navigate—when she loses track of Aamir, who is kidnapped by Lineage's minions in an attempt to turn him to the evil side of Inhumanity—her precursor, Carol Danvers, arrives to help her focus her power and strengths. When Danvers appears, she looks like a cyborg out of a sci-fi flick, especially in her new outfit: so fluid are Danvers's cyborg identities that the line between where her costume—especially her mask—ends and her hairline begins is unclear. Danvers is a human/alien Kree hybrid, not an Inhuman, yet, like Khan, she is still an outsider. Danvers proves the biggest help with Khan's earth-bound "family" problems, providing Khan with outside mentorship to teach her to prioritize emergencies and take care of herself psychologically as well as physically.

Location is still key, however, and GPS is referenced a third time, when Danvers is preparing to say goodbye to Khan.

MS. MARVEL: "It's your star and my lightning bolt."
CAPTAIN MARVEL: "Yeah, it is. It's also a GPS locator, so don't lose it."
MS. MARVEL: "Gorgeous yet functional."
CAPTAIN MARVEL: "That's how we roll."
(*Last Days*, issue 18, 12–13)

Danvers explains that Khan can employ this pendant if she ever needs backup again. The gesture represents a touching connection between these two "cyborg" figures, yet again raises the question of how GPS is supposed to work in an apocalypse. Is this a special superhero version of GPS that operates on its own network? Or maybe Danvers has created her own locators, which continue to work even if larger systems crash? As Haraway has always pointed out, many of our utopian technologies were born—or "birthed"—out of "the reproductive apparatuses of war" (*HR* 3), and knowledge of those origins proves one of the best ways to subvert them. What is the best method "to produce some better ways of mediating the sense of a historical moment that is affectively felt but undefined in the social world that is supposed to provide some comforts of belonging, so that it would be possible to imagine a potentialized present that does not reproduce all of the conventional collateral damage?" (263), asks Lauren Berlant in *Cruel Optimism*. Carol Danvers does not fully succeed in circumventing this "conventional collateral damage" because this third reference to GPS again suggests a blind spot in the story, an overreliance on invisible corporate networks that, because of their military and hierarchical origins, might not prove trustworthy in the long run. Danvers is also recreating systems set up by male superheroes, without fully escaping them as she would if she were to imagine something entirely—or at least significantly—new.

"From one perspective," writes Haraway in her manifesto,

> a cyborg world is about the final imposition of a grid of control on the planet, about the final abstraction embodied in a Star Wars apocalypse waged in the name of defence.... From another perspective, a cyborg world might be about lived social and bodily realities in which people are not afraid of their joint kinship with animals and machines, not afraid of permanently partial identities and contradictory standpoints. The political struggle is to see from both perspectives at once." (CM 295)

—or from a myriad of perspectives, as Haraway has spun out in her most recent work, and as Wilson, for the most part, succeeds in weaving together. This glaring blind spot, however, Wilson seems to share with her millennial characters: a blind dedication to some "grids of control"—GPS, cell networks, video games, and even, in Khan's case, control of her own superhero body—that, rather than scrutinizing the big picture, many prefer to see as personal, individual, and protected. Who controls these grids? Why are Khan, Bruno, and Danvers unable to devise solutions to crises without the help of a consumer device?

Wilson references the loss of cell phone service at the advent of the seeming apocalypse that opens *Last Days*. When panicked citizens gather around Ms. Marvel asking for help, their fear seems less focused on bodily harm than on the loss of network communication: "There's no cell service anywhere!" one of them tells her. "All the TVs and radios are jammed too!" (*Last Days* issue 16, 5). The high school teens with their community know-how save the day once again, and suggest a workable techno-hack—which implies a do-it-yourself construction from scratch—rather than the overly simple "technofix," which implies a stronger reliance on outside systems, and against which Haraway warns.[23] When Khan visits the gym, her former "jock" antagonist, Josh, now protecting the school with a baseball bat, explains, "The AV club is using the school mailing list to contact everybody. They did some weird stuff with tin foil and coat hangers and managed to get a 4G signal in the gymnatorium" (*Last Days* issue 16, 15).

Is the distinction between "techno-hack" and "technofix" too narrow, however? Is a hack like the one the Coles AV Club pulled off really possible? Would any network keep running to even be hackable if a planet—or, in a more current real-world scenario, a hurricane or a nuclear warhead—were heading for Manhattan? In "How to Survive a Disaster," Rebecca Solnit shares multiple stories of makeshift online networks, such as hurricanehousing.org, that have sprouted up in recent climate-related emergencies (Solnit "How to Survive"). Similar networks are becoming increasingly common, one recent example created for fellow Houston citizens to save each other from rising water after Hurricane Harvey (Roberts). Yet the question remains: in a national or global rather than regional disaster, how far off the grid can you go and still communicate beyond your immediate location? Part of Wilson's point, however, seems to be that when a large-scale disaster hits, we will be in worse shape not only if we look too far afield but also if we have not even imagined any positive possibilities.

Further, the best solutions will need to come from a diverse range of perspectives, a younger generation imagining new types of solutions, an older generation contributing a lifetime of technical expertise, especially in what has already been tried and does not work. Danvers explains to Khan that what looks like an approaching planet is really an "incursion zone," which is "what happens when two separate realities collide with each other" (*Last Days* issue 17, 2). Out of all the dichotomies and dichotomy breakdowns we have seen in these early issues of Ms. Marvel's development, generational differences have played the most central role—and these generational gaps can certainly seem massive enough to create an "incursion zone."[24] Yet when Khan, in the face of apocalypse, confesses her superhero identity to her mom, her mom is instantly supportive, saying that she knew all along—a scenario drastically different from earlier superhero stories in which the parents "just don't understand," and the superprotagonist needs to break away from family to finish with her or his identity formation. In Khan's case, however, both her imam and her mom have encouraged her success up to this point—it was Sheikh Abdullah, the imam of the Khan family's mosque, who presaged Khan's meeting with Wolverine in the second collected trade, telling Khan that a teacher would appear when she needed it most (*Generation Why* issue 6, 4–5). Even Aamir—close to Khan's age, but representing a much more traditional religious model—turns out to be on her side: still maddeningly pious and conservative, but supportive. The influence of Loki's mom, the aforementioned more traditional version of a "goddess," likewise ends up a key part of the constellation of beliefs that protects the gym, since she sent Loki on his original mission. These are all positive and diverse religious role models representing a range of generations. These figures also show readers similarities more than differences at a time when mainstream religious narratives attempt to oversimplify and demonize not only all Muslims but, in many cases, "all" of any one religious category.

Wilson addresses the importance of this diverse representation in Mir's interview at the end of this volume. "My husband is Egyptian, I'm American: we both come from the racial and religious majorities from our respective countries where we grew up. It's been a struggle for both of us to learn how to be a minority and prepare kids who are going to be both/and, neither/nor in the ways that Kamala is."[25] In the interest of her own and her children's imagined future, Wilson manages to unite the many identities and "realities" that make up Khan's world at the end of this fourth collected trade. "Here it is. The house that Ms. Marvel built," Khan thinks when she first surveys the scene at the gym. Despite the encouragement and support showered on her when she enters the gym, however, Khan remains worried, insecure about her ability to protect her community in the face of a possible apocalypse, adding,

"Was it all for nothing?" (*Last Days* issue 19, 8). After gathering support from Captain Marvel, her mom, her brother, and Bruno, however, she returns to the "gymnatorium" much more confident, with psychological as well as physical backup. Wilson makes a point of showing everyone reaching across all sorts of boundaries—not just religious boundaries, but also ancient, "sacred" high school boundaries such as jock and nerd—to protect what they have all built together. Alphona's illustrations likewise cross all these boundaries and more: in the final dance-party gym scene, he throws in a teen biomech with spikes coming out of his head—one of Khan's fans from the first story arc—along with pigeons wearing headdresses and Viking helmets, a pig, two unspecified figures in yellow hazmat suits, and a Tibetan monk (*Last Days* issue 19, 14). Aamir smiles and waves from the "nondenominational, nonjudgmental prayer area" (ibid., 11), where Sheikh Abdullah and Khan's *hijab*-wearing friend Nakia, along with a few less visually identifiable worshippers, were sitting with the Tibetan monk a few frames earlier. "Staying with the trouble requires making oddkin," writes Haraway. "[T]hat is, we require each other in unexpected collaborations and combinations, in hot compost piles. We become-with each other or not at all" (*ST* 4). Subverting dichotomies also subverts restrictive and rigid mindsets. Wilson suggests that small subversions, like when Khan's "mean-girl" classmate Zoe apologizes to her for earlier slights (*Last Days* issue 19, 9), can lay the groundwork for subverting larger threatening structures, whether fascist, eugenic, or—in this case—even apocalyptic.

As Solnit asks in a recent interview, however, "How can we get [to a real sense of community] without going through the disaster?" (Solnit "Falling Together"). Why does it take a major disaster—in this case, a looming apocalypse[26]—to build community? "I cannot welcome disaster," Solnit clarified later on *LitHub*, "but I can value the responses, both practical and psychological" ("How to Survive"). Berlant also emphasizes the importance of imagining scenarios and solutions, noting, "In scenarios of cruel optimism we are forced to suspend ordinary notions of repair and flourishing to ask whether the survival scenarios we attach to those affects weren't the problem in the first place" (49). The psychological, the imaginative, are too often devalued and pushed aside in the face of disaster and its threat to bodily safety, but these theorists, along with both Wilson and Haraway, remind us of the necessity of creative, big-picture thinking in the process of forging positive solutions.

As Haraway asserts in an interview at the end of her *Haraway Reader*, "categories are not frozen. We are more inventive than that. The world is more lively than that, including us, and there are always more things going on than you thought" (*HR* 335). In *Staying with the Trouble,* Haraway also notes how, "In urgent times, many of us are tempted to address trouble in terms of making an imagined future safe, of stopping something from happening that looms in the future, of clearing away the present and the past in order to make futures for coming generations" (*ST* 1).[27] As much as we should try not to restrict youth in an attempt to make their world safe, we also need to encourage a youth culture on the verge of overimmersion in technology to see where productive spaces already exist in the real world, in real bodies situated right next to them, and in their communities. Both Wilson and Haraway help us realize not only that we cannot protect these future generations but also that we need to subvert the young/old dichotomy—among many other dichotomies—to move forward as a society.

We sit at a point of cultural and political excess, of feeling that there are too many "issues" to handle all at once, too many identities to protect. That overwhelmed paralysis, however, stems largely from overcategorization, from expending energy unnecessarily by hanging onto and upholding dichotomies, divisions, categories—in other words, from superficially code-switching and trying to please everyone rather than shapeshifting and honoring the many identities we hold within our own bodily boundaries. By breaking down the myriad categories analyzed in this essay to find interconnections rather than divisions, we all can stay focused on what each of us brings to the table that is new and unique and that needs to be nurtured and complicated and spun into stories, rather than ossified, essentialized, and (over)protected. As Haraway writes in *Modest_Witness,* "There is no way to rationality—to actually existing worlds—outside stories, not for our species, anyway" (*MW* 44). By revisiting one early definition and explanation of the cyborg, and by using the storytelling power of popular comics to chip away at this initial boundary between a cyborg generation and the (supposed) rest of us, perhaps we can all make better sense of each other, ditch the infighting, and move forward—because what the new Ms. Marvel highlights more than anything else is that we all have a lot of work to do.

NOTES

1. My coeditor on this volume, Hussein Rashid, points out that this rant also parodies the film *The Matrix.*

2. See, for example, Graham.

3. See, for example, Arjana, as well as Lewis and Lund's collection *Muslim Superheroes,* especially the essays by Wanner, Yanora, and Reyns-Chikuma and Lorenz.

4. As Sophia Arjana writes of the moment of Khan's transformation into a superhero, "Visually it is represented as a religious experience, complete with clouds, an Urdu poem,

and references that are both Christological (the scene resembles the paintings of Jesus's [Ascension]) and Islamic" (the inclusion of birds has resonances of Attar's classic text on spiritual transformation) (55).

5. Recent online conversations among comics scholars have questioned the accuracy of the details of Ms. Marvel's Jersey City as the series has developed but have affirmed the more general New Jersey milieu as accurate, per both G. Willow Wilson's and Sana Amanat's backgrounds, which are rooted in the north New Jersey suburbs.

6. Wilson is Muslim too, but converted later in her life.

7. In "Cold War Culture and the Birth of Marvel Comics," Robert Genter traces the history of the Cold War alongside the development of many of Marvel's seminal characters, but especially Iron Man. After sustaining a Vietnam War wound, Tony Stark adapts to his new cyborg status of needing his suit to survive, and converts himself into a "modern knight, . . . a protective force against the subversive influence of communist infiltration" (966). In *Zombies: A Cultural History*, Roger Lockhurst also traces connections between comics and the Cold War, in particular, the "zombiefication" of youth for which cultural commentators of the time loved to blame comics, especially horror comics.

8. See, for example, Kuang and O'Neil. As an added connection, an interview with O'Neil in the *Guardian* sells the piece in a tagline by highlighting how "[t]he Harvard PhD and data scientist . . . ponders how people's fear and trust of math is akin to worshipping God" (Chalabi).

9. One of my readers notes that these bots can be seen as failed "companion species"—failed, I would argue, precisely because of the Inventor's efforts to restrict and control them rather than to forge affinities with them.

10. The pods inside the bots also look a bit like the pods in *Invasion of the Body Snatchers* (1956), which Lockhurst analyzes alongside the post–Cold War period. See his chapter 6, "After 1945: Zombie Massification."

11. My coeditor notes that the Inventor's tactics also echo the steps to radicalization—as he puts it, "being given a sense of purpose, taking action, and not being present to experience the result of that action." Because these teens are passive batteries, they are being used a lot like suicide bombers, which has obvious resonance with stereotypes employed against Muslims in the United States.

12. This quotation echoes Audre Lorde's essay "The Master's Tools Will Never Dismantle the Master's House," which, like "A Cyborg Manifesto," was first published in 1984.

13. See, for example, Polo.

14. Lockhurst notes one specific iteration of this association of Islam with passive, unthinking worship in the rhetoric of World War Two: "Since 'Muslim' derives from the Arabic meaning 'submission to God,' it was presumably evoked by prisoners as a slang term for resignation to fate. . . . In Primo Levi's account of his year in Auschwitz, he defines the Musulman [from the German *Muselmann* for Muslim] as 'the weak, the inept, those doomed to selection' for inevitable death in the gas chambers" (113).

15. As Arjana notes, this series is also crucial in its visual complication of clothing associated with Islam, since "visual narratives offer an alternative space in which we can see Muslims through a different lens that more accurately reflects reality" (24). Khan's Turkish

friend, Nakia, wears a headscarf, and although Khan's brother looks ultraconservative, he delivers a satisfying takedown of sexism when he chews out Khan's former love interest, Kamran (59).

16. See Mir's interview of Wilson at the end of this volume, in which Wilson calls *Ms. Marvel* an "*anti*-assimilation story" ("Coda: Conversations").

17. In the second trade volume, Wolverine at first thinks Khan might be a mutant like him, but he delivers her to New Attilan and Queen Medusa once he finds out that her powers were triggered by a mist.

18. I thank Elizabeth Coody for this amusing but relevant question: "Is Superman some sort of Methodist because his parents were?" she asked in a panel discussion of the essay collection *Muslim Superheroes* (*Muslim Superheroes: A Celebration in Categories*).

19. Arjana quotes Martin's 1994 *New York Times* article but changes "hated" to "hunted." The typo originated in a secondary source, P. Andrew Miller, "Mutants, Metaphor, and Marginalism: What X-actly Do the X-Men Stand For?" *Journal of the Fantastic in the Arts* 13, no. 3 (2003): 283.

20. Perhaps aware of the dangers of essentializing gender here, artist Takeshi Miyazawa gently pokes fun at gender norms in the following scene by visually objectifying Bruno's body as he rushes to help Kamala: when the alert first comes in, Bruno's low-slung pants reveal, instead of the front-side, chest cleavage most often employed in images of women in comics, back-side "plumber's cleavage." Later, when Bruno is running with Khan, his shirt rides up to show his bellybutton. Ms. Marvel's costume, notably, consistently keeps her fully covered. Whereas "good" women in superhero comics are usually drawn to be consumed (Arjana 2), Khan here is clearly the one to be emulated and even feared, rather than consumed.

21. And perhaps a third character—the guy spilling his coffee—does bear a resemblance to William Shatner's Captain Kirk.

22. I thank Kyle Schlabach for this phrase, as well as this observation.

23. Pop culture semantics are telling here: even the word "hack" has been watered down, particularly in the word "lifehack," to signify consumerist, "lifestyle"-related solutions that do not require the mechanical or technical skill that the word denotes. Lifehack.org, for example, contains more psychological than physical life improvements, which have little to do with the computer hacking with which the phrase originated. Perhaps readers are drawn to the term because it implies difficult visible work that metaphorically represents what is often quite difficult yet invisible psychological work.

24. The incursion zone runs beyond *Ms. Marvel* and into other Marvel titles. C.f. Berlatsky and Dagbovie-Mullins's essay in this book.

25. See "Coda: Conversations."

26. The origins of the word "apocalypse" in "uncover" and "reveal," thus "revelation," are also useful to consider here.

27. Not surprisingly, Khan and Danvers come to a crisis moment in their friendship over this topic in a later publication, *Civil War II*. The cover for that issue, discussed briefly in the introduction to this volume, reads "Protect the Future. Change the Future," over an image of Khan ripping a poster of Carol Danvers. Danvers here, in her support of technology that can predict "future crimes," represents someone keeping the future "safe" (Bendis and Copiel; Evans).

BIBLIOGRAPHY

Alaniz, José. *Death, Disability, and the Superhero: The Silver Age and Beyond*. Jackson: University Press of Mississippi, 2014. Print.

Aldama, Frederick, ed. *Multicultural Comics: From Zap to Blue Beetle*. Austin: University of Texas Press, 2011. Print.

Arjana, Sophia Rose, and Kim Fox. *Veiled Superheroes: Islam, Feminism, and Popular Culture*. Lanham, MD: Lexington Books, 2017. Print.

Bendis, Brian Michael, and Olivier Copiel. *Civil War II* (1). New York: Marvel, 2016.

Berlant, Lauren. *Cruel Optimism*. Durham, NC: Duke UP, 2011. Print.

Brown, Jeffrey A. *Black Superheroes, Milestone Comics, and Their Fans*. Jackson: University Press of Mississippi, 2001. Print.

Chalabi, Mona. "Interview: *Weapons of Math Destruction*: Cathy O'Neil Adds Up the Damage of Algorithms." *The Guardian*. October 27, 2016. Web. https://www.theguardian.com/books/2016/oct/27/cathy-oneil-weapons-of-math-destruction-algorithms-big-data.

Coogan, Peter. "The Definition of the Superhero." *A Comics Studies Reader*. Eds. Jeet Heer and Kent Worcester. Jackson: University Press of Mississippi, 2009. 77–93. Print.

Evans, William. "Ms. Marvel Ripping Apart a Poster of Captain Marvel in Civil War II Is All of Us." n.d. *Black Nerd Problems*. Web. http://blacknerdproblems.com/ms-marvel-ripping-apart-a-poster-of-captain-marvel-in-civil-war-ii-is-all-of-us/.

Gateward, Frances, and John Jennings, eds. *The Blacker the Ink: Constructions of Black Identity in Comics and Sequential Art*. New Brunswick, NJ: Rutgers University Press, 2015. Print.

Genter, Robert. "'With Great Power Comes Great Responsibility': Cold War Culture and the Birth of Marvel Comics." *The Journal of Popular Culture* 40, no. 6 (2007): 953–78. Print.

Graham, David A. "Trump Says Democrats Want Immigrants to 'Infest' the U.S." *The Atlantic* (June 2018). Web. https://www.theatlantic.com/politics/archive/2018/06/trump-immigrants-infest/563159/.

Grewal, Zareena. *Islam Is a Foreign Country: American Muslims and the Global Crisis of Authority*. New York: NYU Press, 2013. Print.

Haraway, Donna. "Companions in Conversation." Interview by Cary Wolfe. *Manifestly Haraway*. Minneapolis: University of Minnesota Press. 2016. Print.

⸻. "A Cyborg Manifesto" (CM). *The Cybercultures Reader*. Eds. David Bell and Barbara M. Kennedy. New York: Routledge, 2000. 291–324. Originally published 1984. Print.

⸻. "Cyborgs to Companion Species (CCS): Reconfiguring Kinship in Technoscience." *When Species Meet*. Minneapolis: University of Minnesota Press, 2008. Originally published 2003. Print.

⸻. *The Haraway Reader* (HR). New York: Routledge, 2004. Print.

⸻. *Modest_Witness@Second_Millenium* (MW). New York: Routledge, 1997. Print.

⸻. *Staying with the Trouble* (ST): *Making Kin in the Chthulucene*. Durham NC: Duke UP, 2016. Print.

"A History of Superman." Slideshow. *Wall Street Journal*. 2017. Web. http://graphics.wsj.com/embeddable-carousel/?slug=history-of-superman.

Howard, Sheena C., and Ronald L. Jackson II, eds. *Black Comics: Politics of Race and Representation*. New York: Bloomsbury Academic, 2013. Print.

Kuang, Cliff. "Can AI Be Taught to Explain Itself?" *New York Times Magazine* (November 17, 2017), n.p. Web. https://www.nytimes.com/2017/11/21/magazine/can-ai-be-taught-to-explain-itself.html.

Lewis, A. David. *American Comics, Literary Theory, and Religion: The Superhero Afterlife.* New York: Palgrave Macmillan, 2014. Print.

Lewis, A. David, and Christine Hoff Kraemer. "Introduction." Lewis and Kraemer, eds. *Graven Images: Religion in Comic Books and Graphic Novels.* New York: Bloomsbury Academic, 2010. Print.

Lewis, A. David, and Martin Lund, eds. *Muslim Superheroes: Comics, Islam, and Representation.* Mizan Series, volume 1. Boston: Ilex Foundation and Center for Hellenic Studies, 2017. Print.

Lewis, Reina. *Gendering Orientalism: Race, Femininity and Representation.* New York: Routledge, 1996. Print.

Lockhurst, Roger. *Zombies: A Cultural History.* London: Reaktion Books, 2015. Print.

Lorde, Audre. "The Master's Tools Will Never Dismantle the Master's House." *Sister Outsider.* Freedom, CA: Crossing, 1984. 110–13. Print.

Lund, Martin. *Reconstructing the Man of Steel: Superman 1938–1941.* New York: Palgrave Macmillan, 2016. Print.

Martin, Douglas. "The X-Men Vanquish America." *The New York Times* (August 21, 1994): 27.

Murray, Christopher. *Champions of the Oppressed? Superhero Comics, Popular Culture, and Propaganda in America During World War II.* New York: Hampton Communication Series, 2011. Print.

"*Muslim Superheroes*: A Celebration in Categories." Roundtable discussion. Joint session of the Religion and Popular Culture Unit and Study of Islam Unit. Annual Meeting of the American Academy of Religion. Boston, MA, November 18, 2017. Podcast, "Live at AAR 2017," posted November 28, 2017. Web. http://www.sacredandsequential.org/.

O'Neil, Cathy. *Weapons of Math Destruction: How Big Data Increases Inequality and Threatens Democracy.* New York: Crown, 2016. Print.

Polo, Susana. "Marvel Exec Insists Wave of Cancellations Not Motivated by Books' Diversity." *Polygon.com.* Dec 22, 2017. Web. https://www.polygon.com/comics/2017/12/22/16810138/marvel-exec-insists-wave-of-cancellations-not-motivated-by-books-diversity. Web.

Roberts, Shadrock. "Online Volunteers Respond to Hurricanes Harvey and Irma." Ushaidi.com (September 8, 2017). Web. https://www.ushahidi.com/blog/2017/09/08/online-volunteers-respond-to-hurricanes-harvey-irma.

Singer, Marc. *Grant Morrison: Combining the Worlds of Contemporary Comics.* Jackson: University Press of Mississippi, 2012. Print.

Solnit, Rebecca. "Falling Together." Interview with Krista Tippet. *OnBeing.* May 26, 2016. Web. https://onbeing.org/programs/rebecca-solnit-falling-together/.

———. "How to Survive a Disaster," excerpt from *A Paradise Built in Hell: The Extraordinary Communities That Arise in Disaster.* New York: Viking/Penguin 2009. Posted on Lithub .org, 11/15/16. Accessed 12/17. http://lithub.com/rebecca-solnit-how-to-survive-a-disaster/.

Swanson, Heather, Anna Tsing, Nils Bubandt, and Elaine Gan. "Introduction: Bodies Tumbled into Bodies." *Arts of Living on a Damaged Planet: Monsters of the Anthropocene.* Minneapolis: University of Minnesota Press, 2017. Print.

Wilcox, Lauren. "Embodying Algorithmic War: Gender, Race, and the Posthuman in Drone Warfare." *Security and Dialogue* 48:1 (2017): 11–28. Print.

Wilson, G. Willow. "Diversity in Comics, Part II." gwillowwilson.com. May 28, 2017. Web. http://gwillowwilson.com/post/161173844153/diversity-in-comics-part-ii.

Wilson, G. Willow, and Adrian Alphona. *Ms. Marvel: Last Days*. New York: Marvel Now!, 2015. Print.

———. *Ms. Marvel: No Normal*. New York: Marvel Now!, 2014. Print.

Wilson, G. Willow, Adrian Alphona, and Jacob Wyatt. *Ms. Marvel: Generation Why*. New York: Marvel Now!, 2015. Print.

Wilson, G. Willow, Elmo Bondoc and Takeshi Miyazawa. *Ms. Marvel: Crushed*. New York: Marvel Now!, 2015. Print.

HOPE AND THE *SA'A* OF MS. MARVEL

A. DAVID LEWIS

"In life," he said, "there are no essentially major or minor characters. To that extent, all fiction and biography, and most historiography, is a lie. Everyone is necessarily the hero of his own life story."
(BARTH 59)

Perhaps superheroes are supposed to fight to their very last breath, to the bitter end, but Kamala Khan in *Ms. Marvel: Last Days* models a different form of heroism. As the end of the world draws near, Khan chooses to protect her immediate community, a choice that reflects both her position as a young, fledgling superheroine and also, arguably, the Islamic principles that inform her altruism. As Ms. Marvel, she does not look to play either savior or sacrifice. Rather than dramatically flinging herself into the center of the conflict, she stays grounded, watching over her community and, at the same time, drawing meaning from it.

Hope at the End of the World

When the end of the world comes, what do we do about hope? Hope is, in many ways, the defining antithesis of apocalyptic prophesy. All other prophesy has hope as an integral element: hope for a better day, hope for a certain event, even hope for what comes after a foreseen disaster. "The prophet is the voice of hope. Apocalypse, by contrast, is the voice of despair," says Jonathan Sacks in *Not in God's Name: Confronting Religious Violence* (231). The apocalyptic eschaton, if understood as the end of this world, has no "after," and, thus, one might suspect, no place for hope.

Yet, hope may have a place in the apocalyptic,[1] assuming we can distinguish between the end of this world and the end of all existence. Though

Sacks claims, "Apocalypse is what happens to prophecy when it loses hope" (Sacks 232), he omits a crucial phrase: "when it loses hope *in this world.*" Bible scholar Greg Stevenson posits that this view of apocalypse "confuses content with function. Language about the future functions in apocalyptic to provide perspective on the present, . . . perspective along the lines of hope and optimism for the future—whether that is the future of this world or of the world to come" (Stevenson 83). While Stevenson's own perspective on the present is largely steeped in a Christian view of a world to come, his observations are easily extendable to any faith system's thanatology, soteriology, or eschatology. One way that hope can function within apocalyptic is if the end is seen as an opportunity for greater transition.

It is in this manner that the apocalyptic best fits alongside or even within the modern superhero genre: "both offer perspective on life by getting us to view the normal through the lens of the divine, the human through the lens of the superhuman" (Stevenson 97). Individually and together, the apocalyptic and the superheroic offer to take audiences outside the customary, mortal frame, addressing morality and mortality on a far greater scale. They elevate, with the potential to transcend—lofty ambitions but not rare ones, as Jane Idleman Smith and Yvonne Yazbeck Haddad are clear to point out in *The Islamic Understanding of Death and Resurrection.* "The hope of something better to come has informed both theology and socio-political expectations, and the translations of the promise of a time of universal peace and justice is easily made from this age to the next (and back again)" (Smith and Haddad 70).

Therefore, while apocalyptic thought may have appeared allergic to hope in Sacks's view, it can just as easily be an essential generic element of hope. Discussing the diabolical *Batman* issue 666 and *Superman* issue 666, Stevenson centers on hope itself as the plots' respective source of conflict (Stevenson 93). "In these stories, the superhero embodies the values, anxieties, fears and hope of the wider culture. They inspire because they demonstrate metaphorically that humans can overcome the various threats and obstacles they face and so become more than they thought themselves capable of" (84). While this is all true, Stevenson's reading does lessen his earlier emphasis on "the lens of the divine." Operating as quasi-or pseudodeities is not what makes the superheroes' struggle with hope vital; rather, it is their demonstration of the very human struggle for hope on a large scale that gives their narratives spiritual value.

To be greater than the moment and yet still entirely human is the second way in which hope can function in apocalyptic, and this is the manner in which hope is experienced in *Ms. Marvel*—a manner that could be read as Islamic.

"The Fate of the World Is out of Your Hands. It Always Was."

In the summer of 2015, Marvel Comics culminated a years-long storyline in their companywide crossover event *Secret Wars*, headed by writer Jonathan Hickman. The origins of this storyline date back at least to the 2012 appointment of Hickman as writer for both the *Avengers* and *New Avengers* titles. Arguably, its genesis began even earlier, with Marvel's 2000 launch of the "Ultimate Universe" in which longstanding superhero properties were reimagined and restarted, such as *Ultimate Spider-Man* returning Peter Parker to high school or *Ultimate X-Men* depicting a twenty-first-century formation of the team. Admittedly, the company had done something similar in 1996—"killing" a number of top-tier superheroes in the *Onslaught* series, recreating them with '90s sensibilities and art styles in the *Heroes Reborn* pocket universe, and then returning them somewhat rejuvenated to the main reality in *Heroes Return*. The Ultimate line initially differed from the *Heroes Reborn* scheme in that it was entirely disconnected from that "main reality" (designated as Earth-616), which had been in effect continuously since at least 1961's *Fantastic Four* 1.[2] While the *Heroes Reborn* universe was understood as the result of the *Onslaught* series set in the Earth-616 reality, there was initially no clear connection (and, likely, no intended connection) between Marvel's primary titles and its growing number of Ultimate titles. Only in 2005 was it suggested that the Ultimate titles were part of the wider Marvel multiverse (Millar, Land, and Ryan), later given the designation Earth-1610. *Secret Wars*, therefore, finally brought Earth-616 and Earth-1610 into direct conflict with each other, as Hickman intended.

Secret Wars and its lead-in, multititle story arc "Time Runs Out" chronicled the near-total collapse of the multiverse, of all alternate or parallel existences toppling into nothingness. Of the potentially infinite realities that once existed, only Earth-616 and Earth-1610 remained, and the boundaries that once separated them started failing. The destructive overlap point, dubbed "an incursion zone," allows for heroes from each Earth to enter into battle with each other, presumably so that their own cosmos might be the last and thus remain stable. Some, such as Reed Richards of the Fantastic Four and his Earth-1610 doppelganger, recognize that the conflict will end in a stalemate of mutually assured destruction, so they outfit "lifeboat" crafts to survive even the annihilation of all outside reality. Others, such as Richards's nemesis Dr. Doom and sorcerer supreme Dr. Strange, set out to confront the source of the multiversal collapse. On the far fringes of reality, Doom and Strange find and challenge the Beyonders, near-omnipotent beings whose experiments have caused the incursions.[3] Doom, with the aid of reformed supervillain Owen Reece (a.k.a. the Molecule Man), brings about the Beyonders' own demise and uses their remaining energies to construct the last broken sliver of the multiverse, Battleworld.

Ultimately, the two Reeds' lifeboats and Doom's Battleworld will result in the restoration of the multiverse,[4] but in *Last Days*, the final incursion appears to be just that: final. And, as comics critic Noah Berlatsky observes, it gets treated far differently by the creators of *Ms. Marvel*, largely due to what comprises her character: "Ms. Marvel, a.k.a. Kamala Khan, is a Pakistani-American, a Muslim, and a woman of color; as such, she's got a different relationship to apocalypse, and to violence. The end of the world, it turns out, looks different from the margins" (Berlatsky). Even young Ms. Marvel's idol, Captain Marvel (Carol Danvers), cannot sincerely give her protégé the false reassurances that all will eventually be well:

> CAPTAIN MARVEL: How much do you know about what's happening right now in Manhattan?
> MS. MARVEL: I was just there. It looks like the end of the world.
> [NO DIALOGUE]
> MS. MARVEL: This is where you're supposed to tell me I'm wrong.
> CAPTAIN MARVEL (GLANCING AWAY AWKWARDLY): Yeah. Absolutely. Totally **not** the end of the world. Minor glitch is all. We've faced worse. (Wilson and Alphona 26)

The extreme peril of such an incursion zone—"what happens when two separate realities collide with each other," as Captain Marvel quickly glosses (26)—is underscored when Danvers tells Khan that no other reinforcements will be coming to Jersey City; all the other superheroes are either on the zone's front line or defending their own home turf. Ms. Marvel, a character already awash in marginality, is not only at the periphery of the current crisis: she is also on her own.

Admittedly, Danvers does delay her departure back to the incursion zone in order to offer the young hero some brief help and advice. It is here, away from the acknowledged center of the conflict, where some of the most clear-eyed responses to such cataclysm can be witnessed. The superheroes fighting at the incursion zone are playing their common roles as larger-than-life defenders of life. After all, this is their common function, as notes Berlatsky: "Giant purple dudes show up with funny hats and plans to devour the planet; psychic gorillas conquer the world. The apocalypse, in forms terrifying and ludicrous, is a monthly occurrence, not to mention a marketing plan" (Berlatsky). Far less common is Ms. Marvel's position in the face of this apocalypse: she is placed in a far more mundane, far less empowered state, a state much like that of her readers. "Kamala doesn't understand what is going on, what kind of mission Captain Marvel has to run off to complete, or even what the nature of the threat is, so the reader's disorientation stemming from these unexplained elements parallels that of the protagonist," observes reviewer Aaron Pound. Berlatsky agrees: "Wilson and Alphona use Ms. Marvel's marginality as an opportunity to focus on the things that usually get lost in the apocalypse" (Berlatsky).

To locate Ms. Marvel at the margins or to link Kamala Khan with marginality is not, it must be noted, to consider her marginal. Quite the opposite, this position affords her maneuvers not commonly available to central characters like Richards, Doom, or Strange. Khan can operate in what political scientist Tony Smith terms a *pericentric framework*, an analytical model that focuses on the pronounced effects and intensity of "junior actors" on a system (570). Like some of the feminist theologians that Jerusha Tanner Lamptey considers in *Never Wholly Others: A Muslima Theology of Religious Pluralism*, Khan has the space to effect "new stories, the creation of a feminist midrash, and the development of interfeminist dialogue" (104). She is afforded an agency that a character like Captain Marvel may, in fact, lack.

What most often gets lost in narratives of predicted or experienced apocalypse is community. There is a dark logic to this absence: if the world ends, then community is void, so community can be abandoned in the face of apocalypse if only to fight for its continued existence.[5] Usually, superheroes fulfill their place as our mythic figures best because they can abandon any human trappings (e.g., their likelihood to return to their mortal families, their dedication to defend their homes, etc.) and act as "divine-like beings" when faced with reality's potential demise; such narratives, claims Stevenson, help "make sense of a group's varied and oft-confusing experiences with the world" (81). Often, superheroes in apocalyptic circumstances exit the communities they defend by taking the battle to a greater stage—Batman departs Gotham, Superman flies off from Lois, and Spider-Man leaves behind his Aunt May—if only to save them.

Yet, as the end approaches, Ms. Marvel still stands with her community as a whole, a rarity in the genre. In reviewing *Last Days,* Pound notes the novelty of Khan's choice: "In the midst of chaos, rather than rushing off to punch a villain in the head, Khan spends her time and uses her powers to help those around her in relatively mundane ways, and becomes the glue that holds together her community" (Pound). In some ways, Ms. Marvel is heeding Captain Marvel's advice, since the young woman's impulse is, in fact, to play the expected role of the superhero and fight to the finish. But, Captain Marvel warns, "I know you want to help them. You're like—you're like me. You don't want to pick and choose. You want to save *everybody.* But, you can't save everybody. Not without damaging yourself" (Wilson and Alphona 39). Had Khan been called by, say, the Avengers to the incursion zone for one final surge, she might have gone. But, when Captain Marvel allows Khan to choose her place, she chooses to "keep fighting" by *remaining* with her community (29).

Perhaps Ms. Marvel's response to the coming apocalypse has more to do with her religious upbringing than readers might initially think. The first hint of an Islamic influence on her actions comes during her talk with Captain Marvel.[6] As Khan frets over how she can safeguard her friends and family, the more seasoned superheroine says, "You can't stop what's coming but you can decide *how* you meet it. The fate of the world is out of your hands. It always was. But *your* fate—what you decide to do right now—is still up to you" (Wilson and Alphona 29). It is this sentiment that triggers, in internal dialogue, a memory for Khan of her imam:

> CAPTION: What she's saying—weirdly, it makes me think of one of Sheikh Abdullah's lectures. We all face the end alone, he said. And we alone have to account for our time on Earth.
> CAPTION: The good and the bad.
> CAPTION: "What will be in the book of your life?" he used to ask. "How will you be remembered?" (29)

Such a sermon (or, more rightly, *khutbah*) could lead some to use the last moments of their lives making some grand gesture. Rushing to the front line of existential conflict is a glorious final mark in the book of life, sure—but that sort of action also speaks to one's perceived role in this life. Any number of superheroes, after saving the universe so many times already, may have come to accept their status, consciously or otherwise, in the superhero's role as "an agent of transcendence" (Stevenson 84). Khan, thus far, has placed herself outside that mythology, "embiggening" herself only to human limits, not to a degree proximal to *shirk* (i.e., not considering Allah supreme, putting anyone or anything as central or on Allah's divine level).

Ms. Marvel may be the hero, but she is not, necessarily speaking, the protagonist—that is the lie of an apocalypse, that anyone can thwart it. This is the fiction, however inspiring, of the superhero, too. Berlatsky puts his finger directly on this connection when he says, "Part of the reason the world ending doesn't need to lead to violence in *Ms. Marvel* is that *Ms. Marvel herself isn't at the center of the world*" (Berlatsky, my emphasis). She is most concerned with maintaining order and immediate safety, even as reality may crumble. Her reasoning is unassailable: "When people panic, they make bad decisions. That's how the rule of law breaks down. It breaks down when people think the rules no longer matter.... That's how really bad things start to happen" (Wilson and Alphona 10). From her position outside the center, from her identities along the margins, Khan can maintain her core principles. Social order remains a top priority for her, even during the downfall of natural order.

Khan prioritizes the keen tie to her family and multifaith community that is emphasized, not rejected, by the final hours. Berlatsky posits that her peculiar reaction, at least in terms of generic superhero conventions, likely lies in her particular mixture of identities: "As a Muslim, as a woman, as a hero, *Ms. Marvel* offers a different narrative, about how people on the margins matter, and care for each other" (Berlatsky), regardless of a larger crisis finally drawing more "central" attention. She remains a hero to her community *within* her community instead of having to journey off and act as a detached protagonist in the greater crisis. Collecting her friends, loved ones, and fellow Jerseyans together at the high school "gymnatorium," Khan is able to watch over her microcosm. Though they neither know about the Earth-616/Earth-1610 conflict nor can directly affect it, Khan takes solace from her community coming together, praying together, and even dancing together. "This is it. My whole world in one room. People I care about.... People I want to protect," she thinks. "They expect me to fix things. But how do I fix something this big?" (Wilson and Alphona 23). Eventually, the truth of Captain Marvel's words sinks in: "The fate of the world is out of your hands. It always was."

To what degree does Khan's dedication to community and her conviction to hope reflect her Muslim identity? It is impossible to say for certain, but there are a number of compelling reasons to see these factors as linked.

Coincidentally—or not—other prominent Muslim characters occupy similar positions during the *Secret Wars* "incursion-zone" event, as well as in the fractured Battleworld splinter universe. As one of the call-center volunteers in *The Mighty Avengers*, Soraya Khorasani maintains her post, and she promises to stay with a caller "right here, on the other end of the line, for as long as you need me" because "this . . . this is what we do" (Ewing and Ross 14). The "we" in her sentence is, presumably, what the Avengers do, but also, with fellow call-center volunteer Dave Griffin beside her, what people of good character and principle do. Notably, *The Mighty Avengers* series was written by Al Ewing, who also penned the *Secret Wars* limited series *Captain Britain and the Mighty Defenders*, set on Battleworld. In it, Faiza Hussain, the modern-day wielder of legendary Excalibur, finds herself with memories of the lost Earth-616 universe. Only those aboard the "lifeboats" or those closely allied with Doom seem to have this awareness; yet, she recalls, "I dream of a very good, very kind man—a friend—who died to help save the world. The *last* Captain Britain. Before he died, he *passed* that name—that duty—on to *me*. I *know* that was real. I know it *happened*" (Ewing, Davis, and Farmer 16). Moreover, she knows, speaking to She-Hulk and her comrades, that Doom's near omnipotence is artificial.

> SHE-HULK: Doom is *God,* and his *law* is—
> CAPTAIN BRITAIN: No. I'm *sorry,* but . . . *No.* That's not *true*. It's not *right*. Doom is a *man*—a man with *power,* but human all the same. He's not *any* kind of *god.*
> SPIDER HERO: . . . *Wow.*
> BARON HO YINSEN: Wow *indeed.* I believe that's what's known as *heresy plus.*
> BARON HO YINSEN: And the *worst* thing is . . . She's absolutely *right.*
> (Ewing, Davis, and Farmer 17)

While other versions of Kamala Khan may exist on Battleworld, it is her fellow Muslima Hussein who maintains Islamic *tawhid* (i.e., faith in Allah's omnipresent unicity) in a landscape shrouded in *fitna* (i.e., widespread distress, whether secular and external or spiritual and internal). She retains her focus, despite whatever else is blurred, on the truth of Allah's omnipotence and unification, even as the warped reality all around her challenges this conviction.

Additional connections can be made between Khan and Islamic eschatology, particularly in regards to the Prophet Muhammad's own role in his time.[7]

Evaluating how Khan comports herself at the brink of universal annihilation depends, in this analysis, on what Muslims have varyingly been instructed to expect and how to behave. Enough of the initial signs (*ishārāt al-sā'a*) and then greater signs (*'alāmāt al-sā'a*) can be read into the fictive events of *Secret Wars*, such that a Muslim character could recognize the crisis as *'amr*, as the onset of God's command to end existence (Smith and Haddad vii, 65–66). With a second Earth choking the atmosphere, the incursion zones themselves are a haze of crimson light, enticingly interpretable, as in the following Qur'anic prediction: "When the sky is rent asunder and it becomes red like ointment" (Rustomji 46, quoting 55:35–36).[8] And, as the situation worsens and the "lifeboats" are engaged, one could read the dissipating environment as being like "[w]hen the trumpet is blown and life ceases to exist, [when] earth is moved and its mountains . . . are crushed to powder at one stroke" (69.14) (49). Indeed, "at the end of time, Allah takes apart his creation. The firmament will shatter, and the mountains fall apart," confirms Rustomji in *The Garden and the Fire*, referencing *surah al-Tur*, the fifty-second chapter of the Qur'an known as The Mount, 1–15 (44). The Qur'an has a good deal to say about the circumstances of *'amr*, of God's decreed end, despite Islam, as a modern world religion, being not generally considered an end-focused faith in practice.

In his book *The Death of a Prophet: The End of Muhammad's Life and the Beginnings of Islam*, religion scholar Stephen Shoemaker examines the eschatological origins of the faith. Comparing Muhammad to Jesus as "an eschatological prophet," Shoemaker suggests that "what often slips through in many accounts is the urgency with which Muhammad seems to have expected the impending arrival of the Hour or 'God's command,' [believing that] even within his own lifetime it would appear" (121). He adds later, "Indeed, it is rather difficult to imagine Muhammad as primarily a social reformer, as [University of Edinburgh's W. Montgomery] Watt suggests, if in fact he expected the social order itself to disintegrate soon along with the rest of the world" (132).

Inasmuch as it may be "difficult" to hold an image of Muhammad as simultaneously social reformer and doomsday prophet, this seeming clash does not make the image any less true or valuable. In fact, credits Shoemaker, this double lens in viewing Muhammad defies Occam's razor, providing a complex and complicated figure rather than a straightforward portrait. This difficulty, too, can be found as much in the holy text as in the holy man. "[A]s David Cook rightly notes, there is some degree of tension between the Qur'an's frequent eschatological exclamations, with their vision of impending doom, and other material focused on defining the nature and structure of the early community" (Shoemaker 159). Rather than eschew one for the other, as Shoemaker suggests many have done, perhaps both can be held in view together, like an image of early Islam with depth perception.

If comic art is, as Charles Hatfield observes in *Alternative Comics: An Emergent Literature*, a medium of tension (132), then where better to showcase this complex image of a Muslim? The opportunity here is to parse "an understanding of Muhammad as someone who saw the social order and the world itself as swiftly passing away [even while] engaging in protracted struggle to bring equality and social justice to those on the margins of society" (Shoemaker 189). Of course, comics may not be the place to examine the Prophet himself nor any of Islam's revered personages, but readers can witness a Muslim balancing this tension in the figure of Ms. Marvel. It takes very little imagination, in fact, to conflate the qualifier of *inshallah* ("god willing") with Captain Marvel's admonishment that "[t]he Fate of the world was out of your hands." Khan is a very human superhero, maintaining her *taqwa* (i.e., her consciousness and reverence of Allah) even when imbued with incredible powers. She puts the lie to John Barth's famous observation that one must place oneself as the main character in his or her narrative; Khan's purity of focus comes from operating at the margins rather than rushing to the center.[9] Moreover, Khan seeks to better her society even as it stands on the precipice rather than leap off the precipice itself. It is not the end of the world that makes her noble but rather her ability to remain noble even when confronted by the end of the world.[10]

It is a tribute to Khan's character and her groundedness that, as the situation becomes increasingly bleak, she prioritizes her relationships above much else. When the moment presents itself, she takes her mother aside to admit her secret identity as Ms. Marvel:

> KHAN: I have something to tell you.
> KHAN: I'm telling you now because I might not ever have a chance to tell you again, and I don't want—I don't want to die without telling my Ammi. I don't want the last thing the angels write in my book to be a lie. (Wilson and Alphona 66)

Quietly buried in the superhero drama of that moment is an acknowledgment of Khan's own religiosity. Moreover, when Khan's mother surprises her by saying she has known all along, the elder Mrs. Khan explains her lack of anger at her daughter's duplicity: "If the worst thing you do is sneak out to help suffering people—then I thank God for having raised a righteous child" (Wilson and Alphona 70). Khan's mother can see beyond any minor infractions (e.g., going out after curfew, dissembling to her parents, fraternizing with unknown men, even risking her well-being) to larger ethics and greater ambitions. Mrs. Khan has, indeed, raised a "righteous child." Khan's religious identity is not peripheral to her mission as a superhero; it is quietly integral.

"Sometimes You Have to Face the End of the World"

As an odd mix of social supporter and apocalyptic witness, Ms. Marvel models that rare brand of hero that many superhero tales might override: the character of faith. This faith is not specifically or exclusively Islamic, but it does correlate strongly to some of the more intricate portrayals of a historical Muhammad. Moreover, this version of faith is not hope for hope's sake, an empty or mindless optimism. It is a worldview that leads Khan to new insights, not only about herself and her community but also about her mother and her most cherished friends. The same young woman who began this story arc bellyaching about a broken heart ("Is it supposed to feel like the world is coming to an end?" she asks the *halal* hot dog vendor[11] [Wilson and Alphona 2]) arrives through this dedication to her community at a greater wisdom. "Sometimes you have to face the end of the world," she realizes, "to find the beginning of something *better*" (Wilson and Alphona 71).

In the introduction to *The End Will Be Graphic: Apocalyptic in Comic Books and Graphic Novels*, editor Dan Clanton argues that comic books are an apt space for modern-day consideration of age-old concerns. "[C]omic books are the medium that comes the closest to approximating the imaginative malleability found in biblical interpretation" (Clanton xvi). In the superhero genre, this sort of hermeneutic may be more potent in the stories where characters deviate from the traditional "duking it out with powerful villains," as Pound puts it. While even the incursion zone–battling heroes invoke "the mythological language of apocalyptic" (Clanton xvii), a deeper analysis can be discerned when the characters are not, as Berlatsky puts it, "blast[ing] away to prevent the apocalypse. G. Willow Wilson . . . places Khan as a bystander to the main story; the apocalypse isn't about her. Even Carol Danvers's presence doesn't so much connect Khan to the Marvel Universe as emphasize her off-to-the-side position within it" (Berlatsky). Wilson gives Khan the narrative space to engage in alternative approaches to loss and hope. And as Stevenson notes, "although apocalyptic mythology relies heavily on conflict, conflict is not the ultimate point. Rather, conflict is one mythological trope employed to afford perspective" (Stevenson 82). Ms. Marvel is afforded room to engage in another trope, that of communal connection and inward self-reflection. Khan is left to ask herself, "What are you supposed to do when you know you're not gonna win this time? How do you be a hero when things have gone too wrong for you to fix them? How do you cope with the end of the world?" (Wilson and Alphona 62).

In the customary superhero apocalypse, hope can only be found in battling to—and against—the bitter end. In his discussion of the similarly reality-shattering storyline *X-Men: Age of Apocalypse* (which just as easily could have been *Heroes Reborn, Zero Hour, Crisis on Infinite Earths*, or any other doomsday story arc), Stevenson argues, "This vision of a dystopian alternate world generates hope by implying that the vision can be avoided, that people can fight for a better future (Stevenson 97). This proves true, ultimately, of *Secret Wars* and Doom's Battleworld dystopia. Ms. Marvel, however, finds this hope—this word she had been looking for just pages earlier—to be "something you can't break" (83), even as the world looks to falter. On the rooftop of her school, moments before reality collapses, her best friend, Bruno, says of Khan's tone, "You say that like there's still *hope*. Like we're gonna make it through this, somehow." To which she responds, "Yeah, I think there is still hope" (85).

Ms. Marvel's hope at the edge of apocalypse emerges not from opposing its coming but from remaining true to her views even in the face of disaster. As the cosmic light begins to overtake their whole existence, Bruno asks, "How much hope?" and Khan replies, "A little bit. A tiny bit. But maybe it's *enough*" (Wilson and Alphona 88). Fighting to the last is not the only way a superhero can inspire. Hope lies elsewhere, too, beyond the superhero's inspiring-yet-simple fiction and back within the principles that are just as much universal as they are Islamic. It is not the amount of hope one has, but the fact one has it, that proves enough.

NOTES

1. I will be using the term "apocalyptic" both in its adjective form (i.e., that which relates to apocalypse in its sense of final catastrophe and eschaton, not necessarily the more literal "revelation" or "revealing") and in its noun form, for the genre of apocalyptic narrative.

2. I emphasize "continuously" here, since the earlier Golden Age origins of heroes like Captain America or the Human Torch were retroactively incorporated into the Marvel universe's continuity well after 1961.

3. In part, *Secret Wars* gets its title from the 1984 series of the same name, where a lone Beyonder sets Earth's many superheroes and supervillains against each other. In that

storyline as well, Doom wrests power from the cosmic being, only to lose control of it, eventually; in 1985's *Secret Wars II*, that Beyonder is only defeated by channeling his energies into the creation of a new universe, presumably one of the realities that collapses in "Time Runs Out."

4. It is outside the scope of this chapter to examine whether this apocalypse neatly matches or significantly conflicts with Islamic *fanā'* or "extinction of all save God" (Smith and Haddad 71). That said, many of the elements discussed by Islamic scholars of not only the *sa'a* —the "appointed hour" of the eschaton leading to resurrection (Rustomji 41)—but also figures like al-Dajjal or a *mahdi* (i.e., an eschatological savior figure or redeemer), along with the resurrection of the dead, could be ambitiously mapped onto this storyline, given the proper motivation and respect (Rustomji 41). In all likelihood, however, these features were not consciously on Hickman & Co.'s mind when writing the epic.

5. In fighting against—excuse the paraphrase—the dying of the light, our heroes are modeled not to go gently but, instead, to battle quite hard. "Nothing says, 'you can commit violence now' like the end of the world. If the zombies are coming, who can blame you for shooting them? If the aliens are invading, you have every excuse to shoot you some aliens. That's part of the reason the news is always filled with apocalyptic warnings about how ISIS is the greatest threat the U.S. has ever faced, or how we live in uniquely dangerous times. We need to convince ourselves that we're more at risk than during World War II, or how else can we justify bombing people?" (Berlatsky).

6. The first hint in this collected trade, at least. The first collected trade, *No Normal*, contains multiple such references. –Eds.

7. Though Khan and the Prophet are being compared here, please understand they are not being equated—not any more than a given Muslim might aim to embody his principles and example.

8. Admittedly, as my editors rightly point out, this is a highly idiosyncratic translation on Rustomji's part, with the line more commonly translated as "There will be unleashed upon you a flash of fire and a smoke; then you will not be able to help one another."

9. For more on how a character can occupy the most attention or character-space and yet defy the label of protagonist, see Woloch.

10. "The famous female mystic Rabi'a al-'Adawiyya (713–801) proclaimed that she wished that the Garden and the Fire did not exist because they were becoming objects of people's desire and replacing the sole and necessary preoccupation with Allah" (Rustomji 58).

11. "I think that's pretty standard, yeah," he snarks.

BIBLIOGRAPHY

Barth, John. "The Remobilization of Jacob Horner." *Esquire* (July 1958): 59.
Bendis, Brian Michael, and Mark Bagley. *Ultimate Spider-Man, v. 1.* New York: Marvel, 2000.
Berlatksy, Noah. "The Surprisingly, Insistently Low-Key Last Days of Ms. Marvel." *Random Nerds*. Random Nerds.com. December 23, 2015. Web. February 8, 2016.
Clanton, Dan W., Jr. Introduction. *The End Will Be Graphic: Apocalyptic in Comic Books and Graphic Novels.* Ed. Dan W. Clanton Jr. Sheffield, UK: Sheffield Phoenix, 2012. xi–xix. Print.

David, Peter, Salvador Larroca, and Art Thibert. *Heroes Reborn: The Return* 1. New York: Marvel, December 1997.

Ewing, Al, and Luke Ross. "Sorry, We're Closed." *Captain America and the Mighty Avengers* 9. New York: Marvel Comics, June 2015.

Ewing, Al, Alan Davis, and Mark Farmer. "Theirs Is a Land with a Wall around It..." *Captain Britain and the Mighty Defenders* 1. New York: Marvel Comics, September 2015.

Hatfield, Charles. *Alternative Comics: An Emerging Literature.* Jackson: University Press of Mississippi, 2006. Print.

Hickman, Jonathan, and Esad Ribic. *Secret Wars.* New York: Marvel 2015.

Lamptey, Jerusha Tanner. *Never Wholly Other: A Muslima Theology of Religious Pluralism.* New York: Oxford University Press, 2014.

Millar, Mark, Adam Kubert, and Andy Kubert. *Ultimate X-Men v. 1.* New York: Marvel, 2001.

Millar, Mark, Greg Land, and Matt Ryan. *Ultimate Fantastic Four* 21–23. New York: Marvel 2005.

Pound, Aaron. "Review—*Ms. Marvel: Last Days* by G. Willow Wilson and Adrian Alphona." *Dreaming about Other Worlds.* Blogspot. January 27, 2016. Web. February 8, 2016.

Rustomji, Nerina. *The Garden and the Fire: Heaven and Hell in Islamic Culture.* New York: Columbia University Press, 2009. Print.

Sacks, Jonathan. *Not in God's Name: Confronting Religious Violence.* New York: Schocken Books, 2015. Print.

Shoemaker, Stephen. *The Death of a Prophet: The End of Muhammad's Life and the Beginnings of Islam.* Philadelphia: University of Pennsylvania Press, 2012. Print.

Smith, Jane Idleman, and Yvonne Yazbeck Haddad. *The Islamic Understanding of Death and Resurrection.* New York: Oxford University Press, 2002. Print.

Smith, Tony. "New Bottles for New Wine: A Pericentric Framework for the Study of the Cold War." *Diplomatic History* 24, no. 4 (Fall 2000): 567–91.

Stevenson, Gregory. "On Beasts and Men: The Book of Revelation and the Apocalyptic Superhero." *The End Will Be Graphic: Apocalyptic in Comic Books and Graphic Novels.* Ed. Dan W. Clanton, Jr. Sheffield, UK: Sheffield Phoenix, 2012. 81–99. Print.

Wilson, G. Willow, and Adrian Alphona. *Ms. Marvel: Last Days.* New York: Marvel, 2015. Print.

Woloch, Alex. *The One vs. the Many: Minor Characters and the Space of the Protagonist in the Novel.* Princeton, NJ: Princeton University Press, 2003. Print.

PART THREE

Pedagogy and Resistance

THE TRANSFORMATIONAL RESISTANCE OF MS. MARVEL IN AMERICA

PETER E. CARLSON AND ANTERO GARCIA

Good is not a thing you are. It's a thing you *do*.
—KAMALA KHAN

As Kamala Khan places the signature Ms. Marvel lightning bolt on her costume for the first time, her narration is a call to action. In this pivotal moment of issue 5 of *Ms. Marvel*, Khan declares that she will be defined by her actions and not simply her state of being. The first five issues of *Ms. Marvel* (2014) are collected in a trade paperback entitled *No Normal*, and this title speaks to Khan's struggle to define herself and establish her agency over the course of her origin story arc. We first meet Kamala Khan as a teenage girl and a fan of the Avengers. She is a child of Pakistani immigrants and a practicing Muslim. She is a sister, a daughter, a friend, and a seemingly normal American youth attending an urban public school in Jersey City, New Jersey. Some of these qualities entitle and empower Khan in certain spaces of her life; however, the various aspects of Khan's developing identity are more often in conflict with each other. It is over the course of these five issues that Kamala Khan engages with this internal conflict, her struggle for an active identity. In issue 1, Khan ponders, "Everybody else gets to be **normal**. Why can't I?" By issue 5, Khan establishes herself as an agent of transformational resistance, a civic voice prepared to protect and support a more inclusive community.

In this chapter, we explore conceptions of civic resistance and social justice in the actions of Kamala Khan and her alter-ego, Ms. Marvel. Bringing a critical race theory (CRT) analysis to Khan's actions within her community, in this chapter, we examine how the contemporary *Ms. Marvel* comic provides lessons and models for youth civic engagement. We analyze how the series depicts an ideological stance of actions motivated by social justice. We seek to frame and understand the models of resistance within this comic, guided by the following questions: How does Ms. Marvel illustrate an enactment of resistance and define social justice? What lessons do readers glean from Ms. Marvel's ideological stance? How can educators support and guide civic and critical learning from author G. Willow Wilson's text?

Grounded in our own disciplinary work as teachers and teacher educators, in this chapter, we consider the pedagogical possibilities of mapping Kamala Khan's civic resistance and what her actions can mean vis-a-vis youth civic learning today. Ultimately, we map the civic shifts of Khan's growth across the first five issues of *Ms. Marvel* as a means not only of highlighting her individual civic ideology and agency but also for unpacking the civic possibilities depicted in comics as well as in the lives of their readers. Kamala Khan's civic voice and agency are intertwined with her personal identity; her growing, adolescent sense of self; and her initially conflicted feelings about how her superpowers are presented. By focusing on Khan's identity struggles over the first five issues, we intentionally go deeper into a single narrative arc, pinpointing the opening framing of Khan as a critical and transformational agent. While this focus poses some limitations in recognizing the wider developments of inclusion in Khan's community, it also offers a lens for interpreting her actions and their transformational ramifications in future stories that arise in later issues of the ongoing series.

Critical Race Theory and the Possibilities of Transformational Resistance

This chapter builds on critical sociological and educational research that assumes that learning and systems of education are inherently tied to the contexts of power and politics in which they are enveloped (Apple; McLaren). We are utilizing sociological tools with Wilson and her cocreators' literary text to reflect on how Kamala Khan represents a contemporary political standpoint, as well as how such a text could inform the civic learning of its readers—particularly youth of color.

In developing our pedagogical approach to *Ms. Marvel*, we draw from research that builds on critical pedagogy (Freire, *Pedagogy*) and critical race theory (Matsuda). Specifically, Paulo Freire's notion that education can foment "critical consciousness" guides how we see youth engagement with texts like comics as part and parcel of youth identity construction. Further, CRT, as first articulated in legal scholarship, emphasizes the role that race plays specifically in its *intersections* with other forms of marginalization.

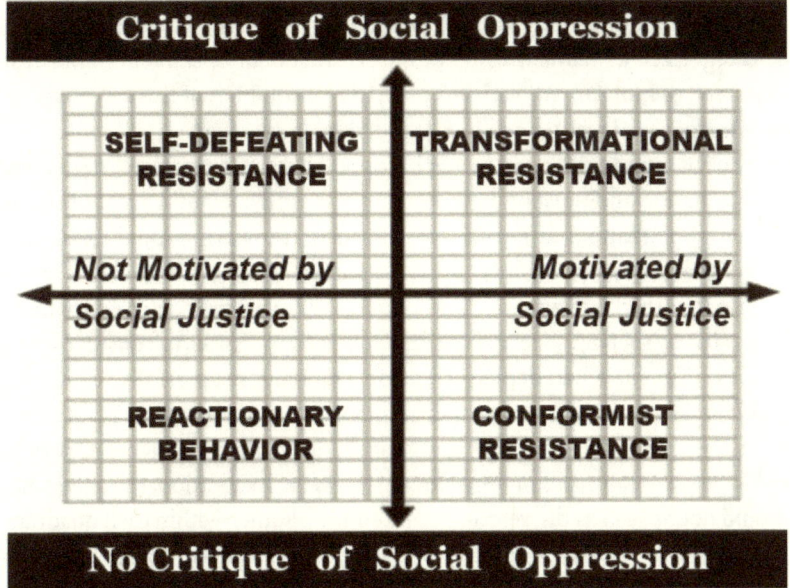

Figure 5.1 A conceptual framework for resistance; adapted from Solórzano & Bernal, 2001

CRT scholars actively identify and develop strategies to eliminate racial subordination primarily by challenging dominant ideology about race, intersectionality, and systems of power. It is important to acknowledge that CRT is not a literary theory. Instead, as a means of understanding and enacting social change, CRT is a more explicitly *actionable* theory; we posit our use of CRT and the frameworks we describe below by Solórzano and Bernal as steps toward pedagogical engagement in schools, with youth. Our analysis of Khan mirrors both the work we see happening with students, and the possibilities of leveraging popular culture in schools as a means of sustaining critical consciousness (e.g. Morrell).

In their 2001 article "Examining Transformational Resistance through a Critical Race and LatCrit Theory Framework," Solórzano and Bernal look at the internal and external dimensions of student resistance to identify the ways youth "negotiate and struggle with structures and create meanings of their own" through their enacted resistance (315). Building on Giroux's recognition of intersecting dimensions of resistance, Solórzano and Bernal developed the framework we have adapted in figure 5.1. Specifically, this image highlights the four kinds of oppositional behavior found when considering to what extent such behavior actively critiques social oppression and to what extent such resistance is motivated by social justice.

In looking at the four quadrants of these dimensions, youth behaviors can be categorized as *self-defeating resistance, reactionary behavior, conformist resistance,* or *transformational resistance*. The possibilities of this last category, transformational resistance, are that individuals enacting it hold "some level of awareness and critique of her or his oppressive conditions and structures of domination and must be at least somewhat motivated by a sense of social justice" (Solórzano and Bernal 319). As such, transformational resistance "offers the greatest possibility for social change" (ibid.). We used this spectrum established by Solórzano and Bernal, looking at how resistance can be motivated by social justice and critical of social oppression, to consider when and how Kamala Khan depicts "transformational resistance."

We want to emphasize the fluidity with which youth resistance can move from one quadrant to another and that the distinction of each category is not inclusive of all types of oppositional behavior. In addition, the quadrants should not be seen as discrete and static entities. Rather, within each quadrant is a range of a student's critique of social oppression and motivation for social justice (Solórzano and Bernal 317). Further, it is important to clarify that we emphasize *youth* resistance in this work, as Solórzano and Bernal specifically looked at contexts of youth activism and resistance. We also aim to underscore the kinds of youth civic agency typically ignored in civic research (Kirshner).

Analysis

Solórzano and Bernal are intent on measuring various classifications of student resistance in order to bring to light "other forms of resistance that may lead to social transformation" (Solórzano and Bernal 310). They assert that much of the examination of "the phenomenon of school resistance tends to focus primarily on working-class males and their self-defeating resistance" (Solórzano and Bernal 310). Solórzano and Bernal insist that actions of resistance that involve both a critique of social oppression and a motivation for social justice are transformative actions because they initiate social transformation instead of social reproduction. Therefore, by analyzing the origins of an act of resistance, specifically the social critique and the motivation for justice inherent in the action, we can assess the transformative possibility of an action. Using this method of sociological analysis on a fictional character offers readers insight into both the transformative power of a character's actions in her fictional communities and the author's social commentary for our real-world communities. Through this process, a character may become a model of transformative agency for student readers.

Recognizing the movement of youth agency across the framework of transformational resistance, we engaged in a discourse analysis of the first five issues of *Ms. Marvel*. Focused on a multimodal analysis of the "interpretative resources" of language and images in *Ms. Marvel* (Wetherell and Potter), we identified instances of youth agency exhibited by Kamala Khan in each issue. We then *mapped* where such behavior fit within the figure adapted from Solórzano and Bernal.

Our analysis of each of the first five issues of *Ms. Marvel* focused on four different readings of the first issues:

1. Actions of protagonists—We looked at how Kamala Khan understands the world around her while redefining her role within it through the choices she makes. We also looked at the nuanced entanglement of identity in the process of coming to terms with one's power.
2. Contexts of intertextuality—What are the lessons, visual cues, and linguistic nods that the creators imbue their comic with to establish a framework for resistance?
3. Referencing the past canon—As this character has a long lineage within the Marvel universe, we looked at how this incarnation of Ms. Marvel is a shift in representation of social justice.
4. Depictions of the broader world and setting of the comic—We explored how this comic book character is part of a broader ecosystem of networked learning (boyd; Castells).

This chapter will focus primarily on the analysis of Kamala Khan's actions. We see this work as an opportunity to reflect for youth the ways individuals' resistance grows and changes over time. In doing so, we are reminded of Larrick's framing of the function of children's literature as a series of both "windows" and "mirrors" that metaphorically reflect and reveal lived experiences for readers. Ultimately, by reading *Ms. Marvel* and informing one's pedagogy, an educator can use comics to allow their students to better their "understanding of resistance as a site of possibility and of human agency" (Solórzano and Bernal).

Findings

OPENING CONFLICT

Throughout the opening issues of *Ms. Marvel,* Kamala Khan is "motivated by a sense that individual and social change is possible" (Solórzano and Bernal), while seeking answers to questions regarding personal identity and societal purpose. Sana Amanat, the cocreator of Kamala Khan and the *Ms. Marvel* series editor, believes Khan's struggle to understand herself and the world around her is something readers "can all connect with" because we are all "just kind of figuring out where we are in the world and what our place is and where we want to be" (qtd. in Hennon). This inner conflict is introduced in the opening panels of issue 1. We meet Khan as she smells "delicious infidel" bacon while staring at a BLT sandwich for sale at the Circle Q, a local convenience store. This bacon is something she cannot access because of a tenet of her Muslim faith. Khan's conflict is contrasted by her nonplussed childhood friend, Nakia. We discover Nakia used to be known by an Americanized nickname, Kiki. When Khan calls her Kiki, Nakia reminds her, "I told you not to call me Kiki anymore." In this scene, Nakia is Khan's foil, somewhat more at peace with her familial and cultural heritage.

Khan continues to reveal her conflict with traditions and societal expectations when the tall, thin, blonde, and peppy Zoe enters the Circle Q. Khan describes Zoe as "so adorable and happy," while Nakia argues that Zoe is "only nice to be mean," and Bruno, Khan's friend who works at the Circle Q, simply states, "I hate her." In three pages, Wilson reveals Khan at odds with her friends and her cultural identity. She breathes bacon-filled air and wants to ensure the most societally popular girl is not ostracized. Khan is balancing social expectations with her personal perspective although not yet enacting resistant measures. Without action, however, Khan nurtures a feeling of exclusion, which is summarized when she laments her feeling of isolation, believing that "[e]verybody else gets to be normal." Khan does not want to eat the bacon, but she also does not want to be forbidden by someone else's command. She does not want to exchange a friendship with Nakia for a friendship with Zoe, but she does not want these friendships to be mutually exclusive. That evening, Khan employs her first act of resistance when she can no longer balance how things are with how she wants them to be.

At the Circle Q, Zoe's boyfriend, Josh, invites Khan to a party on the waterfront, "If, uh, you're **allowed** to do that kind of stuff." Despite the foreshadowing that she will not be allowed to attend, Khan plans to ask her parents' permission to go to the party. At dinner that night, her father forbids it, declaring that "it's not safe for a young girl to be out late at night with strange boys, **drinking** God knows what and thinking God knows what." Khan argues, "If I was a boy, you'd let me go to the party." She attempts to highlight a critique of the sexism embedded in her father's explanation. Her desire is simply to attend a social event that she believes should be inclusive.

SELF-DEFEATING YOUTH AGENCY

The refusal of Khan's father to grant her permission to attend the party puts her at a crossroads. She has identified a social oppression at play. Her motivation to resist this social oppression and attend the party is predominantly personal and not truly motivated by social justice. Therefore, when Khan decides to sneak out of her house, she employs an action of self-defeating resistance. Her resistance is similar to, but less dramatic than, "the high school dropout who may have a compelling critique of the schooling system but then engages in behavior (dropping out of school) that is self-defeating and does not help transform her or his oppressive status" (Solórzano and Bernal). Khan's actions, at best, will allow her to attend this one party, but they will not initiate any transformation of the oppression that made the party forbidden in the first place. Predictably, Khan is caught and grounded. Her resistance within the society of her home defeats her hope to change the practices of that society.

This act of resistance highlights Khan's struggle with her desires to act upon social oppressions she identifies without losing the aspects of her identity that offer her comfort and understanding. Khan does not want to lie to her parents, but her resistant act shows that she is no longer willing to allow social oppressions to continue. Sneaking out to the party does not enact a transformational change at home, and it also fails to give Khan the social access and acceptance she was seeking. The act, however, does change her.

CONFORMING AS MS. MARVEL

Amanat describes Khan as "awkward and unsure in terms of where she fits in and what she wants and who to believe about who she is" (qtd. in Hennon). This characterization is revealed throughout the first issue. Once Khan is at the party, she is greeted by Josh and Zoe. Khan accepts a cup of orange juice. Once she takes a sip, Josh reveals that there is also vodka in the drink. Meanwhile, the "adorable" Zoe tells Khan that "she smells like curry." Khan spits the drink out and walks away, embarrassed and hurt. She wanders the city, recognizing, "I can never be them. No matter how hard I try. I'll always be poor Kamala with the weird **food rules** and the **crazy family**." Despite being offended by the kids at the party, she focuses her anger and shame on her family and culture.

Before Khan can continue her thoughts, a mist envelops her, and she falls unconscious. She has a vision of Captain Marvel, Iron Man, and Captain America. In this dream state, Khan openly declares that she wants to be "beautiful and awesome and butt-kicking and **less complicated**." She wants to be "you," she tells Captain Marvel, the former Ms. Marvel, also known as Carol Danvers. Khan explains that if she could, she "would wear the classic, politically incorrect" Ms. Marvel costume, which is best described as a legless, armless black unitard with a yellow lightning bolt. With that declaration, Khan reveals an act of conformist resistance. She is no longer critiquing a social oppression. In fact, her reference to the "politically incorrect" suit contradicts her earlier resistance to sexism in society. Those enacting conformist resistance want "life chances to get better for themselves and others, but are likely to blame themselves, their families, or their culture for the negative personal and social conditions" (Solórzano and Bernal). In response to her wishes, Khan awakes in her mist-empowered body, physically transformed into the tall, thin, blonde Ms. Marvel of old, complete with the boots and the revealing black unitard she wished for.

This first bodily transformation is a subconscious action of social conformity, representing, as G. Willow Wilson reports, "the pressure young women feel to live up to unrealistic media images," a pressure "more intense still for those of minority backgrounds" (qtd. in Hennon). Khan's enactment of this conformist resistance is a portrayal of Wilson's statement, as the entire scene is filled with visual cues and linguistic nods from the comic's creators, to help young readers connect Khan's struggle to similar struggles in the real world.

Sneaking out to the party went against Khan's familial identity. After feeling ostracized at the party, Khan blames herself for her isolation. This shame manifests itself in her change of shape, which visually eradicates the Pakistani American brown girl and replaces her with a tall, thin, and blonde white woman. Khan's struggle with identity is of relevance for student readers, especially young women of color. The struggle for identity is a common theme in young adult literature for "it is in this struggle for identity and selfhood that 'newness enters the world'" (Bhabha, qtd. in Moje et al.). Paulo Freire explains that "in order for this struggle to have meaning, the oppressed must not, in seeking to regain their humanity (which is a way to create it) become in turn oppressors but rather restorers of the humanity

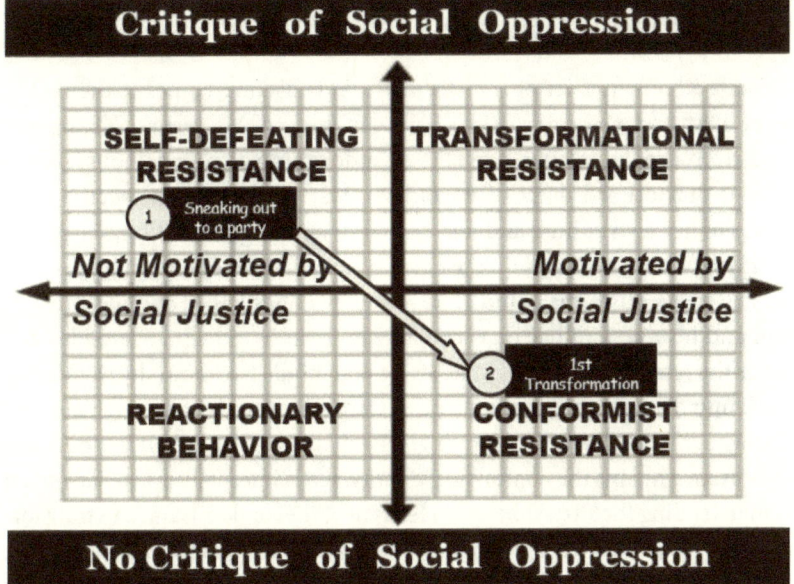

Figure 5.2 Mapping Khan's resistance through issue 1

of both" (Freire *Pedagogy* 44). However, Khan's conformist resistance seeks only to empower herself while reproducing social norms. She believes that, as Wilson reveals, "if I'm going to be a superhero, this is how I should look. This is how I've been told a superhero must look" (qtd. in Hennon). At the end of issue 1, Khan has enacted a self-defeating resistance and a conformist resistance. After being introduced to the framework for resistance developed by Solórzano and Bernal, student readers can track Khan's acts of resistance on a chart, represented by figure 5.2.

Even though Khan initially models self-defeating resistance and then conformist resistance, young readers referencing the framework are reminded that the "distinction between the four behaviors is not static or rigid" (Solórzano and Bernal). Even as Khan stumbles along the way, she is not fixed in her mindset or actions. Any progression is essential for readers to recognize in order to find a model for transformative actions. Critiques of social oppression and motivations for social justice are learned and guided; therefore, it is useful for young readers to note that Khan's creators felt that "the idea of making her a shape-shifter nicely paralleled her personal journey" (Hennon). Khan's physical malleability personifies the fluid development of her social critique and motivations for social justice. Through tracking her changes, readers can come to understand "resistance as a site of possibility and of human agency" (Solórzano and Bernal).

STEPS TOWARD TRANSFORMATIONAL RESISTANCE

Kamala Khan's first act of transformational resistance comes at the end of issue 2. After transforming into a replica of the "old" Ms. Marvel, Khan saves Zoe from drowning after Zoe falls off a dock into a river. Although Khan retains the outward shape of the old Ms. Marvel, she acts on specific principles of her own culture and family. Before jumping into action, she recalls an *ayah* from the Qur'an that teaches "whoever saves one person, it is as if he has **saved all of mankind**." She remembers her father quoting this lesson and how he told her that "people who rush in to help . . . are blessed." After the rescue, she escapes a gathering and inquisitive crowd by wandering back into the mist. Still in the shape of Carol Danvers, Khan recognizes that "being someone else isn't liberating. It's exhausting." Although her outward appearance retains the conformist identity, she is internally awakening to an understanding that "true liberation leads us . . . beyond resistance to transformation" (hooks). It is not her looks or the permission others grant her that empowers her and gives her purpose and joy, but it is her decisions to act on behalf of others. The lessons of her faith and her family prompted her to action. She saves Zoe, the person who mocked her earlier. In that moment, she models a transformational resistance. While Khan understands Nakia and Bruno's earlier assessment of Zoe, she reflects that "even though [Zoe] makes everybody feel like crap . . . I'm glad I was there. I'm glad she lived."

Khan returns home and accounts for her disobedience before her parents, and then she looks to a new future, a new existence that involves being "part of something **bigger**." Issue 2 ends with Khan standing and imitating the curled-fist pose of her Captain Marvel poster. She is modeling Carol Danvers, leader of the Avengers, a superhero striking an empowered pose. This transformation is an internal resistance, a behavior that "is subtle or even silent and might go unnamed as transformational resistance" (Solórzano and Bernal). This behavior "appears to conform to societal and maybe parental expectations," but it is "not conformist resistance because on further and deeper analysis," there is a "social justice agenda to 'give back' to her community" (ibid.).

Through issue 3, readers follow Khan as she continues developing her internal, transformational resistance. She attends mosque and school, navigating these different social spaces while pondering the extent of her new powers. She cannot answer what these changes mean for her identity, whether her abilities altered her identity enough, or whether she can "still be Kamala." She carries this question while walking to meet Bruno at the Circle Q, where she stumbles upon a robbery. Bruno is arguing with a masked gunman inside the convenience store. Khan knows she must step in to save Bruno, saying to herself, "I **am** 911!"

However, her declaration is undercut with a sudden doubt regarding the legitimacy of a hero with her appearance. Khan expresses her doubt in the moments before acting, fearing to reveal herself because "everybody's expecting **Ms. Marvel**. Ms. Marvel from the **news**. With the hair and the spandex and the **Avengers** swag. Not a sixteen-year-old brown girl with a 9 pm **curfew**." Khan once again transforms into another identity. This time, more informed of her abilities and motivation, she appears as Captain Marvel, the hero from the poster on her wall. Still tall, thin, and blonde, this transformation conforms to social expectation. This shift represents another act of conformist resistance, only this time her costume is less revealing, and she is not promoting the "politically incorrect" depiction of female superheroes. However, she is still denying her own identity. Therefore, we assess this act of resistance to be more critical of social oppression and more motivated by social justice than her first transformation (figure 5.2) but still short of the transformational resistance promised at the end of issue 2. In her subsequent fight with the armed robber, the gun accidentally fires, and Khan, still appearing as Captain Marvel, is shot in the stomach.

Issue 4 opens with Bruno calling for an ambulance while the masked gunman flees the scene. Khan returns to her normal appearance and explains to Bruno what she can of her new abilities—one of which, she discovers, is rapid healing. Once Bruno realizes that it was Khan who saved Zoe from drowning, he asks her why she does "it all behind someone else's face?" Khan once again expresses her fear that the public expects "a **real** super hero. With perfect hair and big boots. Not Kamala Khan from Jersey City." Bruno tells her that she should not care what people expect, but instead recognize what the people in their community need. "What **we** need—is **you**." This is an example of a dialogue Paulo Freire describes as involving "people who are attempting, together, to learn more than they now know" (Freire *Pedagogy*). As Freire continues in more detail, "Dialogue further requires an intense faith in humankind, faith in their power to make and remake, to create and re-create, faith in their vocation to be more fully human (which is not the privilege of an elite, but the birthright of all)" (Freire *Pedagogy*, 71). Through this dialogue, Khan leaves her conformist resistance behavior, moving toward a new transformational resistance. When the police arrive, the responding officers ask to see Ms. Marvel. A crudely masked Khan declares "**I'm** Ms. Marvel," redefining Ms. Marvel for Jersey City and the Marvel Comics

Universe. One officer contests her claim, protesting that Ms. Marvel is "tall, blonde, with big . . . **powers**." Khan triples in size and replies, "**I've** got big powers." With that response and transformation, Kamala Khan exists. Once again, her actions personify Freire's explanation that

> [h]uman existence cannot be silent, nor can it be nourished by false words, but only by true words, with which men and women transform the world. To exist, humanly, is to name the world, to change it. Once named, the world in its turn reappears to the namers as a problem and requires of them a new naming. Human beings are not built in silence, but in word, in work, in action-reflection. (Freire *Pedagogy* 90)

Khan's act of transformational resistance is now an external act. As she redefines Ms. Marvel for the attending police officers, she commits a "more conspicuous and overt type of behavior, and the behavior does not conform to institutional or cultural norms and expectations" (Solórzano and Bernal 88). This public act is informed by Khan's reflections on her earlier acts of resistance, reflections aided by her dialogue with Bruno and her identification of the self-defeating and conformist nature of her previous actions. Additionally, while Khan's earlier internal resistance was a transformation act in word, this act of transformational resistance is more critical of social oppressions and more motivated by social justice because "the self and world are engaged with each other in a developing situation" (Dewey 132). Khan now acts "in word, in work, in action-reflection" (Freire *Pedagogy*) as a transformational agent.

Khan's act of transformational resistance is also an act of potential. Because acts of resistance are fluid (Solórzano and Bernal), lasting transformation will only occur if acts of transformational resistance continually take place. Through the rest of issue 4, Khan prepares to enact a more lasting transformation. She learns from Bruno that the masked gunman in the Circle Q was actually Bruno's younger brother, Vick. As the elder brother, Bruno feels compelled to help his troubled sibling. Khan argues that she will be the one to rescue Vick from the ominous Inventor. She explains, "You protect me from stuff all the time. You have since we were **kids**. But now I'm the stronger one, and I'm gonna protect you, and that totally **freaks** you out." Her humanity is transformed through action. As Khan fights to rescue Vick, she reflects, "Maybe what I said to those cops wasn't a joke. Maybe the name belongs to whoever has the courage to fight." So she informs Vick's captors, "You can call me **Ms. Marvel**."

The fifth issue of *Ms. Marvel* shows Khan escaping from her fight with Vick's captors, but not rescuing Vick. She returns home to design a new rescue plan. However, she is once again caught coming home after sneaking out. Khan's mother, seeing her daughter dressed in a homemade costume, exclaims, "[M]y beautiful daughter is destroying her life" and "**ruining** this family." Her mother leaves, exasperated, while Khan's father sits down with his daughter and talks. He seeks to understand his daughter's resistance, and he begins by asking questions. Khan tells him, "I had to go out tonight. To help a friend who was in **trouble**." Her answer alludes to the *ayah* from the Qur'an that her father taught her. In contrast to their shouting match at the dinner table in issue 1, when they argued about attending the party, Khan's father calmly replies to his daughter, replying with hope but also trepidation, "I want to believe you, *jaanu*. But I am terrified of this new Kamala." Their relationship transforms during this conversation into a dialogue that relies on hope and trust instead of debated expectations. Through dialogue, through action and reflection, Khan employs a transformational resistance "that is political, collective, conscious, and motivated by a sense that individual and social change is possible" (Solórzano and Bernal). Khan is still grounded, and now her relationship with her father is not contentious. Before setting out to rescue Vick, she enhances her homemade costume with the symbolic Ms. Marvel lightning bolt. While applying the symbol, she declares, "**Good** is not a thing you are. It's a thing you **do**" (figure 5.3).

Khan's transformation does not occur because of her new powers; however, her new powers do force her to take action in her world. As Ms. Marvel, she saves a woman from drowning, a friend from an armed robber, and the same armed robber from a gruesome genetically mutated terrorist. As Kamala Khan, she reconciles with her friends and parents, while she is also promoting social equity and access for all genders. Further, she establishes herself as an unapologetically bicultural young woman. Khan's development as an agent of transformational resistance occurs as she confronts "social inequalities linked to racism, sexism, class discrimination and ethnocentrism" (Morgan) in her community. During the first five issues, Khan's conflicts are internal and societal. The example of Khan transforming her relationship spheres is an essential model for readers, necessary because "the education of citizens might have some direct bearing on the well-being of the social and ecological places people actually inhabit" (Gruenewald).

Khan's literal transformation into Ms. Marvel is only one extension of her transformative resistance, not the single culmination of her resistant efforts. The evolution of her actions as an agent of transformational resistance is broader than her origins as a costumed superhero. It is the Ms.

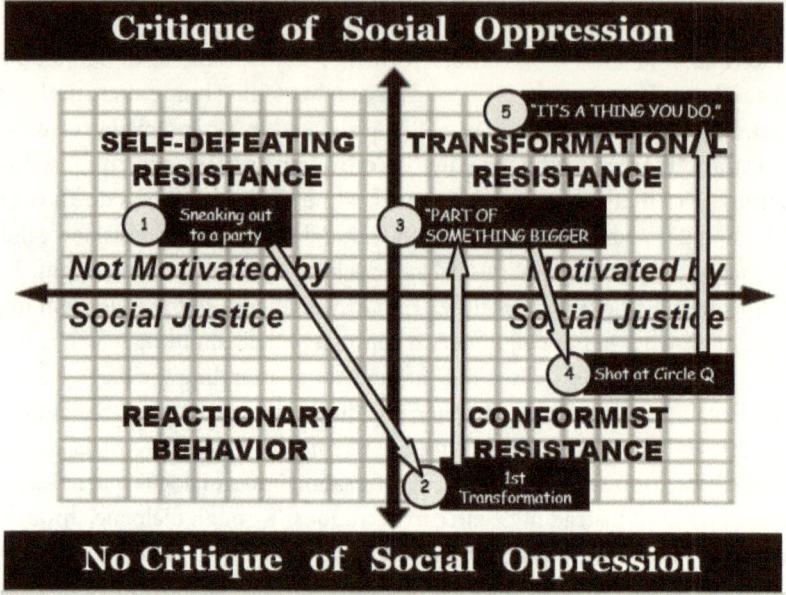

Figure 5.3 Mapping Khan's resistance from issue 1 through issue 5

Marvel persona that embodies Khan's critique of social oppressions she has experienced, a critique guided by her desire for social justice in her community. Readers find a model of transformational resistance in Khan because of her human situations, relationships, and actions. These "shared traits that transcend cultural particularities and may therefore reflect the general human condition" (Tuan) allow readers of all kinds to connect with Khan. While Solórzano and Bernal focus on historical events, we assert that models of transformational resistance can be acquired not only through interpersonal relationships but also to a reader from a text. Therefore, author G. Willow Wilson, editor Sana Amanat, and artist Adrian Alphona are also transformational models, offering various examples of resistance through the actions of their protagonist, Kamala Khan.

The Classroom Implications of Khan's Resistance

In a 2014 interview, comic book writer Brian Michael Bendis reflected, "I would like there to be more of a connection between why people read these stories and how they act. You should see Peter Parker and then want to act like Peter Parker" (Riesman). As we consider the possibilities that this new Ms. Marvel reflects both the external and internal instantiations of civic resistance, Khan's actions can be seen as clear heraldry for the civic possibilities found within each of the adolescent readers that may turn the pages of Wilson, Amanat, and Alphona's text. As Solórzano and Bernal's explanation of transformational resistance—both in the framing for this chapter and in later work—suggests, internal forms of transformational resistance are built over time. On the other hand, external transformational resistance may be "more conspicuous and overt behavior." Through Khan, Wilson's text reflects the internal developments of civic resistance, and through Ms. Marvel, her external transformation. These are two visualizations of an individual's growth: a convergence of powerful identity.

As we see a young woman come to terms with her own *power* while negotiating her various forms of intersectional, historical marginalization, we see her growth as helping shape readers' civic identities. Particularly in considering the representation of characters by race, class, gender, and sexuality, we consider how historically marginalized readers see their forms of resistance realized or ignored by the comics they read. The framework of "transformational resistance" (Solórzano and Bernal) offers "a social critique of the systems and structures which oppress them, and the motivation for social justice" (Giroux).

Therefore, introducing young readers to the transformational resistance framework as a means of character analysis allows educators to guide students through lessons focused on the theme of empowering individuals to overcome personal and communal conflicts. Using *Ms. Marvel* as a classroom text prepares students to address essential questions, such as, What does it mean to be empowered? For whom or to what are individuals responsible? How does adversity shape our character, or who we are? and How can conflicts or obstacles in my life create opportunities for growth? A close reading of the first five issues of *Ms. Marvel* also promotes the following outcomes from the anchors standards for the Teaching Tolerance Anti-Bias Framework:

> Students will recognize that people's multiple identities interact and create unique and complex individuals.
> Students will develop language and knowledge to accurately and respectfully describe how people (including themselves) are both similar to and different from each other and others in their identity groups.
> Students will plan and carry out collective action against bias and injustice in the world and will evaluate what strategies are most effective.
> (Teaching Tolerance)

Mapping Khan's forms of resistance onto the framework developed by Solórzano and Bernal, we are struck by two possibilities from the findings shared above. On the one hand, the activity of identifying the salient moments of resistance in one's own life could be a powerful, autoethnographic activity to develop in classrooms and to parallel the life captured in the pages of *Ms. Marvel*. We could see such work as an area of future study through which readers could consider resistance as an active model of reading and analyzing. At the same time, such work points to the other key area of civic-focused research, at which Kamala Khan's growth hints. While we have thus far emphasized and focused singularly on Khan's growth, we want to briefly peel back the curtain to consider how transformational resistance scales to comic creators, and—eventually—to sustaining transformational readers who directly impact the world. As such, we consider the layered nature of transformational resistance; it is an active state found in more than simply characters on a page:

> Transformational characters: Looking at the actions and beliefs of characters in comics
> Transformational creators: Looking at the paratextual statements (Genette) and writing of comics creators
> Transformational readers: Enacting one's civic agency through an understanding of the possibilities of resistance depicted in comics
> Transformational world: Networking one's actions more broadly to those of a larger youth network (Mirra, Garcia, and Morrell)

We see these layers as rippling changes in concentric circles, as depicted in figure 5.4.

Though we acknowledge that this chapter primarily focuses on the possibilities of civically transformational characters, the layers above are areas for necessary scholarly and pedagogical reflection. As comic book creators can weave in intertextual references and make deliberate connections to the "real" world beyond the pages of comics, they share a political responsibility in both their creation and their *naming* of the world around them. Much as Freire and Macedo suggest reading the word is always preceded by reading the world, the transformational potential of comics characters is preceded by the agency and choice-making of their creators. Likewise, the onus of civic learning is placed on readers (and the mentors of readers within formal K–12 settings). Such reading guides *how* the narratives of characters like Kamala Khan are interpreted and what is to come of such analysis. Does the reading

Layers of Transformation

Figure 5.4 The layers of transformational resistance

of resistance stop within the cerebral headspace of mandated curriculum? Or do critical educators extend the actions and agency depicted in comics onto the lives of students in their classrooms?

To this last point, we want to suggest that we may be describing transformation in broad strokes and that the layers between characters and creators or creators and readers are rife with additional civic agents; the responsibilities of publishers, reviewers, and "brick and mortar" comic book stores—to echo the active intent in this chapter's opening quotation—all wield the potential for powerful civic *goodness*.

Conclusion

As noted above, we see the mapping of Kamala Khan's transformational resistance as a first step in both educational research and classroom engagement with youth. Unpacking Khan's growth begets unpacking the world of Jersey City, as well as the civic duties of the authors, artists, and creative participants around the *Ms. Marvel* series. Ultimately, such work treads a path to the insular analysis of readers and our civic imprint on the world around us. As teachers, students, readers, and fans, transformational resistance is both reflected on us and embodied *by* us. We write with full awareness that the development of such resistance and its enactment by students is significant *work.* To echo once again the words of bell hooks, "[T]rue liberation leads us . . . beyond resistance to transformation" (hooks) while active reading and teaching of *Ms. Marvel* should be a process of fundamentally changing and metamorphosing the civic identities of young people. At the same time, we are cognizant of Kamala Khan's reflection that "being someone else isn't liberating, it's exhausting." We see transformational resistance as an agentic activity that looks and feels different for each of us.

At the time that we conclude this chapter, we are entering an era in which the civic voice and leadership of Kamala Khan are more imperative than ever. As the United States ushers in a president who ran on a campaign grounded in xenophobia and religious intolerance (alongside racism, sexism, and misogyny), the nuanced *identity* of Kamala Khan as a Muslim woman of color cannot be overstated. Her intersectional identity is a crucial aspect of how and why her transformational resistance is so necessary for young people to read and bear witness to. Antonia Darder writes, "If bicultural students are to become competent in the democratic process, they must be given the opportunities to experience it actively as it gradually becomes part of their personal history." We see comics functioning as a bedrock for critical action and transformational resistance in schools and society. By reading Ms. Marvel and informing one's pedagogy, comics can allow students to better their "understanding of resistance as a site of possibility and of human agency" (Solórzano and Bernal).

BIBLIOGRAPHY

Apple, Michael. *Education and Power.* New York: Routledge, 1995.

boyd, danah. *It's Complicated: The Social Lives of Networked Teens.* New Haven, CT: Yale University Press, 2014.

Castells, Manuel. *The Network Society: From Knowledge to Policy.* Eds. M. Castells and G. Cardoso. *The Network Society: From Knowledge to Police.* Washington DC: Center for Transatlantic Relations, 2005. 3–22.

Darder, Antonia. *Culture and Power in The Classroom: Education*al *Foundations for the Schooling of Bicultural Students.* Boulder, CO: Paradigm, 2012.

Dewey, John. *Democracy and Education: Complete and Unabridged.* Lexington, KY: Feather Trail, 2009. Original work published 1916.

Freire, Paulo. *Pedagogy of the Oppressed.* New York: Herder and Herder, 1970.

Freire, Paulo, and Donaldo Macedo. *Literacy: Reading the Word and the World.* Westport, CT: Bergin and Garvey, 1987.

Genette, Gerard. *Paratexts: Thresholds of Interpretation.* Cambridge: Cambridge University Press, 1997.

Giroux, Henry. "Introduction: Literacy and the Pedagogy of Political Empowerment." *Literacy: Reading the Word and the World.* Eds. Paulo Freire and Donaldo Macedo. Westport, CT: Bergin and Garvey, 1987.

Gruenewald, David A. "The Best of Both Worlds: A Critical Pedagogy of Place." *Educational Researcher* 32, no. 4 (2003): 3–12.

Hennon, Blake. "Ms. Marvel": G. Willow Wilson, Sana Amanat on Khan's Transformation. *Hero Complex*, 2014. http://herocomplex.latimes.com/comics/ms-marvel-g-willow-wilson-sana-amanat-on-kamalas-transformation/#/0.

hooks, bell. *Outlaw Culture: Resisting Representations*. New York: Routledge, 1994.

Kirshner, Ben. *Youth Activism in an Era of Education Inequality*. New York: New York University Press, 2014.

Larrick, Nancy. "The All-White World of Children's Books." *The Saturday Review*, 1965. 63–65.

Matsuda, Mari J. "Voices of America: Accent, Antidiscrimination Law, and a Jurisprudence for the Last Reconstruction." *Yale Law Journal* 100 (1991): 1329–1407.

McLaren, Peter. *Life in Schools: An Introduction to Critical Pedagogy in the Foundations of Education*. Boston: Pearson, 2007.

Mirra, Nicole, Antero Garcia, and Ernest Morrell. *Doing Youth Participatory Action Research: Transforming Inquiry with Researchers, Educators, and Students*. New York: Routledge, 2016.

Moje, Elizabeth Birr, Kathryn McIntosh Ciechanowski, Katherine Kramer, Lindsay Ellis, Rosario Carrillo, and Tehani Collazo. "Working toward Third Space in Content Area Literacy: An Examination of Everyday Funds of Knowledge and Discourse." *Reading Research Quarterly* 39, no. 1 (2004): 38–70.

Morgan, John. "Critical Pedagogy: The Spaces That Make the Difference." *Pedagogy, Culture & Society* 8, no. 3 (2000): 273–89.

Morrell, Ernest. *Linking Literacy and Popular Culture: Finding Connections for Lifelong Learning*. Norwood, MA: Christopher-Gordon, 2004.

Riesman, Abraham. "Comics Legend Brian Michael Bendis on Guardians of the Galaxy, Sexism, and Making a Nonwhite Spider-Man." *Vulture* July 21, 2014. http://www.vulture.com/2014/04/comics-brian-michael-bendis-spider-man-guardians-x-men.html.

Solórzano, Daniel G., and Dolores Delgado Bernal. "Examining Transformational Resistance through a Critical Race and LatCrit Theory Framework: Chicana and Chicano Students in an Urban Context." *Urban Education* 36, no. 3 (2001): 308–42.

Teaching Tolerance. *Teaching Tolerance Anti-Bias Framework*. Southern Poverty Law Center, 2014. https://www.tolerance.org/sites/default/files/general/TT%20anti%20bias%20framework%20pamphlet_final.pdf.

Tuan, Yi-Fu. *Space and Place: The Perspective of Experience*. Minneapolis: University of Minnesota Press, 1977.

Wetherell, Margaret, and Jonathan Potter. *Mapping the Language of Racism: Discourse and the Legitimation of Exploitation*. New York: Columbia University Press, 1992.

Wilson, G. Willow, and Adrian Alphona. *Ms. Marvel Vol 1: No Normal*. New York: Marvel, 2014.

CLASSROOM HEROES

Ms. Marvel and Feminist, Antiracist Pedagogy

WINONA LANDIS

Comics have been receiving increased attention in both K–12 and college classrooms, especially in English courses, where they are used to illustrate concepts such as narrative sequence and symbolism. In addition, graphic narratives have become popular objects of study in the academy, as is evident by the number of special collections, academic journals, and even doctoral programs dedicated to the genre. While using graphic texts as instructional tools in these settings works to expand the canon and allow for innovative pedagogy, in this chapter, I explore the use of comics beyond the writing classroom in interdisciplinary courses such as gender and ethnic studies. In this way, I am contributing to foundational work in comics pedagogy in higher education, such as in Lan Dong's anthology *Teaching Comics and Graphic Narratives: Essays on Theory, Strategy, and Practice*, which demonstrates how comics "can be useful primary texts and learning tools in classes that range from literary studies, composition, cultural studies, ethnic studies, [and] gender studies, to other disciplines and interdisciplinary fields" (6). More specifically, this chapter heeds the call put forward by Jenny E. Robb and Rebecca Wanzo to formulate an archive for comics studies that is framed specifically by race and ethnicity, a process that they note is a complex endeavor: "Constructing a canon of multicultural or multiethnic texts, for example, raises a host of questions. What groups would be included? . . . Does the canon include the representation of racial and ethnic minorities, texts produced by racial and ethnic minorities, or both?" (203–4). To this point, I investigate the ways in which the popular superhero comic *Ms. Marvel* helps to answer some of these questions about "canon formation" (as troubling an activity as this might be). More importantly, *Ms. Marvel* exemplifies feminist and anti-racist pedagogy and therefore could be taught in classrooms based around this pedagogy. Although *Ms. Marvel* is a superhero comic and is subject to the expectations of that particular graphic genre, the text also demonstrates and depicts an awareness of contemporary racialization and politics related to ethnicity, culture, and gender, which many other popular serialized comics seek to avoid.[1] By framing my textual analysis of the comic through gender and critical race theorists, I bring to light the ways in which Kamala Khan, the protagonist, grapples with villains and difficulties that reflect and mediate the societal issues of sexism, racism, and Islamophobia. *Ms. Marvel*, through its humor and imagery, is an approachable and "relatable" text for readers, but it is one that also disrupts both generic expectations and hegemonic structures of oppression. In this way, Khan's battle against injustice resonates with many readers' everyday experience; thus, she can be read as a model for how to combat oppressive forces in our lives. By teaching *Ms. Marvel* through the lens of gender studies and critical ethnic studies, this text enables students to gain a new perspective on heroism and terror, which allows them to be more just and empathic learners and community members.

Building on the theoretical work of scholars like Sara Ahmed, Robyn Wiegman, and Jack Halberstam,[2] I argue that *Ms. Marvel* holds a kind of productive power as a specifically interdisciplinary text. That is, the fact that it is a popular visual text, rather than a more conventional literary object, disrupts certain ideas about the objects of study that we use in our classroom. Moreover, the content of the text—the story of a teenage Muslim girl who is bequeathed with superpowers—speaks to its applicability in courses and classrooms that take up cultural, racial, and gender issues from a variety of perspectives and through a multitude of (inter)disciplines and genres. In other words, *Ms. Marvel* has pedagogical value not simply in terms of style and narrative but also through its thoughtful engagement with contemporary social and political subjects within its story. Halberstam, in speaking to the possibilities inherent in less traditional methods and objects of study, emphasizes that "knowledge practices that refuse both the form and content of traditional canons may lead to unbounded forms of speculation, modes of thinking that ally not with rigor and order but with inspiration and unpredictability" (10). Comics in college classrooms, although they adhere to their own particular canons, also rebuke canonicity and traditional form in such innovative ways that they invite (re)imagination of the self and society, which is so often a topic of discussion in women's and gender studies and ethnic studies courses. Since the university as an institution typically seeks out academic and scholarly "rigor," *Ms. Marvel* as a text rejects certain traditional classifications of "rigorousness" in favor of the imaginative possibility of new forms, new characters, and new and effective means of engaging with the lived experiences of those who are frequently marginalized as "other."

As a consumer of comic books and a critic of popular culture, I assumed that fans would be dismissive if not outright offended by the decision to change Ms. Marvel from her original iteration as the buxom blonde Carol Danvers to a Muslim teenager of color. Since the common assumption is that the majority of comic book readers are heterosexual men, most consumers, myself included, feel that comics are created with a specifically "male gaze" in mind, although recent data suggests that readership is divided along gender lines, closer to 65 percent male and 35 percent female.[3] This growth in female readership, as well as growing comic fandom among people of color, correlates with increasing representation of dynamic female and nonwhite characters within comics themselves, such as Kamala Khan as *Ms. Marvel*. Nonetheless, considering the historical context of comics readership, recharacterizing Ms. Marvel as a young woman of color and a Muslim seemed to suggest that there would be waves of discontent in the fan community.[4] Therefore, I assumed that procuring a copy of the first issue would be all too easy when it was initially released in February 2014. To my amazement, I visited two comic book shops known for having a wide selection, and neither of them had the comic in stock. A clerk told me that they had even gotten in a second shipment, but they simply "couldn't keep it on the shelves." The popularity of the new *Ms. Marvel* comic surprised me, and I became interested in discovering the reasons for the eager consumption of *Ms. Marvel*, as well as considering the power and potential of this emerging fan community. I have since used *Ms. Marvel* as one of the primary texts in several classes, including a first-year composition course, an interdisciplinary ethnic studies course (Asian and Asian American Studies), and a literature survey course. This chapter investigates the textual aspects of *Ms. Marvel*, as well as practical classroom engagements with the comic that highlight its significance as a not simply entertaining, but also a feminist, anti-racist pedagogical tool.

Ms. Marvel, Diversity, and Interdisciplinarity

In an interview with the *Washington Post*, Sana Amanat, editor and cocreator of the *Ms. Marvel* series, notes that part of the genesis of Kamala Khan's character came about from her own experience in "what it was like to grow up in this country as a Muslim-American" (Murphy). Like Khan, Amanat says that she "had all these questions" about her identity: "Am I Muslim? Am

I American? Am I Pakistani?" It is clear, then, that Ms. Marvel is noteworthy not only for being a female-created comic in a male-dominated industry but also for demonstrating the ways in which authors and editors, even in serialized pop culture, often embed something of themselves in their work. Significantly, as a Muslim woman of color, Amanat has helped create a character who, although obviously not exactly like her, does provide something of a heroic counterpart—one whom many other young Muslim women in the United States would also undoubtedly admire.

The inclusion of a racial minority in the comic book canon might, in this way, be a move toward greater "diversity," a move with which we as teachers and academics are already too familiar and that we often greet with some degree of skepticism. Sara Ahmed, in discussing the use of the term "diversity" as an ideal in our classrooms and institutions, writes, "The circulation of the word 'diversity' creates the very idea of the 'diverse institution,' and in turn, this idea gives the word 'diversity' its circulatability" (56). Thus, in this tautological relationship, including the term "diversity" as an institutional commitment and practice for a university becomes the very definition of "diversity" and diversity in action. Not unlike other terms such as "interdisciplinary," it becomes a happy buzzword of sorts, which institutions can point to as an indicator of their progressive atmosphere and pedagogical approach. The crux of Ahmed's critique, however, is that "[w]e might want to be cautious about the appealing nature of diversity and ask whether the ease of its incorporation by institutions is a sign of the loss of its critical edge" (4). That is, because diversity and like terms are tossed around frequently in institutions like the university, the terms may be rendered unable to do their crucial work, and in some cases their actual meanings may be overlooked and forgotten. The same could be said of Kamala Khan's presence and popularity—another example of American diversity and neoliberal multiculturalism in popular media. The question emerges: How do we continue to combat the much-too-easy incorporation of ideas like diversity, and even intersectionality, into our texts and our teaching practices, an incorporation that dulls their once sharp "critical edge"?

Rather than ignoring uncomfortable terms and concepts, Ahmed would rather we critically examine such moments of failure, as identification may be the only means of preventing the repetition of problems related to racism and sexism. She says, "The promise of diversity *is* the promise of happiness: as if in becoming happy or in wanting 'just happiness' we can put racism behind us" (165). But putting racism "behind us" cannot and should not be the goal because the very existence of diversity practitioners and departments of women's, gender, and ethnic studies demonstrates that racism is still a major problem in academic institutions. Rather than happiness, then, Ahmed encourages a productive refusal, a "getting in the way," as a means of engaging with antiracist and antisexist practices. In her terms, "The very practical work of doing diversity work brings a wall to the surface. A wall can be defined as that which you do not get over. It is not over if you don't get over it" (179–80). Ahmed seeks to validate the continued study and practice of feminism and antiracism while also pointing to a more productive method. Instead of "playing nice," Ahmed advocates for being a "killjoy" or a "blockage," an interruption, which relies on uncomfortably uncovering failures and mistakes, of the happy narrative of progress. Kamala Khan's characterization in *Ms. Marvel* may allow her to be conceived of as a productive "killjoy" insofar as her character and conflict are presented in a frank and straightforward manner. As Miriam Kent explains, "Issues around Muslim identity are not up for debate within the narrative—they are naturalized aspects of the characters." More crucially, Khan's "naturalized" religious and ethnic identity is integral to the kind of hero that she becomes, since "[t]he racism she experiences, for example, is specific to her race and nationality" (Kent 524). Therefore, issues related to racialized and gendered oppression are not merely for Khan to "get over" or overcome. Rather, readers are compelled to see the way she recognizes and internalizes injustices, both experienced and observed, in order to become her heroic counterpart, Ms. Marvel.

While the intention of women's studies and ethnic studies classes is often to bridge the wide gaps in experience between differently positioned individuals, I contend that it is far more productive to point out to students the ways in which they can fail to know and may even be complicit in unjust acts. Naturally, this is a pedagogical move often avoided in favor of making students feel better about themselves and the state of the world at large. Robyn Wiegman articulates a more decentered and disruptive methodology in the rejection of conventional notions of authority, disciplinarity, and "expertise," instead seeking out alternative (or at least the somewhat overlooked) ways of making and approaching knowledge related to identity politics and interdisciplinary fields. A comic such as *Ms. Marvel* thus exemplifies these interdisciplinary methods and alternative objects of knowledge creation that help to rethink or even reject the academic status quo. In my classrooms, for example, I have used *Ms. Marvel* to demonstrate the ways in which students come from remarkably diverse backgrounds—or, to encourage students to recognize their own privilege and the ways in which their own positionality prevents them from wholly and completely understanding the issues facing marginalized groups such as women of color and women in the developing world. In the popular blog, *Women Write about Comics*, Nancee Reeves details an experience parallel to my own in which she taught *Ms. Marvel* in an honors section of multicultural American literature. She highlights the ways in which the racial and ethnic aspects of Kamala Khan's story were what captured her students' attention the most. She recalls, "Speaking for the whole class, one student commented that '[b]efore reading [*Ms. Marvel vol. 1: No Normal*], I had no idea what life was like for Muslims in the United States. I never considered it. If asked, I would have no idea of how to answer" (Reeves). This student, in reading *Ms. Marvel*, was able to recognize their own ignorance on a particular racial, cultural issue and turn to this text as a productive and useful means of overcoming this ignorance.

My own literature students were similarly captivated by Khan's identity, superheroic and otherwise, and were able to make deep connections and observations about race and gender, even within a more general literary studies course. In a response to the text that echoes many of Reeves' students, one female first-year English major wrote that, in her view, the majority of the text focused on "the internal struggle of being a second-generation individual living under the same roof of her first-generation parents who don't know what it is like growing up in America," and the subsequent construction of Khan's "own identity." *Ms. Marvel* thus invites teachers to take an inter- or multidisciplinary approach to classes even in more conventional disciplines, such as English literature, where comics have already begun to gain analytical ground. That is, *Ms. Marvel* invites instructors to discuss how narrative and form *intersect* with race, gender, and identity, as well as to put a more empathetic, social justice–oriented pedagogy into practice. A large part of what allows *Ms. Marvel* to be read and discussed in this way is its intertextual and intercultural nature. Not only does Khan recall selections from the Qur'an when she first transforms into Ms. Marvel to save her classmate but she and her friends also make thinly veiled references to other media and popular culture and even to other works of literature. When giving herself an internal pep talk before facing down a villain, Khan states for the reader, "I tell myself I can do this. I tell myself I'm exactly where I was meant to be. It's like that Persian guy Rumi said. 'Wherever you are . . . was circled on a map for you'" (Wilson issue 5). This reference to the famous Persian poet asks readers to question who Rumi is and what purpose this quotation serves in this text and at this moment. Moreover, by including references to both Western and non-Western media and literature, *Ms. Marvel* also compels students and instructors beyond the context of American superhero culture and into the realm of global media and readership, which is especially useful when this broadening of traditional American students' horizons is done in a course and a discipline so highly predicated on Western methods and canons.

"Relatability" and Reading across Difference

With these issues in mind, it is crucial when teaching a comic like *Ms. Marvel*, that we consider it and frame it as a potentially disruptive text, one that elicits surprise, discomfort, and other types of aforementioned "bad feeling," but to positive ends. Although the possibility for creating cross-cultural connection is productive, and the ability for readers to "relate" to a female Muslim character is noteworthy, as Ahmed cautions, this "relatability" cannot come at the expense of simplifying or minimizing difference. Indeed, based on reception of *Ms. Marvel*, it is all too possible to frame the comic in this oversimplified manner. Kent notes that for many critics and readers, "Rather than focusing on the specificity of Khan's female-teen-American-Muslim subjectivity, [they] concentrated on how the themes of the book fit into their experiences.... The aspects of the book which arguably make it most feminist and intersectional were thereby cast aside" (524). Often students respond in this way, as they do with many texts, by "fitting the book into their experiences" to make better sense of the characters and cultures with which they are unfamiliar. This is an appropriate starting point for generating discussion, but as Kent emphasizes, to highlight the feminist and antiracist qualities of *Ms. Marvel*, students should be encouraged to reflect on how to connect and comprehend across difference, more than to focus on perceived similarities. Foregrounding the disruptive, critical, and political aspects of the comic enables students to recognize more keenly their positions as readers and their attendant differences from Khan, her friends, and her family.

Even though Amanat disavows any political motivations, one wonders if it is ever possible to create a strong Muslim character completely separate from the political atmosphere in which he or she is embedded, particularly in a post-9/11 United States, and particularly by foregrounding the experiences of a young Muslim woman in the culturally diverse (and tense) Jersey City. "Muslim" and "Islam" are terms that carry heavy connotations and biases, and they often evoke either the hypermasculine, extremist terrorist or the oppressed, veiled woman at risk of arranged marriage and honor killing, who needs to be "rescued" from her patriarchal oppressors. Sunaina Maira writes that, especially in the wake of the post-9/11 war on terror and earlier acts of (often violent) discrimination, there is a need to investigate the experiences of South Asian American youth in order to "help us understand the possibilities and limitations of agency and resistance in these everyday encounters with the state" (26). Within *Ms. Marvel,* it is evident that Khan decides that to protect Jersey City, she cannot rely on "the state" but instead must take matters into her own hands. While vigilante justice is a common plot point in superhero comics, Khan's identity also illuminates the fact that "the state" already excludes, overlooks, and chooses not to protect certain citizens and locations. Therefore, Khan becomes her city's alternative to state protection—often from state violence.

Similarly, South Asian American consumers, who are not frequently interpellated as comics readers, demonstrate the discursive absence and the material presence of their subjectivity through their eager consumption of *Ms. Marvel,* what Maira would call an "expression of cultural citizenship" (13). Tamara Bhalla, in her investigation of South Asian American readership practices, notes that this group is made up of eager readers who use texts to think through and make sense of their identities in the United States. Based on her observations, not only does the act of reading literature on South Asian and South Asian American themes produce a sense of community for these readers, but also, "practices of reading among South Asian Americans reveal unease about and acquiescence to the conditions of neoliberal multiculturalism" (Bhalla 5). More specifically, "pervasive and contradictory cultural ideologies of authenticity produce ambivalence as a structuring feature of South Asian belonging in the United States" (Bhalla 5). In this way, a simultaneous desire for and suspicion of authentic representation in texts and media produces an active and (dis)identificatory audience—one that celebrates characters who resemble themselves, while also being wary of multicultural pandering. Although Bhalla's subjects read popular novels rather than comics, because *Ms. Marvel* is so focused on themes surrounding South Asian, Muslim, and immigrant identity, the readers that make up her study would likely respond to *Ms. Marvel* in much the same way, using it as a tool to articulate their difference *and* their belonging. From this perspective, reconceiving a canonical Marvel superhero does hold important political power, whether the creators realize and claim this power or not. And Khan's power is tied directly to (dis)identification and imaginative possibility, not only for Muslim American readers but for Americans and Asian Americans more broadly.

The broad "relatability" of *Ms. Marvel* for many readers was not lost on my students, who found themselves connecting with Khan despite, or perhaps because of, her difference. My English literature students found Khan especially easy to connect with, as one young woman (and self-avowed Khan fan) explained: "We know exactly what Kamala is thinking and why. We go through her journey of self-discovery with her, which makes her relatable to readers who aren't Pakistani-American Muslim teenage girls (like myself)." And a male student and avid comic book reader reflected on the fact that he could not quite articulate a reason, ideological or otherwise, that "explains why I'm able to connect with Kamala Khan . . . so much better than I can with a character I *should* have more in common with like Iron Man." In a powerful moment of identification, the most dominantly situated reader found himself relating to Khan in spite of, and by fully recognizing, their material differences. One of Reeves's students likewise remarked, "I didn't really care about the superhero plot, but I loved seeing Khan's family life. Her parents cared more about her being happy than about her being a traditional Muslim girl. They were no different than my parents, who push me to attend mass and not eat meat on Fridays, but who I know will always have my back." In all of these examples, college students found themselves connecting with Khan outside of her heroic form and, in the case of the latter example, even found ways to think about their own religious upbringings and familial structures that rendered the seemingly distinct terrain of Muslim culture much more familiar, thereby counteracting many of the dominant negative popular narratives surrounding Islam. These counternarratives operate beyond simply a United States framework, as is evident from other such emergent heroes in Muslim nations, like Egypt's web-based comic series about a veiled vigilante entitled *Qahera the Superhero,* as well as Pakistan's children's cartoon *Burka Avenger,* featuring a burka-clad schoolteacher who fights with books and pencils to defend girls' access to education.[5] These heroes, including Ms. Marvel, fight injustice and inequality on the streets of their respective home nations, but their simultaneous use and reconceptualization of various visual modes of being Muslim, female, and superheroic connects them in a transnational web of diasporic freedom fighters and defenders of justice. These female heroes become an axis of connection for their readers and viewers, thus illustrating their usefulness to courses framed by feminist and antiracist praxis.

When working with comics such as *Ms. Marvel,* it is also crucial that readers do not downplay what makes her a distinct character in favor of foregrounding details that make her the same. It is certainly true that *Ms. Marvel* serves to correct preconceived notions about the severity and strictness of Muslim values and family structures. This educational purpose, for obvious reasons, is helpful, even necessary, in the United States' current sociopolitical climate. However, Shenila Khoja-Moolji and Alyssa Niccolini approach the pedagogical possibility of *Ms. Marvel* with some wariness. They write, "The heroic Muslim girlhood embodied by Kamala is constructed as a foil to unflattering, and, at times, almost villainous, conceptualizations of male Muslim characters in the series" (24). In other words, they read Khan's emergence as a heroic subject as simultaneously reifying certain stereotypes or misreadings of Muslim men, whom she seemingly must "defeat." In particular, Khoja-Moolji and Niccolini read the visual construction of Khan's father in the first issue of the comic as a wrathful caricature, particularly when he is shown transforming almost instantaneously from kind and patient father to mad, sputtering patriarch. Because there is no "gutter" or space between panels in these scenes of anger, they argue that this scene "denies the reader any space, or we might say, even, agency, to create a 'unified reality,' and suggests that this reality is instead already-established and pre-determined. Through the lack of temporal space or gutter, the Muslim man does not *become* angry and violent, he *is* already this" (Khoja-Moolji and Niccolini 32).

While I do share some of the same concerns about *Ms. Marvel*'s tendency to pit "good" Muslim subjects against "bad" ones,[6] I also think this reading of Khan's father is incomplete. Because of the caricature-like quality of his depiction in his moment of anger toward his daughter, I believe students and readers more generally can respond to his visual construction with humor, rather than disgust, especially when compared to the equally humorously exaggerated scowl on Khan's face in the same panel. Furthermore, because his visible frustration stands in stark contrast to his characterization in previous panels, often students encounter this moment as disruptive, and therefore worth analyzing and pausing over in its seeming contradictions. In this way, Khan's father, and his relationship with Khan, promotes discussion of family and love in various cultural contexts, rather than presenting an easily dismissed simplification. Moreover, in numerous scenes in which Khan must negotiate her heroic identity in relation to her everyday life, the comic depicts not her father, but rather her mother decrying Khan's secretive and unsafe behavior as "ruining the family," which is a line often associated with hypertraditional immigrant patriarchs. By contrast, Khan's father takes her aside and calmly, albeit seriously, discusses with her her seemingly rebellious actions (sneaking out, wearing disguises, etc.). He explains to her why she is named Kamala: "It's a special name. *Kamal* means perfection in Arabic. ... That's why we gave you your name. You don't have to be someone else to impress anybody. You are perfect just the way you are" (Wilson issue 5). My students typically react to this moment with fascination and affection. It stands in stark contrast to conceptions of Muslim and South Asian fatherhood as depicted in other popular and news media, wherein fathers marry off their daughters to strangers and enforce strict patriarchal values. Even characters within *Ms. Marvel* assume that Khan's family members place unjust restrictions on her as a young woman and forbid her from going out. However, Khan's Abu and her uptight but nonetheless caring mother paint a more complete picture of immigrant and second-generation Muslim life and familial love. A white male student in my Asian American studies class reflected that "Kamala is very relatable to people who in reality know nothing about Islam itself" and that specifically observing the diversity of the supporting characters, such as the members of the Khan family, helped him to recognize the multiplicitous ways of displaying one's faith and ethnic background. Speaking with regard to the cultural and dogmatic differences between Khan's father and brother, the student explained: "I believe it is critical for the author to portray both characters/personality types that appear in Islamic culture/family for people to recognize stereotypes are never true for every individual."

Although in some regard this upending of cultural stereotypes and expectations plays into normative and hegemonic notions of US assimilation, one cannot overlook its pedagogical importance, especially in our society rife with xenophobia and Islamophobia. *Ms. Marvel* crucially represents and imagines a narrative alternative to the popular stereotypes of Muslim and South Asian subjectivity, with which students are too often inundated. And, as my student emphasized, these representations are especially crucial for reading audiences that have *no* conception or prior knowledge of Islam. The beginning of the sixth issue of *Ms. Marvel* contains a nuanced example of this corrective pedagogical intervention. The reader finds that Khan's parents have ordered her to visit the youth leader of her local mosque, Sheikh Abdullah, to seek penance for sneaking out and breaking curfew—which she did, unbeknownst to them, to fulfill her secret heroic duties. Khan goes to the meeting with dread and assumes that Sheikh Abdullah will chastise and lecture her. Instead, he listens to her (admittedly incomplete) explanation for her behavior—that she has been going out to help others who cannot help themselves—and advises her to seek out a teacher. Khan is stunned by his response and asks, "Wait—you're not going to tell me to be a good girl, focus on my studies, and do *istaghfar* [penance] or something?" (Wilson issue 6). Sheikh Abdullah replies, "If I told you that, you'd ignore me. I know how headstrong you are. So instead, I will tell you to do what you are doing with as much honor and skill as you can" (ibid.). This exchange illustrates the complexity with which this text defies mainstream conceptions of Islam without relying on distance and disavowal. It is certainly the case that the dialogue between Khan and Sheikh Abdullah serves to "correct" certain misconceptions about Islam, particularly those related to the severity of its teachings and its attitude toward young women. However, it is also noteworthy that Sheikh Abdullah recognizes Khan's unique identity as independent and "headstrong," a word that the letterer chooses to set in bold for the reader and that the text does not necessarily equate with "Americanization" and assimilation. Sheikh Abdullah encourages Khan's vocation and character in a decidedly Islamic context and through his position as a religious leader. The reader cannot overlook these religious details because both Abdullah and Khan are depicted in traditional dress (headscarf, cap, and *salwar kameez*) and seated on the floor of the mosque. This visual and narrative framing invites readers to direct their gaze toward a traditional and even intimate religious and cultural space. In this way, readers, especially students, also see the way in which the text of *Ms. Marvel* itself becomes "an Islamic teaching text—one that presents Islamic values and difficult issues that affect American Muslims, and offers theology in the form of a graphic narrative" (Arjana 65). The graphic vehicle of this cultural and theological teaching is key for it is not simply by telling the story of Khan as Ms. Marvel but also in visually showcasing her growth and change that the significance of *Ms. Marvel* as a South Asian and Muslim text with feminist and antiracist potential is made most apparent.

As the above scene indicates, *Ms. Marvel* and her creators are careful not to simply rewrite dominant stories in more palatable and socially acceptable ways. Khan, as a young woman and a hero, thoughtfully reflects on and integrates her upbringing and ethnic background into her actions and choices, both personal and at the community level. Moreover, what is significant about *Ms. Marvel*, and should be emphasized when using it in the classroom, is that the text and the characters productively create connections between various ethnic, religious, and racialized groups, without relying on binaries or equivalencies. To turn to another example from the text, it is worth considering the interracial friendship and relationship between Khan and her Italian American best friend, Bruno. Bruno has been in love with Khan for as long as he can remember, a fact that is likely obvious to just about everyone but Khan herself. Despite being assured by Khan's brother, Aamir, that a romantic relationship with Khan is an impossibility, Bruno insists, "We're not that different. We're both from immigrant families. My Nonna is as crazy-religious as you are, no offense.... She and my pop-pop got married when they were nineteen back in Napoli and worked their way to the U.S. I know where you guys are coming from because I've been there" (Wilson issue 14). Just as Bruno sees important and useful connections between himself and Khan, despite their noted differences, so too students may be invited to locate connections between their lives and Khan's, and by extension, between themselves and other variously marginalized groups. Conversations like these also provide readers and students an opportunity to apply the characters and events of *Ms. Marvel* directly to "real-world" issues affecting similarly racialized youth and communities in the United States and beyond. Khan invites a comparison to the young education advocate Malala Yousafzai (also Pakistani), who was shot by the Taliban for standing up for girls' education. *Ms. Marvel* also gave my own students reason to pause and rethink their positions on refugees, especially the Syrian refugee crisis. A female Chinese international student in my Asian American Studies class wrote that

> Kamala, the main character in this book, is Muslim; the same as the Syrian refugees. In this book, we can see that Kamala is a confident, helpful, and brave girl. When she has super power, she would like to help people around her, which is a contrast with the people who join in the terrorist attacks. They have the same faith, [but] we should define a group of people because some of them threaten our society. A person who has faith is not a wrong thing, and we cannot determine [if] their faith is good or bad.

These comments reflect a simple, yet deceptively powerful, act of self-reflection. More important than strictly defining feminist and antiracist critical terms, this student learned an empathetic and reflexive methodology and ethics for the classroom and for life more generally. The student has recognized her own previous misconceptions and mistakes and shows a real desire to grow from them, demonstrating the larger goal of interdisciplinary work embedded in social justice: encourage mistakes, point out where we have previously done wrong or committed harm, and channel the subsequent feelings of surprise and discomfort into an attitude geared toward productive connection with others.

Significantly, though, Aamir sees the impracticability of Bruno's love for Khan, and while he assures Bruno, "My parents love you. . . . You're like their adopted *gora* nephew or something," he also frankly states, "[M]y parents expect Kamala to marry someone like us. Because they don't want our heritage to die out. They want their grandkids to feel connected to their religion, their language—They want their daughter to be proud of who she is and to pass that pride down to the next generation" (Wilson issue 14). This scene is, in some ways, a problematic articulation of ethnic and religious isolationism, but it is also worth noting that Aamir does not discount the validity of Bruno's feelings for Khan or overlook his own family's affection for Bruno. Instead, Aamir emphasizes his family's religious and cultural pride, an evocation that stands in contrast to narratives of immigrant assimilation so prevalent in both literature and popular media.[7] Khan, as a second-generation South Asian Muslim, does indeed make certain moves toward "Americanization," with her interest in Marvel superheroes and US-based nerd culture, but her claiming of her racial and ethnic identity in her personal and superheroic life—indeed, the fact that her religion and culture have a direct effect on how she constructs her heroic identity—helps to provide a more nuanced, sometimes imperfect, but politically and pedagogically provocative portrayal of immigrants and Muslims. Therefore, while *Ms. Marvel* does indeed recuperate negative portrayals of Islam in popular media, it does so in a way that does not simplify it or minimize its importance to Khan's subject formation and even heroism.

Framing *Ms. Marvel* in this pedagogical manner demonstrates its necessary inclusion in a canon of texts grounded in intersectional and transnational feminism. Moreover, the text enables readers to have a greater awareness of their own subject positions and to recognize that which cannot be known about the lives of others, both components of a feminist and antiracist praxis that are crucial to enacting change within the classroom and eventually beyond it. Maria Lugones describes this type of stance as "playful," an attitude and methodology that involves an "openness to risk the ground that constructs us as oppressors or as oppressed or as collaborating or colluding with oppression" (96). By instilling the notion of "playfulness" and openness to making mistakes to our students, we are also demonstrating the inherent messiness of our relations and interactions with each other. It is, of course, uncomfortable for students to confront these facts and to consider their potential collusion with oppressive structures, in large part due to the feeling of vulnerability that notions of failure produce. Yet, as theorist Erinn Gilson identifies, "Vuler*ability* is not just a condition that limits us but one that can *enable* us. As potential, vulnerability is a condition of openness, openness to being affected and affecting in turn" (310, italics in original). In this way, vulnerability is constructed not as weakness but as potential—not as passive but rather as an active "ability" that can and should be embraced as a way of producing helpful and just connections with others. Therefore, while vulnerability is often the feeling that is to be most avoided, in a women's and gender or ethnic studies classroom, an affect of vulnerability is what can allow for the openness necessary for the balanced, tempered, and empathetic forms of social justice that we currently seek.

Readers of *Ms. Marvel*, even and especially those who are dominantly situated, are invited to figure out these moments of connection, as well as notable differences, as Khan also navigates her own heroic *becoming*, which is complicated by conformity in addition to a desire for critical reimagination. This experience will likely often generate moments of discomfort or fail to produce clear-cut answers. A white male student in the aforementioned Asian American studies course noted that reading *Ms. Marvel* showed him a unique way that Asian Americans and Asian American studies can be represented and, most importantly, allowed him to focus on "the state of understanding, and the act of placing yourself in another person's shoes." This was, I am sure, not an easy feat: to confront one's privilege and acknowledge another perspective. What Ms. Marvel might be asking readers to do is dwell in certain contradiction. Critical race theorist Shireen Roshanravan asks: "What if the attempt to 'correct the mistake' was oriented towards dialogue between those with whom we are mistaken instead of with those who do the mistaking as a justification for violence?" (155).

Ms. Marvel has been constructed to speak to a specific multiethnic and multiracial generation of comic book readers and invite them to respond in turn. Moreover, it encourages those who are dominantly situated, in the classroom and outside of it, to reflect on their privilege and connect with Khan's heroism in a different, but no less progressive and antiracist way. A female student from my English composition class, who hoped one day to be a high school humanities teacher, wrote, "We have to work to reform education in order to make diverse students like Kamala feel more sure of and comfortable with their ethnic identities in American culture." She cited *Ms. Marvel* as a possible text that she could see herself using in her classroom one day, to help her develop a more socially just and empathetic environment. Thus, despite its creators' reliance on the neoliberal rhetoric of sameness amidst difference, it is Khan's distinct difference that creates an axis of identification for her readers, especially those who are members of the South Asian American and Muslim diaspora. A fellow educator called attention to this comic's potential in a fan letter published in the backmatter of *Ms. Marvel*:

As a high school English teacher in a diverse district with many Muslim students and the fifth highest rate of refugee enrollees, I want to thank the creators and editorial staff for the blessed gift of Kamala Khan.... [M]y students adore her—my students of ALL races.... Through Kamala, I have been able to draw out some of my shy, displaced and culturally isolated students through a character who they relate to and for that I can never repay you. (Wilson issue 11)

Ms. Marvel is by no means a perfect text, one that is beyond critical analysis and careful reading, but it is the nuance and imperfection therein that allows this comic, as the above letter indicates, to reach wide audiences and to affect students in noteworthy and powerful ways. By forcing us to confront sticky and complicated subjects related to identity, racism, oppression, and cultural expectations, *Ms. Marvel* urges us to relate to and connect with our fellow learners and community members in ways that allow us to question, if not outright disrupt, dominant means of knowledge making and social engagement. One female student in an English composition class of mine considered *Ms. Marvel* a kind of "guide to life" and noted that it could help audiences learn to identify and avoid discrimination and racism. She explained that these comics "break down the concept of treating everyone equally into the simplest of terms, because even adults can benefit from learning things like children: plain, simple, and straightforward." To provide a more generous take on this sentiment, perhaps it is that comics like *Ms. Marvel* are not so simple at all, but rather push readers to confront uncomfortable ideas and images related to racism, sexism, and xenophobia in contemporary America, ideas that we all must diligently learn to combat.

NOTES

Portions of this chapter were published previously by the author in "Diasporic (Dis)identification: The Participatory Fandom of *Ms. Marvel,*" in *South Asian Popular Culture* (October 2016).

    1. Notably, Marvel Comics has done a great deal to "diversify" (for lack of a better term) its comic book heroes in recent years, including not only the Muslim Ms. Marvel but also a Korean American Hulk and an Afro-Cuban Spider-Man. I would argue, though, that not all of Marvel's titles engage with political, social, and racial issues as directly as *Ms. Marvel* often does.

    2. Although Halberstam published *The Queer Art of Failure*, which I reference here, as Judith Halberstam, I refer to him in this chapter as Jack in respect to his current identity.

    3. These numbers are based on data gathered at New York Comic Con (NYCC) in October of 2017. Statistical data was gathered by Kristen McLean of the market research

engine NPD BookScan: https://icv2.com/articles/news/view/38709/nycc-insider-sessions-powered-icv2-a-demographic-snapshot-comics-buyers.

4. There are several bloggers and online writers, including Corrina Lawson or "GeekMom" at *Wired*, who have written on the varied fan reactions to "reboots" of well-loved series. But the comments posted at the end of the articles are the best way to get an understanding of how the fans felt. This example also gives a helpful overview of the changes in DC's reboot of their comic book canon, which they dubbed the "New 52": http://the-artifice.com/current-state-of-the-comic-book-industry-dc-and-the-new-52/.

5. Given the scope of this chapter, I do not have the time or space to address *Qahera the Superhero* and *Burka Avenger* in greater detail, but, in future projects, I plan to more fully unpack these visual narratives as a means of thinking through the construction and circulation of Muslim female embodiment and Muslim feminism in visual and digital media. For more information on both texts at present, see Arjana.

6. In issues 14 through 16, for example, Khan becomes enamored with a handsome young Muslim man, who quickly transforms into her superpowered enemy. The way in which his character, as compared to Khan, evokes images of the dangerous "terrorist" is admittedly quite problematic. Khan's conservative yet peaceful brother Aamir counteracts this negative reading of Muslim male youth, however.

7. Compellingly, in the most recent plot arc, Aamir courts and marries a black Muslim woman, whose parents are African American Christians. With more space and time, this cross-racial, cross-ethnic relationship and engagement with the oft overlooked black Muslim community would merit further analysis.

BIBLIOGRAPHY

Ahmed, Sara. *On Being Included: Racism and Diversity in Institutional Life*. Durham, NC: Duke University Press, 2012.

Arjana, Sophia Rose. *Veiled Superheroes: Islam, Feminism, and Popular Culture*. Lanham, MD: Lexington Books, 2017.

Bhalla, Tamara. *Reading Together, Reading Apart: Identity, Belonging, and South Asian American Community*. Urbana: University of Illinois Press, 2016.

Dong, Lan. *Teaching Comics and Graphic Narratives: Essays on Theory, Strategy, and Practice*. Jefferson, NC: McFarland, 2012.

Gilson, Erinn. "Vulnerability, Ignorance, and Oppression." *Hypatia* 26, no. 2 (2011): 308–32.

Halberstam, Judith (Jack). *The Queer Art of Failure*. Durham, NC: Duke University Press, 2011.

Haroon, creator. *Burka Avenger*. Television series. Unicorn Black, Pakistan, 2013–2016.

Kent, Miriam. "Unveiling Marvels: *Ms. Marvel* and the Reception of the New Muslim Superheroine." *Feminist Media Studies* 15, no. 3 (2015): 522–27.

Khoja-Moolji, Shenila S., and Alyssa D. Niccolini. "Comics as Public Pedagogy: Reading Muslim Masculinities through Muslim Femininities in *Ms. Marvel*." *Girlhood Studies* 8, no. 3 (2015): 23–39.

Landis, Winona. "Diasporic (Dis)identification: The Participatory Fandom of *Ms. Marvel*." *South Asian Popular Culture* 14, nos. 1–2 (October 2016): 33–47.

Lugones, Maria. *Pilgrimages/Peregrinajes: Theorizing Coalition against Multiple Oppressions*. New York: Rowman and Littlefield, 2003.

Maira, Sunaina Marr. *Missing: Youth, Citizenship, and Empire After 9/11*. Duke University Press, 2009.

Mohamed, Deena. *Qahera the Superhero*. Webcomic. http://qaherathesuperhero.com.

Murphy, Zoeann. "Meet the New Ms. Marvel: A Muslim Teenager." Interview with Sana Amanat. *Washington Post TV*. 2014. Web. November 23, 2014.

Reeves, Nancee. "Comics Academe: Teaching *Ms. Marvel*—Part One." *Women Write about Comics*. January 26, 2016. http://womenwriteaboutcomics.com/2016/01/26/teaching-ms-marvel-part-one/. Accessed January 8, 2018.

Robb, Jenny E., and Rebecca Wanzo. "Finding Archives/Making Archives: Observations on Conducting Multicultural Comics Research." *Multicultural Comics: From Zap to Blue Beetle*. Ed. Frederick Luis Aldama. Austin: University of Texas Press, 2010. 202–19.

Roshanravan, Shireen. "Post 9/11 Shifts in Racial Formation: Tracing Complicity and Mapping Possibility for U.S. South Asian Community." *Works and Days* 29, no. 57/58 (2011): 143–57.

Wiegman, Robyn. *Object Lessons*. Durham, NC: Duke University Press, 2012.

Wilson, G. Willow. *Ms. Marvel*. Issues 1–15. New York: Marvel Comics, 2014.

MORE THAN A MASK, BURKINI, AND TIGHTS

Fighting Misrepresentations through Ms. Marvel's Costume

KRISTIN M. PETERSON

In contemporary portrayals of Muslim women in American TV and films, the headscarf is often used to reduce the women to their religion, which becomes an all-encompassing force in their lives. Such representations suggest that the only way to fully "liberate" Muslim women, so they can assimilate into American culture, is to remove the veil and abandon Islam—hence, the common visual trope of Muslim women unveiling and disrobing. As the veil becomes a tried-and-true symbol of the oppression of Islam, it is rare to see a Muslim woman without a headscarf in mainstream media, which is especially problematic since Muslim American women express their religious identities through a multitude of visual styles and practices. This overreliance on the headscarf as a symbol reduces Muslim women to one-dimensional characters who are motivated only by their religion.

The popular culture figure of Kamala Khan/Ms. Marvel emerged in 2014 as an antidote to this tired stereotype of Muslim women as covered, oppressed, and voiceless victims of Islam and Muslim men. Khan is easily one of the most complex Muslim American characters to be exposed to a mainstream American audience. She is a sixteen-year-old Muslim American who lives in Jersey City, but the series focuses on other aspects of her identity besides her religion, such as her identity as the daughter of Pakistani immigrants, a fan of comic books, and an Inhuman superhero trying to save the world from evil. Instead of presenting Khan as a one-dimensional stereotype, the creators, Sana Amanat and G. Willow Wilson, drew from their own experiences as Muslim women to create a complex and multidimensional character who is defined by much more than her religion.

The complexities of Khan's identity are presented visually in her appearance and clothing. In this chapter, I focus on how the clothing, specifically

Ms. Marvel's costume, can be seen as a political statement of resistance to common misrepresentations of Muslim women. Through an examination of scholarship on fashion as political action, I argue that the character of Ms. Marvel does important political work to shift public perceptions of Muslim Americans. The creators visually portray her as a character who seamlessly moves between various categories. Her superhero costume, which she created herself, highlights different aspects of her identity. Her complex representation allows readers from different backgrounds to relate to Ms. Marvel as a Muslim American, daughter of immigrants, fan of nerd culture, and teenager who does not fit in. While the character of Ms. Marvel also does political work in what she says and does throughout the series, this essay focuses on her image and her fashion not only because of their uniqueness but also because of how fans have used her image in cosplay, fan art, and posters to represent her positive values. Khan is proud of her background as a Muslim, daughter of Pakistani immigrants, superhero, and nerdy teenager. All of those aspects of her identity are exhibited in her costume as Ms. Marvel.

This chapter addresses how everyday practices, aesthetics, and fashion have been theorized as forms of political action. Within the current political context, more and more individuals are kept out of the spaces of legitimate political action, and the aesthetic styles of popular culture become important avenues for alternative politics. Specifically, fashion and visual styles can provide a space for political resistance against overgeneralized representations of Muslim Americans. Since Muslim women are sometimes prohibited from participating in formal political spaces and conversations, aesthetic spaces become an avenue where they can assert different understandings of fashion, modesty, and beauty. In connection to theories on fashion and aesthetic styles as political action, this chapter analyzes the physical appearance of Khan/Ms. Marvel throughout the series, focusing on the transformation of her costume as these changes connect to Khan's larger identity issues. Finally, I examine how fans have engaged with the image of Ms. Marvel through online artwork, creating and wearing Ms. Marvel cosplay outfits and using Ms. Marvel's image to counter hate.

The Emergence of Ms. Marvel in the Current Political Moment

Currently, as spaces of political action continue to narrow and political parties increasingly serve corporate interests, individuals seek opportunities for political resistance through creative projects, popular culture, daily practices, and new media spaces. Muslim American women are further marginalized from traditional political spaces because of compounding factors such as their presumed foreignness, their gender, and their religion. The popular form of comics and the aesthetic styles of fashion provide spaces to highlight these marginalized perspectives, and a sixteen-year-old Muslim American nerd turned superhero can become a relatable figure to also highlight the diverse experiences of young Americans.

Jacques Rancière theorizes the current postpolitical moment as a time in which marginalized voices cannot offer alternative perspectives in order to induce social change. Rancière understands real politics as reliant on what he calls "dissensus" or different ways of sensing the world. What we might typically consider as politics is really a way of maintaining consensus—one standard way of experiencing ideas through the senses. Politics should be about allowing for dissensus or creating "an intervention in the visible and the sayable" (Rancière *Dissensus* 37). Political action creates spaces for people to appear and new avenues for making sense of the world. As Rancière explains, politics "begins when they make the invisible visible, and make what was deemed to be the mere noise of suffering bodies heard as a discourse concerning the 'common' of the community" (139). In other words, for the creators of the Ms. Marvel comic series to demonstrate through aesthetic elements and fashion styles that Muslim American lives deserve to be visible and valued in American public life constitutes political action.

The popular medium of comics can be a flexible space for creators to present alternative perspectives and to experiment with hybrid visual styles. Instead of being portrayed as oppressed and voiceless, Ms. Marvel is consistently shown as a complex and vocal individual. She is strong, moral, independent, creative, funny, and caring. Because of her intersectional identity, readers of various backgrounds can connect to Ms. Marvel, making her one of the most relatable Muslim American characters in popular culture. Ms. Marvel's appearance is also political because of how she uses her clothing to demonstrate pride in her faith and her Pakistani culture. Additionally, Ms. Marvel enacts political work through her visual style because she is shown as a modest, intelligent, and assertive young woman instead of as mindless, submissive, or hypersexualized, as women in comics have too often been represented.

The idea for Kamala Khan came from Marvel editor Sana Amanat and conversations she had with her fellow editor Steve Wacker about her experiences growing up as a Muslim American and the child of Pakistani immigrants. Amanat explains in a TEDx talk how she wanted to create a character who related to her experiences growing up, as a girl who did not fit into the categories that were pushed upon her. Amanat states, "Kamala Khan is so much larger than just a pop culture icon. She came together in response to that global subconscious desire for representation. For those Muslim American bacon-sniffing, short, nerdy girls like me, and for anyone else, regardless of their gender, sexuality, race, religion who just feel like misfits themselves" (Amanat). The creation of Ms. Marvel came out of a desire for more complex representations of Muslims, but Amanat has frequently stated that Khan is about more than just being a Muslim. As Amanat explained in another interview, "As much as Islam is a part of Kamala's identity, this book isn't preaching about religion or the Islamic faith in particular. It's about what happens when you struggle with the labels imposed on you, and how that forms your sense of self. It's a struggle we've all faced in one form or another, and isn't just particular to Kamala because she's Muslim. Her religion is just one aspect of the many ways she defines herself" (Wheeler). Amanat wanted to create a character who would represent more of the universal experiences of all teenagers who do not feel like they fit into the mainstream, popular aspects of high school culture.

Amanat and Wacker then asked G. Willow Wilson to write the *Ms. Marvel* series because of Wilson's experiences writing both graphic novels and more traditional novels about Muslim characters. Wilson, who is also Muslim American, has discussed how she and Amanat "wanted to ... paint a much more realistic portrait of what life is like for a young American Muslim girl, and not to paint over the uncomfortable parts" (Werdine). As Wilson continued, "We try to show the reader that Islam is not monolithic, that there are divisions of belief and practice within the community and within individual families" (ibid.). The creators of *Ms. Marvel* set out to present an alternative representation of a Muslim American teenager that went beyond just reacting to negative stereotypes of Islam. Instead, Amanat and Wilson strove to break out of these stereotypes altogether and to present a teenager who is struggling with her identity, with Islam as only one aspect of her background.

Everyday Practices as Politics

To counter dominant assumptions of Muslim American lives, the character of Ms. Marvel employs not just the popular space of comics but also her dress and daily practices. In his book *The Practice of Everyday Life,* Michel de Certeau argues that the majority of people who are left out of politics find space to resist through the actions of everyday life. Instead of focusing on countercultures that try to live separate from the dominant culture, he argues that most people "consume" the dominant culture, but the resistance resides in what the individuals do with that dominant culture (de Certeau xiii). The culture is not static; people use and transform culture in whatever ways benefit their interests. De Certeau writes, "Users make (*bricolent*) innumerable and infinitesimal transformations of and within the dominant cultural economy in order to adapt it to their own interests and their own rules" (de Certeau xix–xv). These actions to transform and reshape the culture, de Certeau would argue, are political. For example, there are certain social norms around fashion and dressing, but Muslim women who might feel restricted are able to resist and remake social rules around fashion through their daily choices of what to wear.

De Certeau acknowledges that structures are powerful, but in his examination of the tension between structure and agency, he narrows in on moments when individuals have the agency to resist dominant powers. De Certeau engages with Michel Foucault's work on how individuals are caught in "nets of discipline" (qtd. in de Certeau xvi). Within Foucault's understanding, power is not top-down, but dispersed throughout society. Since individuals are exposed to small moments of power and discipline, de Certeau focuses on how "these procedures and ruses of consumers compose the network of an antidiscipline" (ibid.). In other words, if power is dispersed in society through multiple tactics of discipline, then individuals cannot resist through what Foucault calls a "grand refusal," but instead through tactics of resistance, or what de Certeau calls a "multitude of 'tactics' articulated in the details of everyday life" (xv). For de Certeau, then, these tactics of resistance are political actions. Since the majority of people are left out of institutions of power, they can only resist through their everyday practices. Even though these actions do not cause major disruptions in society, these small acts build up broader resistance against dominant powers.

As a Muslim woman and the daughter of Pakistani immigrants, the character of Kamala Khan finds herself in a situation similar to that of other people who experience the marginalization of their voices in formal political spaces. Khan is shown using everyday tactics in her dress and actions to emphasize her religious and cultural background and to reinforce her right to be seen and heard in public spaces. Instead of embracing the Western values that most superheroes espouse, Ms. Marvel proudly incorporates values into her superhero work that she has gained from her religion and her family's culture, as a way to fight for justice and protect the weak. Khan's choice of clothing is a daily gesture that allows her to create not just resistance but also her own way of dwelling in the world.

When not dressed as a superhero, Khan's daily fashion as a teenager is a creative technique to display her multifaceted identity. She frequently wears shirts that show her love of comics, such as a Ms. Marvel sweatshirt and a shirt featuring Captain America's stars and stripes. Khan also wears clothing that incorporates her family's culture and faith. For instance, on the cover of the first volume of the series, she is wearing a bracelet on her right hand that spells out "Kamala" in Arabic script. The bracelet points to a touching moment in the series when Khan's father explains that her name means "perfection" in Arabic. Additionally, on the cover of the third volume of the series, Khan is shown in her Ms. Marvel costume, punching with one hand and sporting henna designs on her other hand, which again point to her cultural heritage. As a counterpoint to dominant Western stereotypes of Islam as backwards, foreign, and threatening, the visual portrayal in the comic series celebrates the beauty of Khan's religion and culture.

There are also several scenes throughout the series when Khan wears Pakistani cultural dress to go to a social event with her family. In the third collected trade, an interesting sequence of events transforms Khan's clothing in its symbolism and purpose. At the start of the scene, Khan is wearing a casual *shalwar kameez*, a Pakistani-style long tunic, along with the same red *dupatta* that she wears as Ms. Marvel. Khan is running late to go to the mosque with her brother, so she is shown running down the stairs, her *dupatta* flowing behind her like it does in a Ms. Marvel action shot. When she is at the mosque, the red scarf that is used as a superhero cape doubles as a head covering for prayer. After prayer is over, Khan puts her Ms. Marvel lightning bolt sweatshirt on over her Pakistani tunic and drapes her scarf back over her neck. She is then shown (figure 6.1) walking down the street with a unique combination of clothing items: her Pakistani-style tunic, a Ms. Marvel sweatshirt, and her cape/headscarf. Khan does not appear bothered by what might be seen as contradictions in her appearance since she uses these clothing items to negotiate her various subject positions. The red scarf, for example, a single piece of fabric, allows Khan to seamlessly move among her identities. The everyday tactics of dress allow the creators of Ms. Marvel to demonstrate something elemental but too often forgotten in our current political moment: Muslim Americans are complex individuals who incorporate Islamic values into their lives but hold values and interests outside of religion as well.

Figure 6.1 Wilson and Alphona, *No Normal*

Fashion as Politics

As discussed in the introduction of this essay, the specific daily practice of dressing can act as a political action that allows subjects to communicate certain values and to negotiate various identity markers. Through the development of Khan's sartorial identity as Ms. Marvel, fashion becomes a useful tool to demonstrate the multifaceted experiences of Muslim Americans. Fashion has been understood in academic studies as not only the commercialized institutions of high fashion but also the everyday practices of dressing that associate an individual with a larger social group or trends. While work on the fashion styles of subcultures by scholars like Dick Hebdige has been significant in understanding how certain groups engage with the political potential of fashion to resist dominant powers (Hebdige), Joanne Entwistle builds on his work by examining how such clothing interacts with the body and analyzing the process of getting dressed as an "embodied activity" (10). Entwistle studies the "complex dynamic relationship between the body, dress, and culture," instead of just interpreting the meaning of clothing (11). In other words, fashion and the process of getting dressed should be understood as private activities that individuals undertake in relationship to larger social forces. According to Entwistle, clothing is the mediated space in between the individual self and society; getting dressed is always both a private and a public activity. As Entwistle explains, "Our bodies are not just the place from which we come to experience the world, but it is through our bodies that we come to be seen in the world" (29). Fashion grants individuals some autonomy, but they are always situated within larger social structures.

The positioning of fashion in between structure and agency is significant to Entwistle's work. Dress is a way for individuals to negotiate between larger social norms, the fashion system, and individual social positions, such as class, gender, or race. As Entwistle writes, "structures such as the fashion system impose parameters around dress; however, within these constraints, individuals can be creative in their interpretations of fashion and their practices of dress" (40). Fashion allows for a degree of individual resistance without disregarding the power of social structures. Susan Kaiser also argues that individuals use fashion as a way of negotiating one's subject position within larger power structures, and she explains further that subject formation is "dynamic, because individuals generally have some degree of *agency*: the freedom or ability to exert one's voice and to resist power relations in some way" (Kaiser 21). When someone chooses what to wear, she has individual agency but within the limits of regulations that come from different aspects of her life. For example, a Muslim woman may face restrictions based on her religion, ethnicity, and gender. Fashion does not offer individuals complete freedom to resist social structures, but fashion does provide individuals with agency to resist in small moments, as de Certeau suggests.

Kaiser is also focused on how fashion allows individuals to negotiate varied and interconnected subject positions. According to Kaiser, fashion "highlights the multiple intersections and entanglements among gender, race, ethnicity, national identity, social class, sexuality, and other facets of our identities" (4). Studies of fashion should focus on these intersections, complexities, ambivalences, and contradictions, all reflected in an individual's choice of what to wear. Individuals have multiple subject positions that they are always negotiating in their fashion decisions. Kaiser is especially interested in "the overlapping or 'in between' spaces, through which fashion subjects exercise agency and articulate more than one subject position simultaneously" (37). Kaiser's emphasis on intersectionality and in-between spaces is useful for examining the experiences of American Muslim women who repeatedly use fashion to negotiate competing tensions within their identities.

Figure 6.2 Wilson and Alphona, *No Normal*

The Political Power of Ms. Marvel and Her Costume

A character like Ms. Marvel is under constant pressure to use her clothing and visual style to represent Islam in a positive light, to present herself as an independent teenager who is not oppressed by Islam, to exhibit pride in her religion and culture, and to avoid portraying herself as a hypersexualized female superhero. Ms. Marvel must work against several competing stereotypes and pressures based on her intersectional identity. Fashion provides an effective means of negotiating these pressures and resisting oversimplification. These in-between spaces also have the potential to produce effective political action, as Muslim women claim that their hybrid fashion styles are just as aesthetically attractive and stylish as dominant Western styles.

Khan's identity struggles are key to both her development as a superhero and to how her clothing and costume transform throughout the series. The transformation of her clothing demonstrates Entwistle's emphasis on getting dressed as a private activity that individuals like Khan undertake while conscious of the way they will appear in public spaces. We are first introduced to Khan in a scene with her friends at the local convenience store and high school hangout, Circle Q. In this opening scene (figure 6.2), Khan is presented in contrast to both her Muslim friend, Nakia, who wears the headscarf, and a popular girl at school, Zoe, who wears a revealing top and short shorts. Zoe is the only female character in the scene not wearing a jacket or sweater, which highlights how she is also using style, but here, to perform her identity as a popular and attractive student who wants to call attention to her body.

Figure 6.3 Wilson and Alphona, *No Normal*

Khan's clothing in this scene highlights her identity in a different way; she is wearing more modest clothing than the popular girl, but she is not wearing a headscarf. Khan's identity is marked by her sweatshirt, which illustrates her love of comics: the lightning bolt is the symbol of the original Ms. Marvel. Instead of wearing clothing that would mark her as popular and trendy like Zoe, Khan chooses clothing that is comfortable and unique and that showcases her comic book fandom. While she does not wear the headscarf, her clothing is still modest. When Khan occupies her own identity, she never wears revealing clothing, and she is never portrayed as overtly sexualized.

Khan's difficulty in negotiating her identity is demonstrated clearly in her visual portrayal, from her first moments as a superhero to her finalized costume as Ms. Marvel. When Khan first develops her shapeshifting powers, she immediately shifts into looking just like her idol, Carol Danvers as Ms. Marvel. She transforms from a short, brown-haired, brown-skinned teenager to a tall, slim white woman with blond hair and blue eyes (figure 6.3). While

Figure 6.4 Ms. Marvel by Frank Cho, writer Brian Reed, *Best of the Best*

Khan is not quite as voluptuous as Carol Danvers was in the original Ms. Marvel series (figure 6.4), she still appears as sexually attractive: the costume is tight and reveals her shoulders and upper legs.

Khan wears this costume, as well as Danvers's identity, when she performs her first rescue: to save her fellow student and earlier tormentor, Zoe, from drowning. When Khan first transforms into a superhero, she embodies the hypersexualized feminine style from traditional comics and superhero films, a style similar to Zoe's. While such sexualization is the dominant way that women are portrayed in American popular culture, Khan appears physically uncomfortable and even weak in these clothes. She discusses how she always dreamed about being a superhero like Captain Marvel, but living in the skin of another person is "exhausting." As she states in the second collected trade, "I always thought that if I had amazing hair, if I could pull off great boots, if I could fly, that would make me feel strong. That would make me happy. But the hair gets in my face, the boots pinch and this leotard is giving me an epic wedgie." Khan discovers in this scene that what really matters is how she is able to help people, not what she looks like. This example also illustrates

Figure 6.5 Wilson and Alphona, *No Normal*

Entwistle's assertion about how clothing is the mediated space in between the individual self and the social space. Instead of choosing an outfit that is comfortable and practical for rescuing people, the initial Ms. Marvel costume demonstrates that Khan is more focused on fitting into a particular social ideal of beauty traditionally associated with female superheroes' strength.

In her next appearance as Ms. Marvel, Khan dresses in the full bodysuit of Captain Marvel, the later incarnation of Carol Danvers. This costume (figure 6.5) is less revealing, but Khan still adopts the body shape and blond hair of Carol Danvers.

After transforming into these two versions of Carol Danvers, Khan decides that instead of pretending to be someone else, she needs to create a costume that will highlight her unique identity. For her final appearance, Khan stops shapeshifting her body and creates a costume that features different elements of her own background. She adapts a blue burkini—a type of modest swimwear developed for Muslim women—adding the gold lightning bolt of the earlier Ms. Marvel and wearing it over a long-sleeved red shirt and red leggings. She also wears a red scarf, a blue mask, and blue boots. The burkini and the modesty of the costume both reflect Khan's faith. The incorporation of red, blue, and yellow, as well as the lightning bolt, are homages to Carol Danvers. Later in the series, Khan meets Captain Marvel, who admires Khan's costume and approves of her use of the lightning bolt. Finally, Khan drapes the *dupatta* over her shoulders to further represent both her culture and her faith.

Khan's final costume (figure 6.6) is significant because of its successful incorporation of multiple elements of her background. Instead of hiding her identity or trying to be someone that she is not, Khan finally embraces and celebrates her background. Illustrating Susan Kaiser's theory of agency, fashion provides an avenue for Khan to easily incorporate these intersecting elements of her identity. In a time when negative popular rhetoric presents Muslims as forever foreign enemies of the American way of life, it is clearly a political action to portray a young Muslim American character like Ms. Marvel as a hero and defender of justice and morality without sacrificing her background as a Muslim and daughter of immigrants. It is also significant that Ms. Marvel never apologizes for any aspect of her background. Even though she struggles with her identity, she is still proud of her faith and culture and how they both have influenced her as a superhero. Ms. Marvel appears awkward in her early costumes, but she is most often shown strong and confident in her final, self-made costume.

Aesthetics as Politics

The aesthetic styles of the Ms. Marvel comic—specifically, the visual appearance of Khan/Ms. Marvel—provide another assertion of radical equality for those who are left out of formal political spaces. As Rancière discusses, the politics of aesthetics is a way for marginalized groups to equalize themselves with those in positions of power. Rancière explains that through the distribution of the sensible—what one is able to see, touch, taste, hear, and feel—those in power determine who is able to experience certain forms of aesthetics. Rancière focuses on "aesthetic acts as configurations of experience that create new modes of sense perception and induce novel forms of political subjectivity" (*Politics of Aesthetics* 3). In other words, aesthetics is the way that people experience the world through their senses, and politics is the struggle over what people can experience and who is included and excluded in these sensory experiences. Ultimately, it is not through participation in the traditional modes of politics, which Rancière would call policing, that

Figure 6.6 *No Normal* issue 3 cover by Jamie McKelvie and Matthew Wilson

individuals are able to challenge dominant power. Rather, it is through art, aesthetics, embodiment, visual culture, and other sensible modes that people can reconfigure the "sensorium" in a way that will provide everyone with equal access to political spaces.

The creators of *Ms. Marvel* use aesthetics to shift the way Muslim women are presented. In turn, this aesthetic work allows the voices of young Muslim women to be heard in public. Ms. Marvel is a strong, independent, and intelligent young woman, in direct opposition to the stereotype of Muslim women as voiceless victims. The creators also shift the aesthetics of how female superheroes appear in comics by presenting Ms. Marvel in modest clothing instead of a hypersexualized costume. Instead of using the traditional aesthetics of comic books, the creators are promoting, in the visual style of the *Ms. Marvel* series, a different distribution of the sensible in order to present a distinct aesthetic in terms of fashion, beauty, modesty, creativity, and individual agency. This work should be seen as political because not only does it allow Muslim women the chance to express themselves in public, but it also asserts that Muslim women are radically equal to all participants in the political space.

Furthermore, emerging work on Islamic fashion addresses how clothing and style become significant modes of resistance, as Muslim women assert their rights to be seen as equal and valued members of society. Annelies Moors and Emma Tarlo argue that fashion can be a political statement for young Muslim women in Western countries, where their voices are often unheard. As Moors and Tarlo explain, "Through their visual material and bodily presence, young women who wear Islamic fashion disrupt and challenge public stereotypes about Islam, women, social integration and the veil even if their voices are often drowned out in political and legal debates on these issues" (Moors and Tarlo 3). The visual presence of Muslim women wearing Islamic fashion contradicts stereotypes of veiled and oppressed Muslim women. When Muslim women use fashion to show themselves as individuals with creative styles, who participate in contemporary consumer culture, they overturn common misconceptions of Muslim women as "dull, downtrodden, oppressed, and out of sync with modernity" (20). Muslim women often create hybrid styles that blend contemporary trends, while still adhering to an Islamic style and rules of modesty. The character of Ms. Marvel is able to use her fashion and aesthetic styles to demonstrate that Islamic values and non-Western cultural styles make positive contributions to American culture. Ms. Marvel not only wears a modest, long-sleeved burkini to rescue people, but she also incorporates explicitly Islamic values of doing good and helping the less fortunate rather than emphasizing characteristics of patriotism that might be advanced by the current political regime.

Creating Connections to Ms. Marvel through Fashion

The political impact of the character of Ms. Marvel can be seen in how this series has connected with fans, both Muslim and non-Muslim. Readers have especially embraced Khan's costume and created their own cosplay outfits. Numerous online photos show grown women, teenage girls, and younger girls in their own versions of Ms. Marvel's costume, often posing in her signature style with clenched fists or hands on the hips. Unlike with many other female superheroes, dressing up as Ms. Marvel does not pressure women to have the perfect body or to wear revealing outfits. The fact that women of various backgrounds, and men as well, have embraced Ms. Marvel illustrates that her multifaceted identity provides many opportunities for readers to connect with her. Fans can relate to being a teenager who does not fit in, a smart and independent young woman, a member of a religious minority, the daughter of immigrants, a young woman who is not a sexualized object, and a fan of nerd culture. The embodied act of creating and wearing the costume of Ms. Marvel is a way for fans to both embrace and express the values that Ms. Marvel represents, such as equality, diversity, creativity, and justice. Again, these practices provide marginalized individuals ways to assert, through aesthetic styles, the radical equality and value of marginalized lives.

Fans have also shown their connection to Ms. Marvel and her positive values through other creative projects. After the release of the first issue, which featured a portrait image of Khan from her nose to her waist, people posted images on social media with their eyes and the tops of their own heads completing Khan's face. Photos of women, men, and kids from all racial backgrounds who had merged their faces with Khan's face highlighted the relatability of her character. In addition to traditional fan art that celebrates Ms. Marvel as a superhero, a good portion of Ms. Marvel fan art addresses political topics, especially in the aftermath of President Trump's election. Several images feature Khan's statement, "Good is not a thing you are. It's a thing you do," emphasizing ethics over strength. Other fan images show Khan crying over the announcement of the Muslim Ban, tearing up an image of Trump,[1] and participating along with other comic book heroines in the January 21, 2017, Women's March. Khan's image also appeared on posters that people displayed at the various women's marches throughout the country (Romano).

These art projects illustrate how fans not only connect with Khan's multifaceted identity but also see her as a representative young person who strives to do what is right and just in the world despite her flaws and challenges. Ms. Marvel fan art also demonstrates how aesthetics can be deployed to do the political work of redistributing the sensible that Rancière describes—in this case, by illustrating the positive values that Muslim American youth bring to public life. Rather than portray a Muslim character like Khan as an enemy to the American way of life, the creators visually demonstrate that the intersectional values that Ms. Marvel represents are essential to American culture.

Even before the influx of anti-Islam hatred coming from the Trump administration, the character of Ms. Marvel was deployed in a creative act of

Figure 6.7 Facebook: Street Cred—Advertising for the People and Bay Area Art Queers Unleashing Power

resistance in January 2015, when Ms. Marvel's image began appearing pasted over anti-Islam ads that ran on the outside of buses in San Francisco. The original ads were created and distributed by the American Freedom Defense Initiative, which the Southern Poverty Law Center classifies as a hate group. The ads showed images of Adolf Hitler meeting with Haj Amin al-Husseini—a Palestinian Arab Nationalist and anti-Zionist, whom the ads called "the leader of the Muslim world." The ads also featured the quotation "Islamic Jew Hatred: It's in the Quran. Stop the Hate." A guerilla campaign (figure 6.7) was launched to counter these ads by pasting an image of Ms. Marvel over the offending photograph of Hitler, then plastering a new quotation over and among the words in the ads, either "Free speech isn't a license to spread hate" or "Calling all bigotry busters."

This guerilla ad campaign is an example of what de Certeau calls a tactic of resistance, as the activists interfered in the cultural space to offer a positive Muslim individual as a counterimage. It is notable that Ms. Marvel, one of the few Muslim American characters in popular culture fighting misrepresentations through her complex identity, was chosen to counter these Islamophobic ads. While the group behind this ad would like to portray Muslim women as oppressed victims of Islam, Ms. Marvel is instead shown as a multidimensional character who is positively influenced by Islam but not reduced to it.

Conclusion

As has been discussed in this chapter, fashion, daily practices of getting dressed, and aesthetic styles can all be avenues for marginalized individuals to assert the equal value of their lives. The character of Kamala Khan/Ms. Marvel, along with the fan art and cosplay around this comic, illustrates how visual styles and creative projects can be used to demonstrate the value that Muslim Americans contribute to the American landscape. Instead of rejecting these religious and cultural elements as too "foreign" for an American superhero, Khan embraces these aspects and incorporates them into her costume as well as her life.

The costume and fashion of Ms. Marvel are also key to her character's political work to shift misconceptions about Muslims, as well as women more generally and other categories of immigrants. Ms. Marvel fights against stereotypes through her appearance. Her costume highlights her creativity, independence, cultural pride, religious faith, and strong moral character. Besides resisting stereotypes of Muslim women, Ms. Marvel also connects with readers who might never have encountered a relatable Muslim character in pop culture. Because of her complex identity, as reflected in her costume and daily fashion, readers can relate to one or more of the many aspects of Ms. Marvel's background. Furthermore, it is particularly striking how many fans connect to Khan through aesthetic avenues by cosplaying as Ms. Marvel, creating fan art that uses Ms. Marvel's image for political demonstrations, or taking self-portraits that merge the fan's face with Khan's face.

Finally, Ms. Marvel is a character who shifts assumptions of how female superheroes should appear. Ms. Marvel is a smart, confident, creative, and assertive superhero who does not need to be portrayed as a sexual object in order to relate to readers. While the character of Ms. Marvel does unprecedented work to subvert assumptions about Muslims through her actions and words, Ms. Marvel's appearance, specifically her costume and daily fashion, has the political potential to resist misrepresentations of Muslim women. In the current political context, with fewer opportunities for those outside of the dominant group to express their opinions through traditional forms of political action or speech, the political potential of creative action through aesthetic style and fashion allows individuals to express the radical equality of their lives. As fans use her image in art and embody her identity in cosplay, Ms. Marvel's fight against injustice and ignorance extends into the real world.

NOTES

1. This image revisits an image from *Civil War II* of Khan ripping up a photo of Carol Danvers. See our discussion of this image in our introduction. –Eds.

BIBLIOGRAPHY

Amanat, Sana. "Myths, Misfits & Masks." *Tedx Teen*, March 17, 2014. http://tedxteen.com/talks/tedxteen-2014/217-sana-amanat-myths-misfits-masks. Accessed December 16, 2015.

de Certeau, Michel. *The Practice of Everyday Life*. Berkeley: University of California Press, 1984.

Entwistle, Joanne. *The Fashioned Body: Fashion, Dress and Modern Social Theory*. Cambridge, UK: Polity, 2000.

Franich, Darren. "Marvel Introduces Muslim Superhero in 'Ms. Marvel #1.'" *Entertainment Weekly*. January 18, 2015. http://www.ew.com/article/2013/11/05/marvel-muslim-super hero-ms-marvel. Accessed December 16, 2015.

Hebdige, Dick. *Subculture: The Meaning of Style*. London: Methuen, 1979.

Kaiser, Susan B. *Fashion and Cultural Studies*. London: Berg, 2012.

Moors, Annelies, and Emma Tarlo, eds. "Introduction." *Islamic Fashion and Anti-Fashion: New Perspectives from Europe and North America*. London: Bloomsbury, 2013.

Rancière, Jacques. *Dissensus: On Politics and Aesthetics*. Ed. Steven Corcoran. London: Continuum, 2010.

———. *The Politics of Aesthetics: The Distribution of the Sensible*. Ed. Gabriel Rockhill. London: Bloomsbury, 2004.

Romano, Aja. "Muslim American Superhero Kamala Khan Has Become a Real-world Protest Icon." *Vox*. February 2, 2017. https://www.vox.com/culture/2017/2/2/14457384/kamala-khan-captain-america-protest-icon. Accessed October 19, 2017.

Werdine, Maria. "Comics and Human Rights: An Interview with G. Willow Wilson." *London School of Economics Human Rights Blog*. February 3, 2015. http://blogs.lse.ac.uk/humanrights/2015/02/03/comics-and-human-rights-an-interview-with-g-willow-wilson/. Accessed December 16, 2015.

Wheeler, Andrew. "All-New Marvel Now! Q&A: Ms. Marvel." *Marvel.com*. November 6, 2013. http://marvel.com/news/comics/21466/all-new_marvel_now_qa_ms_marvel. Accessed December 16, 2015.

Wilson, G. Willow, Adrian Alphona et al. *Ms. Marvel*. Issues 1–15. New York: Marvel Comics, 2014–15.

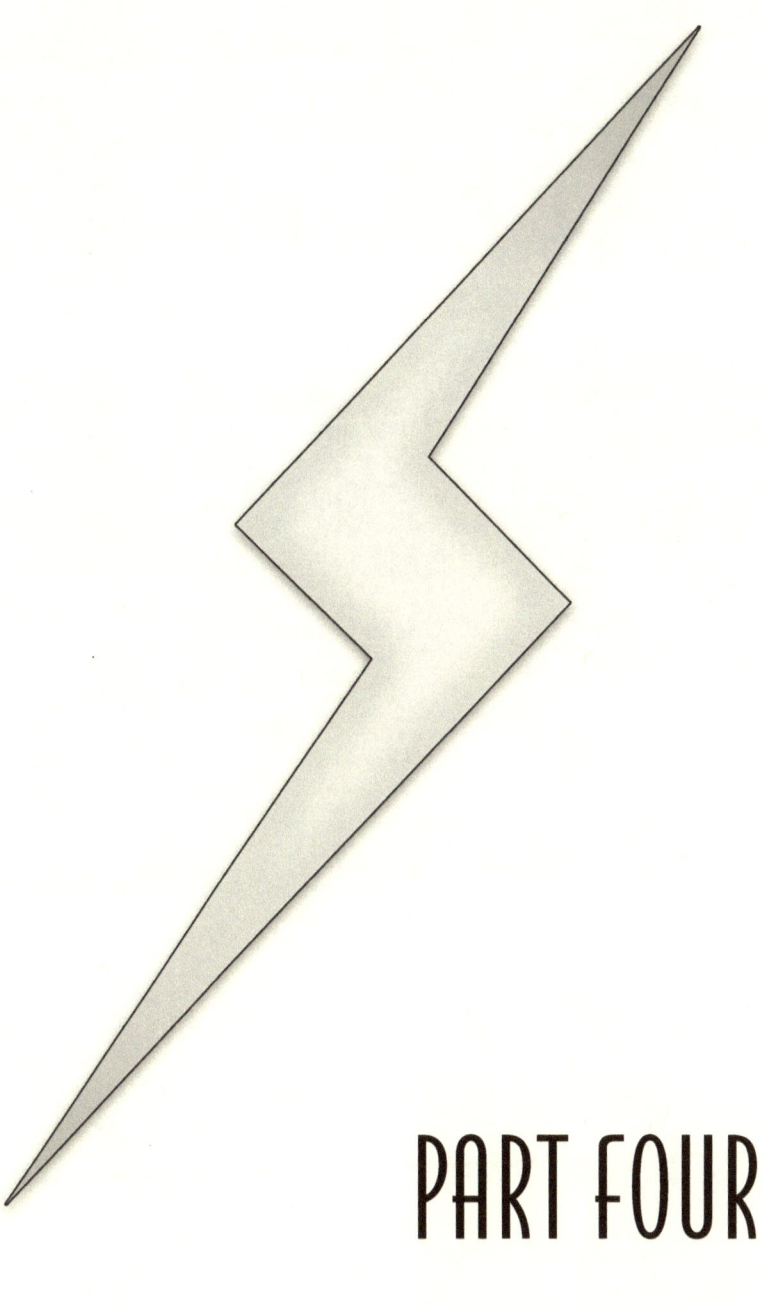

PART FOUR

Fangirls, Fanboys, and
the Culture of Fandom

"WOW. MANY HERO. MUCH SUPER. SUCH GIRL"

Kamala Khan and Female Comics Fandom

AARON KASHTAN

> You're WOLVERINE! My Wolverine-and-Storm-in-Space fanfic was the third-most upvoted story on Freaking Awesome last month! I had you guys fighting this giant alien blob that farts wormholes!
> MS. MARVEL 1, ISSUE 6

Kamala Khan's first words to Wolverine demonstrate one of the many things that distinguish her from the vast majority of superheroes: Khan is a fangirl. Here and on many other occasions in Khan's stories, we are reminded that not only is she a superhero herself, but she is also a fan—and not a passive fan. In addition to following the exploits of her fellow superheroes, she uses those same superheroes as inspirations for her own creative activity.

The fact that Khan is a fan of superheroes, comic books, video games, and Internet culture is not unusual; since at least the beginning of the Silver Age, superheroes have been depicted as fans of other superheroes and of superhero comic books.[1] What makes Khan unique is the kind of fan she is. Prior to Khan, when fans of comics or other areas of geek culture (to use a loaded term) were depicted in superhero comic books, they tended to be teenaged to middle-aged, socially inept, white men. In other words, the fan character tended to be very much like the assumed reader. Readers of superhero comic books could be assumed to be nerds or geeks since reading superhero comic books was a geek hobby. It was also relatively safe to assume that most readers were white, male, and young adult to middle-aged since that was who bought most superhero comic books.[2] As a result, some fan characters, like Barry Allen (the Flash) or Mark Grayson (Invincible), acted as surrogates for the reader, showing him that his passion for comics was

191

justified. Other fan characters, like Evan Dorkin's Eltingville Club, analyzed later in this essay, acted as negative examples for the reader—showing the reader how fans should not behave or telling the reader to take pride in not being that kind of fan.

If earlier fan characters often served as surrogates and positive examples for the reader, then Khan fulfills a similar role, but for a very different fan population. As a fan who is neither white nor male and who writes her own superhero texts as well as consuming superhero narratives created by others, Khan is very different from the traditional superhero demographic. However, Khan has much in common with the new reader base that Marvel, and to a lesser extent DC, has been increasingly seeking to attract. Khan demonstrates that comics are not the exclusive property of white male fanboys, and that traditional comics fandom is not the only way to be a fan. Khan is proof that, as a popular slogan declared in 2014, comics are for everyone.

In order to demonstrate this increasing fan-base diversity, I begin by describing and characterizing Khan's fandom; that is, I explain what kind of fan Khan is. I then move on to an explanation of how her style of fandom is different than that of most previous geek characters in superhero comics. I conclude by suggesting that although *Ms. Marvel*'s representation of Khan's fandom may be seen as cynical or uncritical, it at least represents an improvement on previous efforts at outreach to nontraditional fans, as well as an official acknowledgment that there is more than one way for fans to engage with comics.

What Kind of Fan Khan Is
WHAT KHAN IS A FAN OF

Khan is an avid participant in numerous areas of fan culture. As indicated in the quotation that begins this essay, Khan's first and most obvious fandom is superheroes.[3] She knows everything there is to know about Marvel superheroes, and she looks up to them as a source of inspiration. When Khan meets Wolverine and Captain Marvel, and later when she joins the All-New All-Different Avengers, Khan exhibits the reaction known as "fangirling" or "squeeing," reacting with exaggerated excitement.

However, Khan's most frequently referenced hobby is not superheroes but gaming. Khan has been playing video games and pen-and-paper RPGs since early childhood (1.4.13).[4] She frequently meets her friends Nakia and Bruno at Funtimes Arcade (1.13.5), also referred to as Funtime World (1.19.7). However, her favorite video game is World of Battlecraft, obviously based on World of Warcraft. Khan plays this game and other MMORPGs[5] constantly; she tells her new love interest Kamran that until she met him, she was planning to stay home on Valentine's Day leveling her orc shaman character in this game (1.12.10); and she also says she likes to "stay up late running dungeons" (1.13.8). In addition, she participates in a biweekly dungeon group in "Ancient Scrolls Online," that is, Elder Scrolls Online (2.1.4). Khan often uses video game terminology to describe events in her life; she compares her fight with one of the robots that belong to the Inventor, the first major villain she faces, to a boss fight in World of Battlecraft (1.4.18) and complains that learning about the limitations on her powers is "like when you get a really good build going, then the devs decide to nerf your class" (1.9.12).[6] Khan and Kamran's mutual interest in World of Battlecraft is the beginning of their short-lived romance, which I will examine in more depth below.

Besides superheroes and video games, Khan has a wide variety of other nerd hobbies. She reads manga, including "every volume of Manga Love Rainbow Special XVI" (1.13.10). Planet Unicorn, mentioned in Khan's first fanfic (1.1.4), is another obvious My Little Pony reference, and Khan has a My Little Pony doll in her room (1.4.13). Khan is also a fan of science fiction literature, or at least Frank Herbert's *Dune* (2.4.2), and science fiction and fantasy films; *Star Wars* is mentioned at least twice in the series (1.9.21—although it is Bruno who mentions it here—and 1.15.21), and she once snuck out of the house at midnight to see the final Harry Potter film (1.2.15). Surprisingly, Khan is *not* primarily a fan of comic books. She is not often seen engaging in standard comic book fan practices, including attending comic book conventions and hanging out at the comic book store. On one occasion, Khan is shown making her regular trip to Roy's Comics for the latest issue of *Magical Pony Adventures* (another stand-in for *My Little Pony: Friendship Is Magic*), and she is on first-name terms with the owner, Roy (1.6.6). However, we never see her actually enter the store. By contrast, other comic books often depict the comic book store as the central location of comics fan activity, as will be further discussed below. We also never see Khan cosplaying (unless her superhero costume counts) or attending comic book conventions.

More generally, Khan is deeply immersed in Internet and social media culture. The series frequently references social media websites with tongue-in-cheek names such as Pictagram (1.7.10), MeTube (1.2.12), and Facehead (1.8.5).[7] Khan is intimately familiar with Internet memes, and she references them on a regular basis. In the scene discussed at the start of this essay, Khan describes Wolverine as "Wow. Such athletic. Very claws. So amaze," using the syntax associated with the popular "doge" meme. In this meme, a specific picture of a Shiba Inu dog is combined with a series of two-word captions, each consisting of "so," "many," "very," "such," or "much," followed by a grammatically incorrect word (McCulloch). Khan's battle cry "Embiggen!" is a reference to the *Simpsons* episode "Lisa the Iconoclast," in which Springfield founder Jebediah Springfield's motto is "A noble spirit embiggens the smallest man." However, since this episode aired in 1996, probably before Khan was born,[8] it is likely that she learned the word not from the episode itself but from references to it on social media. Like the doge meme, the word "embiggen" (and its partner "cromulent") has been detached from its original context and has now become part of the general repertoire of Internet pop culture. Long before *Ms. Marvel* issue 1, the word "embiggen" was used in a peer-reviewed physics paper ("Lisa the Iconoclast") and the phrase "click to embiggen" often appears on the Internet. Thus, Khan's use of this word is a symbol of her familiarity with Internet culture in general rather than with *The Simpsons* in particular.

In short, Khan is a fan of a lot of things. In the next section, we examine how Khan expresses her fandom, and what she does with the texts of which she is a fan.

WHAT KHAN DOES WITH FANDOM

Khan is not just a passive fan of superheroes, video games, and other similar phenomena; she uses these texts actively, both as a means of connecting with other people and as motivation for her own creative activity.

One important way in which Khan uses fandom is as a means of connecting with other people. We learn early on that Khan bonded with her best friend, Bruno, thanks to their shared love of geek hobbies. When Khan and Bruno first meet in elementary school, they bond over their shared love for Tween Mutant Samurai Turtles, that is, Teenage Mutant Ninja Turtles (2.10.3).[9] When Khan meets Kamran, she instantly bonds with him upon discovering that he, too, plays *World of Battlecraft* and enjoys old Bollywood movies. In much later issues, Khan develops an instant rapport with her future sister-in-law, Tyesha, when she discovers that Tyesha also read the science fiction novel *Dune* twice but hated the movie. Khan uses geek identity as a means of transcending differences in other parameters of identity; it enables her to connect with Bruno, Kamran, and Tyesha, all of whom differ from her in gender, race, or both.

A second way that Khan uses her fan interests is as inspiration for her own creative activity. As already mentioned, in her first full issue, Khan is seen writing a fan fiction story in which the Avengers visit Planet Unicorn—an example of the common genre of crossover fanfic. Khan's Wolverine-and-Storm fanfic, as we have again already seen, was the third-highest-voted story of the month on Freaking Awesome, which is possibly based on the actual fan site Freakin' Awesome Network. In *All-New All-Different Avengers* Annual 1, we see Khan visiting freakingawesome.com to see how people have reacted to her latest fanfic about "evil Cyclops versus good Ultron."

Fan fiction is often degraded as a second-rate creative act because it legally cannot be published and because, by definition, it depends on preexisting characters and concepts rather than original ones. However, G. Willow Wilson avoids this sort of stereotyped portrayal of Khan's fan fiction. Instead, *Ms. Marvel* presents fan fiction as a legitimate creative act and as a means by which Khan participates actively in a larger fan community. Catherine Tosenberger suggests that fan fiction is distinguished from published children's and young adult literature because its readers and writers are the same: fan fiction is written by and for members of a specific fan community, to the extent that it is often unintelligible to readers outside that community:

> Young people as readers are often constructed by both the publishing industry and children's/young adult literature scholarship as a silent Other, who must passively swallow the narratives adult institutions allow them. Fanfiction enables young readers to speak for themselves: to talk back to the narratives given to them and develop aesthetic forms and traditions to suit themselves, outside of the direct control of adults. (Tosenberger 22)

Khan's fan fiction allows her not merely to passively consume other people's narratives about superheroes but also to create her own superhero narratives. These narratives are addressed to other people who share her passion for and comprehensive knowledge of superheroes. In turn, Khan's readers may be expected to write their own fan fiction, which Khan will then read, as we see her doing in *All-New All-Different Avengers* (*ANADA*) Annual 1. This high level of back-and-forth between readers and writers is unusual in other types of creative pursuits.

A further irony is that as we see in *ANADA* Annual 1, Khan is not just a reader and a writer but also a subject of fanfic. Visiting freakingawesome .com, Khan discovers a number of fanfic stories *about* her, many of which present her in a shockingly negative light.[10] For example, in GATR95's "The Once and Future Marvel" (actually written by G. Willow Wilson and drawn by Mahmud Asrar), Ms. Marvel temporarily becomes the new Captain Marvel after Carol Danvers dies, but Mar-Vell then returns from death and reclaims the Captain Marvel title, telling Khan, "Allow me to explain it to you, for it's simple enough even for *your* gender. It's called a *mantle,* not a *womantle.*" Ms. Marvel accepts the "error of my ways" and vows to stop engaging in "social justice warrioring." This short piece parodies some traditionalist male fans' efforts to act as gatekeepers and to exclude women and minorities from participating in comics fandom. In a different type of parody, "An Evening with Ms. Marvel: A True Story," by Kenneth Raymond (actually Scott Kurtz), Ms. Marvel falls in love with the author and beats up his stepfather. Khan hates most of these stories and demands that one of them—a story by "BadMachine1999" about a love triangle between herself, Nova, and the Miles Morales version of Spider-Man—be removed from the website. (Ironically, BadMachine1999 actually *is* Miles Morales, so Miles is in the unusual position of writing fanfic about himself.) However, it is hypocritical for Khan to criticize anyone else for writing fanfic about her, since she herself writes fanfic about other superheroes. The main difference between Khan's fan fic and that of GATR95 or Kenneth Raymond is that Khan is the more skilled writer.[11]

In other words, *All-New All-Different Avengers* Annual 1 is not a critique of fan fiction as such, but of bad fanfic. This focus is clear from the fact that the annual is addressed to a readership that already knows about and appreciates fanfic. At least some of the bad fan fiction stories in the Annual are examples of specific genres of fan fiction. The Captain Marvel story is an example of "character bashing," or fanfic that trashes a character the author does not like. Kenneth Raymond is instantly recognizable as a Gary Stu, "an original [male] character in a fanfic who obviously serves as an idealized version of the author mainly for the purpose of [w]ish [f]ulfillment" ("Mary Sue"). Zac Gorman and Jay Fosgitt's "Up Close and Fursonal" is an example of an animal transformation fanfic. Natasha Allegri's "The Adventures of She-Hulk" appears to be a depiction of a fanfic written by a barely literate child. In order to get any of these jokes, the reader needs to already have some familiarity with the various kinds of bad fan fiction. Therefore, this annual should be read as parodying fan fiction from an affectionate rather than a hostile perspective. It ultimately shows that Khan's fan fiction has made her part of a community that, even though it includes a lot of stupid people, is a locus of genuine creative activity.[12] This annual also responds to the backlash against characters like Khan from traditionalist fans who are real-life equivalents of characters like Kenneth Raymond. This backlash derives from the fact that Khan's mode of fandom is *not* the dominant mode of superhero comics fandom, as we will see when we compare *Ms. Marvel* to earlier comics that depict superhero comics fans.

How Khan Differs from Earlier Fan Characters

Kamala Khan is certainly not the first comic book character, either in the Marvel Universe or elsewhere, who is a fan of popular culture, but she differs significantly from earlier such characters, both because of her creative (or "transformative") fan practices and because her fandom is presented in a generally positive light. While Khan is not purely a fan of comics, in this section I will focus on comparing Khan's fandom to that of other comic book characters who are fans of comics since, naturally enough, comic book fandom is the most common type of fandom depicted in comic books.

Comic book fans were being depicted in superhero comics even before superhero comics fandom existed as an organized phenomenon. In *Showcase* issue 4 (1956), readers learn that the Silver Age Flash, Barry Allen, chose his secret identity because he is a fan of the Golden Age Flash comics. Barry Allen's comics fandom is the subject of a much later story, "The Riddle of the Runaway Comic," from Flash issue 268. In *Fantastic Four* issue 5, the Human Torch is shown reading a Hulk comic book.[13] Other superheroes who are comic book fans include Robert Kirkman's Invincible and Mark Waid and Barry Kitson's version of the Legion of Super-Heroes. Superhero comic books have also depicted numerous fans who are not themselves superheroes. In Dan Slott's *She-Hulk*, the law firm of Goodman, Lieber, Kurtzberg, and Holliway maintains a complete collection of Marvel comic books, which are legally admissible as evidence because they are approved by the Comics Code Authority, a government agency. This collection has its own librarian, Stu Cicero. *Astro City* volume 2, issue 21 is about a comic book company that exists within a superhero universe, and part of the issue takes place at a comics convention. Superhero comics fans have also been depicted in nonsuperhero comics, such as Alex Robinson's *Box Office Poison* and Evan Dorkin's aforementioned *Eltingville Club* stories.

However, all the characters just mentioned are different from Khan in several ways. First, most of the characters just mentioned are white men. Female and persons-of-color comic book fans are very rare in comic books themselves; besides Khan, the only other major examples are Gertrude Yorkes from *Runaways* and Waid and Kitson's version of Phantom Girl from the Legion of Super-Heroes. Ironically, however, comic books sometimes portray their own fans in a negative light. The Eltingville Club is the most notable example of such a negative portrayal. The four Eltingville Club members are ugly, socially inept, jobless basement dwellers who cause harm to themselves through overinvestment in their fandom. Superboy-Prime, the villain of DC's *Infinite Crisis,* is often read as a stereotype of comic book fans. Outside comic books, similarly stereotypical depictions of comic book fans include the troglodytic Comic Book Guy from *The Simpsons* and the protagonists of *The Big Bang Theory*.[14]

Even when comic book fans are depicted in a more positive light, their fan practices tend to be different than Khan's. Characters like Barry Allen, Stu Cicero, and Mark Grayson engage with comics by collecting them and by visiting comic book stores or comics conventions. Their fandom is "affirmational" rather than "transformative," as a fan named Obsession_Inc explains:

> In "affirmational" fandom, the source material is re-stated, the author's purpose divined to the community's satisfaction, rules established on how the characters are and how the universe works, and cosplay &etc. occur. It all tends to coalesce toward a center concept; it's all about nailing down the details.... "Transformational" fandom, on the other hand, is all about laying hands upon the source and twisting it to the fans' own purposes.

As both Obsession_Inc and Tosenberger observe, affirmational and transformational fandom tend to be associated respectively with male fans and female or younger fans. "Since the vast majority of English-language Western literature and entertainment assumes a default straight, white, cisgender male audience, it's not surprising that transformational fandom is often populated by those considered marginal audiences, who are more likely to feel a need to rework a beloved story to suit their own desires" (Tosenberger 8). Furthermore, affirmational fandom is associated with traditionally male-dominated hobbies like sports and comic books, while transformational fandom is associated with media and TV, whose fandoms have typically been female-dominated. The paradigmatic example of this split is *Star Trek,* whose fandom is the primary case study in Camille Bacon-Smith's pioneering work, *Enterprising Women.*

Stu Cicero is a paradigmatic example of affirmational fandom, as might be expected from the fact that he is a male participant in a traditionally male hobby. Within Stu's universe, Marvel comics are authoritative legal documents, and his job is to know everything about them. In this sense, he resembles the real-world comic fan who takes pride in (usually) his encyclopedic knowledge of comic book continuity and history. Some such fans, like Mark Waid (*Legion of Superheroes*) and Kurt Busiek (*Astro City*), eventually become professional comic book writers themselves, but Stu seems to have no interest in creating comic books of his own. Since about the 1980s, Marvel and DC have cultivated fans like Stu as their standard target audience. In earlier periods, comic books' readership was far broader and more diverse, and many comics were specifically directed at girls, but an explanation of this recent demographic shift is beyond the scope of this essay.[15]

Examples like Cicero suggest that prior to Kamala Khan, comic books typically depicted comics fandom as an affirmational rather than a transformative practice. As a transformational superhero fan, Khan is unusual in that she participates in a stereotypically male fandom, but she engages in fan practices that are stereotypically associated with female fans.

What Khan Does for Her Fans

This comparison between Kamala Khan and earlier fictional depictions of superhero fans is instructive because it helps us understand how Kamala Khan is performing a different kind of rhetorical work. Prior to Khan, when superhero fans or comics fans were depicted in comic books, they tended to reinforce existing stereotypical notions of fan identity. Characters like Mark Grayson, Stu Cicero, and the Eltingville Club resemble the stereotypical real-world comic book reader: they are white males between the ages of fifteen and forty, often of a nerdy persuasion (although Grayson is more of a jock than a nerd). When portrayed positively, such characters serve as a validation of the reader's fan practices, which tend to be affirmational rather than transformative. When portrayed negatively, such characters serve as parodies of harmful fan practices and as examples of behaviors that fans ought to avoid. In either case, however, the assumption is that the reader resembles these fans in one way or another.

An example of the use of fan characters to validate particular fan practices occurs in *Invincible* issue 117, where Mark Grayson has this conversation with his store owner:

GRAYSON: Man, I hate it when a book has been going for over a decade and they start changing things so drastically to keep the story engaging and new. Sure, it has a chance of keeping things interesting, . . . but it's just as likely to alienate the dedicated readers that have supported you all these years.

The owner agrees, saying, "I hear you. . . . I hate change. That's why I mostly read the corporate comics." Grayson and the owner then reveal that they are both joking. The reader laughs at this realization because (presumably) he knows that unlike "corporate" (i.e., Marvel and DC) comics, *Invincible* changes its status quo constantly and the good guys often lose. For example, in the issues just prior to issue 117, Grayson became a father, was raped, and decided to leave Earth after it was conquered by a villain. The implicit message here is that you, the reader, should be like Grayson: instead of lamenting the recent changes in *Invincible*'s direction, you should admire *Invincible* for its audacity and its refusal to maintain the status quo.

Conversely, the Eltingville Club represents a negative depiction of fan practices. Through the members' sexism, their social ineptitude, and their obsessive behavior (such as staying up all night to watch a *Twilight Zone* marathon), they model how fans should not behave. However, instead of allowing readers to feel superior to the Eltingville Club, Dorkin demands that readers see the Eltingville Club members as dark mirrors of themselves. The *Eltingville Club* stories are addressed to readers who are already comic book fans; their humor only makes sense to readers who are familiar with the fan practices that the stories satirize. Therefore, simply by virtue of the fact that one is reading the *Eltingville Club* stories, one must already be a little bit like the Eltingville Club. While the Eltingville Club stories are a much more negative portrayal of comic book fans than *Invincible* issue 117, they equally assume a reader who fits the default stereotype of the comic book fan.

These examples suggest that when fans are depicted in superhero comics, they tend to serve as fictional surrogates for actual comics fans. They model what fans look like and how fans should (or should not) act. But if the fan character is a surrogate for the reader, and the fan character is usually a white male nerd, then the implication is that the reader is also a white male nerd. In other words, depictions of fan characters, even when ironic, tend to reinforce stereotyped ideas about who reads or should read superhero comics. Moreover, because fans in comic books are mostly shown engaging in affirmational rather than transformative fan practices, the implication is that the standard mode of comic book fandom is affirmational—that fans should express their fandom by buying, reading, and discussing comic books, but not by writing fanfic, making fanvids, or engaging in other more involved fan-related processes.

Kamala Khan is similar to these past depictions of fans in that she also acts as a surrogate for the reader. The reader is supposed to see Khan as a model of positive fan practices. The difference is that Khan, as discussed in other essays in this collection, does *not* look or act like a typical comic book reader. She is a young woman of color rather than a white man, and her fandom is transformative and not affirmational. Therefore, G. Willow Wilson's and other writers' depictions of Khan's fandom serves to normalize the idea that fans can look and act like Khan—that you can be a superhero fan even if you do not look like a stereotypical comic book geek or if you prefer writing fan fiction to attending comic book conventions and hanging out at the comic book store. In the spirit of the #WeNeedDiverseBooks campaign, *Ms. Marvel* seeks to present fans who do not match the traditional stereotype of the comic book fan with a fictional representation of themselves. In doing so, it suggests that reading comic books is normal, no matter what you look like or how you engage with them.

One reason *Ms. Marvel* helps to achieve this normalization of nontraditional fans or fan practices is because it presents Khan's fan practices in a completely positive light. Khan is never bullied, abused, or even criticized for being a fan. Her mother does not understand her hobby, asking, "Fan feek ... [W]hat is fan feek?!" (1.5), but seems to have no objection to her involvement in it. (In contrast, Khan's parents are strongly opposed to her brother's extreme piety.) Indeed, rather than exposing her to ridicule or disapproval, Khan's involvement in fandom inspires her creativity and helps her make new friends, as discussed above. Khan's love for superheroes, together with her Islamic faith, is her primary inspiration for becoming a superhero herself when she acquires shapeshifting powers.

Khan's fandom is depicted in a way that normalizes both nontraditional fan practices and participation in fandom by people who do not match the standard comic book fan stereotype. The implicit message of Kamala Khan is that anyone can be a comic book fan and that it is okay to participate in fandom in the transformational style typically associated with female fans rather than the affirmational style typically associated with male fans. In sending this message, Khan plays an important part in Marvel's ongoing efforts to expand its audience.

How Khan Fits into Marvel's Broader Strategies

Kamala Khan is the flagship character of Marvel's ongoing initiatives to attract readers from outside the target demographic, including female, younger, and nonwhite readers. These initiatives have led to titles ranging from Matt Fraction and David Aja's *Hawkeye*, to Ta-Nehisi Coates and Brian Stelfreeze's *Black Panther*, to Ryan North and Erica Henderson's *Unbeatable Squirrel Girl*. *Ms. Marvel* acts as a gateway to these other titles by encouraging readers to see comic book reading as a legitimate hobby.

Ms. Marvel's portrayal of comics fandom as a broad and inclusive hobby seems to have had at least an indirect impact on other comics that portray comic book fans. Another recent Marvel comic with a fangirl protagonist is Gwen Poole (a.k.a. Gwenpool), a comic book fan from the "real" world who has somehow transported herself into the Marvel universe.[16] Gwenpool originated as a joke character, a hybrid of Gwen Stacy and Deadpool created for a variant cover, but became popular enough to star in her own ongoing series (Hastings). Gwenpool is just as fanatical about comic books as the average comic book fan. She knows even more about the Marvel Universe than Stu Cicero does because she also knows all the superheroes' secret identities, which has gotten her into trouble. The fact that Gwenpool is female is not problematized; the text takes it for granted that women can be comic book fans too. Gwenpool is hardly as positive a character as Ms. Marvel—indeed, her obsession with superheroes causes her to make a series of awful decisions—but she at least shows that female fans can be just as obsessive as the Eltingville Club and can engage in equally disastrous behaviors as a result of their excessive devotion to their source texts. If anything, Gwenpool's gender makes her more sensitive to the frequent casual sexism of superhero comics than male fans tend to be. For example, in her guest appearances in *Rocket Raccoon & Groot*, Gwenpool castigates the writer and artist for depicting her in sexually exploitative ways (Kocher and Walsh). This strong, positive portrayal of a female fan has become easier for traditional fans to accept because of *Ms. Marvel*'s work to normalize the concept of female superhero fans.

Marvel's treatment of characters like Khan and Gwenpool contrasts significantly with representations of fangirls in other media. Anastasia Salter and Bridget Blodgett observe that in media franchises like *Sherlock* and *Supernatural*, female fans are presented as "objects of suspicion and desire, often serving narratives as possessions rather than actors. . . . The fanboy image is dominant; the fangirl, even when part of the 'original' demographic of the show, is marginalized in her own space" (152–53). They suggest that "fandom doesn't really have room for women authors and fans.... The fangirl turned auteur remains an easy figure of disdain" (181). By depicting fangirls as positive protagonists, Marvel makes at least token efforts to counteract these negative attitudes toward female fans—even at the risk of alienating entitled male fans, who are angry that Marvel comics no longer presuppose their mode of fandom as the default. Marvel has further helped to promote the fangirl as a legitimate participant in fandom by hiring actual female fans as creators, including G. Willow Wilson herself, as well as Rainbow Rowell, whose novel *Fangirl* is a classic exposition of female fan identity (see Rowell and Anka, *Runaways*).

Ms. Marvel still remains at what Gray, Sandvoss, and Harrington call the "Fandom Is Beautiful" stage of fan studies, which seeks to "not so much deconstruct the binary structure in which the fan had been placed as ... to differently value the fan's place in said binary" (3). In other words, *Ms. Marvel* advocates for the value of female fan practices within fandom at large but does not interrogate fandom itself as an institution.

Furthermore, its celebration of fandom may be seen as disingenuous when coming from a corporation that profits from fandom. Despite these considerations, *Ms. Marvel* represents an advance on the comics industry's previous complete lack of acknowledgment of fangirls. Since the 1980s, when male geeks became entrenched as the default audience for comic books (a development I hope to examine elsewhere), Marvel and DC have generally made only token efforts to acknowledge other modes of fandom. Therefore, *Ms. Marvel* is an important title not just for Khan's racial and religious identity but also because of the message it sends to female and other nontraditional fans. It suggests that fandom is not the exclusive domain of white male fans who engage in traditional affirmational fan practices. Even (or especially) if you do not look like a stereotypical fanboy, or if you prefer to hang out at freakingawesome.net rather than at the comic book store, comic book fandom can be the place for you.

NOTES

1. For some analyses, the categories of fans of superheroes, fans of comic books, and fans of superhero comic books are all distinct; the third category is a subset of the first two. In this essay, I sometimes blur these categories.

2. This article presupposes that the primary audience for superhero comics is straight white men. Of course, this is not a natural or inevitable condition; indeed, it was only true for approximately three decades, from the 1980s to the 2010s. There have always been comic books targeted toward other audiences, ranging from *Young Love* to *Archie* to *Wimmen's Comix,* and even superhero comics have always been read by populations other than

straight white male geeks. The straight-white-male-geek mode of comics fandom has historically been considered "real" fandom, while other fan practices that don't fit this mode are considered lesser—just as, in the culture at large, male-identified fan practices such as sports fandom are often considered more acceptable than female-identified fan practices like fan fiction. For reasons of scope, this chapter takes for granted the assumption that superhero comics fandom, at least since the Silver Age, is primarily a straight-, white-, male-, and geek-oriented activity. However, my other current work seeks to complicate that assumption.

3. Of course, Khan lives in a universe where superheroes are real, so it is not entirely accurate to describe her superhero fandom as simply a geek or nerd hobby, as it would be in real life. However, it is well documented that superhero fandom exists in the Marvel Universe and is very similar to real-world superhero fandom. For example, the fact that Marvel comics exist in the Marvel Universe was established as early as *Fantastic Four* issue 10 (1963).

4. Individual issues from *Ms. Marvel* within this essay are referenced by volume, issue number, and page number. For example, 1.4.13 is page 13 of issue 4 of volume 1.

5. MMORPG stands for "massively multiplayer online role-playing game." –Eds.

6. In other words, "when you're playing a really powerful character and then the developers of the game decide to lower the power level of that type of character."

7. Instagram, YouTube, and Facebook.

8. In keeping with Marvel's sliding time scale, Khan's birthdate, like the precise location of the Simpsons' hometown of Springfield, is unknown. It should also be noted that since 2009, the Jebediah Springfield statue and its attached plaque, which displays the word "embiggen," have appeared in *The Simpsons*' opening sequence.

9. This is a little anachronistic because this franchise had its peak of popularity in the late '80s and early '90s, before Khan and Bruno were born. The franchise has been revived repeatedly since then, including in two movies released in 2014 and 2016; however, these movies came out after the current *Ms. Marvel* series began.

10. This annual begins with a framing sequence in which Khan visits freakingawesome.com and starts reading fanfic. The rest of the annual consists of the six stories she reads, each of which is written and drawn by a different creator or creative team.

11. Because Khan lives in a world where the Marvel superheroes are real, her fan fiction and all of the other fanfics represented in *ANADA* Annual 1 are examples of real person (RP) fic. The ethics of this type of fanfic are a subject of heated ongoing debate: c.f. Beazley.

12. As the editors suggest, this annual may additionally be read as a response to some of the hostile feedback Ms. Marvel received from real-life fans. As such, it participates in a long tradition, going back at least to Fantastic Four issue 11, in which superheroes explicitly or implicitly address fan criticism.

13. I thank Jack Ayres for this reference.

14. As the editors suggest, these cases are not strictly equivalent: the Comic Book Guy is a purely negative stereotype, while the *Big Bang Theory* characters are attracted to comics for reasons with which the reader can sympathize.

15. On the history of comics readership, see Gabilliet, as well as Beaty, Woo, and Sousanis's ongoing *What Were Comics?* project.

16. Squirrel Girl is also a fangirl (or fansquirrel), as shown by the fact that she carries around trading cards that depict all the villains she encounters.

BIBLIOGRAPHY

Bacon-Smith, Camille. *Enterprising Women: Television Fandom and the Creation of Popular Myth*. Philadelphia: University of Pennsylvania Press, 1991.

Bates, Cary and Irv Novick. *The Flash*. Issue 268. New York: DC, 1978.

Beaty, Bart, Benjamin Woo, and Nick Sousanis. *What Were Comics?* http://www.whatwerecomics.com/.

Beazley, Malory. "The Ethics of Real Person Fiction." *Fan/Fic Magazine*. March 6, 2016. https://fanslashfic.com/2016/03/06/the-ethics-of-real-person-fiction/. Accessed January 1, 2018.

Busiek, Kurt, and Brent Anderson. *Kurt Busiek's Astro City*. Issue 21. New York: DC, 2000.

Coates, Ta-Nehisi, Brian Stelfreeze, et al. *Black Panther*. Issues 1–18. New York: Marvel, 2016–2017.

Dorkin, Evan. *The Eltingville Club*. Milwaukie, OR: Dark Horse, 2016.

Fraction, Matt, David Aja, et al. *Hawkeye*. New York: Marvel, 2012–2015.

Gabilliet, Jean-Paul. *Of Comics and Men*. Jackson: University Press of Mississippi, 2009.

Gray, Jonathan, Cornell Sandvoss, and C. Lee Harrington, eds. *Fandom: Identities and Communities in a Mediated World*. New York: New York University Press, 2017.

Hastings, Christopher, Gurihiru, et al. *The Unbelievable Gwenpool*. New York: Marvel, 2016–2018.

Kanigher, Robert, John Broome, and Carmine Infantino. *Showcase*. Issue 4. New York: DC, September–October 1956.

Kirkman, Robert, and Ryan Ottley. *Invincible*. Issue 117. Portland, OR: Image, 2015.

Kocher, Nick, and Michael Walsh. *Rocket Raccoon and Groot*. Issues 8–10. New York: Marvel, 2016.

Lee, Stan, and Jack Kirby. *Fantastic Four*. Issues 5, 10, and 11. New York: Marvel, 1962.

"Lisa the Iconoclast." *Wikipedia*. Accessed January 1, 2018.

"Mary Sue." Tvtropes.org. http://tvtropes.org/pmwiki/pmwiki.php/Main/MarySue/. Accessed January 1, 2018.

McCulloch, Gretchen. "A Linguist Explains the Grammar of Doge. Wow." *The Toast*. The-toast.net. February 6, 2014. http://the-toast.net/2014/02/06/linguist-explains-grammar-doge-wow/. Accessed January 1, 2018.

Montgomery, Paul. "Jordie Bellaire Colors Her World." *Comic Book Resources*. CBR.com. May 25, 2014. https://www.cbr.com/cbr-sunday-conversation-jordie-bellaire-colors-her-world/. Accessed January 1, 2018.

North, Ryan, and Erica Henderson. *The Unbeatable Squirrel Girl*. Issues 1–8. New York: Marvel, 2015.

Obsession_Inc. "Affirmational Fandom vs. Transformational Fandom." Dreamwidth.org. https://obsession-inc.dreamwidth.org/82589.html. Accessed January 16, 2018.

Robinson, Alex. *Box Office Poison*. Marietta, GA: Top Shelf, 2001.

Rowell, Rainbow. *Fangirl*. New York: St. Martin's, 2013.

Rowell, Rainbow, and Kris Anka. *Runaways. Volume 2: Best Friends Forever*. New York: Marvel, 2018.

Salter, Anastasia, and Bridget Blodgett. *Toxic Geek Masculinity in Media: Sexism, Trolling, and Identity Policing.* New York: Palgrave Macmillan, 2017.

Slott, Dan, Juan Bobillo, et al. *She-Hulk.* Issues 2–12. New York: Marvel, 2004–2005.

Tosenberger, Catherine. "Mature Poets Steal: Children's Literature and the Unpublishability of Fanfiction." *Children's Literature Association Quarterly* 39, no. 1 (Spring 2014): 4–27.

Vaughan, Brian K., and Adrian Alphona. *Runaways.* Issues 1–18. New York: Marvel, 2003–2004.

Waid, Mark, and Barry Kitson. *Legion of Super-Heroes.* Issues 1–15. New York: DC, 2005–2006.

Wilson, G. Willow, and Adrian Alphona et al. *Ms. Marvel.* Issues 1–19. New York: Marvel, 2014–2015.

Wilson, G. Willow, Mahmud Asrar, et al. *All-New All-Different Avengers Annual.* Issue 1. New York: Marvel, 2016.

KAMALA KHAN, MILES MORALES, AND MARVEL NOW!

Challenging the Traditional White Male Fan

NICHOLAUS PUMPHREY

In 2012, Marvel introduced the new campaign Marvel NOW! with the motto: "Join the RE-evolution" (Morse). The campaign, which ended in 2015, was Marvel's attempt to create several nonwhite characters and focus on female heroes in the Marvel Universe. Marvel NOW! included all-female teams, Captain Marvel (Carol Danvers) receiving her own series again, and the introduction of a female Thor. The centerpieces of the campaign were Kamala Khan, a young Muslim Ms. Marvel with Pakistani parents, and Miles Morales as the Ultimate Spider-Man, a hero with African American and Latino heritage.

This campaign can be read as an effort to create diverse characters and attract new readership; however, Marvel NOW! received significant backlash from many white male fans. Critics included David Gabriel, Marvel's vice president of sales, who blamed falling numbers on the inclusion of racial and gender diversity (Cain).[1] This response reminds us that Marvel is a corporation concerned with money and sales, begging the question of whether this seemingly inclusive character development is really a challenge to the status quo or a strategic marketing campaign. In this chapter, I examine the racist and sexist commentary from white male fans that arose from the creation and casting of various Marvel characters, especially Khan and Morales, as well as the growing fan base that continues to challenge the traditional white male reader.

Who Reads Comics?

It is impossible to gauge precisely who reads comic books. Comic book subscriptions and the free market nature of store purchases do not allow for accurate demographics. Regular consumers typically create "pull lists" from various comics dealers, but these consumers do not provide any biographical information. Many walk-in consumers purchase comics at a specialty store or even a large-scale bookstore without leaving any record of their identities. To complicate matters further, fans and readers are often two different categories: fans often consume all comics-related media, but they might not be full-time readers. However, the main readers for many years have been heterocisgender white men, often called "fanboys." The loose term "fanboy" signifies the unequal power dynamics associated with institutionalized norms and hierarchies of power within US society. Throughout this work, I use the term "fanboy" to represent the privileged white male reader, who often, in his fandom of comic books, unknowingly participates in institutionalized racism, sexism, and heterosexism.

According to communication scholars Randy Duncan and Matthew J. Smith, the term "fanboy" was first used in correlation with comic book readers (174). Although applied to other subcultures, the designation "fanboy" typically signifies white male readers, privileged within the comics fan subculture.[2] Fanboy culture is intertwined with facets of culturally embedded white supremacy, institutionalized racism, and (hetero)sexism. These sociocultural norms are validated through multifaceted institutions that typically function to uphold the status of groups already in power through religious, political, and socioeconomic status, as well as gender, race, ethnicity, and sexuality. Therefore, anyone operating outside of the context of a cisgender, heterosexual, white, and Christian male is immediately labeled as "Other." In many cases, the obsession of a fan is deemed unhealthy, nonnormative, or not masculine. As this status is usually sexually and gender diminutive, the designation is "fanboy" rather than just "fan" (Stanfill).

Both the fanboy reader and the white male comic creator still dominate much of comics culture; however, the readership is disputed, considering the only way to collect data on comic book readership is to poll readers. In recent years, several studies have been published in order to gauge these readers, either through Facebook "likes" or through polling at comic book stores. Oddly enough, many of these surveys actually disagree with one another, either reinforcing the fanboy stereotype or strongly countering it. One 2005 survey by pop culture studies scholar Neil Shyminsky found that 95 percent of the respondents at comic book stores were male, and 83 percent identified as white or Caucasian (391). This survey, of course, could simply be showing that fanboys still prefer the culture, physicality, and space inherent in the comic book store, without effectively representing broader readership. According to the Nielsen Company, which surveyed readership of DC Comics' *New 52*, a 2011 revamping of DC's entire lineup and a restart of almost all of their titles, 93 percent of the readers were male, only 5 percent were new readers, and only an estimated 2 percent were younger than eighteen (Hudson).

To counter the fanboy stereotype, Brett Schenker of *The Beat* recently reported that 46.67 percent of Facebook users who "like" comic books are women, which contradicts previous surveys, as well as the classic stereotype (Schenker). As Marvel editor in chief Axel Alonso stated in 2014, "While we don't have any market research, the eyes don't lie. If you go to conventions and comic book stores, more and more female readers are emerging. They are starved for content and looking for content they can relate to" (Melrose). One explanation for the varied results is that Alonso really means "fans" rather than "readers." These types of fans may rarely read actual comics, but they may consume comics-related materials and attend the conventions.

Another factor may be the process of "gatekeeping" where "real" fans attempt to police who reads comics. The comic book store can feel like an exclusionary space being policed by white fanboys, which keeps many female readers from buying comics outside of bookstores, which also are often not counted in available metrics. Fandom scholar Benjamin Woo suggests that even if consumers are not all "default fanboys," they represent much of the community of fans online and elsewhere. As a result, conversations about fans almost always focus on white fanboys, which further perpetuates institutionalized racism and sexism. Woo states that there is a "yawning void" within fandom studies where more discussions of race should be held (Woo). Matt Hills, another fandom scholar, agrees and suggests that the way fandom is studied needs to include critical analysis of race (Hills). One of the main reasons that this scholarship does not exist is that a large part of fandom scholarship and comics scholarship has historically been performed by fans themselves, who represent the same normative demographics.

Regardless of the data, the fact that both Marvel and DC actively tried to shift their readership to a more nonwhite and/or nonmale audience suggests that both companies believed in the traditional dominance of the white fanboy. DC Comics, the older of the two companies, is known for heroes such as Wonder Woman, Superman, and Batman, all of which were created either during the Great Depression or World War II. As Dan Didio, copublisher of DC Comics, states, "We realized that our characters were created 40, 50, 60, 70 years ago. And the world has changed, and we've got to change our characters along with them and diversify our cast, our voice, and really be able to connect with as many of our readers as possible" (Johns). Didio expresses the need for a simple investment in the future. According to National Public Radio commentator Rafael Johns, "From the mid-to-late 2000s, comic books' largely white male cast of characters had attracted largely white male fans—older ones. And because of it, readership and profits flat-lined for more than half a decade" (Johns). Both DC and Marvel realized that to stay relevant, they needed to reach just as many white girls and women and people of color as traditional white male readers.

Starting in 2012, Marvel NOW! was meant to shake things up and attract new readership, especially female, with new solo series for *Black Widow, Elektra, She-Hulk,* and *Ms. Marvel.* As Axel Alonso stated in 2016, "We'll provide at least one great reason for readers—old, lapsed or new—to go into a comic store each week" (Morse). Unlike DC's *New 52,* Marvel NOW! was not planned as a complete reboot. The team at Marvel did not want to alienate its traditional readers, so for the most part, it developed some new characters instead of changing the old ones (Morse). As one *Comic Book Resources* article noted in 2012, "The core Marvel readers are the base audience for the Marvel NOW! initiative, but Alonso and his colleagues hope to build upon that base by making the books accessible to new and lapsed comic book readers" (Richards). Despite Marvel's efforts, the change elicited plenty of hateful responses.

According to Mel Stanfill, the diminutive designation of "fanboy" often encourages the white male reader/consumer to "over compensate" and police their subculture with slurs (Stanfill). The impulse to create these slurs correlates with the culture of hypermasculinity among male athletes. These two groups have stereotypically been seen as opposites, yet, as Stanfill notes, they perform in similar ways. Although fanboys depict themselves as oppressed nerds, this designation "serve[s] to reinforce rather than undermine American culture's essential connection between whiteness and privilege" (Stanfill). If white privilege is the subtle and overt benefits that white and light-skinned people inherently receive within a white-dominated society, then white fanboy privilege equates the privilege they gain from characters, writers, and artists being primarily white as well. Shyminsky uses the phrase "invisible knapsack," originated by activist Peggy McIntosh, to explain this privilege based on societal power, status, and hierarchy. As Shyminsky explains, because "the advantages of being male and/or white in North American society [derive] not simply from the perspective of education and professional opportunities, but as an 'invisible knapsack' of unearned assets, advantages [can be] simple, but important to one's sense of safety and well-being" (Shyminsky 388; see McIntosh). White male comics fans have more than seventy-five years of standards in place within comics, and they have benefitted from the fact that comics have rarely deviated from white male norms. Since consumers have partial control over the product, superheroes have consistently reflected this white male reader (DiPaolo 15). Given this long history, the white fanboy's identity is also intertwined into the narratives, which creates a sense of personal investment within the classic depiction of heroes among this traditional fan base.

This personal identification begins when the fan is in his adolescence, and it becomes interlaced with characters from comics, movies, and other media. As a result, the formative years of the fanboy's life are directly associated with their media consumption. In his analysis of the backlash to the 2016 women-led *Ghostbusters* film, pop-culture scholar William Proctor reads this nostalgia as similar to a mental illness that will not allow the fan to see change (Proctor). Instead, the fanboy reacts in a toxic manner because he literally feels that his childhood and identity are in jeopardy. This reaction poses more of a threat than mere nostalgia because of the sheer volume of the fanboy voice (Woo). As long as fanboys have the power and ability to police and control the media, their nostalgia is appeased, and their white, cis-hetero, male identity remains secure.

Within comic books, identity entanglement comes from two generic formulae inherent in most comics titles: the secret identity and the outcast hero. If the secret identity of a character is a nerd who is bullied, a white male fan who identifies with this character might feel that he is in the minority, experiencing oppression and discrimination despite the fact that he holds more societal power as a white, cisgender, heterosexual man. The height of this association in comics came with Spider-Man's creation in 1962, when Stan Lee wrote Spider-Man's secret identity, Peter Parker, to represent the constantly bullied, nerdy white teenager. Stan Lee's creation of Spider-Man took the stereotype of the nerdy, teenage sidekick and flipped it, making him the hero. Although the teenage hero had existed before, in characters such as Billy Batson as Captain Marvel, many comics creators point to the appearance of Spider-Man as the pivotal moment that brought the secretly bullied hero into the mainstream.

The second stereotype, the outcast hero, is exemplified in Marvel's X-Men, who, as Martin Lund argues, "reinforce the notion that a majority white group can still be considered 'minorities' in their roles as outcasts" (38). The X-Men are a group of superpowered mutants shunned by larger society because they were born "different." The X-Men typically defend other mutants from an unsympathetic society and fight injustice perpetrated by "evil" mutants; however, they have been primarily white and male, and live in a mansion in New York (Lund 42).³ As Shyminsky states,

> As a substantially young, white, and male group of heroes within a genre whose creators and readers are nearly uniformly white males, the X-Men actually solicit identification from a similarly young, white, and male readership, allowing these readers to misidentify themselves as the "other." ... Most readers are being taught to identify with oppressions that are unfamiliar and, I would argue, unequal to their own. Additionally, the use of racialized and gendered victim positions by white male readers is particularly troubling when one considers that, despite the obvious difficulties associated with being a teenager or a geek, these readers still often benefit from 'unearned advantage[s] . . . of our arbitrarily awarded power.'" (388; internal quote from McIntosh)

The outcast hero and the secret identity have the power to lull traditional white male readers into a false sense of minority status and persecution, regardless of their privilege (Lund 43).

As a result, these fans, believing they are the ones being oppressed and that their identity is under attack, lash out in anger when the status quo is changed. In the eyes of these fans, because they are losing the narrative attention that they once had, any "diversity" changes in traditional comics characters only reinforce the claim that the cis-hetero, white male is currently the most discriminated against group. Shyminsky states,

> [T]hese privileged white male readers are allowed to collapse the distance between their own experiences of marginalization and the experiences of those who have been historically outside and have been marginalized by institutions of white masculinity. While the possibility that a reader can lay claim to both the socio-economic privileges of white masculinity and the victim positions of women and people of color may seem a contradiction in terms, it is a feat managed by the X-Men themselves. (391–92)

In other words, if a white male reader sacrifices his 93 percent male-created comics percentage to 80 percent, he feels that some discrimination has occurred, even if his side of the ratio is still well above percentages that would more closely reflect the racial and gender balance in the US population as a whole.

One recent example of white male fan backlash is the reaction to the female spy Mockingbird, whose writer, Chelsea Cain, was harassed on Twitter after the October 2016 release of *Mockingbird* 8. The cover, drawn by Joelle Jones, depicted the main female protagonist wearing a shirt that read, "Ask me about my feminist agenda." As Cain stated soon after the harassment began, "My day job is writing thrillers. Bestsellers. Sold millions of copies. Never had to block people until I started writing comics" (Clark). Cain had underestimated the deep investment of the fanboy's identity in its characters. Adding overtly feminist writing and characters jeopardizes an identity rooted in misogyny.

As evidence of this misogyny, here are the top two most "liked" comments (which I leave anonymous) from Marvel's Facebook page on October 21, 2016, just after they posted the cover of *Mockingbird* 8. Both comments received more than eight hundred likes. The first commenter stated, "Feminism is dead and the third wave wants pandering not equality."[4] The second wrote, "This is ... the reason DC is outselling them these days."[5] Axel Alonso responded to the harassment, saying that the Marvel Universe, as well as the industry, "benefits & grows from diverse creators & characters" (Clark). The series was ultimately canceled, however, although supposedly not as a direct result of this backlash. As Cain tweeted when she announced the cancellation, "We need to make sure Marvel makes room for more titles by women about women kicking ass" (Clark). These recent reactions to *Mockingbird* echo the responses Marvel received when creating the Marvel NOW! campaign, which suggests that the racist and sexist outbursts are likely to continue.

Miles Morales, the Ultimate Spider-Man: Continuity Arguments and Institutionalized Prejudice

Spider-Man is arguably the most popular Marvel comic book character. He has super strength and a nerdy alter ego, Peter Parker. Created in 1962, Parker receives superpowers when he is bitten by a radioactive spider, and for the most part, his backstory depicts him as an awkward white kid from Queens. In many instances, Spider-Man–related media has dominated Marvel's popularity, whether through blockbuster films or television cartoons. In 2010, Sony Pictures Studios rebooted the Spider-Man movie franchise. With questions of who will play the "web-slinger" circulating the Internet, one narrative suggested that African American actor Donald Glover should be cast as Peter Parker (Dodds). What resulted was an all-out Twitter war disputing whether Marvel's most famous hero could be black. Sony Picture Studios ultimately cast white actor Andrew Garfield in the role of Spider-Man and later told Marvel that if it wanted to regain movie rights of Spider-Man for another reboot, Peter Parker had to remain white (Biddle).[6] *Gawker* leaked pieces of the contract between Marvel and Sony, which made a point of distinguishing between Spider-Man and Peter Parker. According to section A of the contract, Spider-Man must always be male, and section B, regarding the character of Peter Parker, states:

PETER PARKER CHARACTER TRAITS

Depiction of Peter Parker or his Spider-Man alter ego must conform to the following character traits:

> His full name is Peter Benjamin Parker.
> He is Caucasian and heterosexual.
> His parents become absent from his life during his childhood.
> From the time his parents become absent he is raised by Aunt May and Uncle Ben in New York City.
> He gains his powers while attending either middle school or college.
> He gains his powers from being bitten by a spider.
> He designs his first red and blue costume.
> The black costume is a symbiote and is not designed by him.
> He is raised in a middle class household in Queens, New York.
> He attends or attended high school in Queens, New York, and he attends or attended college in New York City, New York. (Biddle)

Based on this list, the film depiction of Peter Parker can only be a white, heterosexual male from Queens; however, Spider-Man under the mask could be gay, black, or Latino (Miller).

Within recent Marvel films, traditionally white characters played by nonwhite actors always create a controversy. When black actor Michael B. Jordan was cast as the new Human Torch, a traditionally white character from the Marvel series *Fantastic Four*, many fans used arguments similar to those in the Spider-Man controversy (Rottenberg). When black actor Idris Elba was cast as the god Heimdall in the *Thor* movies, there were cries of corrupting the canon and mythology: How can the narrative historically represent Viking gods if they are not all white (Jones)? Of course, this reasoning ignores the fact that the movie presumes that the Norse gods are in fact aliens—or, of course, that fictional characters from comics can be reimagined again and again.

These traditional fans consistently believe that their resistance is a matter of canon and continuity rather than racism. Duncan and Smith define continuity as "a term used to express the intertextual links among separately published comics narratives" (191). In other words, each comic is historically linked from one to another, unless explicitly defined otherwise.[7] The continuous link developed by these comics is grouped into an authoritative canon, which means that, every Spider-Man comic is historically linked to the first one. Continuity can be pushed, but only so much as to not lose fans (DiPaolo 21). The preservation of continuity directly connects current Marvel comics to a time in which black superheroes did not exist; as a result, emphasis on continuity preserves the institutionalized racism of 1960s America.[8] Thus, arguments to retain the canon perpetuate racist ideology, in both overt and subtle ways. Even the creators do not always recognize the problematic history of the canon. As Stan Lee stated in a 2015 *Washington Post* article, "I wouldn't mind, if Peter Parker had originally been black, a Latino, an Indian or anything else, that he stay that way, . . . but we originally made him white. I don't see any reason to change that" (Miller). While Lee has been praised as inclusive and progressive for creating many nonwhite characters, especially Black Panther, the first black superhero, his refusal to let go of tradition counteracts those positive developments.[9]

The creation of Miles Morales, the Ultimate Spider-Man, in 2011 as part of Marvel NOW! was a clear attempt to not only remedy continuity issues but also to appeal to fans. Marvel editors Joe Quesada, Axel Alonso, and Sana Amanat, as well as illustrator Sara Pichelli,[10] decided that if the president of the United States could be African American, then so could Spider-Man. As Matt Brown states, "Miles is a response to a superhero landscape *in publishing* that tends to be fairly white at the top line. He was a good addition to the universe, not just from a racial representation perspective but from a basic worldbuilding one: Miles is a new, rich character, with good stories to tell and fresh places to go" (M. Brown). Yet *Gawker* points out that "the timing [was] odd," given that the Sony Pictures contract went into effect one month after Miles Morales debuted (Biddle). As the *Gawker* leak suggested, Sony seemed worried that Marvel would allow a nonwhite Spider-Man to swing across "the big screen." After making Miles Morales the main Spider-Man in the comic books, writer Brian Michael Bendis hinted that Sony's fears might come true, stating, "Our message has to be it's not Spider-Man with an asterisk, it's the real Spider-Man for kids of color, for adults of color and everybody else" (Bendis).[11] Donald Glover did have a role in the new film, *Spider-Man: Homecoming*, perhaps hinting that a nonwhite Spider-Man was in the works, starting to disrupt the dominance of white characters in the Marvel universe at last.[12]

Kamala Khan, Ms. Marvel: Female and Muslim Representation

Carol Danvers, the original Ms. Marvel, whom Khan idolizes, debuted in 1977 at the height of the women's rights movement in the United States. She was a leader of the Avengers, and, with the name of the company inherent in her identity, she was designed to be a standard bearer, even though her popularity never outshone Spider-Man. Khan's run as Ms. Marvel debuted three years after the first appearance of Miles Morales, also as a part of Marvel NOW! (Wilson). In her 2014 TedxTeen talk, cocreator Sana Amanat suggested a connection between Khan and Morales, saying that the two characters came "together in response to that global subconscious desire for representation" (Amanat "Myths").

In terms of popularity and branding, Pakistani-American Khan stands in a position closer to the original Ms. Marvel than to Spider-Man, yet her readership and sales are still impressive. Amanat cocreated Khan as a semi-autobiographical reflection on her childhood, especially her idolization of comics characters (Amanat "Myths"). However, Amanat wanted to introduce a character who represented her identity, not just a copy of the characters she loved. Amanat's work illustrates how, as Jeffrey Brown argues in *Black Superheroes*, with characters like Khan, women no longer need to "[resort] to creating their pleasures where they can with the text," even though, traditionally, "[w]omen's reading has been characterized through its necessity to rewrite the texts in ways that serve women's own interests in the face of a male-dominated culture" (J. Brown 97–98). With writer G. Willow Wilson at the helm and Amanat as cocreator, Khan represents this new text for "women's own interests." Khan's popularity, especially online, backs up this assertion.

Many of Ms. Marvel's attributes echo Spider-Man's character: she is also a young, awkward teenage kid struggling to find her place in the world who suddenly wakes up with superpowers. While her heroic identity amasses recognition and popularity, her secret identity still struggles in romantic and platonic relationships. Unlike Spider-Man, who was a white kid from Queens, Khan is a female Muslim teen from Jersey City. She is truly an outsider looking in from multiple perspectives. Khan as a character disrupts the white male fan base in two ways: her outright visibility as a young, female Pakistani American is further complicated by the fact that she is the first Muslim character to carry her own title. Yet as Amanat stated upon Khan's debut, her religion is only one piece of many outsider elements of her identity:

> As much as Islam is a part of Kamala's identity, this book isn't preaching about religion or the Islamic faith in particular. It's about what happens when you struggle with the labels imposed on you, and how that forms your sense of self. It's a struggle we've all faced in one form or another, and isn't just particular to Kamala because she's Muslim. Her religion is just one aspect of the many ways she defines herself. (Wheeler)

As a woman, Khan represents a growing roster of female superheroes created and written by women. Many of the female characters who came before her were written by men for the stereotypical fanboy, within a field "dominated by male characters, creative teams, and consumers" (Davis and Westerfelhaus 806). Most of these characters, such as the X-Men's veiled Muslim character Dust, are simply secondary characters on the periphery, who can be ignored most of the time; however, Khan's starring role puts her in full view, and her popularity, as well as her representation in the rest of the Marvel universe outside of her own title, forces the fanboy to deal with her identity in some form. As Rafael Johns put it, both Khan and Jason Aaron's 2014 female Thor break down the "'boys' locker room feel of the comic book world' in more ways than one" (Johns).

Khan's popularity and ability to be identifiable to nonwhite readers, male and female, as well as white female readers, subverts the need to identify with a hero who looks just like the reader.[13] Winona Landis describes this act as "disidentification," which empowers readers who have long had to deal with reading about white male heroes (Landis). Khan deals with issues similar to those that Peter Parker experienced, like being bullied in school, in a way that even white male readers could potentially relate to. As Wilson states on a 2013 Marvel Q and A page, "I think [*Ms. Marvel*] faces some unusual challenges, but they come on top of a whole bunch of usual ones, i.e., getting people to pick up a book with a fresh face on it. Convincing readers that new and different can be new and good" (Wheeler). Khan represents every kid who struggles with outside influences and tries to decide who she is, as opposed to who people tell her she is. Part of this struggle comes out of her identity as a Muslim, as well as from her identity as the daughter of recent immigrants. Amanat often downplays Khan's identity as a Muslim, which she believes can represent another label imposed on her. Resistance to labels and stereotypes is a common struggle for all adolescents, which suggests Khan's "universal connectivity" with all fans (Couric). As Wilson stated when Khan debuted, "In a sense, she has a 'dual identity' before she even puts on a superhero costume. Like a lot of children of immigrants, she feels torn between two worlds: the family she loves, but which drives her crazy, and her peers, who don't really understand what her home life is like" (Kastrenakes). To help "expand Marvel's efforts in reaching new readers," Khan brings her story home to any kid who struggles with conservative parents and non-relatable siblings (ibid.).

Kamala Khan received just as much positive response as many of the other characters of the Marvel Universe. As Amanat—currently the only female South Asian comic book editor—stated in a recent video,

> For the most part, the reaction has been very very positive. We've also had some negative responses because we are attempting to change these very precious characters [....] W]e have to make sure we are constantly challenging the status quo and reminding people that these characters are mantles for the ideals we aspire to be. They are not genders, they are not races, they are ideas and ideals, specifically. ("Sana Amanat on the Growing Influence")

Ms. Marvel's largest response came from a reaction at the Hugo Awards for science fiction and fantasy in 2015, when she won the award for best graphic story. However, that particular award show was under protest by a group calling themselves the Sad Puppies, who claimed that the Hugo Awards were not fair because white men were not winning recent awards. The Sad Puppies claimed that the awards had not been based on merit but on political correctness. Ms. Marvel was not directly attacked by this group, but she was one of the many award-winning characters created by a nonwhite and not exclusively male team. Not surprisingly, *Breitbart.com* criticized the awards as well, claiming that "social justice warriors did their best impression of the nightmare firemen of Ray Bradbury's classic *Fahrenheit 451*, choosing to burn down the Hugo Awards and damage science fiction instead of seeing works of heretical authors outside of their exclusive clique winning awards" (Yiannopoulos). Ms. Marvel and her otherwise positive reaction represent a shifting of readership; however, many white male readers, especially the more extreme conservatives represented by outlets like Breitbart, are still not comfortable with the growing diversity of comic books.

Conclusion: Real Diversity or Tokenism?

Comic books have functioned as a means of social commentary since their creation, so the recent interpretation of new Marvel titles and characters as subversive is not out of the norm. Comics have, of course, frequently made political statements. As Marc DiPaolo states,

> In fact, comic books have always been political, and have taken stands on controversial issues such as the death penalty, abortion, gay rights, and the environment. They have also reflected the mood of the public by being pro-war during wartime and pacifistic during peacetime almost as often as they have served as the voice of the minority opinion, crying for peace during wartime and advocating going to war when the public is reluctant to do so. (11)

Given this political history, it is not surprising to see comics linked more recently to identity politics. As Rafael Johns stated about his own preference for reading, "It's important for me to see brown characters who aren't muggers and who don't speak in slang. Being able to follow a character who's both brown and gay keeps me interested and invested in a comic book. And it's also what makes me willing to actually invest in one" (Johns). Recent backlash against this diversity is clear from the titles of stories on the conservative website *The Federalist*, such as "How Social Justice Warriors Are Ruining Comic Books for Everyone" and "The Queer Lobby Wants to Make Comic Books Unequal" (Trent). The first article and podcast argue that the "focus has shifted where the fandom is the focus, rather than the actual product" ("How Social Justice Warriors"). Ironically, however, this is precisely the reaction Sana Amanat wants, with her desire to have Marvel NOW! represent "the ever changing world we live in today," of which the traditional white male comics fan is only a subset (Amanat "All-New Marvel NOW!").

However, Marvel NOW! is not without its problems. What Marvel actually lacks is equal representation in artists and authors, who remain predominantly white males. Also, Marvel NOW! risks tokenization, taking random characters and inserting said minority—a practice that, Matt Brown argues, can prove as much a part of the problem as not having diverse superheroes at all. As Brown states, "If racial representation in Marvel comics is a problem with a few really good responses lately (Miles, Kamala Khan, the current run of Captain America), race in the Marvel Cinematic Universe is, right now, an outright disaster" (M. Brown). Jeffrey Brown believes that if many of the depictions of heroes "reinforce racial and sexual stereotypes, they can also present tales that move beyond derogatory stereotypes" (J. Brown "Panthers and Vixens," 134), yet this idea of diversity can serve to just placate the various people represented rather than create real change. Until Marvel employs more nonwhite artists and writers, the company continues to walk a thin line between equal representation and mere tokenism (Rodriguez-Jimenez).

Another recent development to challenge all-white, all-male creative teams came when Marvel hired author and activist Gabby Rivera to write *America*, a queer Latina version of the character Miss America from the Golden Age of comics. The series ran for twelve issues from 2017 through 2018. Rivera emphasized how important it was that Marvel chose her, a queer Latina, to write the comic, "to make sure it's coming from an authentic place to really provide that authentic voice." Rivera was impressed "that Marvel was taking that step and actually reaching out to me" (Rodriguez-Jimenez).[14] In a presentation at the University of Kansas, Rivera expressed that she wants to disrupt white supremacy and white spaces through her writing, but she also wants to contribute to representation and create happy narratives for characters, not just stereotypical, tokenized stories. For Benjamin Woo, this type of representation has "problematized the 'default fanboy' identity more than ever" (Woo).

In contrast, although Miles Morales was cocreated by a Latino male, he was primarily written by white men, which can pose a new problem. As Matt Brown suggests,

> The problem with Miles Morales is that inasmuch as he's a necessary response to representation in comics specifically, everywhere else, he's an excuse. He's a reason we don't have to redress the wider context of representation in these stories; he's the reason an enormous number of people don't even have to think about whether there's a problem with Peter Parker being cast white again. (M. Brown)

Stan Lee's reinforcement of Sony's directive that Peter Parker can only be white functions to support historic institutionalized racism and sexism (Miller). It is not as easy these days as Lee thought it was to invent—and especially to run—new and diverse characters: among other obstacles, new characters are up against seventy-five years of white male continuity. If left to traditional fans or the original creators, characters would essentially stay the same. Visibility does matter. Although titles with Kamala Khan and Miles Morales are flourishing, since some of Marvel's own executives, the fanboys of yesterday, continue to blame lack of sales on inclusion, for real change to take place, diverse representation needs to be mandatory and widespread from the top down.

NOTES

1. Gabriel's response further attests to the institutionalized racism I analyze in this essay, especially considering that there are multiple factors that have led to the decline in comic book sales. *The Atlantic* reported that Gabriel tried to walk back his comments and explain that their data showed that books with "diverse" characters were doing poorly; however, comics without white male leads were selling more (Elbein).

2. The term hit the big screen in 2009, when the movie *Fanboys* parodied "nerd" culture, primarily centered around *Star Wars*, but also included comic books. Most of the characters were stereotypes of nerdy, white males, who spent much of the movie commenting on each other's gender and sexual performance (*Fanboys*).

3. Also see Darowski, whose data supports the assertion that the X-Men team has stayed primarily white and male. Even if the mutants have different skin color, they read as ethnically white and male. The exception came in the 90s, when many of the teams were dominated by women, with characters like Storm, Psylocke, Jubilee, Rogue, and Jean Grey.

4. Marvel's Facebook page, October 21, 2016, https://www.facebook.com/Marvel/photos/a.106017942487.92320.6883542487/10154551000112488/?type=3&theater.

5. Batman titles did lead in sales at the time: "Industry Statistics," *Diamondcomics.com*, http://www.diamondcomics.com/Home/1/1/3/237?articleID=185244.

6. Biddle's interpretation of the leaked document has been disputed. See Alex Abad-Santos, "Sony Can Make a Black Spider-Man Movie, It Just Doesn't Want To," *Vox*, June 25, 2015, https://www.vox.com/2015/6/24/8839485/spider-man-black-gay. –Eds.

7. For further reading on continuity, see Reynolds.

8. For further reading on how continuity reinforces gender roles of the 1950s, see Michael Goodrum's article on Lois Lane, in which he analyzes continuity as a "system that reproduces broader social trends of marginalization and oppression" (Goodrum).

9. Many of Lee's other characters are still tied to the institutionalized racism that contextualizes their earlier creation and exhibit various levels of white privilege, such as the wealthy Iron Man or the white "nuclear family" of the Fantastic Four. When more black superheroes are created, they are often tokenized or stereotyped, such as Luke Cage and Misty Knight. Many of the DC Comics characters, such as Batman, Wonder Woman, and

Green Lantern, were created even earlier, and their canon links to 1940s and 1950s America. The casting of Zendaya as Spider-Man's girlfriend, Mary Jane, in the most recent live-action *Spider-Man* film also caused controversy, which was especially focused on her hair (Surrey).

10. These are all either women, people of color, or, in the case of Amanat, both.

11. Also see Opam.

12. *Into the Spiderverse*, though not live action, has also complicated these arguments in fascinating ways that are too recent to incorporate into this book but that we look forward to following. –Eds.

13. In an interview with Katie Couric, Wilson and Amanat stated, "The fan response was phenomenal. Above and beyond anything we expected for this character and this book. And that's when we knew we had a great story because it very much had a universal struggle. Something I think people of all ages can still connect with about the idea of trying to be yourself and people telling you that you can't be" (Couric).

14. Gabby Rivera was also attacked online, specifically by the reactionary group Diversity & Comics. To try to stop her from writing comics, these attacks escalated to threats on her life.

BIBLIOGRAPHY

Amanat, Sana. "All-New Marvel NOW! Ms. Marvel." *Marvel Entertainment.* November 13, 2013. https://www.youtube.com/watch?v=xxljTKoT4gk.

———. "Myths, Misfits & Masks: Sana Amanat at TEDxTeen 2014." *TEDx.* March 17, 2014. https://www.youtube.com/watch?v=091ev9739zQ.

Bendis, Brian Michael, and Sara Pichelli. *Spider-Man* 2, no. 1. New York: Marvel Studios, 2016.

Biddle, Sam. "Spider-Man Can't Be Gay or Black." *Gawker.* June 19, 2015. http://gawker.com/spider-man-cant-be-gay-or-black-1712401879.

Brown, Jeffrey A. *Black Superheroes, Milestone Comics, and Their Fans.* Jackson: University of Mississippi Press, 2000.

———. "Panthers and Vixens: Black Superheroines, Sexuality, and Stereotypes in Contemporary Comic Books." *Black Comics: Politics of Race and Representation.* Eds. Sheena C. Howard and Ronald L. Jackson II. New York: Bloomsbury, 2013. 133–49.

Brown, Matt. "Destroy All Monsters: The Ghettoization of Miles Morales as Spider-Man." *Screen Anarchy.* April 29, 2015. http://screenanarchy.com/2015/04/destroy-all-monsters-the-ghettoization-of-miles-morales-as-spider-man.html#ixzz3d0psE11P.

Cain, Sian. "Marvel Executive Says Emphasis on Diversity May Have Alienated Readers." April 3, 2017. https://www.theguardian.com/books/2017/apr/03/marvel-executive-says-emphasis-on-diversity-may-have-alienated-readers.

Clark, Noelene. "*Mockingbird* Writer Receives Support Online after Feminist Comic Cover Backlash." *Entertainment Weekly.* October 26, 2016. http://www.ew.com/article/2016/10/26/chelsea-cain-mockingbird-feminist-backlash.

"Comic Book Masculinity and the New Black Superhero." *African American Review* 33, no. 1 (Spring 1999): 25–42.

Couric, Katie. "Rise of the Female Superhero." *Yahoo.com.* August 12, 2015. https://yahoo.com/katiecouric/rise-of-the-female-superhero-ever-since-superman-126459307033.html.

Darowski, Joseph. *X-Men and the Mutant Metaphor: Race and Gender in the Comic Books.* Lanham, MD: Rowman & Littlefield, 2014.

Davis, Julie, and Robert Westerfelhaus. "Finding a Place for a Muslimah Heroine in the Post-9/11 Marvel Universe: New X-Men's Dust." *Feminist Media Studies* 13, no. 5 (2013): 800–809.

DiPaolo, Marc. *War, Politics and Superheroes: Ethics and Propaganda in Comics and Film.* Jefferson, NC: McFarland, 2011.

Dodds, Eric. "There Are So Many Reasons Donald Glover Should Be the Next Spider-Man." *Time.* February 10, 2015. http://time.com/3703175/donald-glover-next-spider-man/.

Duncan, Randy, and Matthew J. Smith. *The Power of Comics: History, Form & Culture.* New York: Bloomsbury Academic, 2009.

Elbein, Asher. "The Real Reason for Marvel Comics' Woes." *The Atlantic.* Theatlantic.com. May 24, 2017. https://www.theatlantic.com/entertainment/archive/2017/05/the-real-reasons-for-marvel-comics-woes/527127/.

Fanboys. Directed by Kyle Newman. New York: Weinstein, 2009.

Fingeroth, Danny. *Superman on the Couch: What Superheroes Really Tell Us about Ourselves and Our Society.* New York: Bloomsbury Academic, 2004.

Goodrum, Michael. "'Superman Believes that a Wife's Place Is in the Home': Superman's Girl Friend, and the Representation of Women. *Gender & History* 30, no. 2 (2018): 442–64.

Hajdu, David. *The Ten-Cent Plague: The Great Comic-Book Scare and How It Changed America.* New York: Picador, 2008.

Hills, Matt. "Always-On Fandom, Waiting and Bingeing." *The Routledge Companion to Media Fandom.* Eds. Melissa A. Click and Suzanne Scott. New York: Routledge, 2018. 18–26.

Howard, Adam. "'Spider-Man' Casting Controversy Revives Racial Tensions." *Nbcnews.com.* August 24, 2016. https://www.nbcnews.com/news/nbcblk/spider-man-casting-controversy-revives-racial-tensions-n637111.

"How Social Justice Warriors Are Ruining Comic Books for Everyone." *The Federalist.* May 13, 2016. http://thefederalist.com/2016/05/13/how-social-warriors-are-ruining-comic-books-for-everyone/.

Hudson, Laura. "DC Comics Survey Reports 'New 52' Readership 93% Male, Only 5% New Readers." *Comics Alliance.* February 10, 2012. http://comicsalliance.com/dc-comics-readers-survey-reports-new-52-readership-93-male/.

Johns, Rafael. "Comic Book Publishers Struggle to Attract New Generation of Readers." *All Things Considered,* NPR. May 1, 2015. http://www.npr.org/2015/05/01/403597712/comic-book-publishers-struggle-to-attract-new-generation-of-readers.

Jones, Sam. "Idris Elba Defends Thor Film Role." *The Guardian.* April 27, 2010. https://www.theguardian.com/culture/2010/apr/27/idris-elba-thor-race-debate.

Kastrenakes, Jacob. "Marvel Pushes for Diversity with Newest Superhero, a Teenage Muslim Girl." *The Verge.* November 6, 2013. http://www.theverge.com/2013/11/6/5074498/new-ms-marvel-is-muslim-teenage-girl-kamala-khan.

Landis, Winona. "Diasporic (Dis)identification: The Participatory Fandom of *Ms. Marvel.*" *South Asian Popular Culture* 14, nos. 1–2 (2016): 33–47. http://dx.doi.org/10.1080/14746689.2016.1241344.

Lund, Martin. "'X Marks the Spot': Urban Dystopia, Slum Voyeurism and Failures of Identity in District X." *Journal of Urban Cultural Studies* 2, nos. 1 & 2 (2015): 35–55.

McIntosh, Peggy. "White Privilege and Male Privilege: A Personal Account of Coming to See Correspondences through Work in Women's Studies." Working Paper 189. Wellesley College, Center for Research on Women, 1988.

Melrose, Kevin. "They Are Starved for Content and Looking for Content They Can Relate To." *CBR.com*. February 5, 2014. http://www.cbr.com/they-are-starved-for-content-and-looking-for-content-they-can-relate-to/.

Miller, Michael E. "Peter Parker, a.k.a. Spider-Man, Should Be Straight and White, Says Co-Creator Stan Lee." *The Washington Post*. June 25, 2015. https://www.washingtonpost.com/news/morning-mix/wp/2015/06/25/peter-parker-aka-spider-man-should-be-straight-and-white-says-co-creator-stan-lee/.

Morse, Ben. "Marvel NOW!" *Marvel.com*. 29 June 2016. http://marvel.com/news/comics/19008/marvel_now.

Nama, Adilifu. *Super Black: American Pop Culture and Black Superheroes*. Austin: University of Texas Press, 2011.

Opam, Kwame. "Miles Morales Will Be the Marvel Universe's Main Spider-Man This Fall." *The Verge*. June 21, 2015. http://www.theverge.com/2015/6/21/8820173/miles-morales-spider-man-marvel-universe.

Osborn, Alex. "Fantastic Four Director and Producer Address Casting Uproar." *IGN.com*. June 3, 2015. http://www.ign.com/articles/2015/06/04/fantastic-four-director-and-producer-address-casting-uproar.

Proctor, William. "'Bitches Ain't Gonnah Hunt No Ghosts': Totemic Nostalgia, Toxic Fandom and the Ghostbusters Platonic." *Palabra Clave* 20, no. 4 (2017): 1105–41. DOI: 10.5294/pacla.2017.20.4.10.

Reynolds, Richard. *Super Heroes: A Modern Mythology*. Jackson: University Press of Mississippi, 1992.

Richards, Dave. "Alonso & Brevoort Make Theirs Marvel Now!" *CBR.com*. July 5, 2012. http://www.cbr.com/alonso-brevoort-make-theirs-marvel-now/.

Rivera, Gabby. "Radical Creativity + Queer Latinx Joy." Keynote Address. The Center for Community Outreach. University of Kansas. April 24, 2018.

Rodriguez-Jimenez, Jorge. "Queer Latina Writer Writing for Marvel's America Chavez." *Mitu*. wearemitu.com. March 13, 2017. https://wearemitu.com/entertainment/queer-latina-writer-writing-for-marvels-queer-latina-america-chavez/.

Rottenberg, Josh. "'Fantastic Four's' Message for Comic Fans Who Hate New Cast." *LA Times*. June 3, 2015. http://www.latimes.com/entertainment/herocomplex/la-et-hc-josh-trank-simon-kinberg-fantastic-four-casting-controversy-story.html.

"Sana Amanat on the Growing Influence of Women in Comic Books." *CCTV America*. June 10, 2016. https://www.youtube.com/watch?v=Mq6wbAIkJfc.

Schenker, Brett. "Market Research Says 46.67% of Comic Fans Are Female." *The Beat*. February 5, 2014. http://www.comicsbeat.com/marketresearchsays46femalecomicfans/.

Shyminsky, Neil. "Mutant Readers, Reading Mutants: Appropriation, Assimilation, and the X-Men." *International Journal of Comic Art* 8, no. 2 (Fall 2006): 387–405.

Sperb, Jason. "Reassuring Convergence: Online Fandom, Race, and Disney's Notorious Song of the South." *Cinema Journal* 49, no. 4 (Summer 2010): 25–45.

Stanfill, Mel. "Doing Fandom, (Mis)doing Whiteness: Heteronormativity, Racialization, and the Discursive Construction of Fandom." *Transformative Works and Cultures* no. 8 (2011).

Stenger, Josh. "The Clothes Make the Fan: Fashion and Online Fandom When "Buffy the Vampire Slayer" Goes to eBay. *Cinema Journal* 45, no. 4 (Summer 2006): 26–44.

Stuller, Jennifer K. *Ink-Stained Amazons and Cinematic Warriors: Superwomen in Modern Mythology.* London: I. B. Tauris, 2010.

Superheroes: A Never-Ending Battle. Directed by Michael Kantor. Arlington, VA: PBS Direct, 2013. DVD.

Surrey, Miles. "Zendaya Is Mary Jane in 'Spider-Man Homecoming,' So of Course There's Racist Backlash." *Mic.com.* August 19, 2016. https://mic.com/articles/152038/zendaya-is-mary-jane-in-spider-man-homecoming-so-of-course-there-s-racist-backlash#.d5XhlQo4C.

Trent, John. "The Queer Lobby Wants to Make Comic Books Unequal." *The Federalist.* February 5, 2016. http://thefederalist.com/2016/02/05/the-queer-lobby-wants-to-make-comic-books-unequal/.

Wheeler, Andrew. "All-New Marvel NOW! Q&A: Ms. Marvel." *Marvel.com.* November 6, 2013. http://marvel.com/news/comics/21466/all-new_marvel_now_qa_ms_marvel.

Wilson, G. Willow, and Adrian Alphona. *Ms. Marvel* 3, no. 1. New York: Marvel Studios, 2014.

Woo, Benjamin. "The Invisible Bag of Holding: Whiteness and Media Fandom." *The Routledge Companion to Media Fandom.* Eds. Melissa A. Click and Suzanne Scott. New York: Routledge, 2018. 245–52.

Yiannopoulos, Milo. "Set Phasers to Kill! SJWS Burn Down the Hugo Awards to Prove How Tolerant and Welcoming They Are." *Breitbart.* August 23, 2015. http://www.breitbart.com/big-government/2015/08/23/set-phasers-to-kill-sjws-burn-down-the-hugo-awards-to-prove-how-tolerant-and-welcoming-they-are/.

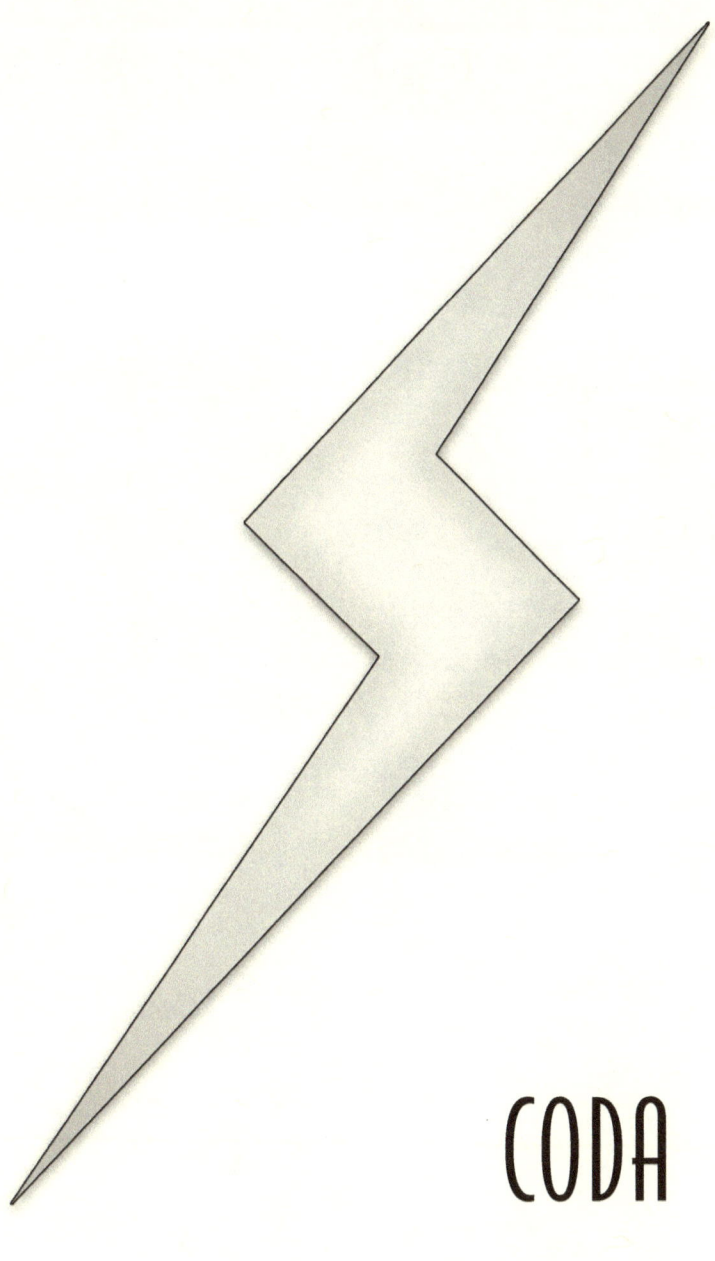

CODA

Conversations

MADINA ON THE LIGHT RAIL (THAT GIRL IS ME)

JOSÉ ALANIZ

THAT GIRL IS ME

FALL, 2016. WE WERE RIDING THE LIGHT RAIL INTO TOWN. I HAPPENED TO HAVE OUT VOLUME ONE OF **MS. MARVEL** ("NO NORMAL"), WHICH I WAS TEACHING THEN. A GIRL IN A VEIL, ABOUT 15, SITTING NEXT TO US, TAPS ME ON THE ARM. SHE GESTURES AND POINTS AT THE BOOK. I SMILE AND LOOK PUZZLED. SHE PULLS OUT HER PHONE AND TAPS, "I AM MADINA. I AM DEAF." SO WE TALK BACK AND FORTH ON MY iPAD. "I AM FROM SOMALIA," SHE SAYS. "MY FAMILY CAME HERE AS REFUGEES. THAT GIRL IS ME." SHE MEANS KAMALA KHAN, MS. MARVEL, A DARK-SKINNED MUSLIM SUPERHERO. AFTER MADINA GOT OFF, MY WIFE SAID, "I'LL NEVER DOUBT THIS COMICS THING AGAIN."

INTERVIEW WITH G. WILLOW WILSON

SHABANA MIR, OCTOBER 2017

Diversity in Comics

Shabana: Do you think Kamala Khan fits into the comic book trend of diverse female characters and characters of color?

Willow: Kamala really predates that conversation by a couple of years. Sana Amanat (editor and cocreator of Ms. Marvel) and I first started talking about this project a little over five years ago. And at the time it was *not* a discussion about "diversity in comics" as such. Of course, among fans there was a groundswell of interest in new, interesting, and diverse characters, but there was no initiative—and I still don't think there's an initiative now as such—among comic book publishers to specifically go out and find "diverse" stories.

The reason this character exists at all is because Sana and her editor at the time, [Stephen] Wacker, wanted to tell not only a diverse story but a very specific story. Sana would tell her editor stories about growing up as a Pakistani-American girl in the United States, the child of immigrant parents, [and] the ways in which her childhood lessons differed from his and from the usual narrative lessons that we see in comics. And they said, "You know what, I'm sure there are a lot of kids out there who are thinking the exact same thing as you are and would love a story like this. So why don't we create a new young American character and give her her own series?" And that's the point at which they called me. And that's all there was.

At the time, I was the only American woman working in superhero comics who had any kind of background in Muslim superhero comics. We spent a solid nine months coming up with a character and her background, her social circle, her school, her childhood, her powers, her costume. And that's one of the reasons I think it worked; it struck a nerve because there was no fishing involved. This is not trying to capture an audience or get an edge on the market or something. It was really about telling a specific story that hadn't been told before.

S: So the story was a specific one, and was not inserted into a trend of diversity. If it can be said to have *entered* a trend of diverse characters, how does Kamala's story enter that trend?

W: Nondiverse in comics usually means cisgender heterosexual white men—in other words, stories that focus on your classic Superman archetype. And I think that the reason such attention is given to this series in particular is because it was successful right after it came out, which shocked everybody. Because the formula that we were using was not supposed to work. It was known throughout the industry that (1) solo titles headed by female characters do not sell; (2) new titles do not sell, ever; and (3) minority characters don't sell. This book should not have sold. It should have been dead on arrival by the old industry manual. This is just five years ago; this is not ancient history. That a character like this, in a solo series—in other words: they're supposed to hold up the entire story, they're not on a team, they're not being carried by more famous characters that they can ride the coattails of . . . this is not Teen Titans, this is not the Avengers. For a series like that to succeed was just wildly, wildly out of the box and shocked a lot of people.

I think that's why the question is still being asked: Why did Ms. Marvel work? What is it about Ms. Marvel that worked when so many other attempts at this kind of story failed in the past? I don't know that I have concrete answers to all those questions, by the way. But when something that you expect to fail succeeds, people's ears kind of prick up, and they start asking why. That's how I think we got drawn into the larger conversation about diversity in comics and what sells and what doesn't.

Comic Book Market and Readership

S: Do you believe the future of comics holds a trend of diverse characters?
W: I think it's anybody's guess because we haven't even decided what that means. That's question one. Question two is what other factors are at play in comics in general, and [with] comics treating diverse characters in particular. There's a lot going on in comic books right now that's unconnected to diversity or lack of diversity—and it's connected to how people read and consume media, what audiences are interested in comics, and whether the comics industry is doing a good job of getting comics into the hands of new

readers. What that really means is: Is this very antiquated distribution system the comic book industry uses still working? And if it isn't, how do you bridge the gap and get into bookstores and get to people that way—people who might not go to their local comic book store or even know where it is but who would go to their local Barnes and Noble, or independent bookstore, or library? Is enough being done to reach those audiences? Do those audiences have different preferences in terms of what they read, [compared to] the older, stereotypical comic-book-guy-from-*The Simpsons* audience, which was the bread and butter of the comic book industry for so long? It's very difficult, in my opinion, to disentangle the issue of *diversity* from these *larger* economic forces that are affecting the entire comic book industry right now. So I don't really have a concrete answer.

S: How would you say comic book readership has shifted?
W: Age is a big one. It used to be that there was almost no point in digitizing comics because no one was reading them on their tablet or Kindle or what have you. Now with the rise of color tablets, the Kindle Fire, and the iPad, tons of people have started reading comic books in digital format. That's one thing. Of course, that readership skews younger than the traditional readership. It's also not entirely clear, but there are a lot of suggestions that that younger audience is also more female. Comics used to be seen as having a male-dominated readership. But now at the bigger comic book conventions there's gender parity: it's 50–50 between men and women.

S: So it used to be that basically Peter Parker was your main reader, right?
W: Yes, exactly. *Yes*. Peter Parker was your Mary Sue or Danny Sue Everyman. He represented exactly the same kind of people who were reading the comic book. I think that's the reason that character works so well. There are a lot of very big questions being asked in the comic book industry right now about what it means to write comics. Are superhero comics kind of a dying breed because they reference so much ancient history? They've got these tangled continuities that stretch back, in the case of somebody like Superman, nearly one hundred years now. How do you bring new audiences into that? Do they care about all of this backstory? If they don't, should you change something, or would that lose your old readership? There are big existential questions being asked right now, of which diversity is a part. But certainly, there are much larger forces at work that make it very difficult to say what's going to happen to those books and those audiences.

S: That's especially interesting because Hussein [Rashid] was interested in what you think of [the death of] Wolverine. How does that relate to Wolverine? Are we going to start burying all of our Wolverines?

W: It could happen! From time immemorial, one of the biggest ways to drum up interest in a title or in a series is to kill off a beloved main character. Think death of Superman back in the 1990s. I was a pimply young comic book reader at that time, and I still remember that story arc and the death of Superman—oh my God! I remember the posters. Even at my local strip-mall dance studio where I took ballet lessons as a kid, there was a big Death of Superman poster. I think these events are a way to drum up interest, but, at the same time, they're inevitably controversial. And they've gotten more so because the trend has been over the last couple of years to either kill off or discredit these beloved decades-old characters (who are usually straight white men) and replace them with, in the case of Wolverine, a female successor—or in the case of the Hulk, with a geeky young Korean American scientist successor, and in the case of Spider-Man, with a black Latino successor.

It really does raise a lot of the issues that we were talking about. Is there a market for those books? Are people attached enough to the old characters for them to be offended to see them be replaced? And the answer varies from character to character. Like in the case of Wolverine, it was done in a way that people really connected to this successor, this X23, Laura. Because it was a movie, everybody saw the movie [*Logan*] in which there's the cute little kid who's also a murderous psychopath running around, and we see that baton handed off from old man Logan who's lost his ability to heal: he's dying, he's got to pass his torch to this girl, he's teaching her about life. You really get a sense of continuity, that that new character belongs there. So X23 has done unusually well in this chain of succession, these characters who have had their mantles of superhero passed down to the next generation.

But there are other cases in which the fans have reacted less well. In the case of the new Hulk—there is some controversy surrounding that because Bruce Banner's end was a bit ignominious, and there was not this sense of passing the torch. You're left to wonder if it's the diversity that people are reacting against or the lack of continuity, the lack of a sense of legacy. Or is it something completely different? Arguments can be made either way. The responses have been so different from book to book, character to character, that it's difficult to generalize.

S: In your [blog] piece "So About That Whole Thing," you wrote: "On a practical level, this is not really a story about 'diversity' at all. It's a story about

the rise of YA [young adult] comics." Different groups of people have laid claim to Ms. Marvel's story as theirs. How are those two stories—YA and diversity—different? How is Ms. Marvel a story primarily about a YA market?
W: I think they're interrelated because the younger you go demographically in America, the more diverse you get. My older daughter was born in 2011, which was the first year since white people landed in the Americas—the first year since we started recording this stuff—that more mixed and nonwhite children were born than white children. And my daughter's part of that: she's half North African and half European. I think younger audiences are more open to picking up stories about characters [who] might not look like them, and are able to identify with those characters. And I think that's a big thing.

The other part of that, though, is that at the time *Ms. Marvel* launched, there really were not a whole lot of YA comics available in the superhero world. There were lots in the literary world—Raina Telgemeier was just coming up. The more literary black-and-white comic books were coming out. But in superheroes, the trend for twenty years had been to go very dark, very gritty, very gory, and very adult. If you took a kid into a comic book shop that specialized in comic books, you could give them almost nothing. We were really tapping into a very underserved market in terms of youth. You know, there's no sex in *Ms. Marvel*; there's no gore. If you wanted a young, G-rated or PG-rated comic book that you could give to a twelve-year-old girl, there were not a whole lot of them around. That, I think, is a huge part of our success....

This is where I think that getting into these very nitty-gritty questions—like, Is it diversity? Is it about Islam? Is it about this?—is unhelpful because there's cross-pollination, and you can serve multiple audiences with the same book.... This is a frustration I have in the publishing industry because of the tendency to overlook the fact that different kinds of people can connect to different parts of the same book. I get as much mail from homeschooling Christian moms saying, "I want to thank you for putting religion in a positive light and giving me something I can give to my kids," as I do from Muslim kids or South Asian kids. So that's a big thing. People just want comics without sex and gore that they want to give to their kids!

The Race and Religion of Superheroes

S: I'm reminded of Charlottesville,[1] and the image of alt-right men chanting, "You will not replace us!" jumped to my mind. You will not replace Bruce Banner!

W: Exactly! It's really interesting because I think there is some cultural anxiety there. When you see a character that you identify with, you aspire to be, become replaced by someone who doesn't look like you, doesn't have the same problems as you, does not aspire to the same things as you—I think that struck *some* people in a particularly emotional way that nobody quite understands.

S: Speaking of markets and readerships, killing off a "white" Hulk and replacing him with a nonwhite person gambles with the readership, positing a political reimagining, [and] assumptions about where readers are.

W: I think you're right, and sometimes the gamble pays off, and sometimes it doesn't. The thing about markets—and especially publishing markets—is that every time you see a success, everybody rushes to replicate that *exact* success in that *exact* way, and it's almost always a bad idea. Because the reason that particular book or particular series succeeds tends to be very specific and individual. Why was it Harry Potter that was massively successful and popular, yet not the million Harry Potter look-alike series that came out afterward—which should have been a sure thing, right? It's the same formula; it's the same age range; it's the same publishing strategy. So why did so many fall by the wayside? We can't even remember their names anymore. Then along comes another series—I don't want to name names now—but it does really well. And you're saying, this is *terrible!* Why has this done so well? There are others that are *better* that crashed and burned. It's tough. Ms. Marvel was something that couldn't be predicted, yet a gamble was made.

A lot of the credit is due to Sana and Steve, who supported Ms. Marvel before it even existed. That's a part of diversity that we don't even talk about. We talk about diversity creators. We don't talk about diversity gatekeepers—the people in positions to make decisions about what gets made and what does not. That's huge. Having someone like Sana, and Steve—supportive and willing to put his own name on the line, like Steve did—made all the difference. . . . At the time, [Steve] was [Sana's] direct editorial supervisor. It's partly how much firepower is a publisher willing to put behind a certain project? And if it's a passion project—if an editor is really willing to champion it and get it the support that it needs and the market that it needs—that can make a huge, huge difference. It did for Ms. Marvel because it had such excellent editors, who were really going to bat for it when all the critical decisions were being made about how it was going to be marketed.

S: What year was Ms. Marvel first floated as an idea?

W: [I]t would've been 2011 or 2012. What was sort of stunning at the time was that Marvel was going to give this legacy title—Ms. Marvel. I mean, like, the name's right there—to a Muslim teenager. That was shocking.

S: Even now it's shocking.

W: Are you crazy? I was like, Do you realize, we're all going to get death threats? We're going to have to hire an intern *just* to manage the death threats. It's going to be crazy. I was like, You're nuts!

S: So were there death threats?

W: You know, the backlash at the beginning was much more muted than I thought it was going to be. I was bracing for an absolute shit storm. There was certainly grumbling—this was going on five years ago when the book came out. This big cultural conversation that we're having now, about who owns America, was not yet in full swing. It was just a groundswell. I think if the book came out today, there'd be riots—maybe not riots, but possibly riots! But, at the time, there was a dull roar, and a much bigger roar was support, which was just amazing to me.

S: Thinking back to the [2016] *Ghostbusters* remake, I guess it helped that [the character shift] was female-to-female.

W: Ms. Marvel wasn't a gender swap.

S: So it's just ethnic color added—and of course religion.

W: Terrorism!

Ms. Marvel as a Relatable Teen

S: One of our volume contributors was curious about how, as Noah Berlatsky put it, "like many a Peter Parker-esque nerd before her, Kamala is out of place and uncomfortable."[2] Was that characterization intentional?

W: Being out of place and uncomfortable? Yes. Because I think that's what made Peter Parker an Everyman. Who feels confident and wonderful at sixteen? Nobody! If you peak at sixteen, your life is going to suck. For most people, sixteen is an age where you're not quite an adult, you're still breaking out in zits, the guy or girl you like won't look twice at you, you can't figure out who you are in relation to your peers, there's peer pressure, there's pressure coming from your adults and teachers about what you're going to be when you grow up—it's a rough time! That age is a very good entry point to get people to empathize with a character [whom] they might not otherwise. Because you might not know what it's like to be in specific family situations, you certainly don't know what it's like to have superpowers, but you know what it's like to be sixteen, out of place, and nobody really gets you. That's really powerful, and it's a very rooted archetype of the superhero world where you have superheroes of two flavors: you have the astronomically good-looking billionaire heir to an empire: your Bruce Waynes, your Tony Starks, your Clark Kents—they're just aspirational. Nobody's ever going to be Superman. Nobody's ever going to have the money of Batman. Nobody's ever going to have the brains and the money of Tony Stark. But they're aspirational.

And then you have your Peter Parkers, whom you identify with. They're not aspirational; they're actual. He's a skinny, geeky, pimply, nerdy kid from a lower-class Queens family. We can get that. That's more our speed. Kamala was created in that vein, tapping into that adolescent anxiety that we've all had—not having the money, not having the great bod, not conforming to whatever ideals you're meant to conform to.

S: I suppose the body of Ms. Marvel also lends itself to the awkward shapes that the adolescent body takes.
W: Yes! All of a sudden, you're like, Oh my God, my feet are huge! And you feel like you're the only person who's ever had this problem.

S: Many nonimmigrants can also relate to Kamala's parents' fobbiness[3] because it's their parents somewhat exaggerated.
W: I guess one thing that's semiuniversal about being in that age range is that you suddenly think your parents don't understand you. They're so embarrassing! Why do they even talk to you? I was like that at sixteen. All of us were. It's a generational gap. You think you're the only person that this happened to and your parents can't possibly understand you. Every suggestion they make is stupid. Readers who might think this isn't for me, this isn't about me, might say, Hey this happened to me—I've had these conversations.

Desi[4] Ms. Marvel

S: Speaking of Kamala's parents, though, as a Pakistani and Punjabi, I always wondered how you use Urdu and Hindi. What resources do you use? I was especially fascinated by Kamala's Terrigenesis, her transformation in the Terrigen Mists, where [Amir] Khusro's Sufi poetry is the musical background. How did you come up with that?

W: That's what my head looks like a lot of the time. As an American Muslim, I find myself in *desi* spaces quite a bit, as do a lot of my friends who aren't necessarily of *desi* background—simply because there are a lot of *desi* mosques. A lot of the big organizations regionally and nationally are led or supported by *desis,* so the vocabulary sneaks in, the norms sneak in. Literally, until two weeks ago, I had no idea that the folding down of the corner of the *saggadah*—you know, the prayer mat—I had no idea that this wasn't from Sunnah.[5] I *just* found out that it's just a *desi* custom. Because it's what we all do! Chances are you've been to a *desi* mosque and had a *desi* imam. We're all sort of pseudo-Hanafis[6] because we pray behind a Hanafi imam. So many of my friends I interact with on a daily basis are of *desi* background, I either use the slang that's crept into my own vocabulary, or I'll get on the phone and will be like, Hey, in this situation, if your mom was going to bawl you out, what would you say? And they'll be like, Oh! Let me tell you.

I'd be nervous about all this stuff were it not for the fact that the last person that everything goes through is Sana. This is her birth community; this is in many ways her story. If something looks weird to her, she just flags it. I'll give you an example. Kamala visits her relatives in Karachi, and I was describing to the artist what she's wearing; I was describing a kind of *shalwar kameez,* and he put her in leggings. And I was like, "I don't know, shouldn't they be looser?" And Sana was like, "No, no, this is what cute girls in Karachi would wear. Those [loose] pants are much more villagey."

S: How does Ms. Marvel's costume reflect who she is?

W: Sana and I had a very specific purpose with the costume. It was going to be DIY. It wasn't ever going to be an Iron Man thing. She's from a middle-class home, with an allowance every week. She will have made her costume herself from things she can find in her own closet. We wanted it to be modest—in the sense that it covers her butt. No undies on the outside. That was a big thing. Jamie McKelvie, British artist, was the one who designed her costume, ultimately. It was a tough thing to do, really. We were like, okay, so we know it has to cover her butt. We'd like it to be sort of long-sleeved—and that already takes you way beyond the pale of the vast majority of superhero outfits on women, where typically you have a boob window, butt floss for underwear, that kind of thing. It made sense for her to use something burqinilike [*laugh*] because it'd be the right fabric. It'd be stretchy, it'd be sweat resistant, and she'd have one probably in her closet. We built from there. And Sana especially was adamant that there had to be a reason for each part of her costume to exist, and it had to be something she could make herself. Her little utility bracelet is repurposed bangles that her friend Bruno welds together and makes little compartments in it that she can hold stuff in. She's not wearing *hijab*, but she's got the scarf she can wear over her head. It had to make sense. And you look at the overall result, and you're like, Well, this is not sexy at all—which was the point. But at the same time, you ask the question, Is this going to fly? Will you have readers look and say, "Where's the butt floss?"

But what was interesting about that—and this was another one of those things you can't predict—is that for a lot of people, a costume like Kamala's is much easier to wear. Because they don't have the bod for the butt floss. I'm a size 12, I'm not going to go out dressed in a skin-tight jumpsuit. I'm going to wear something that makes me feel good in my body as it is, and this is easy to make and easy to wear. And that has made a huge difference. Because you don't need to be a size two to cosplay Kamala.

S: We were talking about relatability vis-à-vis Spider-Man, and it sounds like costume relatability is important, too. Isn't Ms. Marvel's costume pretty unprecedented?
W: *I've* never seen one like it, even for teen superheroes—well, Riri Williams [the new black female Iron Man] came after her, but she's also got body armor. You've got Black Widow, but hers is skintight. So you've got costumes where everything is covered up, but it's covered up with spray paint.

S: How do you place Ms. Marvel in the context of a gender struggle?
W: Oh, my goodness. This isn't a question I thought too, too much about when we were launching the book. I just wanted her to be the best iteration of this, of what we set out to do with the book, rather than to say, Okay, we're going to take a specific stand in the continuum of feminism in terms of clothing or gender relations. That wasn't at the forefront of my mind. I don't personally know how to answer that question. You see both arguments: she's a step forward for women in superhero comics because she does wear something that anybody can wear, and she's not going for the sexified look. But others are like, This is a regressive patriarchal way to dress a superhero. I really have no investment in that conversation.

Ms. Marvel in Public Political Discourse

S: [I'm c]urious to know what you think of how Kamala is being used as a political icon. There's some fan art that shows Kamala responding to the election of Trump. I've also seen political signs at protests that use Kamala. And of course, people are cosplaying as Kamala. Why has Kamala become a political icon in this moment? Why do fans from a variety of backgrounds embrace Kamala as a character who represents their lives and experiences? What role should comic book characters play in real life political spaces?

W: I have to be a little bit careful here. . . . We could have a *whole* other interview just about this, how Kamala might have been brought to life by writers, editors, and artists—but at the end of the day, she is the intellectual property of a giant entertainment corporation that has its own independent interest.

I didn't expect Kamala to enter public discourse outside the comic book. That was a big surprise to me. I think it makes a lot of sense, given what the country is fighting over on a cultural level—in other words, who gets to be American and who gets to represent America. Superheroes have always been a big part of that conversation—kind of our collective iconography. They're sort of our Greek gods. They're the exaggerated representation of our ideals and fears, the new things we're afraid of. On that level, it makes sense that people would see a vital symbol in that tussle over who's American and what is America. But I didn't expect it. It's been very interesting to watch that unfold.

S: A student of Hussein's asks: Are Ms. Marvel's polymorph powers symbolic of her need to fit in? Noah Berlatsky describes Ms. Marvel as an "assimilation fantasy," but at the same time reminds us that she says, "Being someone else isn't liberating. It's exhausting." Where does she fall on that assimilation continuum? In what ways does Ms. Marvel speak to Muslim American and ethnic American trends and challenges?

W: Ms. Marvel is at heart an *anti*assimilation story. The moral of the story of her powers is that she can only heal herself in her true form. The more she heals, the less she can take on the shapes of other people. Which is kind of what the wrap-up of the third act of her first story arc was about. She thought if she had these powers, she was going to be this beautiful, blond Amazon she's always been told she *has* to be. But it turns out [that] in order to use her powers, she cannot be that person. Her real power comes from who she is, not from pretending to be some other person.

She has that great scene with her dad where he says that the reason they chose her name is because she's perfect just the way she is. So that's the message that we really wanted to put across in that first story arc: that you don't have to be a blond Amazon—that you really *can't* be—[and] that to take full advantage of the powers you have, it has to come from a genuine place. It has to come from who you really are, not from who you think you should be.

S: But that is a pretty timeless American theme, too: be yourself. Right?
W: Be yourself, yes. But they say, be yourself as long as you fit into these specific categories. [*laugh*] Be yourself, according to me.

S: I know fans will want to know: How much of Ms. Marvel is a reflection of Willow's inner badass and/or inner conflicts?
W: [*laugh*] I don't know about "inner badass." Mostly, I feel fifteen minutes away from dropping every ball I'm attempting to juggle. For me, really, the heart of the series is making something I could really have used when I was her age—something that would've maybe changed the way I thought about myself when I was sixteen. [It's about] what it means to be a superhero, and what that means you have to *be* like and *do*, but also the way parenthood is a protection for my children who will face things I didn't. My husband is Egyptian, I'm American. We both come from the racial and religious majorities from our respective countries where we grew up. It's been a struggle for both of us to learn how to be a minority and prepare kids who are going to be both/and, neither/nor in the ways that Kamala is. When I had my older daughter, I said, "God, I have to get to work! By the time she's old enough, there has to be a body of books I can give her and say, 'You know, you're not the first person to experience these things. There is a way through, and hopefully adults haven't messed things up so badly that you will not be okay.'"

Islam and Superhero Comic Books

S: A question from one of the academic contributors: Islam, of course, is a global religion and one that has intermeshed with a number of cultures worldwide. Naturally, there is no one monolithic "Islam" nor even one solid "American superhero tradition." That said, are there any principles to the superhero ethos that either clash [with] or must be negotiated by a Muslim superhero? That is, how does the general Islamic sense of "heroism" line up with the modern American superhero tradition in comics?

W: That's an interesting question, and you can answer it multiple ways. My husband is Egyptian and a big superhero skeptic. He thinks superheroes are an attempt by the world's only superpower to normalize its violence. In other words, you're so powerful that it's inevitable that there will be casualties you didn't intend, and it's not your fault because it's just a side effect of being so powerful.

S: How do you live with *that*? [*laugh*]
W: It's made me become a much better writer.

S: But it interrogates your entire endeavor.
W: But there's something to that argument—that superheroes are an outgrowth of being a superpower on the world's stage and an outgrowth of imperialism. In that sense, creating a Muslim superhero in the American superhero continuum was very difficult because most superpowers involve violence. Look at Cyclops. If he opens his special glasses, he will blow stuff up. That's kind of America in a nutshell!

Think of what Superman can do, what Batman does. I didn't want [Kamala] to be a telepath. That's a very archetypal passive superpower often given to women. You know, superpowers where you can know and feel the pain of others—I was like, No, absolutely not. . . . Because, you know, any power we give her will make a statement about how we see Muslims in superherodom. If her powers are violent, then we're going to be making a statement about Islam and violence. If her superpowers are passive, we're going to be making a statement about how we think Muslims should be in modern America—you know, feel the pain of others, just deal with it. Eventually, I was like, What if she can stretch and bend and be as big or as small as she wants? What if you give her something that is kinetic, goofy-looking, fun to draw, and not something that you see every day. Nothing sparkles; she doesn't float—I was like no flying, please, no flying. I'm so sick of flying. No flying, no sparkling.

It was really tough because that's the biggest symbol in a superhero: what their superpowers are. And when it's something as loaded as the first Muslim superhero to get her own ongoing series, you have to think about it really carefully. We made her a polymorph in the sense that she can bend and grow; she has to use her wits to use her powers. In other words, it's not really obvious how those powers can solve anything. That was definitely intentional—to not have powers that involved violence made me really think about what it was to be a superhero.

S: So the opposition to violence was because it was a Muslim superhero?

W: Yes, I think if I was making a random superhero, I wouldn't have thought twice about giving her powers to blow stuff up, laser eye beams, or anything you touch turns into a bomb—those are classic superpowers, superpowers used over and over, and nobody's thought twice about them. But to give them to a Muslim superhero? "Hi, I'm a Muslim superhero and I can turn anything into a bomb." [*laugh*] Is that honestly the message we want to be sending here?

S: You could've done invisibility. But then, "I'm a Muslim woman! I can be invisible!"

W: Right! Anything you do, you're like, Shit! We can't do that. Oh, we can't do that either.

S: Do you *want* Ms. Marvel to be a Muslim superhero?

W: You know—yes. Islam is central to her identity. However, having said that, I'm happy that that's not how she's identified now. With people who talk about Ms. Marvel today, Islam only comes up incidentally. I think it's because we—I use the royal "we"; of course, I'm just a part—we really used her religion as kind of a jumping-off point to define her ethics. The ethics are a part of her that can be connected to anybody, regardless. It was really important to me and to Sana that Islam offer something in the series to anybody—that this isn't just a dot in her identity matrix, that this isn't part of a list: she's female, she's Muslim, and so on. If there was something worthwhile in making Islam part of a superhero, we had to get down to the ethical roots of the religion, bring up something that would be of use to any reader who picked it up. If we succeeded in anything, I hope it's that. Because, I have to say, now the fan art features stuff Kamala has said that's from the Qur'an—"Kill one person and it's like you've killed humanity, save one soul and it's like you saved humanity"—and that hadith about when you find the day of reckoning is upon you, and you have a seedling in your hand, then plant the seedling. We're so used to thinking of religion in general and Islam in particular as part of a secular debate about *identity*, so we forget what Islam is on an ethical level. We got down to the roots of that: *good is not a thing you are, it's a thing you do*. That's not from any particular text, but that's what differentiates Islam from other faiths where it is by faith alone, whereas in Islam, good deeds are an integral part of faith, and you can't do one thing and not the other. It was important to me to make that accessible and timely, and it went into the DNA of the series.

S: Several Muslim women in my research felt they had to represent a "diet" or low-key religiosity to be palatable as Muslim. Do you see that happening, or do you feel that pressure in Ms. Marvel?
W: Yeah, I feel that pressure is there. If people knew how much of a fundamentalist I really am in real life, they'd be alarmed.

S: I'll keep that out of the transcript!
W: You can put it in. I don't care. [*laugh*] It's important to me to show a plurality of ways of practicing and interpreting Islam. You've got Kamala, who's sort of an archetypal—you know, second-generation Muslim—to whom faith is important, but getting the new Drake album on release day is also important! But you also have her best friend [Nakia], who's this woke political *hijabi*, who is political in a very secular sense. You've got Aamir, her brother, who's kind of coded as a Salafi—we don't use the word Salafi; he's just kind of coded that way. He's very, sort of, a strict literalist interpretation of things—he's a *good guy*. That was important to me, too. Like them or love them, the vast majority of Salafis are good people; they're not suicide bombers. And you've got the dad and the mom and Sheikh Abdullah at the mosque—I thought it was very important to have him be a positive figure, even though he's very much a traditionalist, whom you might expect to finger wag and be like, Don't do this and don't do that. He really comes through and supports Kamala the way she needs to be supported at crucial points in the story.

The pressure's certainly there not to get too crazy with Kamala's religiosity because you are aiming it at a wider audience, and America's getting more and more secular. And that's kind of tough. So I sort of make up for that by having positive, much more traditionally conservative characters around her [who] make up the bedrock of her emotional life. They're there. They're a huge part of the series; they're the people she turns to in times of struggle, so that we have a range of ways of practicing Islam. But, yeah, if we had put her in, like, *hijab* and we'd made it so that she'd always take her brother or father along to make it *halal*—I do occasionally get letters like that. Oh yeah. More than one *Salafi* reader will write to say, "I will boycott this series until she wears *hijab*." I was like, Dude, you were never going to buy this series to begin with. You [can] only boycott stuff you've actually bought.

It's an interesting mix, and at the end of the day, trying to be all things to all people will just make you into a panacea and an anodyne nonstory. You can't [do that]. You have to pick the story you want to tell, and tell that story. If you want a different story, that's fine—there are other books. This is not the one.

NOTES

1. On August 12, 2017, a white nationalist gathering in Charlottesville, Virginia, to protest the removal of a Confederate statue escalated to violence. Many were beaten and injured in the clash between protesters and counterprotesters. Counterprotester Heather Heyer was killed when a car driven by an Ohio resident drove into the crowd. For an early account, see Maggie Astor, Christina Caron, and Daniel Victor, "A Guide to the Charlottesville Aftermath," *The New York Times,* August 13, 2017, https://www.nytimes.com/2017/08/13/us/charlottesville-virginia-overview.html. –Eds.

2. Noah Berlatsky, "What Makes the Muslim Ms. Marvel Awesome: She's Just like Everyone," *The Atlantic,* March 20, 2014, https://www.theatlantic.com/entertainment/archive/2014/03/what-makes-the-muslim-em-ms-marvel-em-awesome-shes-just-like-everyone/284517/.

3. "FOB"-ness, or "fresh off the boat"-ness –Eds.

4. South Asian, from Sanskrit, meaning "of our country" –Eds.

5. The verbal teachings of the prophet Muhammad –Eds.

6. One of four Sunni Islamic schools, named after the scholar Abū Ḥanīfa –Eds.

ACKNOWLEDGMENTS

This project started when Jessica reached out to Hussein with some questions about religious references in Ms. Marvel. That initial email turned into a meeting about a possible book project, which eventually turned into this volume. Our conversations have always been "yes, and" ones, where we validate each other's grandest ideas and encourage each other to be better. We have also supported each other when work and life were not always in the best balance. This partnership has been a good one for us both, because of the work the other has put into it.

First, we would like to thank our contributors. They have been timely, communicative, and willing to push us about our ideas. Their essays are profound reflections and analyses of a small book. We were lucky to have gathered such a hardworking, intelligent, and fun group of colleagues.

We are indebted to Vijay Shah, Lisa McMurtray, Kristi Ezernack, and Laura Strong at University Press of Mississippi, Vijay for believing in this project, Vijay and Lisa for shepherding it through many stages, and Lisa and Laura for keeping it on track to the end. Vijay kept asking us why a book on nineteen issues of a comic was important, and that forced us to keep thinking about how best to speak to the variety of our audiences. Our surety is better articulated because of him. Lisa made logistics as frictionless as possible, for which we are truly grateful. Other partners in the publication process we are lucky to have worked with are Camille Hale, our eagle-eyed copyeditor, and our anonymous reviewers, who found the perfect balance between tough and encouraging and helped us shape, polish, and complicate this manuscript into its best form.

Hussein taught Ms. Marvel in a variety of classes and community groups while this volume was coming together. His students and participants always helped him see the material afresh, and their perspectives encouraged him to think through and appreciate the power of Kamala Khan. He also wants to mention his family, who read through Ms. Marvel with him numerous times to see what they could see with him.

Jessica is indebted to Shabana Mir and Svend White, who introduced her to Hussein when she had questions they couldn't answer about Islam and comics. Goshen College provided her with a grant to teach one less class as she finished the book, and her Goshen College colleagues Ann Hostetler and Beth Martin Birky encouraged her in her early forays into the field. Jessica is also grateful to José Alaniz and Eric Berlatsky for welcoming her into and helping her navigate the world of comics scholarship. Eva Cherniavsky provided academic mentorship over many years, as well as comments at a crucial time in the development of the book proposal, while Jane Macdonald proved infinitely generous with her time and expertise in academic publishing. Finally, Jessica can't thank her patient and encouraging family enough, especially all four of her parents, who kept believing in her no matter how many times she messed up. Thomas and Leo and their sharp kid-reader eyes helped her spot details she would otherwise have missed, and Kyle Schlabach, as always, is the most incisive editor and encouraging colleague, as well as the best intellectual sparring partner she could ever hope to have.

G. Willow Wilson offered words of support for this project when she was first told of it. We hope we have validated her trust. "Good is not a thing you are, it's a thing you do." We hope we did "good."

Finally, since Kamala's first run ends with the *Last Days* storyline and a cosmic whimper, we feel obligated to thank Allah for the Big Bang.

Excelsior!

CONTRIBUTORS

José Alaniz, professor in the Department of Slavic Languages and Literatures and the Department of Comparative Literature (adjunct) at the University of Washington, Seattle, has published two books, *Komiks: Comic Art in Russia* (University Press of Mississippi, 2010) and *Death, Disability and the Superhero: The Silver Age and Beyond* (University Press of Mississippi, 2014). His research interests include death and dying, disability studies, eco-criticism, and comics studies. Current book projects include *Resurrection: Comics in Post-Soviet Russia* and *Beautiful Monsters: Disability in Alternative Comics*. His comics have appeared in *The Stranger*, the Seattle anthology *Dune*, and *Tales From La Vida: A Latinx Comics Anthology*.

Eric Berlatsky is professor and chair of the English Department at Florida Atlantic University. He is the author of *The Real, the True, and the Told: Postmodern Historical Narrative and the Ethics of Representation* (Ohio State University Press, 2011) and the editor of *Alan Moore: Conversations* (University Press of Mississippi, 2012). He has also published essays on narrative frames, early Superman comics, and the works of Posy Simmonds, Hanif Kureishi, Paul Auster, Julian Barnes, Virginia Woolf, Alan Moore and Dave Gibbons, Henri Bergson, Graham Swift, Art Spiegelman, and Milan Kundera. He has another article forthcoming with Sika A. Dagbovie-Mullins analyzing Black Lightning and Moon Girl comics, and they are also coediting a book on mixed-race superheroes.

Peter E. Carlson is a literacy curriculum specialist with Green Dot Public Schools, California, where he works as an instructional coach and curriculum writer. As a teacher, Carlson facilitated high school courses in drama, film, broadcast journalism, speech and debate, and English for ninth-, tenth-, and eleventh-grade students in South Central Los Angeles. Carlson's research has appeared in the *Oregon English Journal* and in a chapter of the book *Literacy Enrichment and Technology Integration in Pre-Service Teacher Education*. Carlson worked with the Graduate School of Education and

Information Studies at the University of California, Los Angeles, instructing teacher candidates in critical media literacy. He earned his master's degree in urban education from the University of California, Los Angeles.

Sika A. Dagbovie-Mullins is an associate professor and director of graduate studies in the Department of English at Florida Atlantic University. She is author of *Crossing B(l)ack: Mixed Race Identity in Modern American Fiction and Culture* (University of Tennessee Press, 2013), which examines assertions of a black-centered mixed-race identity where black is not subject to erasure but instead grounds a more expansive identity politics. She is currently co-editing an anthology (with Eric Berlatsky) that examines representations of racial mixedness and the idea of the superhero. Her other research focuses on representations of slavery in contemporary African American fiction and popular culture. Her articles have appeared in journals such as *African American Review*, *The Journal of Popular Culture*, *The Lion and the Unicorn*, *Mississippi Quarterly*, and *Palimpsest: A Journal on Women, Gender, and the Black International*, and she serves on the editorial advisory board of the *Journal of Popular Culture*.

Antero Garcia is an assistant professor in the Graduate School of Education at Stanford University, where he studies how technology and gaming shape both youth and adult learning, literacy practices, and civic identities. Prior to completing his PhD, Antero was an English teacher at a public high school in South Central Los Angeles. Based on his research focused on equitable teaching and learning opportunities for urban youth through the use of participatory media and gameplay, Antero codesigned the Critical Design and Gaming School—a public high school in South Central Los Angeles. His most recent books are *Good Reception: Teens, Teachers, and Mobile Media in a Los Angeles High School*; *Doing Youth Participatory Action Research: Transforming Inquiry with Researchers, Educators, and Students*; and *Pose, Wobble, Flow: A Culturally Proactive Approach to Literacy Instruction*.

Aaron Kashtan teaches at the University of North Carolina, Charlotte, and earned his PhD in English at the University of Florida. His research focuses on the effects of digital technology on the material and visual rhetoric of reading and writing, with particular attention to comics. His first book, *Between Pen and Pixel: Comics, Materiality, and the Book of the Future*, was published in spring 2018. Kashtan's teaching and service work to integrate multimodal composition, comics studies, and media studies into the broad discipline of English studies.

Winona Landis received her PhD in English literature from Miami University (OH), with a graduate certificate in women's, gender, and sexuality studies. Her dissertation project, entitled "Illustrating Empire: Race, Gender, and Visuality in Contemporary Asian American Literary Culture," interrogates the workings of US neoimperialism in the Asia Pacific as represented in popular literature, comics, and graphic novels. She is currently a visiting assistant professor of Asian and Asian American studies in the Department of Global and Intercultural Studies at Miami University. Her future research will tether together her interests in secondary education and multiethnic graphic narratives by investigating the ways in which the latter may enable the use of social justice–framed pedagogical practices in racially and socioeconomically diverse high school English classrooms.

A. David Lewis holds a PhD in religious studies from Boston University, where he developed *Graven Images: Religion in Comic Books and Graphic Novels* with Christine Hoff Kraemer. He is currently an instructor for Massachusetts College of Pharmacy and Health Sciences University in the Greater Boston area. An acclaimed graphic novelist himself for works including *The Lone and Level Sands*, *Some New Kind of Slaughter*, and *Kismet, Man of Fate*, Lewis is a former executive board member for the new Comics Studies Society, a founding member of *Sacred and Sequential*, and the Eisner-nominated author of *American Comic Books, Literary Theory, and Religion: The Superhero Afterlife*. Lewis serves as a board member for the NuDay Syria nonprofit and also coedited both *Muslim Superheroes: Comics, Islam, and Representation* with Martin Lund and, with Christopher Moreman, *Digital Death: Mortality and Beyond in the Online Age*, a winner of the Ray and Pat Browne Award for Best Edited Collection in Popular Culture and American Culture. His latest research in graphic medicine addresses the depiction of cancer in comic books, and his 501(c)(3) organization CYRIC is dedicated to publishing free comic books for Syrian refugee children.

Martin Lund holds a master's degree in theology, history, and anthropology of religion and a PhD in Jewish studies from Lund University, Sweden. He is a senior lecturer of religion at Malmö University. His current research focuses on representations of New York City in American comic books and graphic novels. He is also the author of *Re-Constructing the Man of Steel: Superman,*

Jewish American History, and the Invention of the Jewish–Comics Connection (Palgrave, 2016); coeditor with A. David Lewis of *Muslim Superheroes: Comics, Islam, and Representation* (ILEX Foundation/Harvard University Press, 2017); and coeditor, with Sean Guynes-Vishniac, of the forthcoming anthology *Unstable Masks: Whiteness and American Superhero Comics* (Ohio State University Press). He coedits (with Julia Round and Sean Guynes) the book series *Encapsulations: Critical Comics Studies* at University of Nebraska Press.

Shabana Mir is an associate professor of anthropology and director of undergraduate education at American Islamic College, Chicago, where she teaches Islamic studies, gender studies, and research methods. She is the author of the award-winning book *Muslim American Women on Campus: Undergraduate Social Life and Identity* (University of North Carolina Press, 2014), which received the Outstanding Book Award from the National Association for Ethnic Studies and the Critics' Choice Award from the American Educational Studies Association (2014). She has also written academic chapters, journal articles, children's literature, and a blog. She has taught at Millikin University, IL, University of Southern California online, Oklahoma State University, Indiana University, and Eastern Illinois University. She earned her PhD in education policy studies and anthropology, with a concentration in comparative education from Indiana University, Bloomington; an MA in English literature from Punjab University, Pakistan; and an MPhil in Education from Cambridge University (UK). She is an international public speaker on gender, religion, education, and politics, and speaks English, Urdu, and Punjabi, as well as some Arabic and Farsi.

Kristin M. Peterson is an assistant professor in the Department of Communication at Boston College. She received her PhD in media studies from the University of Colorado Boulder, where she was also a research fellow for the Center for Media, Religion and Culture. Her research focuses on Islam in North America, specifically examining how young Muslims engage with online media sites, images, videos, and creative projects as spaces to explore different discourses, styles, and emotions. Her current research project examines a series of creative projects in which Muslim American youth engage with aesthetics, affects, and hybrid styles to shift assumptions and present the complexities of their lives.

Nicholaus Pumphrey is an assistant professor of religious studies and the curator of the Quayle Bible Collection at Baker University in Baldwin City,

Kansas. He has a master's degree from Vanderbilt University and a PhD from Claremont Graduate University, specializing in ancient Near Eastern history and literature and the history of interpretation of the Hebrew Bible. His work on comics involves the historical influences of religion in comics, how comics reflect religious stereotypes in American culture, and how comic books influence the interpretation of religion and the Bible. Pumphrey wrote "From Terrorist to Tzadik" in *The Ages of X-Men*, which examined the introduction of Judaism to Magneto's backstory. He has two articles on Muslims in Marvel Comics: "Avenger, Mutant, or Allah: A Short Evolution of the Depiction of Muslims in Marvel Comics" and "*Niqab* not *Burqa*: Canon and Reception of Marvel's Dust." He recently published a book with McFarland Press, *Superman and the Bible: How the Idea of Superheroes Affects the Reading of Scripture*. He is an avid Marvel Comics collector and a reader of *X-Men, Ms. Marvel,* and *Silver Surfer*.

J. Richard Stevens is an associate professor in media studies at the University of Colorado Boulder. He is the author of *Captain America, Masculinity, and Violence: The Evolution of a National Icon* (2015) and is currently working on his second book, *Transforming Culture: Hasbro, Marvel, and the Rise of Hypercommercial Media Franchising*. His research delves into the intersection of ideological formation and media message dissemination, comprising studies such as how cultural messages are formed and passed through popular culture and how technology infrastructure affects the delivery of media messages, as well as communication technology policy and related studies in how media and technology platforms are changing American public discourse.

Editors

Jessica Baldanzi is a professor of English at Goshen College, where she teaches comics and graphic novels, as well as twentieth- and twenty-first-century American literature, media and popular culture, creative writing, critical theory, and composition. She has presented papers about Ms. Marvel and the works of Chris Ware and Marguerite Abouet and has helped promote comics for a general readership with a comics review blog, *Commons Comics*. She coedited a Comics and Graphic Novels issue for the *Center for Mennonite Writing Journal* with Mary Roth, and her article "Beyond Hair Bows and Cleavage" was just published in *Lessons Drawn: Essays on the Pedagogy of Comics and Grahpic Novels*. She is also a creative writer, specializing in flash memoir and fiction. Baldanzi earned her PhD from Indiana University Bloomington, with a focus on science and literature, especially representations of eugenic and genetic ideology in twentieth-century and more recent fiction.

Hussein Rashid, PhD, is founder of Islamicate, L3C, a consultancy focusing on religious literacy and cultural competency. He has a bachelor's degree in Middle Eastern studies from Columbia University, a master's degree in theological studies focusing on Islam, and a master's and PhD from Harvard University in Near Eastern languages and cultures, focusing on South and Central Asia. He has taught at Columbia University, Hofstra University, Fordham University, Virginia Theological Seminary, Reconstructionist Rabbinical College, SUNY Old Westbury, and Barnard College. His research focuses on Muslims and American popular culture. He writes and speaks about music, comics, movies, and the blogistan. He has published academic works on Muslims and American popular culture, Malcolm X, *qawwali*, intra-Muslim racism, teaching Shi'ism, Islam and comics, free speech, Sikhs and Islamophobia, Muslims in film, and American Muslim spaces of worship.

INDEX

Page numbers in **bold** refer to illustrations.

Aaron, Jason, 217
Abdullah, Sheikh, xi, 68, 98, 108–9, 121, 162–63, 244
Academy X, 25, 27, 29
Adlakha, Siddhant, 78
Afghanistan, 25–27, 30
A-Force, 13
Ahmed, Sara, 153, 155–56, 158
Air, 81
Aja, David, 202
Alaniz, José, 99–100, 102, 229
Alba, Richard, 58
al-Husseini, Haj Amin, 186
Alif, The Unseen, 81
Allegri, Natasha, 196
Allen, Barry, 191, 197–98
All-New All-Different Avengers, 195-96
All-New All-Different Avengers, 192
Alonso, Axel, 209–10, 213, 215
Alphona, Adrian, 81, 94, 96, 103, 109, 120, 146–47
Alsultany, Evelyn, 79
Alternative Comics, 125
Amanat, Sana, vii, 34, 81, 92, 138, 146–47, 154–55, 158, 170, 172–73, 215–19, 230, 235, 238–39, 243
America, 220
American Comics, Literary Theory, and Religion, 92
American Freedom Defense Initiative, viii, 186
Are We All Postracial Yet?, 74–75
Arjana, Sophia Rose, 100

Arts of Living on a Damaged Planet, 101
Asrar, Mahmud, 196
Astro City, 197, 199
Avengers, 8, 118
Avengers, 4, 7–9, 13, 15, 52, 69, 121, 123, 133, 142–43, 195, 216, 231

Bacon-Smith, Camille, 198
Bakhtin, Mikhail, 57–58
Banner, Bruce, 14, 233–34
Barth, John, 125
Barthes, Roland, xiii
Batgirl, 73
Batman, 117
Batman, 120, 209, 237, 242
Batson, Billy, 211
Battleworld, 119, 123, 127
Bayoumi, Moustafa, 21, 35
Belasco, 27
Bendis, Brian Michael, 146, 215–16
Berlant, Lauren, 106, 109
Berlatsky, Eric, 51
Berlatsky, Noah, 119–20, 122, 126, 236, 240
Bernal, Dolores Delgado, 135–37, 141, 146–48
Beyonders, 119
Bhabha, Homi, 58, 71–72
Bhalla, Tamara, 159
Big Bang Theory, The, 198
Bin Laden, Osama, 74
Black Canary, 73
Black Panther, 202
Black Panther, vii, 30, 215
Black Superheroes, 216
Black Widow, 210

255

Black Widow, 239
Blodgett, Bridget, 202–3
Box Office Poison, 197
Bradbury, Ray, 218
Breitbart.com, 218–19
Brown, Jeffrey, 12, 216, 220
Brown, Matt, 215, 220
Burka Avenger, 160
bus ads, viii, x, xiii, 186
Busiek, Kurt, 199
Butterfly Mosque, The, 81–82

Cage, Luke, 30
Cain, Chelsea, 213
Cairo, 81
Captain America, vii, ix, 9, 13–14, 54, 73, 140, 175, 220
Captain Britain, 123
Captain Britain and the Mighty Defenders, 123
Captain Marvel, 3, 6–7, 10, 16–17
Captain Marvel, vii, 6–7, 10–11, 15, 17, 54–55, 66, 72, 109, 119–22, 125, 140, 142–43, 180–82, 192, 196, 207, 211
Captain Marvel and the Carol Corps, 13
Carol Corps, 11, 13, 16
Carrelli, Bruno, 33, 51–52, 55, 59–61, 69–71, 77, 93, 96, 102–3, 107, 109, 127, 138, 142–44, 163–65, 192–94, 239
Carrelli, Victor, 69, 71, 96, 144–45
Caucasia, 65–66, 69
Chameleon, 69
Champions, 15
Chaplin, Charlie, 94, 96, 103
Cho, Alexander, 66–67
Christian, Mark, 72
Cicero, Stu, 197–99, 202
Civil War, 13–15
Civil War II, ix, 13–16
Clanton, Dan, 126
Claremont, Chris, 8
Clynes, Manfred, 93
Coates, Ta-Nehisi, 202
Cobb, Helen, 10
Colan, Gene, 6

Comic Book Guy, 198, 232
Comic Book Resources, 210
comics conventions, xiii, 122, 193, 197–98, 201, 209, 232
community, xiii–xiv, 48, 51, 53, 70, 75, 80, 90, 92, 100, 103, 108–9, 116, 120–22, 125–27, 133–34, 142–43, 145–47, 153, 159, 164, 172, 195–96, 209
Coogan, Peter, 105
Cook, David, 124–25
cosplay, 171, 184–85, 187, 193, 240
Costello, Matthew, 22
Crisis on Infinite Earths, 127
Critical Approaches to Comics, xi
critical race theory (CRT), 133–50
Cruel Optimism, 106
Cyborg, 73
"Cyborg Manifesto," 89–91, 94, 100–101, 106
"Cyborgs to Companion Species," 93, 97
Cyclops, 195, 242

Dagbovie-Mullins, Sika A., 51
Danvers, Carol, vii, ix, xii, 3–17, 54–56, 66, 68–69, 72, 93, 105–8, 119, 126, 140, 142, 154, 179–82, 196, 207, 216
Darder, Antonia, 150
Darius, Julian, 24
Davé, Shilpa, 76
Davis, Julie, 25
DC Comics, Inc., 81, 192, 198–200, 203, 209–10
Deadpool, 202
Death, Disability, and the Superhero, 99–100
Death of a Prophet, The, 124
de Certeau, Michel, 173–74, 177, 186
DeConnick, Kelly Sue, 10–11
DeFilippis, Nunzio, 25, 27
Didio, Dan, 209–10
DiPaolo, Marc, 219
Disney. *See* Walt Disney Company
District X, 22
Ditko, Steve, 80
diversity, vii, 51, 62, 71, 73, 92, 98, 154–58, 162, 212–13, 219–21, 230–35

Dong, Lan, 152
Dorkin, Evan, 192, 197, 200
Dotbusters, 50
Dragon Awards, 12
Dr. Doom, 119–20, 123, 127
Dr. Strange, 119–20
Duff, Cameron, 22, 32
Duncan, Randy, 208, 215
Dune, xii, 193–94
Dust, xii, 21–36, 217

Eisner Awards, vii
Elam, Michele, 68
Elba, Idris, 214
Elektra, 210
Eltingville Club, 197, 200
Eltingville Club, 192, 198–200, 202
End Will Be Graphic, The, 126
Enterprising Women, 198
Entwistle, Joanne, 176–78, 180–81
Ewing, Al, 123

Fahrenheit 451, 218
fanboys, xiii, 8, 192, 202–3, 208–11, 213, 217, 220–21
fandom, xiii–xiv, 154, 179, 191–203, 208–9, 219
fan fiction, 32, 52, 89, 191, 193, 195–97, 201
Fangirl, 203
Fantastic Four, 118, 197, 214
Fantastic Four, 30, 118
Federalist, The, 219
Flash, 191, 197
Fosgitt, Jay, 196
Foucault, Michel, 174
Fraction, Matt, 202
Freire, Paulo, 134, 140–41, 143–44, 148
Frigga, 98, 108

Gabriel, David, 207
Galactus, 82
Garden and the Fire, The, 124
Garfield, Andrew, 214
Gawker, 214–15
Generation Why, **95**

Ghostbusters (2016), 211, 236
Gilson, Erinn, 165
Giroux, Henry, 135
Glover, Donald, 214, 216
Goldberg, David Theo, 74–75, 77, 80
Gorman, Zac, 196
Gottschalk, Peter, 25
Graven Images, x, 92
Gray, Jonathan, 203
Grayson, Mark, 191, 198–200
Greenberg, Gabriel, 25
Grewal, Zareena, xi, 98
Griffin, Dave, 123
Guggenheim, Marc, 28
Gwenpool, 202

Haddad, Yvonne Yazbeck, 117
Halberstam, Jack, 153
Haraway, Donna, 89–94, 96–101, 103, 106–7, 109–10
Haraway Reader, 109–10
Harrington, C. Lee, 203
Hassan vs. City of New York, 74
Hatfield, Charles, 125
Hawkeye, 202
Hawkeye, 14
Hebdige, Dick, 176
Heimdall, 214
Hellions, 27, 30
Henderson, Erica, 202
Herbert, Frank, xii, 193
Heroes Reborn, 118, 127
Heroes Return, 118
Hickman, Jonathan, 118
Hills, Matt, 209
Hitler, Adolf, vii–ix, 186
hooks, bell, 150
"How to Survive a Disaster," 107
Hugo Awards, vii, 12, 218–19
Hulk, vii, 14, 73, 197, 233, 235
Human Torch, 197, 214
Hussain, Faiza, 123

identity, xiii, 21–22, 28, 36, 65, 70, 90–91, 94, 98, 106, 110, 147, 159, 167, 176, 211–13,

220, 243; civic, 147, 150; cultural, 138; ethnic, 50, 58, 166; fan, 199, 203; geek, 194; generational, 31; immigrant, 33, 159; masculine, 100, 102; Muslim, ix, 25–26, 29, 33, 51, 122–23, 156, 159, 203, 218; national, 28–29, 32–33, 177; outsider, 100; politics, 35, 156, 219; racial, 58, 203; South Asian, 75; superhero, 5, 55, 91, 105, 108; transnational, 32; youth, 134
Immigration and Nationality Act of 1965, 49
Immigration Reform and Control Act of 1986, 49
Infinite Crisis, 198
Internet, 89, 107, 171, 184, 191, 193–94, 209, 213–14, 216
Inventor, 4–5, 89–90, 93–94, 96–97, 100, 105, 144, 193
Invincible, 199–200
Invincible, 191, 197
Iron Man, vii, 13–16, 54, 73, 140, 238–39
Islam, vii–xiv, 3, 12, 21–36, 47–48, 51–54, 56–57, 59–62, 67–68, 71, 73–84, 90–92, 97–100, 104–5, 108–9, 116–27, 133, 138, 142, 150, 153–67, 170–78, 182–87, 201, 203, 207–8, 217–18, 229, 230, 234–38, 240–44
Islamic Understanding of Death and Resurrection, The, 117
Islam Is a Foreign Country, xi, 98
Islamophobia, x, xii–xiii, 24, 33, 36, 80, 82, 100, 150, 153, 162, 186

Jameson, J. Jonah, 7
Jenkins, Henry, xi
Jersey City, NJ, vii, xii, 3, 31–36, 47, 50, 52, 54–55, 57–58, 60, 62, 69, 71, 73–75, 80, 82, 92, 100, 103, 105, 119, 133, 143, 149, 158–59, 170, 217
Johns, Rafael, 210, 217, 219
Jones, Joelle, 213
Jordan, Michael B., 214
Joseph, Ralina, 67–68
Josh, 52, 69, 71, 107, 138–39

Kaboom, 79
Kaiser, Susan, 177, 182

Kamran, xi, 68, 72, 78–80, 101, 104, 193–94
Kent, Clark, 237
Kent, Miriam, 35, 156, 158
Khan, Aamir, xi–xii, 33, 52, 59, 72, 77, 79–80, 98, 104–5, 108–9, 162–65, 175, 201, 244
Khan, Disha, 33, 52, 54–56, 59–62, 66–68, 71, 76, 98, 101, 104, 108–9, 125–26, 139, 145, 160–62, 164–65, 201, 237, 244
Khan, Ghazala, viii
Khan, Kamala: ethnicity, xi, xiv, 48, 58, 61–62, 72, 75, 78, 81, 92, 100, 145, 152–53, 156–57, 165–66, 177, 208, 240; and fan art, ix, **ix**, 185, 187; and feminism, xii, 11–12, 17, 90, 120, 152–67, 239; and gender, vii, xi–xiv, 5, 12, 22, 33, 35, 47, 53–55, 61, 68, 73, 82, 90–92, 97, 101, 105–6, 119, 122, 139–40, 145, 147, 150, 153, 155–60, 166–67, 170–74, 177, 183–84, 194, 196–98, 201–3, 207–21, 230–32, 236, 239, 242; identity, xii–xiii, 3–4, 15, 34, 47–48, 52, 55–59, 62, 65–66, 90–91, 97–100, 104–5, 108, 122, 125–26, 133–34, 137–40, 142–43, 150, 156–57, 159, 161, 163, 165, 170–73, 175–79, 181–82, 185–87, 194, 216–18, 243; Pakistani heritage and culture, vii–viii, xii, 3–4, 15, 31–35, 47–48, 51–55, 57–61, 65–84, 90–91, 101–3, 119, 133, 138, 140, 142, 160, 164–65, 170, 174–75, 178, 182, 187, 207, 216–17, 230, 237–38; as a second-generation immigrant, vii, xiii, 47–62, 66, 76–79, 89–90, 99–100, 103–4, 133, 159, 161–62, 165, 170–71, 174, 182, 185, 187, 218, 230, 237; superpowers, x, 3–4, 47, 54, 65, 67, 69, 71, 90, 92–94, 99–101, 104, 107, 110, 122, 134, 137, 141–42, 144–45, 179, 181, 201, 230, 240–42. See also *Ms. Marvel*; Ms. Marvel
Khan, Khizr, viii
Khan, Yusuf, 33, 52–56, 59–62, 66–68, 76, 82, 97–98, 101, 104, 139, 142, 145, 160–62, 164–65, 175, 201, 237, 241, 244
Khoja-Moolji, Shenila, 161
Khorasani, Soraya, 123
Khusro, Amir, 238
Kinney, Laura, 233

Kirkman, Robert, 197
Kitson, Barry, 197–98
Kline, Nathan, 93
Kraemer, Christine Hoff, x, 92
Kree, 66, 99, 105
Kyle, Craig, 27

Lamptey, Jerusha Tanner, 120
Landis, Winona, 217
Larrick, Nancy, 137
Lee, Stan, 100, 211, 215, 221
Legion of Super-Heroes, 197–99
Lewis, A. David, 92
Lewis, Reina, 103–4
Lineage, 79, 100–101, 103–5
LitHub, 109
Lockjaw, 97, 104
Logan, 233
Loki, 31, 70–71, 82, 98–100, 105, 108
Lugones, Maria, 165
Lund, Martin, 211

Macedo, Donaldo, 148
Madrid, Mike, 7
Maira, Sunaina, 50–51, 158–59
Mamdani, Mahmood, 79
Mani, Bakirathi, 75
Marcus, 7–8
Marvel Cinematic Universe, 220
Marvel Comics, vii, 3, 6, 21–36, 98, 118, 143–44, 192, 199–203, 207, 209–11, 213–15, 218–21
Marvel Entertainment, LLC, 81, 84
Mar-Vell, 6, 15, 196
Marvel NOW!, 207–21
Marvel Studios, 5–6
Marvel Super-Heroes, 6
Marvel Universe, xi, xiv, 13, 32, 82–83, 126, 137, 143–44, 197, 207, 213, 217–18
Marvel Unlimited, 16
Master of the World, 16
McCloud, Scott, 22
McIntosh, Peggy, 210
McKelvie, Jamie, 238
Mighty Avengers, The, 123

Mighty Captain Marvel, The, 15
Mir, Shabana, 108
Miss America, 220
Miyazawa, Takeshi, 81, 102–3
Mockingbird, 213
Mockingbird, 213
Modern Times, 94, **94**
Modest Witness, 91, 110
Mody, Navroze, 50
Mohanty, Chandra, 73
Molecule Man, 119
Moon Girl, 73
Moors, Annelies, 184
Morales, Miles, 73, 196, 207–21
Morrison, Grant, 23–25, 30
Ms. Marvel, **ix**, xi, 3, 9, 12–13, 16, 31–32, 35, 60, 74–84, 97–98, 118–19, 149–50, 152–67, 173, 192, 194–95, 197, 201–3, 210, 217–18, 234; "Best of the Best," **180**; Circle Q, 33–34, 51–52, 60, 68–72, 75, 80, 84, 138, 142, 144, 178; Coles Academic High School, 34, 71–72, 80, 84, 96, 100, 105, 107–9, 122, 230; *Crushed*, 98, **102**; Essential collection, 16; *Last Days*, 105–9, 116, 119–22; Masterworks collection, 16; *No Normal*, xiv, 47, **53**, 61, 70, 76, 133–34, 137–38, 145, 147–48, 157, **176**, **178**, **179**, **181**, **183**, 229; and race, xi–xiv, 21–23, 35, 47–51, 57, 61–62, 65–84, 92, 97, 100, 108, 119, 134–35, 140, 145, 147, 150, 152–67, 173, 177, 185, 194, 196–98, 201–3, 207–21, 230–31, 233–36, 239, 241; and sexuality, xi–xii, 23, 61, 100, 147, 173, 177, 208; and technoculture, 89–110
Ms. Marvel, vii, 5–11, 14, 21–36, 62, 68, 91–92, 96–100, 107–10, 120–21, 125–27, 137, 139–48, 154–57, 160, 166, 171–73, 179, 182–87, 196, 207, 216, 218–19, 229, 230–31, 234–44; costume, xiii–xiv, 4, 6–11, 15, 47, 54–55, 59, 66, 68–69, 72, 100, 105, 133, 140, 143, 145, 170–87, 193, 218, 230, 238–39; sexualization, 5, 55, 172, 178–80, 183, 185, 187, 239. *See also* Khan, Kamala
Murray, Christopher, 99
Muslims. *See* Islam

Nakia, xi-xii, 33, 35, 52, 60, 69, 71, 109, 138, 142, 178, 192, 244
Nee, Victor, 58
Never Wholly Others, 120
New Avengers, The, 9, 118
New 52, 209-10
New X-Men, 23-24, 27, 29-30
New York City, NY, 21-36, 58-59, 62, 71, 74, 82, 92, 119
New York Times, vii, 12
Niccolini, Alyssa, 161
Nichols, Nichelle, 102
Nimoy, Leonard, 102
Nishime, LeiLani, 66
North, Ryan, 202
Not in God's Name, 116
Noto, Phil, ix
Nova, 196

Obama, Barack, 16, 67, 69
Onslaught, 118
Ozawa, Takao, 49

Parker, Peter, 7, 15, 47, 78, 118, 146, 211, 213-15, 217, 220-21, 232, 236-37
PATRIOT Act, 74
Phantom Girl, 198
Pichelli, Sara, 215
Poole, Gwen, 202
Potter, Harry, 193, 235
Pound, Aaron, 120-21, 126
Practice of Everyday Life, The, 173-74
Proctor, William, 211
Professor's Daughter, The, 68-69
Professor X, 8

Qadir, Sooraya. *See* Dust
Qahera the Superhero, 160
Queen Medusa, 66, 79, 99, 101, 103-4
Quesada, Joe, 215
Qur'an, xiv, 56, 97, 124, 142, 145, 157, 186, 243

Raboteau, Emily, 68-69
Rancière, Jacques, 172, 182-83, 185
rape, 7-8, 16

Rashid, Hussein, 233, 240
Raymond, Kenneth, 196-97
Reece, Owen, 119
Reed, Brian, 9
Reeves, Nancee, 157, 160
retroactive continuity (retcon), 12, 15
Rhodes, James Rupert "Rhodey," 14
Richards, Reed, 118-20
Rimmon-Kenan, Shlomith, 23
Rivera, Gabby, 220
Robb, Jenny E., 152
Robinson, Alex, 197
Rocket Raccoon & Groot, 202
Rogue, 8
Roshanravan, Shireen, 166
Rowe, Aimee Carrillo, 67
Rowell, Rainbow, 203
Royal, Derek Parker, 92
Rumi, 157
Runaways, 198
Rushkoff, Douglas, x
Rustomji, Nerina, 124

Sacks, Jonathan, 116-17
Sad Puppies, 218
Sandvoss, Cornell, 203
San Francisco, CA, viii, x, xiii, 186
Salter, Anastasia, 202-3
Schenker, Brett, 209
Secret Wars, 13, 118-27
Senna, Danzy, 65
September 11 attacks, 21, 29-31, 33, 48, 50, 59, 73-75, 82, 158-59
She-Hulk, 197, 210
She-Hulk, 123
Sherlock, 202
Shoemaker, Stephen, 124-25
Showcase, 197
Shyminsky, Neil, 208, 210-12
Simpsons, The, 194, 198, 232
Slott, Dan, 197
Smith, Jane Idleman, 117
Smith, Matthew J., 208, 215
Smith, Tony, 120

social class, 23, 32–33, 35–36, 47, 50, 58–59, 61, 70, 97, 136, 145, 147, 177, 214, 237–38
social justice, 133–34, 136, 139, 141–44, 146–47, 157, 196, 218
social media, 5, 185, **186**, 193–94, 208–9, 213–14
Solnit, Rebecca, 107, 109
Solórzano, Daniel G., 135–37, 141, 146–48
Sony Pictures Studios, 213–16, 221
Southern Poverty Law Center, viii
Spider-Man, 7
Spider-Man, vii, 13–15, 69, 73, 78, 104, 120, 196, 207, 211, 213–17, 233, 239
Spider-Man: Homecoming, 216
Spock, 102, **102**
Squirrel Girl, 73
Stacy, Gwen, 202
Stanfill, Mel, 210
Stark, Tony, 9, 13–15, 237
Star Trek, 102–3, 198
Star Wars, 193
Staying with the Trouble, 91, 110
Stefani, Matt, **ix**
Stelfreeze, Brian, 202
Stephens, Gregory, 70–71, 73
stereotypes, viii, xi–xiii, 6, 9, 21, 24, 31, 36, 49, 51–52, 54–56, 67, 73, 78, 81, 92, 97, 161–62, 170, 173, 175, 178, 183–84, 187, 195, 198–201, 203, 208–11, 217–18, 220, 232
Stevenson, Greg, 117, 120, 126–27
Storm, 191, 195
Street, Paul, 69
Strömberg, Fredrik, 25
Superboy-Prime, 198
Superman, 117
Superman, 99–100, 120, 209, 231–33, 237, 242
Supernatural, 202
Swanson, Heather, 101

Tarlo, Emma, 184
Teaching Comics and Graphic Narratives, 152
Telgemeier, Raina, 234
terrorism, ix, 78–79, 158, 236

Thind, Bhagat Singh, 49–50
Thomas, Roy, 6
Thor (films), 214
Thor, vii, 73, 98–99, 217
Tintin in the Congo, 65
Tosenberger, Catherine, 195
transformational resistance, 133–50, **135**, **141**, **146**, **149**
Trump, Donald, viii–ix, 36, 74, 89–90, 98, 185, 240
Twilight Zone, 200
Tyesha, xii, 194

Uhura, Lieutenant, 102, **102**
Ultimate Spider-Man, 118, 207, 213–16
Ultimate X-Men, 118
Ultimate Universe, 83, 118, 207, 213–16
Ultron, 195
Ulysses, 16
Unbeatable Squirrel Girl, 202
Uncanny X-Men, 8

van Sciver, Ethan, 23
violence, x, xii, 6, 52, 90, 119, 122, 159, 161, 166, 242–43

Wacker, Steve, vii, 81, 172–73, 230, 235
Waid, Mark, 197–99
Walt Disney Company, 5, 81–82
Wanzo, Rebecca, 152
War Machine, 14
Watt, W. Montgomery, 124
Wayne, Bruce, 237
Weir, Christina, 25, 27
Westerfelhaus, Robert, 25
White, John, 68
Wiegman, Robyn, x, 153, 156
Wilcox, Lauren, 103
Williams, Riri, 239
Wilson, G. Willow, vii, xiv, 4, 12, 14, 31, 34, 62, 81–84, 92, 97, 107–10, 120, 126, 134, 138, 140–41, 146–47, 170, 173, 195–96, 201, 203, 216–18, 230–44
Wolverine, 25, 31, 105, 108, 191–92, 194–95, 233

Women Write about Comics, 157
Wonder Woman, 209
Woo, Benjamin, 209, 220

Xavier Institute, 25–27, 29
X-Men, 30
X-Men, xii, 8, 21, 24–25, 27–30, 32, 100, 211–12, 217
X-Men: Age of Apocalypse, 127
X23, 233

Yang, Gene Luen, 100
Yorkes, Gertrude, 198
Yost, Christopher, 27
Young X-Men, 24, 28–30
Yousafzai, Malala, 164

Zero Hour, 127
Zoe, xii, 33, 35–36, 52, 54–56, 60, 62, 69, 71, 80, 109, 138–39, 142–43, 178–80

www.ingramcontent.com/pod-product-compliance
Lightning Source LLC
Chambersburg PA
CBHW030613230426
43661CB00053B/1966